LEVEL FOUR

SCOPE ENGLISH ANTHOLOGY

Literature and Reading Program

Edited by
Katherine Robinson
Editorial Director, Scope Magazine

SCHOLASTIC INC.

The Scope English Story

In 1964, when Scholastic first published it, SCOPE Magazine was a near-revolutionary publication: a magazine designed to bring good literature and reading, and useful skills, to young people. Now, after more than twenty years, SCOPE is the most widely used magazine in junior and senior high school Reading and English programs—reaching nearly 40 percent of all secondary schools in the United States.

Teachers have found SCOPE Magazine so useful in motivating readers that they have asked for a more permanent resource containing the high quality reading selections and activities found in every issue of SCOPE. So we developed SCOPE ENGLISH—a complete English program including both reading and literature as well as a comprehensive writing and language program. Teachers all over America are finding in SCOPE ENGLISH precisely those qualities that made SCOPE Magazine so popular: It makes English easier to learn, more motivating, more teachable. We've included selections from the magazine that are of high interest to students—stories, poems, plays, TV scripts, articles and more—as well as tried-and-true teacher favorites that create a basic curriculum framework. The reading levels of these selections are accessible to all junior and senior high school students, grades 6–12, yet the ideas are challenging and provocative. SCOPE ENGLISH includes an *Anthology* at each grade level, organized by themes, authors, or genres, and a *Writing and Language* text, written in clear, conversational style.

SCOPE ENGLISH contains eye-catching photos and illustrations that actually aid in students' understanding of the important events in a selection. An illustration is provided every three to five pages of text, to make the reading experience less threatening for the students. All the materials motivate secondary students to read more and write better.

More than twenty years after SCOPE Magazine first brought the SCOPE philosophy to the English classroom, we're proud to be able to reach you with the SCOPE ENGLISH program. We hope you will find these materials just as useful and helpful as you've found SCOPE Magazine to be in making English learning easier and more satisfying.

LITERATURE CONSULTANT

Theodore Hipple, Ph.D.
Professor, English Education
University of Florida
Gainesville, Florida

READING CONSULTANT

Virginia B. Modla, Ph.D.
Reading Curriculum Associate
School District of Cheltenham Township
Elkins Park, Pennsylvania

LEVEL FOUR READERS

Mary Anne Brock
Teacher
Lawrence D. Bell High School
Hurst, Texas

Marlene McDaniel
Teacher
Northside High School
Roanoke, Virginia

Gregory Wojcik
Chairperson, English Department
Thorton Fractional Township High
    School North
Calumet City, Illinois

CURRICULUM CONSULTANTS

Barbara Coulter
Director of Language Education
Detroit Public Schools
Detroit, Michigan

Nora Forester
Reading Coordinator
North Side School District
San Antonio, Texas

William Horst
Secondary Section Committee
National Council of Teachers of English

Barbara Krysiak, Ed.D.
Principal
North Hampton Elementary School
North Hampton, New Hampshire

Nancy McHugh
Teacher
Grant High School
Van Nuys, California

Editorial, Design and Art Production: Kirchoff/Wohlberg, Inc.

ISBN 0-590-34669-5

12 11 10 9 8 7 6 5 4 3   0/9

LEVEL FOUR
Contents

List of Skills Lessons 13

SECTION 1 Short Stories

Introduction 18

The Green Door 20
O. Henry

Blue Eyes Far Away 24
Mackinlay Kantor

Gentleman of Río en Medio 28
Juan A. A. Sedillo

Marigolds 32
Eugenia Collier

The Enemy 41
Pearl S. Buck

Future Tense 54
Robert Lipsyte

SECTION REVIEW 62

SECTION 2 Drama

Introduction 68

The Sneeze 70
Neil Simon   based on a story by Anton Chekhov

I Remember Mama 78
John Van Druten   based on stories by Kathryn Forbes

Sudden Death 87
Tom Chehak & Joshua Brand

SECTION REVIEW 100

SECTION 3 Adventure

Introduction. 106

Leiningen Versus the Ants. 108
Carl Stephenson

Flight Into Danger 119
Arthur Hailey

Mind Over Water. 134
Diana Nyad

In the Shadow of a Rainbow 139
Robert Franklin Leslie

The Homecoming of Ulysses 150
based on The Odyssey *by Homer*

SECTION REVIEW 164

SECTION 4 Mystery

Introduction. 170

The Haunted Chess Set 173
Julia Remine Piggin

The Adventure of the Copper Beeches 179
based on a story by Sir Conan Doyle

The Third Level 190
Jack Finney

The President Regrets 196
Ellery Queen

SECTION REVIEW 202

SECTION 5   Poetry

Introduction 208
Narrative Poems 210
Ghosts 210
Sandra Gardner

Frankenstein 212
Edward Field

Last Day at the Job 215
Gretchen Cryer & Nancy Ford

Lyric Poems 217
Hector the Collector 217
Shel Silverstein

Of Kings and Things 218
Lillian Morrison

Still 220
Andrés Purificasion

Medicine 221
Alice Walker

Could Be 222
Langston Hughes

Butterfly 224
Donald James Solomon (student)

A Red, Red Rose 225
Robert Burns

Starting at Dawn 226
Sun Yün-feng
translated by Kenneth Rexroth & Ling Chung

Player Piano. 227
John Updike

The Earth's a Baked Apple 228
Michael Colgrass

Message Poems 231

Thief 231
Tom Whitecloud

A Work of Artifice 232
Marge Piercy

Telephone Conversation 234
Susan Keady

Where the Rainbow Ends 235
Richard Rive

Memo to the 21st Century 236
Philip Appleman

Do Not Go Gentle Into That Good Night. 238
Dylan Thomas

Found Poems and Concrete Poems 240

Right of Way. 240
Marjorie Burns

Food Processor 242
Marjorie Burns

Urban Landscape 243
Spike St. Croix

Tribute to Henry Ford—3 244
Richard Kostelanetz

SECTION REVIEW 246

SECTION 6 Relationships

Introduction. 252

Very Special Shoes 254
Morley Callaghan

Letter to a Black Boy. 260
Bob Teague

Celebration 266
Alonzo Lopez

The Troublemaker 268
from All Things Wise and Wonderful by James Herriot

Since You Left. 275
Ch'ang Ch'u Ling

Road. 276
Larry Libby

Long Walk to Forever 277
Kurt Vonnegut, Jr.

If You Hear That a Thousand People Love You. 283
Guadalupe de Saavedra

Take Over, Bos'n 284
Oscar Schisgall

SECTION REVIEW 288

SECTION 7 Personal Narrative

Introduction. 294

The Story of Little Sure-Shot 296
Fiona Greenbank

The Electrical Wizard 306
John Dos Passos

Clemente—A Bittersweet Story 312
Jerry Izenberg

400 Mulvaney Street 319
Nikki Giovanni

Knoxville, Tennessee 326
Nikki Giovanni

Growing Up. 328
Russell Baker

SECTION REVIEW 336

SECTION 8 Nonfiction

Introduction. 342

Central Park 344
John Updike

Steelworker: Mike Lefevre 347
from Working *by Studs Terkel*

The Acorn People. 353
Ron Jones

Dolphins. 365
Alice Herman Lehrer

Emotion Twists Issues—Stick to the Facts. 370
Kevin E. Steele

Guns: A Serious Problem 375
Ann Landers

A Kitten for Mrs. Ainsworth 380
James Herriot

SECTION REVIEW 386

SECTION 9   Humor

Introduction 392

Fresh Air Will Kill You 394
Art Buchwald

And They Lived Happily Ever After for a While 398
John Ciardi

The Cow Who Liked to Kick 400
Ambrose Bierce

Who's On First? 405
Bud Abbott & Lou Costello

How Beautiful With Mud 410
Hildegarde Dolson

SECTION REVIEW 418

SECTION 10   Identity

Introduction 424

By Any Other Name 426
Santha Rama Rau

The Rocking Horse 433
Doris Halman

A Trip for Mrs. Taylor 446
Hugh Garner

Dirge Without Music 454
Edna St. Vincent Millay

Stevie Wonder: Growing Up in a World of Darkness 456
James Haskins

SECTION REVIEW 472

SECTION 11 The Novel

Introduction. 478

Biography. 480

The Pearl 482
John Steinbeck

    Chapter 1. 482

    Chapter 2. 491

    Chapter 3. 498

    Chapter 4. 512

    Chapter 5. 526

    Chapter 6. 533

SECTION REVIEW 550

Glossary. 554

Handbook of Terms in Literature 561

Author and Title Index 586

LEVEL FOUR
Skills Lessons

UNDERSTANDING LITERATURE

Reading Various Types of Literature

Short Story	20	Message Poetry	231
Play	70	Found Poetry and Concrete Poetry	240
Adventure	108	Biography	296
Myth	150	Autobiography	319
Mystery	173	Nonfiction	344
Narrative Poetry	211	Humor	394
Lyric Poetry	217	Novel	482

Plot

Definition	23	Clues to a surprise ending	61
Purpose of events	23	Suspense and plot	178
Time order	27	Plot and subplot	201

Characterization

Through dialogue	40	Through stated or implied motivation	432
Character motivation	53	Through present and past events	445
Through characters' actions	86	Character traits	471

Conflict

Conflict and resolution	118	Conflict, climax, and resolution	149
Types of conflict	133, 163	Conflict between two people	163
Conflict within one person	138	Conflict between a person and nature	163

Setting

Importance of time and place	31	Stage directions	77
Details about setting	31	Description of setting	195

Point of View

Understanding point of view	305	Third person	311

First person . . . . 305, 325   Changing points of view . . 318, 335
Point of view and character motivation 311   From different stages in life . . . 335

Theme

Symbols reflecting theme 259   Theme and characterization . . . 274
Understanding theme 259   Indirect statement of theme . . . 274
Theme and symbols 259   Theme and plot 282
Theme and main idea 265   Theme in a novel 549

Mood

Definition 189   Mood and setting 195
Mood in mystery 189   Mood through symbols 232
Mood through description . . . 189   Mood in a poem 239

Tone

Tone 346   Imagery and tone 385
Changes in tone . . . . 352, 364   Satire and irony 397
Serious, formal tone 369   Exaggeration 404
Argumentative tone 374   Puns 409
Emotional vs. factual tone . . . 379   Ironical situations 417

READING COMPREHENSION

Building background knowledge . . 18   Drawing conclusions 202
Summarizing 27   Figurative language 246
Interpreting 27   Making inferences 288
Thinking and Discussing 27   Recognizing significant details . . 336
Main idea and details 62   Fact and opinion 386
Supporting details 62   Author's purpose 418
Sequence 100   Critical reading 472
Cause and effect 164   Cloze 550

VOCABULARY/WORD ATTACK

Synonyms 62   Sound words 248
Antonyms 62   Word parts 288
Prefixes 65   Greek word parts 336
Closed compounds 65   Compound words 339
Synonym context clues 100   Technical terms 386
Antonym context clues 100   Suffixes 388
Glossary 103   Idioms 418
Pronunciation key 103   Hyphenated compounds 421
Words from a foreign language . . 103   Open compounds 421

Using experience clues 164
Phonetic respelling and pronunciation 167
Multiple meanings 202
Base words 205
Denotation and connotation . . . 246

Word roots 421
Shades of meaning 472
Context clues 550
Latin word parts 553

ORAL LANGUAGE DEVELOPMENT

Courtroom trial 65
Acting out a scene 103
Newscast 167
Dialogue 205
Reading a poem 249

Persuasive argument 291
Performing a skit 339
Debate 388
Interview 388
Speech 553

PROCESS WRITING

Comparisons 63
Review 101
Paragraph 165
Objective firsthand report . . . 203
Poem 249
Social letter 289

Autobiographical narrative 337
Letter of persuasion 387
Description 419
Character development . . . 473
Story 551

WRITING ABOUT THE SELECTION

Newspaper article 27
Description 31
Letter 53
Surprise ending 61
Dialogue. 77
Monologue 138
New ending 178

Imagery 219
Point of view 374
Satire 397
Exaggeration 404
Puns 409
Character description 549
Story within a story 549

RESEARCH AND STUDY SKILLS

Researching activities 65
Library 65
Card catalog 65
Catalog 65
Encyclopedia 65
Following directions 103
Periodic Guide 167
Special Dictionaries 167
Using photographs 205

Anthologies 249
Reference Sources 291
Periodicals 291
Biographical Dictionary . . . 339
Diagrams 339
Chart 388
Almanac 421
Graph 421

SHORT STORIES

Short-story writers present a setting — a time and a place. They fill the setting with characters who act and speak and feel. They plot a series of events in the lives of the characters. The writers create a world and then invite readers inside.

The Wreck of the Ole '97
Thomas Hart Benton (1889–1975).
Hunter Museum of Art, Chattanooga,
Gift of the Benwood Foundation.

Short Stories

For thousand of years, people have made up stories. The first stories were spoken aloud. Many of these stories were passed down from generation to generation. Later, storytellers began to write down their tales.

In modern times, writers have begun to develop a new literary form—the short story. Thousands of short stories have been written in the past 150 years. Each of these stories is different, but they all have certain elements in common. As you read the six short stories in Section 1, notice how each one presents people, places, events, and ideas in a unique way. Also look at how each writer has included the common elements of setting, plot, character, and point of view to create a powerful effect on you, the reader.

Setting It Up

The *setting* is the time and place in which a story happens. How the characters in each story look, act, and feel is influenced by where and when the story takes place. The stories in this section are presented in very different settings—a big city in the early 1900's; a small town in New Jersey in the recent past; a farming area in New Mexico in the 1940's; a dust-covered small town during the Depression; a Japanese coastal town during World War II; and a school in the here and now, though by the end of the story, you may wonder just exactly where the story took place.

Plotting It Out

The *plot* of a story is made up of the events that take place in the story in the order that the writer presents them. Sometimes the events are presented in the order they actually happened. At other times, writers include *flashbacks*—breaks in the story action that tell us about a time in the past.

As the plot of a story develops, readers begin to get a clear understanding of the events and people in the story. Sometimes readers begin to expect certain things to happen. When readers are a little nervous about what's going to happen, that feeling is called *suspense*. Suspense plays an important part in the overall effect of mystery and adventure stories. When readers begin to expect one thing to happen and something completely unexpected occurs, this is called *surprise* or a *plot twist*. The first two stories in Section 1 contain plot twists. You won't fully understand the mystery "The Green Door" or learn the meaning of "Blue Eyes Far Away" until you reach the end of those stories. Suspense and surprise add to the power of a story plot.

A Real Character

The people in a short story are its *characters*. Good writers make their characters believable. The more believable the story characters seem, the more readers care about what the characters do and what happens to them. Writers use a variety of methods to bring their characters to life. They describe how the characters look; they relate their words and actions; they reveal their inner thoughts and feelings; and they show how the characters affect each other. Writers also help readers understand their characters' *motivation*. That is, they show why characters act the way they do.

Points of View

Every story is told by a *narrator* who views the story from a particular angle. Sometimes the narrator is a story charac-

ter who tells the story from the *first-person* (or "I") point of view. The stories "Gentleman of Río en Medio" and "Marigolds" in this section are written from the first-person point of view. Sometimes a story is told from a *third-person* point of view by an "all-knowing" narrator who stands outside the story and knows what all the characters are doing, thinking, and feeling. The other four stories in this section are written from this viewpoint.

The point of view affects how readers understand the characters. In a story told from a first-person point of view, the narrator adds his or her own *bias*, or slant, to the descriptions of the characters. The first-person narrator, however, cannot reveal exactly how other characters feel inside or what they are thinking. A third-person narrator, such as the one telling the story "The Enemy" from this section, lets readers know where all the characters are, what they are thinking, and what motivates them. The first-person point of view brings readers right into the story action. The third-person point of view can let readers see the action from a place outside the action.

Now it's time to enter six different settings and learn about what happens to several very different characters.

The Green Door

by O. Henry

On the street, a man hands you a card with these words on it: "The Green Door." What does it mean? Rudolf Steiner, the main character of this O. Henry story, aims to find out. Always eager to find adventure, Rudolf goes behind the green door. What does he find there? When O. Henry—one of the most popular authors who ever lived—tells it, there's bound to be a surprise.

Rudolf Steiner was a true adventurer. During the day he sold pianos. In the evening he went out in search of the unexpected. The most interesting thing in life, he thought, might lie just around the next corner.

One evening, Rudolf went out for a walk in the central part of the city. He passed by a man who was handing out cards in front of a dentist's office. The man pressed a card into Rudolf's hand. One side of the card was blank. On the other side were written in ink three words: "The Green Door."

Rudolf noticed that some people before him had tossed their cards on the ground. These fell blank side up. He picked up a few of them and saw that every one had the dentist's address on it and an advertisement for the dentist's work. Rudolf went back down the street and was given another card by the man in front of the dentist's office. Once again, his card said only "The Green Door."

Rudolf could not ignore this chance for adventure. He looked at the building that the dentist's office was in and decided that it was there that his adventure must lie.

The building was five stories high. A small restaurant was in the basement. The first floor seemed to be a fur shop. The second floor was the dentist's. His name appeared in winking electric letters. The next floor had signs for dressmakers, musicians, and doctors. Still higher up, on the fourth and fifth floors, curtains were hung in the windows and milk bottles could be seen on the ledges. It seemed that people lived on these floors.

Rudolf entered the building and walked quickly up two flights of carpeted stairs. He stared down the dimly lit hallway and saw a green door. What would be behind the green door? Danger? Death? Love? Disappointment?

He knocked on the door. Moments passed before the door slowly opened. A young woman stood behind the door, looking ghostly pale and weak. She swayed slightly and Rudolf caught her. He sat her down on an old faded couch. The young woman was totally still and seemed to have fainted. Rudolf fanned her with his hat, and soon she awoke.

Her face was the one that Rudolf's heart was looking for. She was the reward for all his adventures. But she was awfully thin and pale.

She smiled at him. "I fainted, didn't I?" she asked. "Well, who wouldn't? Try going for three days without eating."

Rudolf jumped up and told her that he would be right back. He dashed out the green door and down the stairs. In 20 minutes he was back with both arms full of groceries. He laid them all out on the table—bread and butter, cold meats, cakes, pies, a roasted chicken, milk, and hot tea. They sat down to eat.

The food brought some color and life back into the young woman's face. She began to tell him about her life. It was a story of low wages, illness, lost jobs, and lost hope. To Rudolf the story sounded very important. "To think of your going through all that," he exclaimed. "Don't you have any friends or relatives in the city?" She replied that she did not. "I'm alone in the world, too," Rudolf said.

Suddenly her eyelids drooped and she sighed deeply. "I'm awfully sleepy," she said. Rudolf rose and took his hat. He held out his hand and she took it and said, "Good night." Her eyes seemed to ask a question. "Oh, I am coming back tomorrow to see how you are getting along," he said.

Then at the door she asked, "How did you come to knock on my door?" Quickly he decided that she must never know the truth. "One of our piano tuners lives in this house," he said. "I knocked at your door by mistake." The last thing he saw in the room before the green door closed was her smile.

At the head of the stairway he paused and looked around. He went along the hallway to the other end and noticed that every single door was painted green. He went up a flight of steps and each door on that floor was also green. In fact, every door in the building was green. Surprised, he went outside.

The man giving out the cards was still in front of the building. Rudolf showed the man his two cards. "Why did you give me these cards and what do they mean?" Rudolf asked. The man pointed down the street and said he thought Rudolf was probably too late for the first act.

Rudolf looked where the man had pointed and saw a theater. Above the entrance to the theater was a large electric sign advertising a new play, *The Green Door*.

"I hear it is a first-rate show," the man said. "The manager who represents the theater paid me to hand out some cards along with the dentist's. May I give you one of the dentist's cards, sir?"

READING COMPREHENSION

Summarizing. Choose the best phrase to complete each sentence. Then write the complete statements on your paper.

1. Rudolf Steiner thought that interesting adventures _____ (never happened to him, were dangerous and a waste of time, could happen anywhere).

2. For Rudolf, the cards were _____ (not important, an invitation to adventure, an unusual advertisement).

3. Behind the green door, Rudolf found _____ (a dentist's office, a theater entrance, a pale young woman who needed help).

4. Rudolf thought that the woman's story was _____ (unbelievable, very important, ridiculous).

5. Before he left the building, Rudolf discovered that all the doors were _____ (locked, different colors, green).

6. Rudolf found out that the cards were really _____ (ads for a new play, ads for a dentist, given to him by mistake).

Interpreting. Write the answer to each question on your paper.

1. Why did the young woman behind the green door faint?

2. Why did Rudolf get a second card from the man on the street?

3. When Rudolf first saw the pale young woman behind the door, how did he feel?

4. What was the question Rudolf saw in the eyes of the young woman?

5. What surprised Rudolf when he looked at the other doors in the building?

For Thinking and Discussing

1. Why did Rudolf decide that the girl should never know why he had actually knocked at her door? Do you think he should have told her the truth?

2. If you had been in Rudolf's place, what would you have done after you received the card?

UNDERSTANDING LITERATURE

Plot. The *plot* of a story is the sequence of events in the story. In a good plot, each event has one or more purposes for being presented. Some plot purposes are:

a. to provide background information

b. to show what a character is like

c. to develop or complicate a problem

d. to lead up to other events

Here are five events from the plot of "The Green Door." On your paper, list the numbers 1–5. Beside each number, write the letter of the purpose or purposes the author had for presenting that event.

1. Rudolf went for a walk.

2. Rudolf thought a card given to him was a chance for adventure.

3. Rudolf found a pale young woman behind the green door.

4. Rudolf discovered that all the doors on the floor were green.

5. The man told Rudolf that the cards were really advertisements.

WRITING

If this were the beginning of a longer story, you might read about Rudolf's next visit to the woman. In that visit, the writer might develop the problem further or provide more information to show what the characters are like. Write a paragraph telling what happens when Rudolf goes back to visit the woman.

Blue Eyes Far Away

by Mackinlay Kantor

*Her neighbors are surprised by the way Esther Lee accepts
the news of her husband's death. But there are even more
surprises in store for the husband's killer.*

*The title is an important clue to this suspenseful story. Is the
situation hopeless, or is there someone on hand who can see
that justice is done?*

Esther Lee's neighbors climbed the
steep road to bring her the news. They
found their job easier than they had
expected.

She was sitting on a bench under the
old cedar tree. Her blue eyes seemed very
empty and blank behind her glasses.

"Mrs. Lee," said George Dutton, "we
came to tell you—there's been an accident, and your husband was—they took
him to the hospital. I think you'd better
come, right away."

Joseph Lee's wife didn't say anything.
Slowly she got to her feet. The black bag
on her lap slid to the ground.

George Dutton turned away. His wife
put her arm around Esther Lee's shoulders. "Now, Mrs. Lee—he's hurt bad.
But maybe he'll be all right."

"It was an automobile accident," the
farmer said. "The highway police have
got the fellow that hit him, too. If it's
possible to convict him, we're going to
do it."

Convict, thought Esther Lee. *That
meant, then, that Joseph—*

"Can we go now?" she asked.

"Yes. Our car's right out here at the
gate. Don't you want to lock your house?
And what about this bag of yours?"

"Leave them be," said the woman.

It was not a strong case. It was really
no case at all except that a man had been
killed when his car was hit by the high-
powered red automobile of a young man.

That curve of the road had been deserted at the time of the accident, except
for the two men. Noise from the crash
had brought people from all directions.

The record of the young man who
drove the high-powered red automobile
was checked. It was found that he had
been in other accidents. He was known

for being careless. But you can't convict a man on his reputation, said the young fellow's lawyers.

The young man was charged with manslaughter. But after that, things moved slowly.

There wasn't much interest in the case after a while. Joseph Lee was not a well-known or wealthy man. There were few people in the courtroom. The defense knew that this was a simple matter. The case was the *State of New Jersey* versus *Archie Stolt*. The case would cost money but Archie Stolt could afford it. The defense did not know, however, that the night before the trial began, a small, gray-haired woman in a worn-out dress and old black hat went to call on the prosecutor.

Lawyers for the defense didn't seem to care when they saw her sitting in court. A weak attempt, they whispered, to get sympathy.

Esther Lee was the last witness called by the State. They had tried to bring in Archie Stolt's other accidents and his bad reputation. He watched, comfortably, as the little woman said she was Esther Lee, widow of the dead Joseph Lee.

"Where do you live, Mrs. Lee?" came the prosecutor's question.

"On the first Watchung mountain."

"Were you at home on the afternoon of June 20th, at about 5:30 p.m.?"

"Yes, Your Honor," said Esther Lee.

The lawyer cleared his throat. "Mrs. Lee, how long had you lived there?"

"Well," she said in her mild voice, "quite a while. See, when Joseph and I were first married, we lived down on Barnegat. He fished. We lived there for 40 years. And then his cousin left him a little place up on Watchung; we were getting older, so we moved up there. We lived there almost 11 years. We—"

"Your Honor," said the defense lawyer, "I object. The answers by the witness are beside the point. They are trying to plant sympathy in—"

The judge rapped. "Objection sustained."

The next question came like an explosion through the close air of the courtroom. "Mrs. Lee, did you see the accident in which your husband met his death?"

The woman nodded. Her answer was lost in the sudden stir as people moved forward.

"Tell the court what you saw."

"Well," said Esther Lee, "Joseph had gone to Union with his garden truck. He had good customers there every day. I sat out in front, always, to watch for him. I always used to do that, when he fished on Barnegat—"

The lawyer for the defense was on his feet. The prosecutor motioned him into his chair. "Tell only about the accident, please."

Esther Lee's blue eyes were wet. "I watched Joseph's old car come around a bend in the road," she said slowly, "and he was on the right side of the road. Then the red car came from the other way—on the wrong side of the road. And—Joseph's car swung out toward the middle—to try and miss it, I guess. But

25

the other car swung out, too. . . . They hit. That's all, sir. But the red car was on the wrong side of—"

"Your Honor!" cried the lawyer for the defense.

Archie Stolt settled back into his chair with a grin on his face. They couldn't pull anything like that and get away with it.

"I object. It was impossible for Esther Lee to have seen the accident from so far away. Impossible! The scene of the accident is miles from her home. I—"

The judge turned and looked down at the old woman. "I must remind you," he said, "that lying is a very serious offense.

You have sworn to tell nothing but the truth. How far is it from your home to the scene of the accident?"

"Must be a good three miles," whispered Esther Lee.

Three miles. . . . People in the courtroom shook their heads.

The woman's rough fingers touched the black bag in her lap. "I always watched for Joseph, though," she said. "Just like I used to do when he'd come in with his fish, on Barnegat. He liked to have me, and—"

She held up a shiny brass telescope. "This was his," she explained. "I always watched for Joseph, when he came home."

READING COMPREHENSION

Summarizing. Choose the best phrase to complete each sentence. Then write the complete statements on your paper.

1. Mrs. Lee's neighbors thought it would be hard to _____ (tell her about the accident, climb the steep hill, catch the man in the red car).

2. Archie wasn't worried at the trial because _____ (he knew he wasn't guilty, he thought there were no witnesses to the accident, the victim wasn't well known).

3. The contents of the black bag _____ (showed how lazy Archie was, showed how smart Esther was, explained how Esther had seen the accident).

Interpreting. Write the answer to each question on your paper.

1. What did Esther always do when Joseph went away?

2. Why was it easier for Esther Lee's neighbors to bring her the news than they had expected?

3. Why was it such a surprise to everyone in the courtroom when Esther said she had seen the accident?

4. Why did the judge warn Esther about lying in the courtroom?

For Thinking and Discussing. What kind of person was Esther Lee? Why do you think she waited until just before the trial to speak to the prosecutor?

UNDERSTANDING LITERATURE

Plot and Time Order. The plot of a short story is made up of all the events that happen in the story. The order in which the author presents these events may not be the order in which they actually happened. There is often a reason for telling the events in a particular order.

Here are seven events from the plot of "Blue Eyes Far Away." On your paper, write the list of events. To the left of the events, number them in the order that the author told readers about them in the story. To the right, number the events in the order in which they actually occurred.

a. Esther's neighbors climbed the hill to tell her about the crash.

b. Esther Lee saw the car crash.

c. Joseph Lee was killed in an accident.

d. Mrs. Lee watched for her husband.

e. Mrs. Lee appeared in court.

f. Mrs. Lee called on the prosecutor.

g. Archie Stolt was involved in several car accidents.

WRITING

Imagine that you are a reporter covering the trial in this story. Write a short article telling the main events of the plot in the order in which they occurred. Start your article with the following: *In court today, Mrs. Esther Lee provided convincing evidence that she had witnessed, from three miles away, the crash that killed her husband. She was sitting on her porch . . .*

Gentleman of Río en Medio

by Juan A. A. Sedillo

Don Anselmo's people have lived in Río en Medio for hundreds of years. Now the old man is selling his land to newcomers who are moving in. All the details of the sale seem to be agreed upon. But change can also bring unexpected problems.

It took months of negotiation to come to an understanding with the old man. He was in no hurry. What he had the most of was time. He lived up in Río en Medio, where his people had been for hundreds of years. He tilled the same land they had tilled. His house was small and wretched, but quaint. The little creek ran through his land. His orchard was gnarled and beautiful.

The day of the sale he came into the office. His coat was old, green, and faded. I thought of Senator Catron, who had been such a power with the people up there in the mountains. Perhaps it was one of his old Prince Albert coats. He also wore gloves. They were old and torn and his fingertips showed through them. He carried a cane, but it was only the skeleton of a worn-out umbrella. Behind him walked one of his innumerable kin — a dark young man with eyes like a gazelle.

The old man bowed to all of us in the room. Then he removed his hat and gloves, slowly and carefully. Then he handed his things to the boy, who stood obediently behind the old man's chair.

There was a great deal of conversation, about rain and about his family. He was very proud of his large family. Finally, we got down to business. Yes, he would sell, as he had agreed, for $1,200, in cash. We would buy, and the money was ready.

"Don Anselmo," I said to him in Spanish, "we have made a discovery. You remember that we sent that surveyor, that engineer, up there to survey your land so as to make the deed. Well, he finds that you own more than eight acres. He tells us that your land extends across the river and that you own almost twice as much as you thought." He didn't know that. "And now, Don Anselmo," I added, "these Americans are

FOR SALE

buena gente, they are good people and they are willing to pay you for the additional land as well, at the same rate per acre. So that instead of $1,200, you will get almost twice as much. The money is here for you."

The old man hung his head for a moment in thought. Then he stood up and stared at me. "Friend," he said, "I do not like to have you speak to me in that manner." I kept still and let him have his say. "I know these Americans are good people, and that is why I have agreed to sell to them. But I do not care to be insulted. I have agreed to sell my house and land for $1,200, and that is the price."

I argued with him but it was useless. Finally he signed the deed and took the money but refused to take more than the amount agreed upon. Then he shook hands all around, put on his ragged gloves, took his stick, and walked out with the boy behind him.

A month later my friends had moved into Río en Medio. They had replastered the old adobe house, pruned the trees, patched the fence, and moved in for the summer. One day, they came back to the office to complain. The children of the village were overrunning their property. They came every day and played under the trees, built little play fences around them, and took blossoms. When they were spoken to, they only laughed and talked back good-naturedly in Spanish.

I sent a messenger up to the mountains for Don Anselmo. It took a week to arrange another meeting. When he arrived he repeated his previous preliminary performance. He wore the same faded cutaway, carried the same stick, and was accompanied by the boy again. He shook hands all around, sat down with the boy behind his chair, and talked about the weather. Finally, I broached the subject. "Don Anselmo, about the ranch you sold to these people: They are good people and want to be your friends and neighbors always. When you sold it to them, you signed a document, a deed, and in that deed you agreed to several things. One thing was that they were to have the complete possession of the property. Now, Don Anselmo, it seems that every day the children of the village overrun the orchard and spend most of their time there. We would like to know if you, as the most respected man in the village,

could not stop them from doing so in order that these people may enjoy their new home more in peace."

Don Anselmo stood up. "We have all learned to love these Americans," he said, "because they are good people and good neighbors. I sold them my property because I knew they were good people, but I did not sell them the trees in the orchard."

This was bad. "Don Anselmo," I pleaded, "when one signs a deed and sells real property, one sells also everything that grows on the land, and those trees, every one of them, are on the land and inside the boundaries of what you sold."

"Yes, I admit that," he said. "You know," he added, "I am the oldest man in the village. Almost everyone there is my relative and all the children of Río en Medio are my *sobrinos* and *nietos,* my descendants. Every time a child has been born in Río en Medio since I took possession of that house from my mother, I have planted a tree for that child. The trees in that orchard are not mine, *Señor.* They belong to the children of the village. Every person in Río en Medio born since the railroad came to Santa Fe owns a tree in that orchard. I did not sell the trees because I could not. They are not mine."

There was nothing we could do. Legally, we owned the trees but the old man had been so generous, refusing what amounted to a fortune for him. It took most of the following winter to buy the trees, individually, from the descendants of Don Anselmo in the valley of Río en Medio.

READING COMPREHENSION

Summarizing. Choose the best phrase to complete each sentence. Then write the complete statements on your paper.

1. Don Anselmo refused to take more money for his land because he _____ (had agreed on a price and wanted to keep his word, didn't need the money, thought the land wasn't worth much).

2. The buyers of the land were bothered by _____ (sheep that ate all the grass, the high price they had paid, children playing under the trees).

3. Don Anselmo wouldn't tell the children to leave because _____ (he had already tried and failed, the trees belonged to the children, it wasn't his problem anymore).

Interpreting. Write the answer to each question on your paper.

1. Why did the Americans offer additional money for Don Anselmo's land?

2. Was Don Anselmo the only one to profit from the sale of his land? Explain your answer.

3. Why did it take so long—most of the winter—for the Americans to buy the trees?

For Thinking and Discussing. According to the story title, Don Anselmo was a "gentleman." In what ways did he live up to that title? In what ways did the buyers live up to being called "good people"?

UNDERSTANDING LITERATURE

Setting. The events of a story happen in a certain place at a certain time. The place and time of a story make up its *setting*.

To understand "Gentleman of Río en Medio," it is important to think about the setting. How do the people live in this setting? What is important to them?

Here are eight statements about the setting of "Gentleman of Río en Medio." On your paper, indicate which statements are *true* and which are *false*.

1. The old man's family had lived in Río en Medio for many years.

2. Río en Medio was a wealthy area.

3. The people in the area had a close relationship with each other.

4. Change occurred slowly in Río en Medio.

5. People near Río en Medio lived in a very modern way.

6. The new owners understood the traditions before they moved in.

7. Respect was valued in Río en Medio.

8. Law was more important than tradition in this area.

WRITING

Think about a place you know or have read about. Make a list of some of the ways people live or act in that place. Then develop your list into a short description of the place.

Marigolds

by Eugenia Collier

*Golden marigolds shine in the sun. To an old woman,
marigolds are as good as gold. To young Lizabeth in this
short story, marigolds are too beautiful to live. But what is a
world without beauty? Who can live in such a world?
Perhaps a reckless child—but not the woman she becomes.*

When I think of my home town where I grew up, all that I seem to remember is dust. I remember the brown, crumbly dust of late summer that gets into the eyes and makes them water. It is the kind of dust that gets into the throat and between the toes of bare brown feet. I don't know why I should remember only the dust. There must have been green lawns and paved streets under leafy shade trees somewhere in town.

But memory doesn't always present things as they are, but rather as they feel. And so, when I think of that time and place, I remember only the dry September of the dirt roads and grassless yards of the shantytown where I lived. And the one other thing I remember is a bright splash of sunny yellow against the dust— Miss Lottie's marigolds.

Whenever I remember those marigolds, I feel the mixed emotions of growing up. Emotions that are as hard to grab as smoke, yet as real as the potted flowers before me. The joy and anger, happiness and shame of a 14-year-old going on 15 become mixed together when I think back to that moment years ago.

I think of those marigolds at the strangest times.

While I was growing up, the Depression gripped the country. We children were only a little aware of how poor we were. We were used to living that way. Having no radios, few newspapers, and no magazines, we knew little of the world outside of our own. Poverty was the cage in which we were all trapped, and our hatred of it was like the restlessness of a zoo-bred flamingo who knows nature created him to fly free.

By the time I was 14, my brother Joey and I were the only children left at our house. The older ones had left home to get married or to live in the city. The two babies had been sent to relatives who might care for them better than we. Joey was three years younger than I. Each morning our mother and father walked down the dirt road and around the bend. She walked to her job as a cleaning woman. He walked to his daily search for work. After our few chores around the shanty, Joey and I were free to run wild in the sun with the other children.

The memory of those days runs together like a fresh watercolor painting left out in the rain. I remember drawing a picture in the dust which Joey happily erased with one sweep of his dirty foot. I remember fishing in a muddy creek. The fish went right by my cupped hand as Joey laughed. And I remember, that year, a strange restlessness of body and spirit. It was a feeling that something unknown and scary was beginning.

One day returns to me clearly for some reason. I was resting under the great oak tree in our yard. I was deep in thought which I have now forgotten except that it involved some secret. Joey and a bunch of kids were bored now with the old tire hanging from an oak limb. It had kept them busy for a while. "Hey, Lizabeth," Joey yelled. He never talked when he could yell. "Hey, Lizabeth, let's go somewhere."

I came back from the thoughts of my private world. "Where at, Joey?"

The truth was that we were becoming tired of the empty summer days.

"Let's go see if we can find us some locusts on the hill," someone suggested.

Joey made a face. "Ain't no more locusts there. Y'all got 'em while they was still green."

The argument that followed was short and not really worth it. Hunting locust trees wasn't fun anymore by now.

"Tell you what," said Joey finally, his eyes sparkling. "Let's us go over to Miss Lottie's."

The idea caught on at once. Annoying Miss Lottie was always fun. I was still child enough to run along with the group. We went over old fences and through bushes that tore our already ripped clothes, back to where Miss Lottie lived. I think now that we must have looked partly funny and partly sad. There were five or six of us, all different ages, dressed in only one thing each. The girls wore faded dresses that were too long or too short. The boys wore patched pants. A little cloud of dust followed our thin legs and bare feet as we tramped over the dusty ground.

When Miss Lottie's house came into view, we stopped. We had to make our plans and get a little more courage. Miss Lottie's house was the most rundown of all our rundown homes. The sun and rain had faded its frame from white to a sad gray. The boards seemed to be standing, not from being nailed together, but from leaning together like a house that a child might have made from cards.

As far as I know, it is still standing. It was a gray, rotting thing with no porch, no shutters, and no steps. It was set on a small lot with no grass, not even any weeds.

In front of the house in a squeaky rocking chair sat Miss Lottie's son, John Burke. He was what was known as "queer-headed." He sat rocking day in and day out in a mindless way. He wore a torn hat above his shaggy head to shade him from the sun. John Burke was

not usually aware of anything outside his quiet dream world. But if you disturbed him, he would become very mad. He would strike out at you and curse at you in some strange language that only he could understand. We children made a game of thinking of ways to disturb him and then escape his anger.

But our real fun and our real fear lay in Miss Lottie herself. Miss Lottie seemed to be at least a hundred years old. Her big frame still held traces of the tall, powerful woman she must have been. She was now bent over. Her smooth skin was a dark reddish-brown. Her face had Indian-like features.

Miss Lottie didn't like people who bothered her, especially children. She never left her yard, and nobody ever visited her. We never knew how she managed those things that depended somewhat on other people. For example, how she ate, or even whether she ate. When we were tiny children, we thought Miss Lottie was a witch and we made up tales. We half believed them ourselves. We were far too grown up now, of course, to believe witch stories. But old fears have a way of clinging like cobwebs. And so, when we saw the tumbledown shack, we had to stop and gather our courage.

"Look, there she is," I whispered, forgetting that Miss Lottie could not possibly have heard me from that distance. "She's fooling with them crazy flowers."

"Yeh, look at 'er."

Miss Lottie's marigolds were the strangest part of the picture. They did not fit in with the rest of her yard. Beyond the dusty brown yard, in front of the sorry gray house, rose suddenly and shockingly a bright strip of blossoms. They were clumped together in large mounds, warm and sun-golden. The old, black witch-woman worked on them all summer, every summer, down on her creaky knees. She weeded and arranged while the house crumbled and John Burke rocked.

For some strange reason, we children hated those marigolds. They got in the way of the perfect ugliness of the place. They were too beautiful. They said too much that we could not understand. They did not make sense.

There was something about how the old woman destroyed the weeds that bothered us. It should have been a funny sight—the old woman with the man's hat on her white head, leaning over the bright flowers. But it wasn't funny. It was something we could not name. We had to bother her by throwing a pebble into her flowers or by yelling a dirty word, then dancing away from her anger. Actually, I think it was the flowers we wanted to destroy, but nobody had the nerve to try it. Not even Joey, who was usually fool enough to try anything.

"Y'all git some stones," commanded Joey now. He was met with instant giggling as everyone except me began to gather pebbles from the dusty ground. "Come on, Lizabeth."

I just stood there looking through the bushes. I was torn between wanting to join the fun and feeling that it was all a bit silly.

"You scared, Lizabeth?"

I cursed and spat on the ground.

"Y'all children get the stones. I'll show you how to use them."

I said before that we children were not very aware of how thick the bars of our own cage were. I wonder now, though, if we were not more aware of it than I thought. Perhaps we had some small notion of what we were and how little chance we had of being anything else. Otherwise, why would we have wanted to destroy things so much? Anyway, the pebbles were collected quickly, and everybody looked at me to begin the fun.

"Come on, y'all."

We crept to the edge of the bushes that bordered the narrow road in front of Miss Lottie's place. She was working quietly, kneeling over the flowers. Suddenly, "zing"—an expertly aimed stone cut the head off of one of the blossoms.

"Who out there?" Miss Lottie's head came up as her sharp eyes searched the bushes. "You better git!"

We kneeled down out of sight in the bushes. We tried to stop our laughter that insisted on coming. Miss Lottie looked across the road for a moment. Then she went back to her weeding. "Zing"—Joey sent a pebble into the blooms, and another marigold was beheaded.

Miss Lottie was angry now. She began struggling to her feet, leaning on a cane and shouting. "Y'all git! Go on home!" Then the rest of the kids let loose their pebbles. They were storming the flowers and laughing wildly at Miss Lottie's anger. She shook her stick at us and started toward the road crying, "John Burke, John Burke, come help!"

Then I lost my head entirely. I was mad with the power of creating such anger. I ran out of the bushes in the storm of pebbles, straight toward Miss Lottie. I was chanting madly, "Old witch, fell in a ditch, picked up a penny and thought she was rich!" The children screamed with delight. They dropped their pebbles and joined the crazy dance. They swarmed around Miss Lottie like bees. The madness lasted only a moment. John Burke, startled at last, lurched out of his chair. We dashed for the bushes just as Miss Lottie's cane went whizzing by my head.

I did not join the fun when the kids gathered again under the oak in our back yard. Suddenly I was ashamed. The child in me sulked and said it was all in fun. The woman in me flinched at the thought of the mean attack that I had led. The mood lasted all afternoon. When we ate the beans and rice that was supper that night, I did not notice that my mother was not there. She always worked well into the evening. Joey and I had a bad fight after supper. Finally I stretched out in the room we shared and fell asleep.

When I awoke, somewhere in the middle of the night, my mother had returned. I listened to what I could hear through the thin walls that separated our rooms. At first, I heard no words, only voices. My mother's voice was like a cool, dark room in summer. It was peaceful, comforting, and quiet. I loved to listen to it. It made things seem all right somehow. But my father's voice cut through hers, shattering the peace.

"Twenty-two years, Maybelle, 22 years," he was saying, "and I got nothing for you, nothing, nothing."

"It's all right, honey, you'll get something. Everybody out of work now, you know that."

"It ain't right. Ain't no man ought to eat his woman's food year in and year out and see his children running wild. Ain't nothing right about that."

"Honey, you took good care of us when you had it. Ain't nobody got nothing nowadays."

"I ain't talking about nobody else. I'm talking about me. God knows I try." My mother said something I could not hear, and my father cried out louder. "What must a man do, tell me that?"

"Look, we ain't starving. I git paid every week, and Mrs. Ellis is real nice about giving me things. She gonna let me have Mr. Ellis's old coat for you this winter—"

"Mr. Ellis's coat! You think I want people's old things?" Suddenly my father started to sob loudly and painfully. He cried helplessly and hopelessly in the dark night. I had never heard a man cry before. I did not know men ever cried. I covered my ears with my hands. It still could not cut off the sound of my father's painful sobs.

My father was a strong man who

would whisk a child upon his shoulders and go singing through the house. My father made toys for us and laughed so loud that the great oak seemed to laugh with him. He taught us how to fish and hunt rabbits. How could it be that my father was crying? But the sobs went on. They went on until I could hear my mother's voice, deep and rich, humming softly as she used to hum to a frightened child.

The world had lost its boundary lines. My mother, who was small and soft, was now the strength of the family. My father, who was the rock on which the family had been built, was sobbing like the tiniest child. Everything was suddenly out of tune. Where did I fit into this crazy picture? I do not now remember my thoughts. I only remember a feeling of great confusion and fear.

Long after the sobbing and humming had stopped, I lay on the bed with my hands over my ears. I wished that I, too, could cry and be comforted. The night was silent now except for the sound of crickets and of Joey's soft breathing. But the room was too crowded with fear to allow me to sleep. Finally, with the feeling of terrible aloneness of 4 a.m., I decided to wake up Joey.

"Ouch! What's the matter with you? What you want?" he demanded when I had pinched and slapped him awake.

"Come on, wake up."

"What for? Go 'way."

I was lost for a reasonable answer. I could not say, "I'm scared and I don't want to be alone," so I said, "I'm going out. If you want to come, come."

The promise of adventure awoke him. "Going out now? Where at, Lizabeth? What you going to do?"

I was pulling my dress over my head. Until now I had not thought of going out. "Just come on," I said quickly.

I was out the window and halfway down the road before Joey caught up with me.

"Wait, Lizabeth, where you going?"

I was running as if something was after me. I was running silently and furiously until I came to where I had half-known I was headed: to Miss Lottie's yard.

The half-dawn light was more scary than darkness. In it the old house was like the ruin that my world had become. It looked haunted. But I was not afraid, because I was haunted, too.

"Lizabeth, you lost your mind?" panted Joey.

I had indeed lost my mind. All the feelings of that summer swelled in me and burst. The great need for my mother who was never there, the hopelessness of our poverty, and the fear opened by my father's tears all made me feel crazy.

"Lizabeth!"

I leaped into the mounds of marigolds and pulled madly. I pulled and destroyed the perfect yellow blooms. The fresh smell of early morning and of dew-soaked marigolds pushed me on as I went tearing and sobbing, while Joey tugged my dress crying, "Lizabeth, stop, please stop!"

And then I was sitting in the little garden among the ruined flowers. I was crying and crying, but it was too late to undo what I had done. Joey was sitting

beside me. He was scared and silent and did not know what to say. Then, "Lizabeth, look."

I opened my swollen eyes and saw in front of me a pair of large feet. My eyes lifted to the swollen legs. I saw an old body dressed in a tight cotton nightdress. Then the shadowed Indian face and the short white hair. And there was no anger in the face now—now that the garden was destroyed and there was nothing any longer to be protected.

"M-Miss Lottie!" I jumped to my feet and just stood there and stared at her. That was the moment when childhood faded and womanhood began. That crazy act was the last act of childhood. The witch was no longer a witch but a broken old woman who had dared to create beauty where everything was ugly. She had been born poor and had lived that way all her life. Now at the end of that life she had nothing except a fallingdown hut, a wrecked body, and John Burke. Whatever life there was left in her, whatever love and beauty and joy that had not been squeezed out by life, had been there in the marigolds she so tenderly cared for.

Of course I could not say the things that I knew about Miss Lottie as I stood there ashamed. The years have put words to the things I knew in that moment. As I look back upon it, I know that moment marked the end of innocence. Innocence means seeing things at face value, and not seeing things below the surface. In that moment I looked beyond myself and

into the depths of another person. This was the beginning of having feeling for another person.

The years have taken me worlds away from that time and that place. They have taken me away from the dust and poverty of our lives. They have taken me away from the bright things that I destroyed in a blind, childish striking out. Miss Lottie died long ago and many years have passed since I last saw her hut. It was completely barren at last. She never planted marigolds again. Yet there are times when the image of those yellow flowers returns with a painful sting. For one does not have to be ignorant and poor to find that his life is as barren as the dusty yards of our town. And I, too, have planted marigolds.

READING COMPREHENSION

Summarizing. Choose the best phrase to complete each sentence. Then write the complete statements on your paper.

1. Lizabeth and her friends were used to being _____ (entertained, tired, poor).

2. The children in the story caused trouble because they _____ (were bored and had nothing else to do, wanted to find ways to make money, couldn't read or write well).

3. The one thing of beauty Lizabeth remembered from her childhood was _____ (Miss Lottie's marigolds, her favorite party dress, the view from her window).

4. When Lizabeth heard her father crying, she _____ (went to sleep, comforted him, covered her ears).

5. Lizabeth pulled out the marigolds because she _____ (wanted to destroy something beautiful, wanted to plant them in her own yard, hated Miss Lottie).

6. After Lizabeth destroyed the marigolds in Miss Lottie's garden, she felt _____ (ashamed, relieved, angry).

7. The night she destroyed the marigolds, Lizabeth _____ (blamed the act on someone else, was severely punished when she got home, began to understand other people's feelings).

Interpreting. Write the answer to each question on your paper.

1. How did Lizabeth feel when she heard her father crying?

2. Why did Miss Lottie's marigolds bother Lizabeth so much?

3. What does the author mean by the phrase, "The world had lost its boundary lines"?

4. Why did Lizabeth cry after she destroyed the marigolds?

5. How did Lizabeth's feelings about Miss Lottie change during the story?

6. Why is the image of the marigolds still painful to Lizabeth years later?

For Thinking and Discussing

1. In this story, the marigolds are more than flowers in someone's garden. They have a special meaning. What did the marigolds mean to Miss Lottie? Why do you think she never replanted the flowers after Lizabeth destroyed them?

2. What does the author tell us about Lizabeth's family life? How do you think her experiences influenced the way she acted?

UNDERSTANDING LITERATURE

Characterization. One of the important keys to understanding a short story is knowing what the characters are like. Here are some of the ways in which a writer can show what the characters in a story are like:

a. by describing their physical appearance

b. by detailing their words and actions

c. by revealing their thoughts and feelings

d. by showing the ways in which they affect the other characters in the short story

Here are four quotations from "Marigolds." Find each quotation in the story. On your paper, write down which character each quotation is about. Then write one or two sentences explaining what is revealed about the character from the quotation.

1. "He never talked when he could yell."

2. "He sat rocking day in and day out in a mindless way."

3. "The child in me sulked and said it was all in fun. The woman in me flinched at the thought of the mean attack that I had led."

4. "What must a man do, tell me that?"

WRITING

Many years later, Lizabeth still felt ashamed at having destroyed Miss Lottie's marigolds. Pretend you are Lizabeth. Write a letter to Miss Lottie in which you explain why you ruined her marigolds and apologize for your actions.

The Enemy

by Pearl S. Buck

Doctor Sadao Hoki is a highly skilled Japanese doctor. He takes pride in his ability to help save human lives. But what will the doctor do when a wounded American sailor suddenly washes up on the shore near his home? This is during World War II, and America is the enemy. What is the doctor's responsibility—to save the enemy or to kill him?

Dr. Sadao Hoki's low, square stone house was set upon rocks well above a narrow beach that was outlined with bent pines. Sadao had been sent at 22 to America. He had come back at 30, famous not only as a surgeon but as a scientist. Because of his medical research, he had not been sent abroad with the troops. Also, he knew, there was some slight danger that the old General might need an operation for a condition for which he was now being treated medically, and for this possibility, Sadao was being kept in Japan.

Looking at the fog coming in over the beach, Sadao thought of his wife, Hana. He had met Hana in America, but he had waited to fall in love with her until he was sure she was Japanese. He wondered often whom he would have married if he had not met Hana, and by what luck he had found her in the most casual way at an American professor's house.

Now he felt her hand on his arm and was aware of the pleasure it gave him, even though they had been married years enough to have the two children. She laid her cheek against his arm.

It was at this moment that both of them saw something black come out of the mists. It was a man. He was flung up out of the ocean—flung, it seemed, to his feet by a breaker. He staggered a few steps, his body outlined against the mist, his arms above his head. Then the curled mists hid him again.

"Who is that?" Hana cried. Now they saw him again. The man was on his hands and knees, crawling. Then they saw him fall on his face and lie there.

"A fisherman, perhaps," Sadao said, "washed from his boat." He ran quickly down the steps and behind him Hana came, her wide sleeves flying.

"He is wounded!" Sadao exclaimed. He made haste to the man, who lay motionless, his face in the sand. Sadao stooped, Hana at his side, and turned the man's head. They saw the face.

"A white man!" Hana whispered.

A wet cap fell away and there was his wet yellow hair, long, as though for many weeks it had not been cut, and upon his young and tortured face was a yellow beard. He was unconscious and knew nothing that they did to him.

Now Sadao remembered the wound, and with his expert fingers he began to search for it. On the right side of his lower back, Sadao saw that a ragged gun wound had been reopened. The flesh was blackened with powder.

"What shall we do with this man?" Sadao muttered. But his trained hands seemed of their own will to be doing what they could to stop the fearful bleeding.

"If we sheltered a white man in our house, we would be arrested, and if we turned him over as a prisoner, he would certainly die," Sadao said.

"The kindest thing would be to put him back into the sea," Hana said. But neither of them moved.

"There is something about him that looks American," Sadao said. He took up the battered cap. Yes, there, almost gone, was the faint lettering, "U.S. Navy." The man was a prisoner of war!

"He has escaped," Hana cried softly, "and that is why he is wounded."

They hesitated, looking at each other. Then Hana said with resolution, "Come, are we able to put him back into the sea?"

"If I am able, are you?" Sadao asked.

"No," Hana said, "But if you can do it alone . . ."

Sadao hesitated again. "The strange thing is," he said, "that if the man were whole I could turn him over to the police without difficulty. I care nothing for him. He is my enemy. All Americans are my enemy. And he is only a common fellow. You see how foolish his face is. But since he is wounded . . ."

"You also cannot throw him back to the sea," Hana said. "Then there is only one thing to do. We must carry him into the house."

"But the servants?" Sadao inquired.

"We must simply tell them that we intend to give him to the police—as indeed we must, Sadao. We must think of the children and your position. It would endanger all of us if we did not give this man over as a prisoner of war.

"Certainly," Sadao agreed. "I would not think of doing anything else."

So, his arms hanging, they carried him up the steps and into the side door of the house toward an empty bedroom.

"He will die unless he is operated on," Sadao said, considering. "The question is whether he will die if he is operated on, too."

Hana cried out in fear. "Don't try to save him! What if he should live?"

"What if he should die?" Sadao replied.

Hana considered this, and when she did not answer, Sadao turned away. "At any rate something must be done with him," he said, "and first he must be washed." He went quickly out of the room and Hana came behind him. She did not wish to be left alone with the white man. He was the first she had seen since she left America, and now he

seemed to have nothing to do with those whom she had known there. Here he was her enemy, a menace, living or dead.

She went to the door and called, "Yumi—Yumi—come with me!"

Then Hana led the way quickly and softly to the kitchen. There two servants were frightened at what their master had just told them. The old gardener who was also a house servant pulled the few hairs on his upper lip.

"The master ought not to heal the wound of this white man," he said bluntly to Hana. "The white man ought to die. First he was shot. Then the sea caught him and wounded him with her rocks. If the master heals what the gun did and what the sea did, they will take revenge on us."

"I will tell him what you say," Hana replied courteously. But she herself was also frightened, although she was not as superstitious as the old man was. Could it ever be well to help an enemy? Nevertheless, she told Yumi to fetch the hot water and bring it to the room where the white man was.

"My master ought not to command me to wash the enemy," Yumi said stubbornly.

There was so fierce a look of resistance upon Yumi's round dull face that Hana felt unreasonably afraid. After all, what if the servants should report something that was not as it happened?

"Then please," Hana said gently, "return to your own work." This left Hana with the white man alone. She might have been too afraid to stay, but her anger at Yumi gave her strength.

"Stupid Yumi," she muttered fiercely. "Is this anything but a man? And a wounded, helpless man!"

She dipped the small clean towel that Yumi had brought into the steaming hot water and washed his face carefully. She kept on washing him until his upper body was quite clean. But she dared not turn him over. Where was Sadao?

"Sadao!" she called softly.

He had been about to come in when she called. She saw that he had brought his surgeon's emergency bag and that he wore his surgeon's coat.

"You have decided to operate!" she cried.

"Yes," he said shortly. "Fetch towels."

He peered into the wound with his bright surgeon's light fastened on his forehead. "The bullet is still there," he said with cool interest. "Now I wonder how deep this rock wound is? If it is not too deep, it may be that I can get the bullet. He has lost much blood."

At this moment Hana choked. He looked up and saw her face was the color of sulfur.

"Don't faint," he said sharply. "If I stop now, the man will surely die." She clapped her hands to her mouth and ran out of the room.

He had forgotten that of course she had never seen an operation. But her distress and his inability to go to her at once made him impatient and irritable with this man who lay as though dead under his knife. In his dream the man moaned, but Sadao paid no heed except to mutter at him.

"Groan," he muttered, "groan if you

like. I am not doing this for my own pleasure. In fact, I do not know why I am doing it."

The door opened and there was Hana again. She had not stopped even to smooth back her hair.

She crouched close to the sleeping face of the young American. It was a very thin face, she thought, and the lips were twisted. The man was suffering, whether he knew it or not. Watching him, she wondered if the stories they heard sometimes of the sufferings of prisoners were true. They came like flickers of rumor, told by word of mouth and always contradicted. In the newspapers the reports were always that wherever the Japanese armies went the people received them gladly, with cries of joy at their liberation. She hoped anxiously that this young man had not been tortured.

At this moment, Sadao felt the tip of his instrument strike against something hard. Then, quickly, with the cleanest and most precise of incisions, the bullet was out. The man quivered but he was still unconscious.

"This man will live in spite of all," Sadao said to Hana and sighed.

The young man woke, so weak, his blue eyes so sad when he figured out where he was, that Hana felt compelled to apologize.

"Don't be afraid," she begged him softly.

"How come . . . you speak English?" he gasped.

"I was a long time in America," she replied.

She saw that he wanted to reply to that but he could not. So she knelt and fed him gently from the porcelain spoon. He ate unwillingly, but still he ate.

"Now you soon will be strong," she said, not liking him and yet moved to comfort him.

He did not answer.

When Sadao came in the third day after the operation he found the young man sitting up, his face bloodless with the effort.

"Lie down!" Sadao cried. "Do you want to die?"

"What are you going to do with me?" the boy muttered. He looked just now barely 17. "Are you going to hand me over?"

For a moment Sadao did not answer. He finished his examination and then pulled the silk quilt over the man.

"I do not know myself what I shall do with you," he said. "I ought of course to give you to the police. You are a prisoner of war . . . no, do not tell me anything." He put up his hand as he saw the young man about to speak. "Do not even tell me your name unless I ask for it."

They looked at each other for a moment, and then the young man closed his eyes and turned his face to the wall.

"Okay," he whispered, his mouth a bitter line.

Outside the door Hana was waiting for Sadao. He saw at once that she was in trouble.

"Sadao, Yumi tells me the servants feel that they cannot stay if we hide this man here anymore," she said. "She says, they are thinking that you and I were so long in America that we have forgotten to think of our own country first. They think we like Americans."

"It is not true," Sadao said harshly. "Americans are our enemies. But I have been trained not to let a man die if I can help it."

"The servants cannot understand that," she said anxiously.

Neither seemed able to say more, and somehow the household dragged on. The servants grew more watchful every day. Their courtesy was as careful as ever, but their eyes were cold upon the pair for whom they worked.

"It is clear what our master ought to do," the old gardener said one morning. "When the man was so near death, why did he not let him bleed?"

"That young master is so proud of his skill to save life that he saves any life," the cook said.

"It is the children of whom we must think," Yumi said sadly. "What will be their fate if their father is condemned as a traitor?"

They did not try to hide what they said from the ears of Hana and she knew that they spoke on purpose that she might hear. That they were right she knew in most of her being. But there was another part of her which she herself could not understand.

As for Sadao, every day he examined the wound carefully. Finally, he pulled out the last stitches. In two weeks, the sailor would be nearly as well as ever.

On the seventh day after the stitches were removed, two things happened. In the morning the servants left together, their belongings tied in large, square cotton kerchiefs. When Hana got up in the morning nothing was done. The house was not cleaned and the food not prepared. She knew what that meant. She was upset and even terrified, but her pride as a mistress would not allow her to show it. Instead, she inclined her head gracefully when the servants appeared before her in the kitchen. She paid them off and thanked them for all that they had done for her.

She made the breakfast and Sadao helped with the children. Neither of them spoke of the servants beyond the fact that they were gone. But after Hana had taken morning food to the prisoner, she came back to Sadao.

"Why is it we cannot see clearly what we ought to do?" she asked him. "Even the servants see more clearly than we do. Why are we different from other Japanese?" Sadao did not answer.

In the afternoon the second thing happened. Hana saw a messenger come to the door in official uniform. Her hands went weak and she could not draw her breath. The servants must have told already. She ran to Sadao, gasping, unable to utter a word.

"What is it?" he asked the messenger and then he rose, seeing the man's uniform.

"You are to come to the palace," the man said. "The old General is in pain again."

When Sadao came to tell Hana good-bye she was in the kitchen, but doing nothing. The children were asleep and she sat merely resting for a moment, more exhausted from her fright than from work.

"I thought they had come to arrest you," she said.

He gazed down into her anxious eyes. "I must get rid of this man for your sake," he said in distress. "Somehow I must get rid of him."

"Of course," the General said weakly, "I understand fully. But that is because I once took a degree in Princeton. So few Japanese have."

"I care nothing for the man, Excellency," Sadao said, "but having operated on him with such success . . ."

"Yes, yes," the General said. "The way you have acted only makes me feel that I need you more. You say you think I can stand only one more such attack as I have had today?"

"Not more than one," Sadao said.

"Then certainly I can allow nothing to happen to you," the General said with anxiety. His long pale Japanese face became blank, which meant that he was in deep thought. "You cannot be arrested," the General said, closing his eyes. "Suppose you were condemned to death and the next day I had to have my operation?"

"There are other surgeons, Excellency," Sadao suggested.

"None that I trust," the General replied. "It is very unfortunate that this man should have been washed up on your doorstep," he said irritably.

"I feel it so myself," Sadao said gently.

"It would be best if he could be quietly killed," the General said. "Not by you, but by someone who does not know him. I have my own private assassins. Suppose I send two of them to your house tonight — or better, any night. You need know nothing about it. If you like, I can even have them remove the body."

Sadao considered. "That perhaps would be best, Excellency," he agreed, thinking of Hana.

He left the General then, and went home, thinking over the plan. In this way, the whole thing would be taken out of his hands. He would tell Hana nothing.

He refused to worry as he went into the room where the American was in bed. But as he opened the door he found the young man out of bed to his surprise, and preparing to go out into the garden.

"Gosh, I feel good again! But will the muscles on this side always feel stiff?"

"Is it so?" Sadao inquired, surprised. He forgot all else. "Now I thought I had provided against that," he murmured. He lifted the edge of the man's shirt and gazed at the healing scar. "Massage may do it," he said, "if exercise does not."

"It won't bother me much," the young man said. His young face was gaunt un-

der the stubbly blond beard. "Say, doctor, I've got something I want to say to you. If I hadn't met a Jap like you, well, I wouldn't be alive today. I know that."

Sadao bowed, but he could not speak.

"Sure, I know that," he went on warmly. His big thin hands gripping a chair were white at the knuckles. "I guess if all the Japs were like you there wouldn't have been a war."

"Perhaps," Sadao said with difficulty. "And now I think you had better go back to bed."

Sadao slept badly that night. Time and

again he woke, thinking he heard the rustling of footsteps, the sound of a twig broken or a stone displaced in the garden.

The next morning he made the excuse to go first into the guest room. If the American were gone, he then could simply tell Hana that the General had directed this. But when he opened the door, there, on the pillow, was the shaggy blond head. He could hear the peaceful breathing of sleep, and he closed the door again quietly.

But certainly, he thought, the second night must be the night. There rose a wind that night, and he listened to the sounds of bending boughs and whistling

doors. But the next morning the American was still there.

Then the third night, of course, must be the night. The wind changed to quiet rain and the garden was full of the sound of dripping leaves and running springs. Sadao slept a little better, but he woke at the sound of a crash and leaped up.

"What was that?" Hana cried. "I must go and see."

"Don't go," he said fearfully. "Don't go!"

Yet, when he opened the door of the guest room in the morning, there was the young man. He had already washed and was on his feet. He had asked for a razor yesterday and had shaved himself, and today there was a faint color in his cheeks.

"I am well," he said joyously.

Sadao drew his kimono around his weary body. He could not, he decided suddenly, go through another night. It was not that he cared for this young man's life. No, simply, it was not worth the strain.

"You are well," Sadao agreed. He lowered his voice. "You are so well that I think if I put my boat on the shore tonight, with food and extra clothing in it, you might be able to row to that little island not far from the coast. It is so near the coast that it has not been worth fortifying. Nobody lives on it because in storms it is submerged. But this is not the season of storms. You could live there until you saw a fishing boat pass by. They pass quite near the island because the water is many fathoms deep there."

The young man stared at him, slowly comprehending. "Do I have to?" he asked.

"I think so," Sadao said gently.

The young man nodded, understanding perfectly. "Okay," he said simply.

Sadao did not see him again until evening. As soon as it was dark, Sadao had dragged the stout boat down to the shore and in it he put food and bottled water that he had bought secretly during the day, as well as two quilts he had bought at a pawnshop. The boat he tied to a post in the water, for the tide was high. There was no moon and he worked without a flashlight.

He went into the guest room that night before he went to bed and checked carefully the American's temperature, the state of the wound, and his heart and pulse.

"I realize that you are saving my life again," he told Sadao.

"Not at all," Sadao said. "It is only inconvenient to have you here any longer."

He had hesitated a good deal about giving the man a flashlight. But he had decided to give it to him after all. It was a small one, his own, which he used at night when he was called.

"If your food runs out before you catch a boat," he said, "signal me two flashes at the same instant the sun drops over the horizon. Do not signal in darkness for it will be seen. If you are all right but still there, signal me once. You will find fish easy to catch but you must eat them raw. A fire would be seen."

"Okay," the young man breathed.

He was dressed now in the Japanese clothes which Sadao had given him, and at the last moment Sadao wrapped a black cloth about his blond head.

"Now," Sadao said.

The young American, without a word, shook Sadao's hand warmly. Then he walked quite well across the floor and down the step into the darkness of the garden. Once . . . twice . . . Sadao saw his light flash to find his way. But that would not be suspected. He waited until he saw one more flash from the shore. Then he closed the door. That night he slept.

"You say the man escaped?" the General asked faintly. He had been operated upon a week ago, an emergency operation to which Sadao had been called in the night. For 12 hours Sadao had not been sure the General would live.

After a week Sadao had felt the General was well enough to be spoken to about the prisoner.

"That prisoner," the General said with some energy, "did I not promise you I would kill him for you?"

"You did, Excellency," Sadao said.

"Well, well," the old man said in a tone of amazement. "So I did! But you see, I was suffering a good deal. The truth is, I thought of nothing but myself. In short, I forgot my promise to you."

"I wondered, Your Excellency," Sadao murmured.

"It was certainly very careless of me," the General said. "But you understand it was not lack of patriotism." He looked anxiously at his doctor. "If the matter should come out, you would understand that, wouldn't you?"

"Certainly, Your Excellency," Sadao said. He suddenly understood that the General was in the palm of his hand and, therefore, he himself was perfectly safe. "I can swear to your loyalty, Excellency," he said to the old General, "and to your zeal against the enemy."

"You are a good man," the General murmured, and closed his eyes. "You will be rewarded."

But Sadao, in searching the spot of black in the twilighted sea that night, had his reward. There was no flash of light in the dusk. No one was on the island. His prisoner was gone — safe, doubtless, for he had warned him to wait only for a Korean fishing boat.

He stood for a moment on the veranda, gazing out at the sea from which the young man had come that other night. For some reason, he began to think of other white faces he had known. He remembered the old teacher of anatomy, who had insisted that Sadao show mercy with his knife. Then he remembered the face of his landlady and the difficulty he had had in finding a place to live because he was a Japanese. The Americans were full of prejudice. It had been bitter to live with it because he knew he was better than they were. It was a relief to be openly at war with them at last.

Now he remembered the young, drawn face of the prisoner again. It seemed white and repulsive to him now.

"Strange," he thought. "I wonder why I could not kill him."

READING COMPREHENSION

Summarizing. Choose the best phrase to complete each sentence. Then write the complete statements on your paper.

1. Sadao had studied medicine in _____ (Japan, the United States, Australia).

2. Sadao worked to stop the man's bleeding because _____ (he didn't yet realize the person was an enemy, Hana hated the sight of blood, his instincts as a doctor immediately took over).

3. Sadao sent the young man to the island so that he could be _____ (alone, rescued, with other Americans).

Interpreting. Write the answer to each question on your paper.

1. How did Sadao know the young man was an American prisoner of war?

2. Why was the young man sad and bitter when he awoke from the operation?

3. Why did Sadao tell the General about the sailor in the first place?

4. When Dr. Sadao was convinced that the American was safe, how did he feel about the decision to let him go free?

For Thinking and Discussing

1. How did Sadao feel about Americans? Why? Why did he save the sailor anyway?

2. How did Hana feel about having an enemy in the house? Why do you think she supported her husband?

UNDERSTANDING LITERATURE

Character Motivation. Short story characters usually have a clear reason, or *motivation,* for speaking or acting as they do. In a well-written story, the characters' motives should fit their personalities.

Select the best choice to complete each statement below about one of the characters in "The Enemy." Write the letter of the answer on your paper.

1. No matter how she felt about having the sailor in her house, Hana always _____.
   a. looked for help from others
   b. thought first of her children
   c. supported her husband

2. Sadao's actions were most strongly influenced by his _____.
   a. concern for his family
   b. values as a physician
   c. loyalty to his country

3. Whenever he appeared in the story, the General _____.
   a. seemed concerned only with himself
   b. demonstrated love for his soldiers
   c. showed hatred for Americans

WRITING

Imagine the American writing a letter of thanks to Sadao after the war. Pretend you are Sadao, writing a letter in response. Explain why you saved the American's life.

Future Tense

by Robert Lipsyte

Gary, the top creative writer in school, was anxious to meet his new English teacher. When he found him too ordinary to be true, his imagination took over.

Gary couldn't wait for tenth grade to start so he could strut his sentences, parade his paragraphs, renew his reputation as the top creative writer in school. At the opening assembly, he felt on edge, psyched, like a boxer before the first-round bell. He leaned forward as Dr. Proctor, the principal, introduced two new staff members. He wasn't particularly interested in the new vice-principal, Ms. Jones; Gary never had discipline problems, he'd never even had to stay after school. But his head cocked alertly as Dr. Proctor introduced the new Honors English teacher, Mr. Smith. Here was the person he'd have to impress.

He studied Mr. Smith. The man was hard to describe. He looked as though he'd been manufactured to fit his name. Average height, brownish hair, pale white skin, medium build. Middle age. He was the sort of person you began to forget the minute you met him. Even his clothes had no particular style. They merely covered his body.

Mr. Smith was . . . just there.

Gary was studying Mr. Smith so intently that he didn't hear Dr. Proctor call him up to the stage to receive an award from last term. Jim Baggs jabbed an elbow into his ribs and said, "Let's get up there, Dude."

Dr. Proctor shook Gary's hand and gave him the County Medal for Best Composition. While Dr. Proctor was giving Jim Baggs the County Trophy for Best All-Round Athlete, Gary glanced over his shoulder to see if Mr. Smith looked impressed. But he couldn't find the new teacher. Gary wondered if Mr. Smith was so ordinary he was invisible when no one was talking about him.

On the way home, Dani Belzer, the prettiest poet in school, asked Gary, "What did you think of our new Mr. Wordsmith?"

"If he was a color he'd be beige," said Gary. "If he was a taste he'd be water. If he was a sound he'd be a low hum."

"Fancy, empty words," sneered Mike Chung, ace reporter on the school paper. "All you've told me is you've got nothing to tell me."

Dani quickly stepped between them. "What did you think of the first assignment?"

"Describe a Typical Day at School," said Gary, trying unsuccessfully to mimic Mr. Smith's bland voice. "That's about as exciting as tofu."

"A real artist," said Dani, "accepts the commonplace as a challenge."

That night, hunched over his humming electric typewriter, Gary wrote a description of a typical day at school from the viewpoint of a new teacher who was seeing everything for the very first time, who took nothing for granted. He described the shredded edges of the limp flag outside the dented front door, the worn flooring where generations of kids had nervously paced outside the principal's office, the nauseatingly sweet pipe-smoke seeping out of the teachers' lounge.

And then, in the last line, he gave the composition that extra twist, the little kicker on which his reputation rested. He wrote:

> The new teacher's beady little eyes missed nothing, for they were the optical recorders of an alien creature who had come to earth to gather information.

The next morning, when Mr. Smith asked for a volunteer to read aloud, Gary was on his feet and moving toward the front of the classroom before Mike Chung got his hand out of his pocket.

The class loved Gary's composition. They laughed and stamped their feet. Chung shrugged, which meant he couldn't think of any criticism, and Dani flashed thumbs up. Best of all, Jim Baggs shouldered Gary against the blackboard after class and said, "Awesome tale, Dude."

Gary felt good until he got the composition back. Along one margin, in a perfect script, Mr. Smith had written:

You can do better.

"How would he know?" Gary complained on the way home.

"You should be grateful," said Dani. "He's pushing you to the farthest limits of your talent."

"Which may be nearer than you think," snickered Mike.

Gary rewrote his composition, expanded it, complicated it, thickened it. Not only was this new teacher an alien, he was part of an extraterrestrial conspiracy to take over Earth. Gary's final sentence was:

> Every iota of information, fragment of fact, morsel of minutiae sucked up by those vacuuming eyes was beamed directly into a computer circling the planet. The data would eventually become a program that would control the mind of every school kid on earth.

Gary showed the new draft to Dani before class. He stood on tiptoes so he could read over her shoulder. Sometimes he wished she were shorter, but mostly he wished he were taller.

"What do you think?"

"The assignment was to describe a typical day," said Dani. "This is off the wall."

He snatched the papers back. "Creative writing means creating." He walked away, hurt and angry. He thought: *If she doesn't like my compositions, how can I ever get her to like me?*

That morning, Mike Chung read his own composition aloud to the class. He described a typical day through the eyes of a student in a wheelchair. Everything most students take for granted was an obstacle: the bathroom door too heavy to open, the gym steps too steep to climb, the light switch too high on the wall. The class applauded and Mr. Smith nodded approvingly. Even Gary had to admit it was really good—if you considered plain-fact journalism as creative writing, that is.

Gary's rewrite came back the next day marked:

Improving. Try again.

Saturday he locked himself in his room after breakfast and rewrote the rewrite. He carefully selected his nouns and verbs and adjectives. He polished and arranged them in sentences like a jeweler strings pearls. He felt good as he wrote, as the electric typewriter hummed and buzzed and sometimes coughed. He thought: *Every champion knows that as hard as it is to get to the top, it's even harder to stay up there.*

His mother knocked on his door around noon. When he let her in, she said, "It's a beautiful day."

"Big project," he mumbled. He wanted to avoid a distracting conversation.

She smiled. "If you spend too much time in your room, you'll turn into a mushroom."

He wasn't listening. "Thanks. Anything's okay. Don't forget the mayonnaise."

Gary wrote:

The alien's probes trembled as he read the student's composition. Could that skinny, bespectacled earthling really suspect its extraterrestrial identity? Or was his composition merely the result of a creative thunderstorm in a brilliant young mind?

Before Gary turned in his composition on Monday morning, he showed it to Mike Chung. He should have known better.

"You're trying too hard," chortled Chung. "Truth is stronger than fiction."

Gary flinched at that. It hurt. It might be true. But he couldn't let his competition know he had scored. "You journalists are stuck in the present and the past," growled Gary. "Imagination prepares us for what's going to happen."

Dani read her composition aloud to the class. It described a typical day from the perspective of a louse choosing a head of hair to nest in. The louse moved from the thicket of a varsity crew-cut to the matted jungle of a sagging perm to a straight, sleek blond cascade.

The class cheered and Mr. Smith smiled. Gary felt a twinge of jealousy. Dani and Mike were coming on. There wasn't room for more than one at the top.

In the hallway, he said to Dani, "And you called my composition off the wall?"

Mike jumped in. "There's a big difference between poetical metaphor and hack science fiction."

Gary felt choked by a lump in his throat. He hurried away.

Mr. Smith handed back Gary's composition the next day marked:

See me after school.

Gary was nervous all day. What was there to talk about? Maybe Mr. Smith hated science fiction. One of those traditional English teachers. Didn't understand that science fiction could be literature. *Maybe I can educate him,* thought Gary.

When Gary arrived at the English office, Mr. Smith seemed nervous too. He kept folding and unfolding Gary's composition. "Where do you get such ideas?" he asked in his monotone voice.

Gary shrugged. "They just come to me."

"Alien teachers. Taking over the minds of schoolchildren." Mr. Smith's empty eyes were blinking. "What made you think of that?"

"I've always had this vivid imagination."

"If you're sure it's just your imagination." Mr. Smith looked relieved. "I guess everything will work out." He handed back Gary's composition. "No more fantasy, Gary. Reality. That's your assignment. Write only about what you know."

Outside school, Gary ran into Jim Baggs, who looked surprised to see him. "Don't tell me you had to stay after, Dude."

"I had to see Mr. Smith about my composition. He didn't like it. Told me to stick to reality."

"Don't listen." Jim Baggs body checked Gary into the schoolyard fence. "Dude, you got to be yourself."

Gary ran all the way home and locked himself into his room. He felt feverish with creativity. Dude, you got to be your-

self, Dude. It doesn't matter what your so-called friends say, or your English teacher. You've got to play your own kind of game, write your own kind of stories.

The words flowed out of Gary's mind and through his fingers and out of the machine and onto sheets of paper. He wrote and rewrote until he felt the words were exactly right:

> With great effort, the alien shut down the electrical panic impulses coursing through its system and turned on Logical Overdrive. There were two possibilities:
> 1. This high school boy was exactly what he seemed to be, a brilliant, imaginative, apprentice best-selling author and screenwriter, or,
> 2. He had somehow stumbled onto the secret plan and he would have to be either enlisted into the conspiracy or erased off the face of the planet.

First thing in the morning, Gary turned in his new rewrite to Mr. Smith. A half hour later, Mr. Smith called Gary out of Spanish. There was no expression on his regular features. He said, "I'm going to need some help with you."

Cold sweat covered Gary's body as Mr. Smith grabbed his arm and led him to the new vice-principal. She read the composition while they waited. Gary got a good look at her for the first time. Ms. Jones was . . . just there. She looked as though she'd been manufactured to fit her name.

Average. Standard. Typical. The cold sweat turned into goose pimples.

How could he have missed the clues? Smith and Jones were aliens! He had stumbled on their secret and now they'd have to deal with him.

He blurted, "Are you going to enlist me or erase me?"

Ms. Jones ignored him. "In my opinion, Mr. Smith, you are overreacting. This sort of nonsense"—she waved Gary's composition—"is the typical response of an overstimulated adolescent to the mixture of reality and fantasy in an environment dominated by manipulative music, television, and films. Nothing for us to worry about."

"If you're sure, Ms. Jones," said Mr. Smith. He didn't sound sure.

The vice-principal looked at Gary for the first time. There was no expression in her eyes. Her voice was flat. "You'd better get off this science fiction kick," she said. "If you know what's good for you."

"I'll never tell another human being, I swear," he babbled.

"What are you talking about?" asked Ms. Jones.

"Your secret is safe with me," he lied. He thought, *If I can just get away from them. Alert the authorities. Save the planet.*

"You see," said Ms. Jones, "you're writing yourself into a crazed state."

"You're beginning to believe your own fantasies," said Mr. Smith.

"I'm not going to do anything this time," said Ms. Jones, "but you must promise to write only about what you know."

"Or I'll have to fail you," said Mr. Smith.

"For your own good," said Ms. Jones. "Writing can be very dangerous."

"Especially for writers," said Mr. Smith, "who write about things they shouldn't."

"Absolutely," said Gary, "positively, no question about it. Only what I know." He backed out the door, nodding his head, thinking, *Just a few more steps and I'm okay. I hope these aliens can't read minds.*

Jim Baggs was practicing head fakes in the hallway. He slammed Gary into the wall with a hip block. "How's it going, Dude?" he asked, helping Gary up.

"Aliens," gasped Gary. "Told me no more science fiction."

"They can't treat a star writer like that," said Jim. "See what the head honcho's got to say." He grabbed Gary's wrist and dragged him to the principal's office.

"What can I do for you, boys?" boomed Dr. Proctor.

"They're messing with his moves, Doc," said Jim Baggs. "You got to let the aces run their races."

"Thank you, James." Dr. Proctor popped his forefinger at the door. "I'll handle this."

"You're home free, Dude," said Jim, whacking Gary across the shoulder blades as he left.

"From the beginning," ordered Dr. Proctor. He nodded sympathetically as Gary told the entire story, from the opening assembly to the meeting with Mr. Smith and Ms. Jones. When Gary was finished, Dr. Proctor took the papers from Gary's hand. He shook his head as he read Gary's latest rewrite.

"You really have a way with words, Gary. I should have sensed you were on to something."

Gary's stomach flipped. "You really think there could be aliens trying to take over Earth?"

"Certainly," said Dr. Proctor, matter-of-factly. "Earth is the ripest plum in the universe."

Gary wasn't sure if he should feel relieved that he wasn't crazy or be scared out of his mind. He took a deep breath to control the quaver in his voice, and said: "I spotted Smith and Jones right away. They look like they were manufactured to fit their names. Obviously humanoids. Panicked as soon as they knew I was on to them."

Dr. Proctor chuckled and shook his head. "No self-respecting civilization would send those two stiffs to Earth."

"They're not aliens?" He felt relieved and disappointed at the same time.

"I checked them out myself," said Dr. Proctor. "Just two average, standard, typical human beings, with no imagination, no creativity."

"So why'd you hire them?"

Dr. Proctor laughed. "Because they'd never spot an alien. No creative imagination. That's why I got rid of the last vice-principal and the last Honors English teacher. They were giving me odd little glances when they thought I wasn't looking. After ten years on your planet, I've learned to smell trouble."

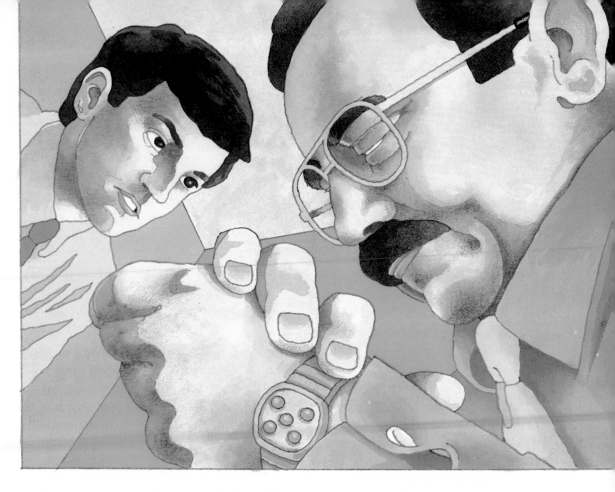

Gary's spine turned to ice and dripped down the backs of his legs. "You're an alien!"

"Great composition," said Dr. Proctor, waving Gary's papers. "Grammatical, vividly written, and totally accurate."

"It's just a composition," babbled Gary, "made the whole thing up, imagination, you know."

Dr. Proctor removed the face of his wristwatch and began tapping tiny buttons. "Always liked writers. I majored in your planet's literature. Writers are the keepers of the past and the hope of the future. Too bad they cause so much trouble in the present."

"I won't tell anyone," cried Gary.

"Your secret's safe with me." He began to back slowly toward the door.

Dr. Proctor shook his head. "How can writers keep secrets, Gary? It's their nature to share their creations with the world." He tapped three times and froze Gary in place, one foot raised to step out the door.

"But it was only a composition," screamed Gary as his body disappeared before his eyes.

"And I can't wait to hear what the folks back home say when you read it to them," said Dr. Proctor.

"I made it all up." Gary had the sensation of rocketing upward. "I made up the whole . . ."

READING COMPREHENSION

Summarizing. Choose the best phrase to complete each sentence. Then write the complete statements on your paper.

1. Gary described Mr. Smith as very _____ (smart, ordinary, exciting).

2. The composition Gary wrote for school was _____ (a mystery, a biography, science fiction).

3. Gary began to believe that Mr. Smith and Ms. Jones were _____ (creative, aliens, crazy).

4. At the end of the story, Dr. Proctor revealed that _____ (he was an alien, Mr. Smith and Ms. Jones were humanoids, he didn't like writers).

Interpreting. Write the answer to each question on your paper.

1. How did Gary feel when Mr. Smith returned his composition and his rewrite?

2. Why didn't Mr. Smith like Gary's composition?

3. Why did Gary begin to think that Mr. Smith and Ms. Jones were aliens?

For Thinking and Discussing

1. What does this story's title mean? Does the title have more than one meaning? Explain your answer.

2. What do you think will happen to Gary next?

UNDERSTANDING LITERATURE

Plot. Some stories have a *surprise ending*. A surprise ending occurs when the reader, and often the characters in the story, are shocked by what happens. The author achieves a surprise ending by creating anticipation for an expected ending. In "Future Tense," the author leads us to suspect that Mr. Smith and Ms. Jones are aliens. We are shocked to find out that it is not they, but Dr. Proctor, who is from another planet.

Read each of the following quotes from the story and copy them on your paper. Decide whether each is a clue to the expected ending, or to the surprise ending. Write *E* for a clue to the expected ending or *S* for a clue to the surprise ending.

1. There was no expression in her eyes. Her voice was flat.

2. "You really have a way with words, Gary. I should have sensed you were on to something."

3. "You'd better get off this science fiction kick . . . if you know what's good for you."

4. He looked as though he'd been manufactured to fit his name.

5. "No self-respecting civilization would send those two stiffs to Earth."

WRITING

In the style of Gary's composition, write a paragraph describing the surprise ending.

Section Review

VOCABULARY

Synonyms and Antonyms. *Synonyms* are words that have almost the same meaning—for example, *moist* and *damp*. *Antonyms* are words that have opposite meanings—for example, *moist* and *dry*.

Each sentence below comes from one of the stories in this section. Notice the word in italics in the sentence. Then look for a synonym and an antonym of each word in italics in the list above the sentences. Write each word with its synonym and antonym on your paper.

empty	respond to	exposed
underwater	stops	exceptional
well-built	spreads	crumbling
medium	pass up	crowded

1. "Rudolf could not *ignore* this chance for adventure."

2. "That curve of the road had been *deserted* at the time of the accident. . . ."

3. "'He tells us that your land *extends* across the river and that you own almost twice as much as you thought.'"

4. "And so, when we saw the *tumble-down* shack, we had to stop and gather our courage."

5. "'Nobody lives on it [the island] because in storms it is *submerged*.'"

6. "*Average* height, brownish hair, pale white skin . . ."

READING

Main Idea and Details. When you read, try to sort the information you learn into main ideas and details. The main idea of a paragraph or selection is the central thought that holds all of the information together. The main idea answers the question "What is this about?" The details are bits of information that support or relate to the main idea.

In much of your reading, the main idea will appear near the beginning of a paragraph or selection. The rest of the paragraph or selection will contain the supporting details.

Here are two groups of statements about two stories you have read in this section. On your paper, write the sentence from each group that states the main idea of that group. Under each main idea, list the details that support it.

Group A

In the evening, Rudolf went out walking.

Rudolf knocked at the green door.

He went back and got another card.

Rudolf was a true adventurer.

He asked what the card meant.

Group B

It took months of negotiations to come to an understanding.

There was a great deal of conversation.

What Don Anselmo had was lots of time.

Finally, everyone got down to business.

He removed his hat and gloves, slowly and carefully.

WRITING

Comparisons. A comparison tells how two things are alike or similar and how they are different. To write a comparison of two things, you need to observe them or think about them carefully. When you do this, you can find similarities and differences between almost any two things.

Step 1: Set Your Goal

Choose one of these topics for a comparison:

1. Write a comparison of the girl Lizabeth and Miss Lottie in "Marigolds." Include similarities and differences between any of the following characteristics: their ages, interests, backgrounds, behavior, and character traits.

2. Write a comparison of Dr. Sadao's ["The Enemy"] life in America and his life in Japan. Include similarities and differences between any of the following aspects of his life: school, work, his home in each place, the physical appearance of each area, and his activities and friends.

Whichever you choose, use your imagination and the information given in the story to make your comparison.

Step 2: Make a Plan

Make two lists of ideas for your comparison: one of similarities, the other of differences. You may want to divide each list into sections for different subtopics. For example, suppose you were writing a comparison of Sadao's life in America and his life in Japan. The lists of similarities and differences might be divided into these categories: the place where he lived; people he knew; the way he spent his time.

Once you have made the lists, you need to decide how to organize the ideas. You can use either of these two methods:

1. In one paragraph, tell all about one subject. Then, in a second paragraph, compare the second subject to the first subject, pointing out similarities and differences between them. For example, in a comparison of Lizabeth and Miss Lottie, you would first write a paragraph describing Lizabeth. Then you would write a second paragraph comparing Miss Lottie to Lizabeth, pointing out how they are alike and how they are different.

   When you use this method, make sure that you compare the same kinds of details in both paragraphs. Also, present your points of comparison in the same order.

2. Discuss each point of comparison, one at a time, with a separate paragraph on each point. For example, in a comparison about Sadao, your first paragraph could discuss the similarities and differences between the places where he lived. Your second paragraph might describe what was alike and what was different about the people he knew. The final paragraph of your composition could tell what was similar and what was different about the way he spent his time.

Step 3: Write a First Draft

Write a first draft, according to the method of organization you have decided on. Refer to your list of similarities and differences and try to include all of them in your comparison. Be careful to follow the same method of organization throughout your composition. If you have chosen the first method of organization, do not switch to the other method halfway through your composition. But if the method you chose doesn't seem to work well, you can begin again and try the other method.

You might also want to include specific examples in your composition to illustrate the similarities and differences. For example, in a comparison about Sadao, you might say, "As a student, he had to report to his professors; as a surgeon, he had to report to the general." Remember that you want your reader to be able to see things more clearly as a result of your comparison.

Step 4: Revise

When you revise your composition, ask yourself these questions:

Do you clearly state the important similarities and differences?

Have you followed the same method of organization throughout?

Did you include details that illustrate your comparisons?

After you have revised your comparison, proofread it and copy it over neatly.

The following is a quiz for Section 1. Write the answers in complete sentences on your paper.

Reading Comprehension

1. What did the card that said "The Green Door" really mean?

2. In "Blue Eyes Far Away," what was Esther Lee doing when her husband died? Why was this important to what happened later?

3. In "Gentleman of Río en Medio," what problem did the new owners face? How did they solve it?

4. In "The Enemy," why was the sailor lucky that a doctor found him?

5. How did Gary's wish to remain the top creative writer in school contribute to the turn of events?

Understanding Literature

6. In "The Green Door," what kind of person was Rudolf? Why was knocking on the door typical of him?

7. How did Mrs. Lee feel about her husband in "Blue Eyes Far Away"?

8. What happened in "Gentleman of Río en Medio" after the land was sold?

9. What is the setting of "Marigolds"? Why is the story's time important?

10. How did earlier events in Sadao's life affect his feelings toward the American sailor in "The Enemy"?

Word Attack

1. In "Future Tense," Gary writes a composition about a teacher who is part of "an extraterrestrial conspiracy to take over the Earth." In the word *extraterrestrial, extra-* means "beyond." *Terrestrial* means "of the earth or its inhabitants." So *extraterrestrial* means "existing outside the earth."

   a. Try to think of other words with the prefix *extra-*. Explain the meaning of each word. You may use the dictionary if you need help.

   b. Make up at least five original words of your own using the prefix *extra-*, *extraloud* for example. Write a definition for each word you create, and use it in a sentence.

2. The word *flashlight* from "The Enemy" is a special kind of word called a *closed compound*. Think of other closed compounds that either begin with *flash* or end with *light* such as *flashcube* or *nightlight*. List the words on your paper. You may use the dictionary to help you.

Speaking and Listening. Get together with some classmates to recreate the courtroom scene in "Blue Eyes Far Away." You will need students to play the judge, the lawyer for the defense, the lawyer for the prosecution, Archie Stolt, and Esther Lee. When you are ready, act out the trial in front of the class. Let the class be the jury.

Researching. Go to the library and find out what you can about the lives of one of these authors: O. Henry, Mackinlay Kantor, or Pearl S. Buck. Find the titles of other short stories and books they wrote. Report to the class what you learned.

Creating. Write a story about what happens to Gary when he reaches the alien planet. Is he put on trial? Is he able to use his creative talents to become a famous writer there? Does he ever manage to get back to Earth?

DRAMA

Drama is alive. On stage, actors become people revealing thoughts and emotions aloud. Drama is an interaction between actors and audience. During a play, members of the audience learn about the characters and about their own lives as well.

Two on the Aisle
Edward Hopper (1882–1967).
Toledo Museum of Art,
Gift of Edward Drummond Libbey.

Drama

In ancient times, actors performed under the open sky. Now they perform in large or small theaters in front of an audience, or in large sound studios in front of movie or television cameras. Whether drama is presented live, on tape, or on film, it is a special form of literature. Drama is alive.

Drama is meant to be seen and heard rather than just read. Words on paper are transformed by a capable actor into statements and emotions that touch the viewer's thoughts and feelings. The interaction between actor and audience is vital to drama. The audience must believe that the actors *are* the people they portray. The actors must sense the audience's belief in them.

The Right Look

Drama even looks different on paper from other literary forms. Characters' names are indicated before the words, or *lines,* that they speak. And there are no quotation marks used to set off a speaker's exact words. The playwright also gives actors and readers clues to how the lines are to be spoken. Special notes, called *stage directions,* are enclosed in parentheses to indicate emotions and actions that are to accompany the lines. The stage directions help the actors know what feelings to display. They also help people who read the plays in books to get a clearer mental picture of how the "live" play would look and sound. Other stage directions describe the setting of a scene and indicate any change in setting.

In a short story, you might read:

A Russian clerk named Cherdyakov found himself sitting directly behind his boss, General Mikhail Brassilhov, at the theater one night. He thought this was an excellent opportunity to make himself known to the General and perhaps to earn a promotion. He introduced himself in as humble a way as possible. The haughty General couldn't have cared less who the pushy man was, however. He was more interested in great actors than in little clerks.

In "The Sneeze," the first play you will read in this section, this same scene appears as follows:

Cherdyakov: Permit me, sir. I am Cherdyakov . . . Ivan Ilyitch. This is a great honor for me, sir.
General: *(turns, coldly):* Yes.
Cherdyakov: Like yourself, dear General, I too serve the Ministry of Public Parks. . . . That is to say, I serve you, who is indeed himself the Minister of Public Parks. I am the Assistant Chief Clerk in the Department of Trees and Bushes.
General: Ahh, yes. Keep up the good

work. . . . Lovely trees and bushes this year. Very nice.

(The General turns back. Cherdyakov sits back, happy, grinning like a cat. The General shrugs back.)

What is the difference between the two forms? In the short story, the reader is told about the characters and their actions. In the play, the characters reveal themselves through what they say and what they do.

The first two dramas in this section, "The Sneeze" and "I Remember Mama," were originally short stories. The playwrights, Neil Simon and John Van Druten, decided to bring the stories to life by adapting them into stage plays. The third drama in this section, "Sudden Death," was written originally for television. It was an episode in the series *The White Shadow.*

Dramatic Elements

Whether dramas are written for the stage, for the large movie screen, for the small TV screen, or for radio, they have certain common elements. Like short stories, dramatic scenes are placed in a certain *setting.* They follow a *plot* line that usually moves in sequence. They examine the thoughts, words, and actions of a group of *characters.* What makes drama different from other literary forms is the close relationship that is developed between the characters and the audience. Dramatic characters are alive. Their problems on stage or on film often seem real to the audience.

In "The Sneeze," Cherdyakov finds himself with the opportunity at the theater to get to know his boss on equal terms. All that stands in Cherdyakov's way are his enormous sneezes and his own lack of confidence. Cherdyakov's particular problems may be unusual, but his desire for recognition is a need that everyone can understand and share.

In "I Remember Mama," a teenage girl grows up as part of an immigrant family in San Francisco at the turn of the century. She needs direction to help plan her future. Her problem is one most of the audience has faced. Her mother shows her the way — by word and example.

In "Sudden Death," a basketball coach and the team members confront a tragedy that was not in their game plan: death. Facing tragedy is a problem all of us must experience.

Drama is a form of literature that calls for audience participation. So, add a little drama to your life. On with the show!

The Sneeze

a play by Neil Simon
based on a story by Anton Chekhov

Have you ever done something that truly embarrassed you? Perhaps you apologized to those you offended. To Ivan Ilyitch Cherdyakov, sneezing on his boss's head is an embarrassment. But Cherdyakov does more than merely offer a simple apology. After all, how can he ever be forgiven for what he has done?

Cherdyakov's story is presented through the eyes of a writer who narrates and takes part in the action.

CHARACTERS

Writer, the play's narrator
Ivan Ilyitch Cherdyakov, a Russian clerk
His wife, Madame Cherdyakov
General Mikhail Brassilhov, Minister of Public Parks and Cherdyakov's boss
Madame Brassilhov, the General's wife

Writer: If Ivan Ilyitch Cherdyakov, a civil servant, a clerk in the Ministry of Public Parks, had any passion in life at all, it was the theater. *(Enter Ivan Cherdyakov and his wife. He is in his mid-thirties, mild-mannered, and shy. He and his wife are dressed in their best, but are certainly no match for the grandeur around them. They are clearly out of place here. They move into their seats. As his wife studies her program, Cherdyakov is beaming* with happiness as he looks around and in back at the theater and its famous audience. He is a happy man tonight.) He certainly had hopes and ambitions for higher office and had dedicated his life to hard work and patience. Still, he would not deny himself his one great pleasure. So he purchased two tickets in the very best section of the theater for the opening night performance of Rostov's *The Bearded Countess.* *(A splendidly uniformed General and his wife enter, looking for their seats.)* As fortune would have it, into the theater that night came His Respected Boss, General Mikhail Brassilhov, the Minister of Public Parks himself. . . .

(The General and his wife take their seats in the first row, the General directly in front of Cherdyakov.)

Cherdyakov *(leans over to the General):* Good evening, General.

General *(turns, looks at Cherdyakov coldly):* Hmm? . . . What? Oh, yes. Yes. Good evening. *(The General turns front again, looks at his program.)*

Cherdyakov: Permit me, sir. I am Cherdyakov . . . Ivan Ilyitch. This is a great honor for me, sir.

General *(turns coldly):* Yes.

Cherdyakov: Like yourself, dear General, I too serve the Ministry of Public Parks. . . . That is to say, I serve you, who is indeed himself the Minister of Public Parks. I am the Assistant Chief Clerk in the Department of Trees and Bushes.

General: Ahh, yes. Keep up the good work. . . . Lovely trees and bushes this year. Very nice.

(The General turns back. Cherdyakov sits back, happy, grinning like a cat. The General shrugs back. Suddenly, the unseen curtain rises on the play and they all applaud. Cherdyakov leans forward again.)

Cherdyakov: My wife would like very much to say hello, General. This is she. My wife, Madame Cherdyakov.

Wife *(smiles):* How do you do?

General: My pleasure.

Wife: My pleasure, General.

General: How do you do?

(He turns front, flustered. Cherdyakov beams at his wife; then:)

Cherdyakov *(to the General's wife):* Madame Brassilhov—my wife, Madame Cherdyakov.

Wife: How do you do, Madame Brassilhov?

Madame Brassilhov *(coldly):* How do you do?

Wife: I just had the pleasure of meeting your husband.

Cherdyakov *(to Madame Brassilhov):* And I am my wife's husband. How do you do, Madame Brassilhov?

(The Writer "shushes" them.)

General *(to the Writer):* Sorry. Terribly sorry. *(The General tries to control his anger as they all go back to watching the play.)*

Cherdyakov: I hope you enjoy the play, sir.

General: I will if I can watch it. *(He is getting hot under the collar. They all go back to watching the performance.)*

Writer: Feeling quite pleased with himself for having made the most of this golden opportunity, Ivan Ilyitch Cherdyakov sat back to enjoy *The Bearded Countess.* He was no longer a stranger to the Minister of Public Parks. They had become, if one wanted to be generous about the matter, familiar with each other. And then, quite suddenly, without any warning, like a bolt from a gray thundering sky, Ivan Ilyitch Cherdyakov reared his head back, and . . .

Cherdyakov: AHHHHHHHH—CHOOOO-OOOO!!! *(Cherdyakov unleashes a monstrous sneeze, his head snapping forward. The main blow of the sneeze discharges on the back of the General's completely bald head. The General winces and his hand immediately goes to his* *now-dampened head.)* Ohhh, my goodness, I'm sorry, your Excellency! I'm so terribly sorry! *(The General takes out his handkerchief and wipes his head.)*

General: Never mind. It's all right.

Cherdyakov: All right? . . . It certainly is not all right! It's unpardonable. It was monstrous of me—

General: You make too much of the matter. Let it rest. *(He puts away his handkerchief.)*

Cherdyakov *(quickly takes out his own handkerchief):* How can I let it rest! It was inexcusable. Permit me to wipe your neck, General. It's the least I can do. *(He starts to wipe the General's head. The General pushes his hand away.)*

General: Leave it be! It's all right, I say.

Cherdyakov: But I splattered you, sir. Your complete head is splattered. It was an accident, I assure you—but it's disgusting!

Writer: Shhh!

General: I'm sorry. My apologies.

Cherdyakov: The thing is, your Excellency, it came completely without warning. It was out of my nose before I could stifle it.

Madame Brassilhov: Shhh!

Cherdyakov: Shhh, yes, certainly, I'm sorry. . . . *(He sits back, nervously. He blows his nose with his handkerchief. Then Cherdyakov leans forward.)* It's not a cold, if that's what you were worrying about, sir. Probably a particle of dust in the nostril—

General: Shh!

(They watch the play in silence, and Cherdyakov sits back, unhappy with himself.)

Writer: But try as he might, Cherdyakov could not put the incident out of his mind. The sneeze, no more than an innocent accident, grew out of all proportion in his mind, until it resembled the angry roar of a cannon aimed squarely at the enemy camp. He played the incident back in his mind, slowing down the procedure so he could view again, in horror, the infamous deed. *(Cherdyakov, in slow motion, repeats the sneeze again, but slowed down so that it appears to us as one frame at a time. It also seems to be*

three times as great in intensity as the original sneeze. The General, also in slow motion, reacts as though he has just taken a 50-pound hammer blow at the base of his skull. They all go with the slow motion of the "sneeze" until it is completed, when the unseen curtain falls and they applaud. They all rise and begin to file out of the theater, chattering about the lovely evening they have just spent. . . .)*

General: Charming . . . charming.

Madame Brassilhov: Yes, charming.

General: Charming . . . simply charming. Wasn't it charming, my dear?

Madame Brassilhov: I found it utterly charming.

(Cherdyakov stands behind them, tapping the General.)

Writer: I was completely charmed by it.

Cherdyakov *(still tapping away at the General):* Excuse me, Excellency.

General: Who's tapping? Somebody's tapping me. Who's that tapping?

Cherdyakov: I'm tapping, sir. I'm the tapper . . . Cherdyakov.

Madame Brassilhov *(quickly pulls the General back):* Stand back, dear, it's the sneezer.

Cherdyakov: No, no, it's all right. I'm all sneezed out. . . . I was just concerned about your going out into the night air with a damp head.

General: Oh, that. It was a trifle. A mere faux pas. Forget it, young man. Amusing play, don't you think? Did you find it amusing?

Cherdyakov: Amusing? Oh, my goodness, yes. Ha, ha. So true. Ha, ha. I

73

haven't laughed as much in years. Ha, ha, ha . . .

General: Which part interested you the most?

Cherdyakov: The sneeze. When I sneezed on you. It was unforgivable, sir.

General: Forget it, young man. Come, my dear. It looks like rain. I don't want to get my head wet again.

Madame Brassilhov: You shouldn't let people sneeze on you, dear. You're not to be sneezed at.

(They are gone.)

Cherdyakov: I'm ruined! Ruined! He'll have me fired from Trees and Bushes. They'll send me down to Branches and Twigs.

Wife: Come, Ivan.

Cherdyakov: What?

Wife: You mustn't let it concern you. It was just a harmless little sneeze. The General's probably forgotten it already.

Cherdyakov: Do you really think so?

Wife: No! I'm scared, Ivan.

Writer: And so they walked home in despair. . . .

Cherdyakov: Perhaps I should send him a nice gift. Maybe some Turkish towels.

Writer: Cherdyakov's once-promising career had literally been blown away. . . .

Cherdyakov *(as they arrive home):* Why did this happen to me? Why did I go to the theater at all? Why didn't I sit in the balcony with people of our own class? They love sneezing on each other.

Wife: Come to bed, Ivan.

Cherdyakov: Perhaps if I were to call on the General and explain matters again, but in such a charming, honest, and humble manner, he would have no choice but to forgive me. . . .

Wife: Maybe it's best not to remind him, Ivan.

Cherdyakov: No, no. If I ever expect to become a gentleman, I must behave like one.

Writer: And so the morning came. It so happened this was the day the General listened to petitions, and since there were 50 or 60 petitions ahead of Cherdyakov, he waited from morning till late, late afternoon. . . .

(Cherdyakov moves into the office set.)

General: Next! . . . NEXT!

Cherdyakov: I'm not next, your Excellency. I'm last.

General: Very well, then. . . . Last!

Cherdyakov: That's me, sir.

General: Well, what is your petition?

Cherdyakov: I have no petition, sir. I'm not a petitioner.

General: Then you waste my time.

Cherdyakov: Do you not recognize me, sir? We met last night under rather "explosive" circumstances. . . . I am the splatterer.

General: The what?

Cherdyakov: The sneezer. The one who sneezed. The sneezing splatterer.

General: Indeed? And what is it you want now? A *Gesundheit*?

Cherdyakov: No, Excellency . . . your forgiveness. I just wanted to point out there was no political or antisocial motivation behind my sneeze. It was an unplanned act of God. I curse the day my nose formed itself on my face. It's a hateful nose, sir, and I am not responsible for its wrong acts. *(Grabbing his own nose)* Punish that which committed the crime, but pardon the innocent body behind it.

74

Exile my nose, but forgive me, your kindship. Forgive me.

General: My dear young man, I'm not angry with your nose. I'm too busy to have time for your nasal problems. I suggest you go home and take a hot bath—or a cold one—take something, but don't bother me with this silly business again. . . . Gibber, gibber, gibber, that's all I've heard all day. *(Going offstage)* Gibber, gibber, gibber, gibber . . .

(Cherdyakov stands alone in the office, sobbing.)

Cherdyakov: Thank you, sir. God bless you and your wife and your household. May your days be sweet and may your nights be better than your days.

Writer: The feeling of relief that came over Cherdyakov was enormous. . . .

Cherdyakov: May the birds sing in the morning at your window and may the coffee in your cup be strong and hot. . . .

Writer: The weight of the burden that was lifted was unmeasurable. . . .

Cherdyakov: I worship the chair you sit on and the uniform you wear that sits on the chair that I worship. . . .

Writer: He walked home, singing and whistling like a lark. Life was surely a marvel, a joy, a heavenly paradise. . . .

Cherdyakov: Oh, God, I am happy!

Writer: And yet—

Cherdyakov: And yet—

Writer: When he arrived home, he began to think. . . .

Cherdyakov: Have I been the butt of a cruel and thoughtless joke?

Writer: Had the Minister toyed with him?

Cherdyakov: If he had no intention of punishing me, why did he torment me so unmercifully?

Writer: If the sneeze meant so little to the Minister, why did he deliberately cause Cherdyakov to writhe in his bed?

Cherdyakov: . . . to twist in agony the entire night?

Writer: Cherdyakov was furious!

Cherdyakov: I AM FURIOUS!

Writer: He foamed and fumed and paced the night through, and in the morning he called out to his wife, "Sonya!"

Cherdyakov: Sonya! *(She rushes in.)* I have been humiliated.

Wife: You, Ivan? Who would humiliate you? You're such a kind and generous person.

Cherdyakov: Who? I'll tell you who! General Brassilhov, the Minister of Public Parks.

Wife: What did he do?

Cherdyakov: The swine! I was humiliated in such subtle fashion, it was almost unnoticeable. The man's cunning is equal only to his cruelty. He practically forced me to come to his office to grovel and beg on my knees. I was reduced to a gibbering idiot.

Wife: You were that reduced?

Cherdyakov: I must go back and tell him what I think of him. The lower classes must speak up. . . . *(He is at the door.)* The world must be made safe so that men of all nations and creeds, regardless of color or religion, will be free to sneeze on their superiors! It is he who will be humiliated by *I*!

Writer: And so, the next morning, Cherdyakov came to humiliate *he*. . . .

(Lights up on the General at his desk.)

General: Last! *(Cherdyakov goes to the general's desk. He stands there glaring down at the General with a faint trace of a smile on his lips. The General looks up.)* Well?

Cherdyakov *(smiles):* Well? Well, you say? . . . Do you not recognize me, your Excellency? Look at my face. . . . Yes. You're quite correct. It is I once again.

General *(looks at him puzzled):* It is you once again—who?

Cherdyakov *(confidentially):* Cherdyakov, Excellency. I have returned, having taken neither a hot bath nor a cold one.

General: Who let this filthy man in? What is it?

Cherdyakov *(on top of the situation now):* What is it? . . . What is it, you ask? You sit there behind your desk and ask, What is it? You sit there in your lofty position as General and Minister of Public Parks, a member in high standing among the upper class and ask me, a lowly civil servant, What is it? You sit there with full knowledge that there is no equality in this life, that there are those of us who serve and those that are served, those of us who obey and those that are obeyed, those of us who bow and those that are bowed to, that in this life, certain events take place that cause some of us to be humiliated and those that are the cause of that humiliation . . . and still you ask, "WHAT IS IT?"

General *(angrily):* What is it? Don't stand there gibbering like an idiot! What is it you want?

Cherdyakov: I'll tell you what I want! . . . I wanted to apologize again for sneezing on you. . . . I wasn't sure I made it clear. It was an accident, an accident, I assure you. . . .

General *(stands and screams out):* Out! Out, you idiot! Fool! Imbecile! Get out of my sight! I never want to see you again. If you ever cross my line of vision I'll have you exiled forever. . . . WHAT'S YOUR NAME?

Cherdyakov: Ch-Cherdyakov! *(It comes out as a sneeze—in the General's face.)*

General *(wiping himself):* You germ spreader! You maggot! You insect! You are lower than an insect. You are the second cousin to a cockroach! The son-in-law of a bedbug! You are the nephew of a ringworm! You are nothing, nothing, do you hear me. . . . NOTHING!

(Cherdyakov backs away, and returns home.)

Writer: At that moment, something broke loose inside of Cherdyakov. . . . Something so deep and vital, so much a part of him that the damage that was done seemed beyond repair. . . . Something drained from him that can only be described as the very life force itself. . . . *(Cherdyakov takes off his coat. He sits on the sofa, head in hands.)* The matter was over, for once, for all, forever. What happened next was quite simple. . . . *(Cherdyakov lies back on the sofa.)* Ivan Ilyitch Cherdyakov arrived at home . . . removed his coat . . . lay down on the sofa—and died!

(Cherdyakov's head drops and his hand falls to the floor. Blackout.)

76

READING COMPREHENSION

Summarizing. Choose the best phrase to complete each sentence. Then write the complete statements on your paper.

1. Cherdyakov purchased expensive tickets because _____ (his hearing and sight were poor, he loved going to the theater, he was rich and famous).

2. After he sneezed on the General, Cherdyakov _____ (apologized greatly, was too proud to say anything, laughed loudly).

3. By making a small incident seem too important, Cherdyakov _____ (got a promotion, was fired from his job, caused his own death).

Interpreting. Write the answer to each question on your paper.

1. How did the General feel when Cherdyakov insisted on speaking to him at the theater?

2. What might have happened if Cherdyakov had dropped the incident after he sneezed?

3. How did Cherdyakov's desire to be more important get him into trouble?

4. What are some examples of the author's use of humor in the play?

For Thinking and Discussing. At the end of the play, "something broke loose inside of Cherdyakov." What broke loose? How did this lead to his death?

UNDERSTANDING LITERATURE

Stage Directions. When a play is printed in a book, it consists of the *dialogue* and the *stage directions*. The stage directions are notes the writer provides for actors and readers. The notes describe the play's setting, explain how characters should look, indicate how characters should say their lines, and tell what actions should take place on stage.

Here are five stage directions from "The Sneeze." On your paper, indicate whether each gives you information about the *setting*, the *plot*, the *characters*, or several different elements. Then write a sentence or two explaining what you learn from each stage direction.

1. *"He and his wife are dressed in their best, but are certainly no match for the grandeur around them."*

2. *"The General and his wife take their seats in the first row, the General directly in front of Cherdyakov."*

3. **General** *(turns, looks at Cherdyakov coldly) . . ."*

4. *"He starts to wipe the General's head. The General pushes his hand away."*

5. *"Cherdyakov takes off his coat. He sits on the sofa, head in hands."*

WRITING

Suppose Cherdyakov hadn't sneezed again. Write a new ending with new dialogue and stage directions.

I Remember Mama

A play by John Van Druten
based on stories by Kathryn Forbes

Katrin wants to be a writer, but no one seems interested in reading or publishing her stories. She is ready to give up until Mama helps her find the perfect subject to write about—her own family.

This play is really two scenes from a longer play about a Norwegian-American family living in San Francisco around 1910. The play is based upon the stories of Kathryn Forbes, who is the real Katrin in the play.

CHARACTERS

Katrin, a teenage girl
Mama, her mother
Papa, her father
Nels, her brother
Dagmar, her younger sister
Christine, her younger sister
Florence Dana Moorhead, a famous writer
Bellboy in Miss Moorhead's hotel

The period of the play is around 1910. The curtains part to reveal a kitchen. Mama and Papa are seated. Mama is darning. Dagmar, a young girl, is seated on a small chest, reading a solid-looking book. Nels enters from back door, carrying a newspaper.

Nels (*hitting Papa playfully on the head with the paper*): Hello! Here's your evening paper, Papa. (*Papa puts down the morning paper he is reading and takes the evening one from Nels.*)

Papa (*at table*): Is there any news?

Nels: No. Oh, I forgot. There's a letter for Katrin. I picked it up on the mat as I came in. (*Going to back door and calling*) Katrin! Katrin! There's a letter for you.

Katrin (*answering from offstage*): Coming!

Mama (*at table*): Nels, you know who the letter is from?

Nels: Why, no, Mama. (*Hands it to her.*) It looks like her own handwriting.

Mama (*gravely inspecting it*): Is bad.

Papa: Why is bad?

Mama: She get too many like that. I think they are stories she send to the magazines.

Dagmar (*closing her book loudly, rising*): Well, I'll go and see if I have any puppies yet. (*Crosses below the table and then turns.*) Mama, I've just decided something.

Mama: What have you decided?

Dagmar: If Nels is going to be a doctor, when I grow up, I'm going to be a— (*Looking at the book title, and stumbling over the word*) vet-vet-veterinarian.

Mama: And what is that?

Dagmar: A doctor for animals.

Mama: Is good. Is good.

Dagmar: There are far more animals in the world than there are human beings, and far more human doctors than animal ones. It isn't fair. (*She goes to the pantry door.*) I suppose we couldn't have a horse, could we? (*This only produces a concerted laugh from the family. She turns, sadly.*) No . . . I was afraid we couldn't. (*She goes into the pantry.*)

(*Katrin comes in. She wears an adult dress. Her hair is up and she looks about eighteen.*)

Katrin: Where's the letter?

Mama (*handing it to her*): Here.

(*Katrin takes it, nervously. She looks at the envelope, and her face falls. She opens it, pulls out a manuscript and a re-jection slip, looks at it a moment, and then replaces both in the envelope. The others pretend not to watch her. Then she looks up, with determination.*)

Katrin (*above table*): Mama . . . Papa . . . I want to say something.

Papa: What is it?

Katrin: I'm not going to go to college.

Papa: Why not?

Katrin: Because it would be a waste of time and money. The only point in my going to college was to be a writer. Well, I'm not going to be one, so . . .

Mama: Katrin, is it your letter that makes you say this? It is a story come back again?

Katrin: Again is right. This is the tenth time. I made this one a test. It's the best I've ever written, or ever shall write. I know that. Well, it's no good.

Nels: What kind of a story is it?

Katrin: Oh . . . it's a story about a painter, who's a genius, and he goes blind.

Nels: Sounds like *The Light That Failed.*

Katrin: Well, what's wrong with that?

Nels (*quickly*): Nothing. Nothing!

Katrin (*moving down*): Besides, it's not like that. My painter gets better. He has an operation and recovers his sight, and paints better than ever before.

Mama: Is good.

Katrin (*bitterly unhappy*): No, it isn't. It's rotten. But it's the best I can do.

Mama: If there was someone we could ask . . . for advice . . . to tell us . . . tell us if your stories are good.

Katrin: Yes. Well, there isn't. And they're not.

Papa (*looking at the evening paper*): There is something here in the paper about a lady writer. I just noticed the headline. Wait. (*he looks back for it and reads.*) "Woman writer tells key to liter-ary success."

Katrin: Who?

Papa: A lady called Florence Dana Moorhead. It gives her picture. A fat lady. You have heard of her?

Katrin: Yes, of course. Everyone has.

She's terribly successful. She's here on a lecture tour.

Mama: What does she say is the secret?

Papa: You read it, Katrin. (*He hands her the paper.*)

Katrin (*grabbing the first part*): "Florence Dana Moorhead, celebrated novelist and short story writer . . . blah-blah-blah . . . interviewed today in her suite at the Fairmont . . . blah-blah-blah . . . pronounced sincerity the essential quality for success as a writer." (*Throwing aside the paper.*) A lot of help that is.

Mama: Katrin, this lady . . . maybe if you sent her your stories, she could tell you what is wrong with them?

Katrin (*wearily*): Oh, Mama, don't be silly.

Mama: Why is silly?

Katrin (*behind table*): Well, in the first place because she's a very important person . . . a celebrity . . . and she'd never read them. And in the second, because . . . you seem to think writing's like . . . well, like cooking, or something. That all you have to have is the recipe. It takes a lot more than that. You have to have a gift for it.

Mama: You have to have a gift for cooking, too. But there are things you can learn, if you have the gift.

Katrin: Well, that's the whole point. I haven't. I know . . . now. So, if you've finished with the morning paper, Papa, I'll take the want-ad section, and see if I can find myself a job. (*She takes the morning paper and goes out.*)

Mama: Is bad. Nels, what you think?

Nels: I don't know, Mama. Her stories seem all right to me, but I don't know.

Mama: It would be good to know. Nels, this lady in the paper . . . what else does she say?

Nels (*taking up the paper*): Not much. The rest seems to be about her and her home. Let's see. . . . (*He reads, walking downstage.*) "Apart from literature, Miss Moorhead's main interest in life is gastronomy."

Mama: The stars?

Nels: No—eating. "A brilliant cook herself, she says that she would as soon turn out a good soufflé as a short story, or find a new recipe as she would a first edition."

Mama (*reaching for the paper*): I see her picture? (*She looks at it.*) Is kind face. (*Pause while she reads a moment. Then she looks up and asks.*) What is first edition?

(*Blackout. Lights up on turntable, representing the lobby of the Fairmont Hotel. A couch against a column with a palm behind it. An orchestra plays softly in the background. Mama is discovered seated on the couch, waiting patiently. She wears a hat and a suit, and clutches a newspaper and a bundle of manuscripts. A couple of guests come through the curtains and cross, disappearing into the wings. Mama watches them. Then Florence Dana Moorhead enters through the curtains. She is a stout, dressy, good-natured, middle-aged woman. A bellboy comes from the right, paging her.*)

Bellboy: Miss Moorhead?

F. D. Moorhead: Yes?

Bellboy: Telegram.

F. D. Moorhead: Oh . . . thank you. (*She*

tips him, and he goes. Mama rises and moves toward her.)

Mama: Please . . . please . . . Miss Moorhead . . . Miss Moorhead.

F. D. Moorhead *(looking up from her telegram):* Were you calling me?

Mama: Yes. You are . . . Miss Florence Dana Moorhead?

F. D. Moorhead: Yes.

Mama: Please . . . might I speak to you for a moment?

F. D. Moorhead: Yes—what's it about?

Mama: I read in the paper what you say about writing.

F. D. Moorhead *(with a vague social smile):* Oh, yes?

Mama: My daughter, Katrin, wants to be a writer.

F. D. Moorhead *(who has heard that one before):* Oh, really? *(She glances at her watch.)*

Mama: I bring her stories.

F. D. Moorhead: Look, I'm afraid I'm in rather a hurry. I'm leaving San Francisco this evening. . . .

Mama: I wait two hours here for you to come in. Please, if I may talk to you for one, two minutes. That is all.

F. D. Moorhead *(kindly):* Of course, but I think I'd better tell you that if you want me to read your daughter's stories, it's no use. I'm very sorry, but I've had to

81

make a rule never to read anyone's un-published material.

Mama (*nods, then after a pause*): It said in the paper you like to collect recipes . . . for eating.

F. D. Moorhead: Yes, I do. I've written several books on cooking.

Mama: I, too, am interested in gastron-omy. I am good cook. Norwegian. I make good Norwegian dishes. Lutefisk. And Kjötboller. That is meatballs with cream sauce.

F. D. Moorhead: Yes, I know. I've eaten them in Christiania, Norway.

Mama: I have a special recipe for Kjötboller . . . my mother give me. She was best cook I ever knew. Never have I told this recipe, not even to my sisters, because they are not good cooks.

F. D. Moorhead (*amused*): Oh?

Mama: But . . . if you let me talk to you . . . I give it to you. I promise it is good recipe.

F. D. Moorhead (*vastly tickled now*): Well, that seems fair enough. Let's sit down. (*They move to the couch and sit.*) Now, your daughter wants to write, you say? How old is she?

Mama: She is eighteen. Just.

F. D. Moorhead: Does she write, or does she just . . . want to write?

Mama: Oh, she write all the time. Maybe she should not be author, but it is hard to give up something that has meant so much.

F. D. Moorhead: I agree, but . . .

Mama: I bring her stories. I bring twelve.

F. D. Moorhead (*aghast*): Twelve!

Mama: But if you could read maybe just one. . . . To know if someone is good cook, you do not need to eat a whole dinner.

F. D. Moorhead: You're very persuasive. How is it your daughter did not come herself?

Mama: She was too unhappy. And too scared . . . of you. Because you are celeb-rity. But I see your picture in the paper.

F. D. Moorhead: That frightful picture!

Mama: Is the picture of woman who likes to eat good. . . .

F. D. Moorhead (*with a rueful smile*): It certainly is. Now, tell me about the Kjötboller.

Mama: When you make the meatballs you drop them in boiling stock. Not water. That is one of the secrets.

F. D. Moorhead: Ah!

Mama: And the cream sauce. That is an-other secret. It is half sour cream, added at the last.

F. D. Moorhead: That sounds marvelous.

Mama: You must grind the meat six times. I could write it out for you. And . . . (*Tentatively*) while I write, you could read?

F. D. Moorhead (*with a laugh*): All right. You win. Come upstairs to my apart-ment. (*She rises.*)

Mama: Is kind of you. (*They start out.*) Maybe if you would read two stories, I could write the recipe for Lutefisk as well. You know Lutefisk. . . ?

(*They have disappeared into the wings, and the turntable revolves out. Katrin is at her desk.*)

Katrin: When Mama came back, I was sitting with my diary, which I called my journal now, writing a Tragic Farewell to

My Art. It was very seldom that Mama came to the attic, thinking that a writer needed privacy, and I was surprised to see her standing in the doorway. *(She looks up. Mama is standing on the steps.)* Mama!

Mama: You are busy, Katrin?

Katrin *(jumping up):* No, of course not. Come in.

Mama *(coming downstage):* I like to talk to you.

Katrin: Yes, of course.

Mama *(seating herself at the desk):* You are writing?

Katrin *(on the steps):* No, I told you, that's all over.

Mama: That is what I want to talk to you about.

Katrin: It's all right, Mama. Really, it's all right. I was planning to tear up all my stories this afternoon, only I couldn't find half of them.

Mama: They are here.

Katrin: Did you take them? What for?

Mama: Katrin, I have been to see Miss Moorhead.

Katrin: Who's Miss . . . ? You don't mean Florence Dana Moorhead? *(Mama nods.)* You don't mean. . . . *(She comes downstage to her.)* Mama, you don't mean you took her my stories?

Mama: She read five of them. I was two hours with her. We have glass of sherry. Two glass of sherry.

Katrin: What did she say about them?

Mama *(quietly):* She say they are not good.

Katrin *(turning away):* Well, I knew that. It was hardly worth your going to all that trouble just to be told that.

Mama: She say more. Will you listen, Katrin?

Katrin *(trying to be gracious):* Sure. Sure. I'll listen.

Mama: I will try and remember. She say you write now only because of what you have read in other books, and that no one can write good until they have felt what they write about. That for years she write bad stories about people in the olden times, until one day she remember something that happen in her own town . . . something that only she could know and understand . . . and she feels she must tell it . . . and that is how she write her first good story. She say you must write more of things you know. . . .

Katrin: That's what my teacher always told me at school.

Mama: Maybe your teacher was right. I do not know if I explain good what Miss Moorhead means, but while she talks I think I understand. Your story about the painter who is blind . . . that is because . . . forgive me if I speak plain, my Katrin, but it is important to you . . . because you are the dramatic one, as Papa has said . . . and you think it would feel good to be a painter and be blind and not complain. But never have you imagined how it would really be. Is true?

Katrin *(subdued):* Yes, I guess it's true.

Mama: But she say you are to go on writing. That you have the gift. *(Katrin turns back to her, suddenly aglow.)* And that when you have written story that is real and true . . . then you send it to someone whose name she give me. *(She fumbles for a piece of paper.)* It is her . . . agent . . . and say she recommend you. Here. No, that is recipe she give me for goulash as her grandmother make it . . . here. . . . *(She hands over the paper.)* It helps, Katrin, what I have told you?

Katrin *(subdued again):* Yes, I . . . I guess it helps. Some. But what have I got to write about? I haven't seen anything, or been anywhere.

Mama: Could you write about San Francisco, maybe? Is fine city. Miss Moorhead write about her home town.

Katrin: Yes, I know. But you've got to have a central character or something. She writes about her grandfather . . . he was a wonderful old man.

Mama: Could you maybe write about Papa?

Katrin: Papa?

Mama: Papa is fine man. Is wonderful man.

Katrin: Yes, I know, but . . .

Mama *(rising):* I must go fix supper. Is late. Papa will be home. *(She goes down the steps to the curtains, and then turns back.)* I like you should write about Papa. *(She goes inside.)*

Katrin *(going back to her seat behind the desk):* Papa. Yes, but what's he ever done? What's ever happened to him? What's ever happened to any of us? Ex-

cept always being poor and having illness, like the time when Dagmar went to hospital and Mama . . . *(The idea hits her like a flash.)* Oh . . . Oh . . . *(Pause—then she becomes the Katrin of today)* And that was how it was born . . . suddenly in a flash . . . the story of "Mama and the Hospital"! . . . the first of all the stories. I wrote it . . . oh, quite soon after that. I didn't tell Mama or any of them. But I sent it to Miss Moorhead's agent. It was a long time before I heard anything . . . and then one evening the letter came. *(She takes an envelope from the desk in front of her.)* For a moment I couldn't believe it. Then I went rushing into the kitchen, shouting . . . *(She rises from the desk, taking some papers with her, and rushes downstairs crying.)* "Mama! Mama!" *(The curtains have parted on the kitchen—and the family tableau— Mama, Papa, Christine, and Nels, sitting around the table. Dagmar is not present. Katrin, out of breath, comes rushing into the kitchen.)* Mama . . . Mama . . . I've sold a story!

Mama *(at table)*: A story?

Katrin: Yes, I got a letter from the agent . . . with a check for . . . *(Gasping)* five hundred dollars!

Nels *(sitting on the chest)*: No kidding? *(He rises.)*

Mama: Katrin . . . is true?

Katrin: Here it is. Here's the letter. Maybe I haven't read it right. *(She hands her the letter. Papa and Mama huddle and gloat over it.)*

Mama *(stopping her, quickly)*: You read us the story. You have it there?

Katrin: Yes.

Mama: Then read.

Katrin: Now?

Mama: Yes. No—wait. Dagmar must hear. *(She opens pantry door and calls.)* Dagmar!

Dagmar *(off)*: Yes, Mama?

Mama *(calling)*: Come here, I want you.

Dagmar *(off)*: What is it?

Mama: I want you. No, you leave the rabbits! *(She comes back.)* What is it called . . . the story?

Katrin *(seating herself in a chair)*: It's called "Mama and the Hospital."

Papa *(delighted)*: You write about Mama?

Katrin: Yes.

Mama: But I thought . . . I thought you say . . . I tell you . . . *(She gestures at Papa, behind his back.)*

Katrin: I know, Mama, but . . . well, that's how it came out.

(Dagmar comes in and joins the whole group around the table.)

Katrin *(reading)*: "For as long as I could remember, the house on Steiner Street had been home. All of us were born there. Nels, the oldest and the only boy . . ." *(Nels looks up, astonished to be in a story.)* "my sister, Christine . . ." *(Christine does likewise.)* "and the littlest sister, Dagmar . . ."

Dagmar: Am I in the story?

Mama: Hush, Dagmar. We are all in the story.

Katrin: "But first and foremost, I remember Mama." *(The lights begin to dim and the curtain slowly to fall. As it descends, we hear her voice continuing.)*

READING COMPREHENSION

Summarizing. Choose the best phrase to complete each sentence. Then write the complete statements on your paper.

1. Katrin became depressed after _____ (her father became seriously ill, receiving another rejection slip from a magazine, meeting with Miss Moorhead).

2. Mama convinced Miss Moorhead to read Katrin's stories by _____ (giving her special Norwegian recipes, paying her a large sum of money, writing her a letter).

3. Katrin sold her first story because _____ (her brother helped her, she followed Miss Moorhead's advice, she gave up).

Interpreting. Write the answer to each question on your paper.

1. What advice did Miss Moorhead give Katrin?

2. Why did Katrin nearly give up trying to write?

3. Why did Katrin decide to write a story about her mother?

4. What might have happened to Katrin's writing career if Miss Moorhead had not read her stories?

For Thinking and Discussing. Describe some of Mama's qualities. What kind of effect did she have on her family?

UNDERSTANDING LITERATURE

Characterization and Actions. One way that characters in a play reveal what they are like is by what they do during the play—their *actions*. For example, Dagmar uses big words. You know she's smart and likes to show off. Katrin argues a lot and changes her feelings quickly, so you know she's emotional.

Here are four words which describe some of Mama's qualities. Below the words are four of Mama's actions in the play. On your paper, match each quality with the action that reveals it. Then write a sentence or two explaining each match.

    a. understanding   **c.** humble
    b. determined   **d.** clever

1. She decided to appeal to Miss Moorhead's interest in gastronomy.

2. She kept telling Miss Moorhead about her recipes until the woman agreed to read Katrin's stories.

3. She suggested Katrin write a story about Papa.

4. She listened carefully as Katrin explained her problems.

WRITING

Miss Moorhead advised Katrin to write about things she knew. Could you write a story about someone you know? Write a paragraph explaining whom you would write about, some of the person's qualities, and some of the actions you would include in your story.

Sudden Death

by Tom Chehak & Joshua Brand

This episode from the television series The White Shadow *is not about a "sudden death" play-off game. The Carver High School basketball team and Coach Ken Reeves have more to lose than the game.*

CHARACTERS

Ken Reeves, the Carver High basketball coach
Sybil Buchanon, vice-principal
Jim Willis, principal
Randy Judd, a freshman basketball player
Henry Judd, Randy's father
Louella Judd, Randy's mother
Nurse, at a local hospital
Doctor Luria, a young doctor at the hospital
Warren Coolidge ⎫
"Salami" Pettrino ⎪
Morris Thorpe ⎪ Carver
Curtis Jackson ⎬ High
James Hayward ⎪ basketball
Milton Reese ⎪ team
Abner Goldstein ⎪
Ricky Gomez ⎭
Paul Wilson, a Carver student

In the gym of Carver High, Coach Reeves is holding basketball tryouts. Randy Judd, a black teenager, is on the court. He is quick and graceful. But he doesn't know the fine points of the game.

Cut to Reeves's office. Randy walks in looking nervous.

Reeves: Randall?
Randy: The name is Randy—Randy Judd.
Reeves: Have a seat. I haven't seen you around here before.
Randy: I'm a freshman.
Reeves: You've got a real feel for the game. Did you ever play team basketball before?
Randy: I've just played a lot of playground stuff.
Reeves: You're good. No, I take that back. I think you can be good. But you don't know the scoreboard from the backboard.
Randy: I can learn!
Reeves: Maybe. I can show you what to do on the court. But it's up to you to learn what I teach you.

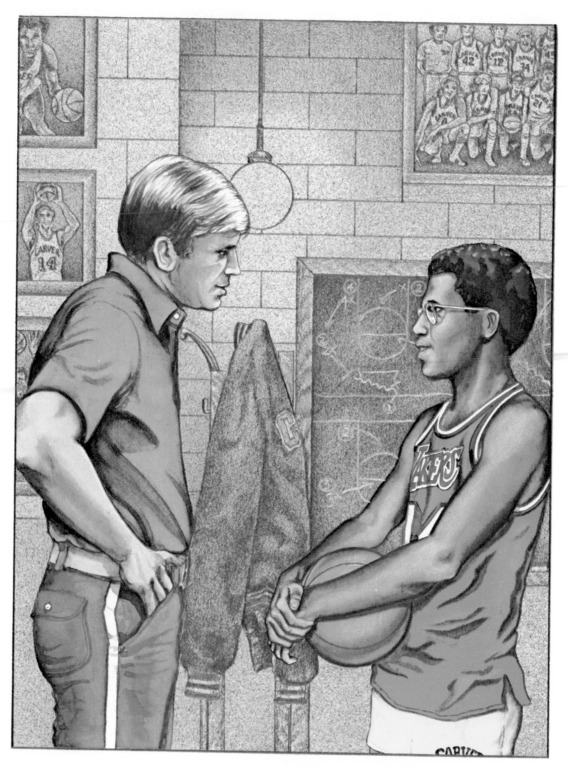

Randy: Why are you interested in me, if you're not sure I can make it?

Reeves: You've got talent. That gives you a head start. Who knows how far your talent will take you? But it's worth my time to try—if you're willing to try.

Randy: I am!

Reeves: Being on this team will mean working hard. Your muscles will hurt for a while. Your lungs will ache. If your grades fall, you'll be off the team. Understand?

Randy: Yes.

Reeves: Here's a permission slip. Have your parents sign it.

Randy: Okay!

(Cut to Sybil Buchanon's office. She is getting ready to go home. Reeves stops by, looking cheerful. She is grumpy.)

Reeves: Are you leaving soon?

Buchanon: You'd better believe it!

Reeves: Good. Could you give me a lift?

Buchanon: Where's your car?

Reeves: It's on strike, in the parking lot. I hope it's just the battery.

Buchanon: You can have a ride on one condition. Wipe that silly grin off your face! I've had a terrible day.

Reeves: Aren't you going to ask me how *my* day went?

Buchanon: All right. How did your day go?

Reeves: I thought you'd never ask. Carver has a new member on the basketball team.

Buchanon: Where did you get this one?

Reeves: I held tryouts. One of the kids, Randy Judd—

Buchanon *(interrupting him):* —is the greatest natural talent you've ever seen.

Reeves: Well, not exactly. But he's only a freshman. I'll have him for four years. He hasn't got as much talent as Coolidge. But he has a lot of desire, and he can learn. He's a coach's dream. Anybody can coach someone like Coolidge and look good. But I'd love to create a good ballplayer out of Randy.

Buchanon: You sound like Dr. Frankenstein.

Reeves: I knew you'd never understand.

(Cut to gym, where the team is practicing the next afternoon. Reeves blows his whistle.)

Reeves: Wait a second! What are you doing, Warren?

Coolidge: I was milking the ball. You told us to.

Reeves: "Milking the ball" doesn't mean "freeze the ball." Salami, you tell Warren. Suppose you were alone with the ball under the basket while we're practicing milking the ball. What would you do?

Salami: Huh? I don't even know what you just said.

Reeves: Thorpe, what do we do?

Thorpe: We shoot.

Reeves: Thank you. Got the idea now, Coolidge?

Coolidge: Yeah. I had it all along.

Reeves: Then why didn't you shoot?

(Randy walks into the gym.)

Randy: Coach Reeves?

Reeves *(to Randy):* Just a minute. *(To Coolidge)* Why didn't you shoot?

Coolidge: I had a cramp. *(The team laughs.)* I think I've got appendicitis. *(He*

89

is annoyed that they don't believe him.)

Reeves: Where does it hurt?

Coolidge: Right here on the left side.

Reeves: Warren, your appendix is on the right side.

Coolidge *(relieved):* Well, it *did* hurt.

Gomez: Warren is a very delicate monster.

Hayward: Coolidge, you have more things wrong with you than a used car.

Coolidge: I'm telling you, I had a cramp!

Reeves *(grinning):* Stay with it, Warren. The great ones play in spite of pain. Now, try it again. *(He goes over to talk to Randy. The team watches.)*

Reese: Who's that guy?

Gomez: He's the new man on the team.

(They return to practice. Randy and Reeves talk.)

Randy: I've got a problem. My mother won't sign the permission slip.

Reeves *(surprised):* Why not?

Randy: She's afraid I'll get hurt playing basketball.

Reeves: You could get hurt crossing the street. You could get hurt eating chicken! She lets you eat chicken, doesn't she? I don't believe this.

Randy: What am I going to do?

Reeves: We'll figure something out.

(Cut to Randy Judd's house. The doorbell rings, and Mr. Judd answers it. Reeves is standing there.)

Reeves: Mr. Judd? I'm Ken Reeves. I'm the basketball coach at Carver High.

Mr. Judd: Oh, yes. Please come in.

(They go into the living room, where Mrs. Judd is.)

Mr. Judd: Louella, this is Mr. Reeves, the basketball coach.

Reeves: How do you do, Mrs. Judd?

Mrs. Judd: Randy speaks very highly of you. At least he speaks highly of your high opinion of him.

Reeves: Randy tells me you won't sign his permission slip for the basketball team.

Mrs. Judd: I believe that Randy goes to school to learn—not to play.

Reeves: The two things can go together.

Mrs. Judd: We don't need more black basketball players. We need more black doctors and scientists. Randy may have the "desire" to play ball. But he's also a gifted student. That's more important to us.

Reeves: Randy's studies won't be hurt by his playing ball. It's unfair to take away his chance to join in.

Mrs. Judd: We appreciate your interest, Mr. Reeves. But the question is settled.

Reeves *(to Mr. Judd):* Won't you give him the chance?

Mrs. Judd: We don't like your interfering. I must ask you to leave. *(Reeves slowly stands up. Mr. Judd stops him.)*

Mr. Judd: Just a moment, Mr. Reeves. My wife feels very strongly about this. Now, I'm not much of a sports fan myself. I have a hard time sharing Randy's excitement. But Randy is our only child. We love him, and we want what's best for him.

Mrs. Judd: And what's best for your team isn't what's best for Randy.

Reeves: It's not a question of what's best for my team. It's what's best for Randy.

Mrs. Judd: We want Randy to go to college. We've always planned on that. So has he. If he gets involved in too many things, his grades might fall.

Reeves: Then let me make a deal with you. If his grades slip one point, he'll leave the team. But if he can handle both sports and schoolwork, then you'll let him play.

Mr. Judd (to his wife): We can't keep him in a glass cage forever. (She doesn't answer.) All right, Mr. Reeves. If his grades stay up, Randy can stay on your team.

(Cut to school doctor's office. Randy is being given a checkup. The doctor says he's in good health.

(Cut to gym. Reeves is teaching his team how to do a "fast break" in practice the next day. Randy misses a basket. He shakes his right arm, as though it hurts.)

Reeves: Pay attention, Randy! Don't take your eyes off the basket. Coolidge, try to make the play in one single motion! (Reeves shows them how to make the shot. Then he sees Randy with his head hanging down and his hands on his hips.)

Reeves: Get your hands off your hips! When a man puts his hands on his hips, he lets the other team know he's tired. Then they'll run you ragged.

(The team goes into the locker room. They are all tired, especially Randy.)

Hayward (to Randy): How's it going?

Randy: I'm worn out.

Hayward: It takes a while to get into shape.

Salami: If you thought that was something, you haven't seen anything yet.

Gomez: The coach will have you running in your sleep.

Coolidge: I lost 10 pounds my first week on the team.

Jackson: I was so sore. I felt like I'd gone 15 rounds with Muhammad Ali.

Randy: I'm so tired that my head hurts.

Goldstein: You'll get used to it.

(Cut to the gym during a game. The score is close. In the stands, we see Mr. Judd watching and cheering. But Randy is sitting on the bench.

(After the game, the Carver team runs into the locker room. They are in a good mood because they have won. Randy's suit is clean, showing that he never got in the game. But the others tease him to show he is one of them anyway.)

Hayward: You're looking good, rookie.

Thorpe: Hey, Randy, did you catch any splinters? (Randy grins and opens his locker. But his grin fades as he looks at his right hand.)

Goldstein: What's the matter?

Randy: My hand feels numb.

Reese: You probably sat on it on the bench.

Randy (laughing): That's probably it.

Goldstein: Rub it down with alcohol.

(Cut to next practice in the gym. Reeves gives the team a talk.)

Reeves: All right, clowns. Let's get the circus started. Reese, why did you foul out in yesterday's game?

Reese: I got carried away.

Reeves: Next time I'll carry you away.

Reese: Hey, I'm only human.

Reeves: Don't flatter yourself. What about you, Jackson? What's with all those fancy passes and dribbles?

Jackson: Cool is my style.

Reeves: Next time you can practice your "style" on the bench. We play basketball. We're not putting on a floor show. That other team came close to beating us. We've got a lot to work on. Hayward, you and Randy bring the ball up. Gomez, Salami, you cover them. Make them work for everything.

(The four players go out on the court. Randy looks good. But he's shaking his right hand, as though it hurts. He makes a basket. Then he stands still, hands on hips.)

Reeves: Don't hang around the basket! Do it again.

Randy: I'm tired.

Reeves: Then you're out of shape. Thorpe, go in for Randy. Randy, run 10 laps around the gym.

Randy: I'm really tired.

Reeves: Is it going to kill you to run 10 laps? (Randy looks embarrassed.) Go on. All right, you guys, let's try it again. (Randy runs very slowly.)

Reeves: Randy! Pick up those feet!

(Randy speeds up. He's breathing hard. Suddenly he grabs his head and screams. Then he falls down. Reeves and the boys rush over to Randy, who doesn't move.

(Cut to a hospital waiting room. Reeves walks around the room and then goes out to the nurse's desk.)

Reeves: Have you been able to reach Mr. or Mrs. Judd yet?

Nurse: Who are you?

Reeves: I'm the boy's coach. I came with him in the ambulance. I was told they couldn't reach his parents.

Nurse: Whose parents?

Reeves: Randy Judd's! He's the boy they took into the Emergency Room.

Nurse: We reached Mrs. Judd a few minutes ago.

Reeves: What took so long?

Nurse: Mrs. Judd was out shopping. Mr. Judd is a bus driver. He was working.

Reeves: Is there any news about Randy?

Nurse: As soon as we have any information, we'll let you know.

(Dr. Luria walks up to speak to the nurse.)

Luria: Have Mr. and Mrs. Judd gotten here yet?

Nurse: They're on their way. This is the boy's coach.

Reeves: How is Randy?

Luria: We won't know for a while.

Reeves: What happened? He was fine. Then all of a sudden, he just fell down.

Luria: Randy had an aneurism.

Reeves: You'll have to speak more plainly for me.

Luria: An aneurism happens when an artery swells up. If pressure is placed on the artery, it could burst. Randy had an aneurism in his brain. There's been a lot of bleeding in there. He's still in a coma.

Reeves: Is he going to live?

Luria: I don't know.

(Mr. and Mrs. Judd arrive.)

Mr. Judd: Is Randy all right?

Luria: Mr. Judd and Mrs. Judd? I'm Dr. Luria. Will you please come with me?

(Cut to the Carver gym at night. The principal, Jim Willis, enters and finds Reeves shooting baskets.)

Reeves: How did you know I was here?

Willis: Where else would an ex-basketball player go to work things out of his system? *(Pause.)* I spoke to Randy Judd's parents.

Reeves: How are they?

Willis: They're doing as well as can be expected. I also spoke to Dr. Luria. He's worried about you. He's afraid you might feel responsible. He wants you to understand there was nothing you could do.

Reeves: Everybody tells me that. Everybody's afraid of what I feel. Well, I feel guilty! I feel responsible!

Willis: Dr. Luria told me that those weak spots in the arteries are there from birth. Most doctors agree with that.

Reeves: Randy told me he was tired. I thought he was faking it. I made him run laps. I wasn't thinking about Randy. I was thinking about how I could create a star player. This might not have happened if it hadn't been for me.

Willis: You are not responsible. He was examined by a doctor before you let him play.

Reeves: If he had bad arteries, why didn't we know about it?

Willis: There's only one test for aneur-

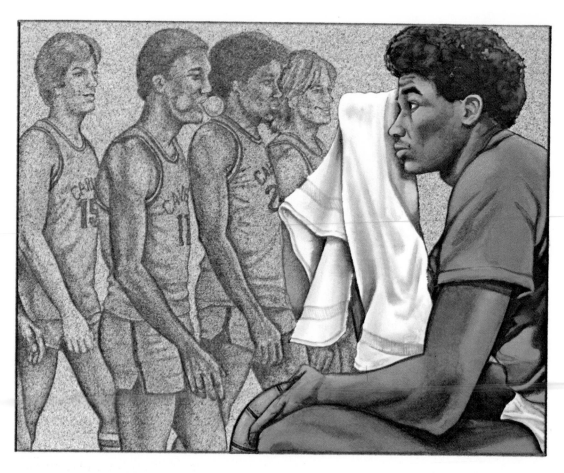

isms. You put dye into the bloodstream. It goes to the brain. Then you X-ray the entire body. Should we do that to everyone who wants to play?

Reeves: All I know is, basketball isn't worth all this.

(Cut to Reeves's office, the next day. Sybil Buchanon enters.)

Buchanon: Any news about Randy?

Reeves: He's still the same.

Buchanon: Have you spoken to his parents?

Reeves: I've tried, but I can't seem to dial the number. I'm afraid to talk to them. Please, don't tell me I'm not re-sponsible. If one more person tells me that, I'll scream.

Buchanon: I'm not here to talk about you. That subject is boring. But I am worried about your team. Those kids are shaken up by what happened to Randy. I think you should try to get them back to normal. *(Reeves looks up at her, admitting she's right.)*

(Cut to practice, that afternoon. Most of the team is warming up. But Coolidge is lying on a bench. Reeves walks over to him.)

Reeves: Warren, are you with us this afternoon?

Coolidge: I've got a headache.

Gomez: Coolidge is afraid he's got what Randy had, because his head hurts. *(This comment hits Reeves hard.)*

Coolidge: My head feels like a time bomb—tick, tick, tick.

Reeves: Just because you have a headache doesn't mean you have an aneurism.

Coolidge: How do *you* know?

Reeves: That's crazy, Warren.

Coolidge: It's my head. I know if it hurts or not.

Reeves: Come on, get up.

Coolidge: If you make me run laps and I drop dead, it's your fault. *(Reeves is really hurt by this.)*

Goldstein: You always think you're sick, Coolidge.

Jackson: Randy did have a headache.

Gomez: But his hand hurt, too. That doesn't mean anything.

Salami: Coach making him run laps is what did it. *(He is embarrassed when he sees he has hurt Reeves.)* I mean, I don't really think that did it.

Reeves: But you do think it had something to do with it.

Salami: Well, maybe it did.

Hayward: Salami just meant it probably speeded things up.

Salami: Yeah, that's what I meant.

Reeves: You're excused from practice, Warren.

Gomez: What a faker.

Coolidge *(getting up):* You get on my nerves, Gomez.

Reeves: Warren, if your head hurts, go see the nurse. *(The team is surprised. Coolidge is always acting sick. Why is the coach worried now?)*

Thorpe: He doesn't need a nurse. He needs a psychiatrist.

(Cut to the hospital. Reeves is bringing candy and flowers to Randy. But when he gets to the room, Mrs. Judd is alone there. She sits by Randy's empty bed. Her eyes are red from crying.)

Mrs. Judd *(to Reeves):* I didn't want him to play. He was my baby. You killed my baby! *(Reeves looks shocked and sad.)*

(Cut to the halls of Carver High School. Students are talking.)

Salami: I never knew anybody who died before.

Reese: I remember when my grandmother died. But she was old.

Thorpe: I saw a guy get shot once. But he didn't die. *(Paul Wilson walks over.)*

Paul: Hey, I heard about that kid dying. Did you know him?

Thorpe: We all knew him.

Reese: I was guarding him in practice.

Paul: You wouldn't catch me playing for Reeves.

Hayward: Why not?

Paul: I heard the kid died because the coach pushed him too hard. He made the kid run laps when he wasn't feeling well.

Hayward: If I were as dumb as you, I'd keep my mouth shut, so no one would know.

Paul: Well, that's the way I heard it.

Thorpe: Coach didn't push Randy any more than he does the rest of us.

Reese: Randy just had bad veins, man.

Paul: You guys are nuts. *(He walks away.)*

(Cut to the Judd house. Mrs. Judd an-

swers the doorbell. Reeves is at the door.)

Reeves: Hello, Mrs. Judd.

Mrs. Judd: Randy isn't here.

Reeves: I was hoping I could talk with you and Mr. Judd.

Mrs. Judd: My husband isn't here. He's out taking a walk.

Reeves: Maybe I should come back.

Mrs. Judd: No, you shouldn't.

Reeves: I want you to know how sorry I am. If there's anything I can do, please name it. It would help me as much as you.

Mrs. Judd: If you're looking for forgiveness, forget it. I hope this bothers you for the rest of your life! *(She closes the door.)*

(Cut to Jim Willis's office. Reeves walks in.)

Willis: Hi, Ken. Sit down. How are you?

Reeves: I'm all right.

Willis: Did you see the *Times* article about our last game?

Reeves *(not listening):* Every year you read about something like this happening to some kid. But you never think you'll be a part of it yourself.

Willis: It was an accident.

Reeves: The funeral's tomorrow. I'll need passes to let the team out of school for it.

(Cut to the street, a few minutes later. Reeves is walking by himself. Coolidge runs up behind him.)

Coolidge: Hey, Coach. Have you got a minute?

Reeves: I have to pick up my car before the garage closes.

Coolidge: Would you mind if I went with you?

Reeves: I guess not. What's on your mind?

Coolidge: You know how the guys get on my back for complaining?

Reeves: Yes.

Coolidge: Well, this thing that happened to Randy scares me. I mean, you think you're going to live forever. Death isn't real. You can fool around, because you've got all the time in the world. You know what I mean?

Reeves: Yes.

Coolidge: I played ball with that guy two days ago. Now he's gone. I don't

know how to deal with it. I'm afraid of dying. Are you?

Reeves: I think almost everyone is.

Coolidge: So how do you handle it?

Reeves: I never knew death was real until my mother died. Even then, I didn't really believe she was gone forever. I kept hoping to see her again. I don't know how to make it easy for you. We're all going to die someday. Sometimes just knowing that helps you to see things better.

Coolidge: What do you mean?

Reeves: It makes you realize what's really important. Your friends, your family— all people are in the same boat. If we don't take care of each other, no one else will. I'm sorry I can't be more help.

Coolidge: What you said makes me feel better. *(They look at each other. They both feel better now.)*

(Cut to Reeves's office. The team walks in. Everyone is wearing a dark suit.)

Goldstein: Are you ready, Coach?

Reeves: Yes.

Salami: I hate cemeteries. They give me the creeps.

Jackson: So maybe we'll just leave you there.

Reeves: Leave him alone. He's just whistling in the dark.

Salami: I'm not whistling.

Reeves: That's an expression. It means you make a joke out of something that scares you. That makes it less frightening.

(*Cut to the cemetery. Mr. and Mrs. Judd stand by the open grave. The team and Reeves stand nearby. Some of his boys look upset.*)

(*A minister gives a short speech about Randy. Then a coffin is put into the grave. Mrs. Judd throws a handful of dirt into the grave. Then she and Mr. Judd walk away. Reeves follows them to their car. He speaks to Mrs. Judd.*)

Reeves: I'm sorry. (*She turns away, coldly. Reeves backs away looking hurt. Then Mr. Judd follows him.*)

Mr. Judd: Mr. Reeves? We had Randy for such a short time. We had so many dreams for him. This is all so hard.

Reeves: I understand.

Mr. Judd: I never saw Randy happier than when he made your team. I'm glad he had that experience. It was a gift. Thank you. (*They shake hands. Then Mr. Judd returns to his wife. Reeves looks grateful, but still very sad.*)

(*Cut to the Judd house. Mr. and Mrs. Judd are packing up some of Randy's things. The doorbell rings. Mr. Judd goes to answer it. He walks back into the room with the Carver basketball team.*)

Mr. Judd: Louella? (*Mrs. Judd turns around and stares.*)

Coolidge: We all thought that maybe you might want this. (*He holds out Randy's uniform. Mrs. Judd takes her husband's arm. Then she walks toward the boys and reaches out for the uniform.*)

(*Fade out.*)

READING COMPREHENSION

Summarizing. Choose the best phrase to complete each sentence. Then write the complete statements on your paper.

1. Coach Reeves was excited about Randy joining the team because he _____ (saw that Randy was a great player, was a friend of Randy's family, thought Randy was talented).

2. At first Randy couldn't join the team because _____ (he was sick, his parents objected, his grades weren't good enough).

3. Mrs. Judd did not want Randy to play on the basketball team because she _____ (was worried about his health, believed his studies were more important, did not like basketball).

4. When Reeves said, "Is it going to kill you to run 10 laps?" he _____ (knew Randy was sick, thought Randy was sick, was trying to get Randy to work harder).

5. The artery problem that led to Randy's aneurism started when he _____ (joined the basketball team, was born, began running laps).

6. After Randy's death, Coach Reeves felt _____ (guilty, relieved, angry).

Interpreting. Write the answer to each question on your paper.

1. Why wouldn't Randy's mother sign the permission slip?

2. What did Mr. Judd mean when he said, "We can't keep him in a glass cage forever"?

3. Why was Coach Reeves so pleased to have Randy on the team?

4. Why did Coach Reeves insist that Randy run 10 laps around the gym?

5. Why did Mrs. Judd tell Reeves she hoped Randy's death bothered him for the rest of his life?

6. How did Reeves feel after Mr. Judd told him that Randy's team experience was a "gift"?

For Thinking and Discussing

1. Do you think Randy's parents were overprotective? Why or why not?

2. How do you think Randy would have felt if he had not been allowed to play basketball?

3. Do you think Reeves was a good coach? Was he fair with the boys on the team? Find some examples from the story to support your opinion.

4. Several people tried to convince Reeves that he shouldn't feel guilty about Randy's death. Do you think he should have felt guilty? Explain your answer.

UNDERSTANDING LITERATURE

Characterization and Dialogue. What characters say to each other in a play is called *dialogue*. Through their dialogue, characters tell the audience a lot about themselves.

On your paper, match the following excerpts of dialogue from "Sudden Death" with the personal qualities listed below them. Each of the qualities is characteristic of the person speaking. Then write a sentence or two explaining each match. Mention other moments in the play when the character showed the same quality.

1. "**Reeves:** . . . But I'd love to create a good ballplayer out of Randy."

2. "**Coolidge:** I had a cramp. I think I've got appendicitis."

3. "**Mrs. Judd:** We don't like your interfering. I must ask you to leave."

4. "**Mr. Judd:** I never saw Randy happier than when he made your team. I'm glad he had the experience."

a. dedicated

b. comforting

c. fearful

d. quick-tempered

WRITING

Suppose Mrs. Judd came to Coach Reeves's office after Randy died. Consider how she was feeling and how she might express this. Also consider Coach Reeves's state of mind. Write a dialogue between the two characters. Try to show Mrs. Judd's intense pain and anger and Coach Reeves's sorrow and regret.

Section Review

VOCABULARY

Synonyms and Antonyms in Context.
You can often find clues to the meaning of
an unfamiliar word in the words or sentences that come before or after the new
word. These clues in the reading material
are called *context clues*.

Two kinds of helpful context clues to
look for are synonyms and antonyms.
Sometimes you can spot a synonym or
antonym of the unfamiliar word nearby in
the reading.

Look for synonym and antonym context
clues to help you understand the words in
italics in the following excerpts from "The
Sneeze." On your paper, list the synonyms
or antonyms you find. Then write definitions for the italicized words.

1. "Cherdyakov: All right? . . . It certainly is not all right! It's *unpardonable*."

2. "Cherdyakov: . . . Punish that which
   committed the crime, but *pardon* the
   innocent body behind it."

3. "Madame Brassilhov: I found it *utterly*
   charming."
   "Writer: I was completely charmed by
   it."

4. "Cherdyakov: I was humiliated in such
   subtle fashion, it was almost unnoticeable."

READING

Sequence. The order in which events
happen in a play or story is called their
sequence. When you follow the sequence
of events carefully, you can understand
why characters act the way they do. For
example, you can understand why Mama
decided to tempt Miss Moorhead with her
recipes if you recall that she had first read
about Miss Moorhead's interests in the
newspaper.

The following events happened in "Sudden Death." On your paper, rearrange the
events in the correct sequence.

1. Coolidge claimed to have a funny
   feeling in his head.

2. Mrs. Judd agreed to let Randy join
   the team.

3. Carver won a game, but Randy didn't
   get to play.

4. Mrs. Judd told Reeves that she hoped
   he would always feel responsible.

5. Reeves and Coolidge discussed the
   value of friendship.

6. Randy told Reeves that his parents
   wouldn't let him join the team.

7. Willis told Reeves that he was not
   responsible for Randy's death.

8. Randy screamed and held his head.

9. Reeves told Randy that he had a lot
   to learn about basketball.

10. Mrs. Judd accepted Randy's uniform.

WRITING

A Review. A *review* gives one person's opinion of something, such as a book, a play, a movie, or a concert. A review can help you decide whether or not something is worth reading, seeing, or hearing. It can also help you better understand a certain work.

Step 1: Set Your Goal

The first step in writing a review is to decide what the topic will be. It will probably be easier for you to write a review about something that you have definite positive or negative feelings about. Choose one of the following topics for review:

1. One of the plays in this section—"The Sneeze," "I Remember Mama," or "Sudden Death."

2. A movie or a television program that you have seen. Be sure it is one you have seen recently, so that you will be able to remember some of the details.

Once you have chosen a topic for review, you can then decide what your purpose is and what you want to say. For example, suppose you were writing about the play "The Sneeze." Your purpose might be to show that "The Sneeze" is a good play because it is clever and funny. Write down your topic and purpose like this:

TOPIC: "The Sneeze"
PURPOSE: To show it is a clever and
              funny play

Step 2: Make a Plan

Before writing a review, you must decide what standards you will be using to judge your topic. If you were writing a review of a food product, for example, standards might include flavor, texture, color, and the kinds of ingredients in the product.

If you decide to review one of the plays in this section, the following list of questions may help you set your standards:

☐ Were the characters believable?
☐ Was the dialogue natural? Was it amusing? Clever?
☐ Was the plot interesting? Was it easy to follow? Was it exciting? Funny?
☐ Was the message, or theme, clear? Was it important?
☐ Was the play original?
☐ How does it compare to other plays I've read?

Write the answers to the questions you have decided to use as your standards. Make a list of specific examples to support your opinion.

Step 3: Write a First Draft

Now that you know what your standards are and have examples to support your opinion, you are ready to write your first draft. At this stage, concentrate on writing down everything you want to say. Don't worry about how your sentences sound or about your spelling or punctuation. You will have time to make changes in the next step.

As you write, be sure to include the following points in your review. You may want to write a paragraph for each.

1. Introduce the work.
   Identify the work specifically and state a general opinion.

2. Summarize the work.
   Be brief but informative.

3. Apply your standards.
   Discuss strengths and weaknesses. Give specific examples to support your opinion.

4. Reach a conclusion.
   Give your personal reaction and include a recommendation to others.

Step 4: Revise

When you revise your review, ask yourself these questions:

☐ Do I begin my review with a statement that expresses my overall opinion? Does it grab the readers' attention?

☐ Do I provide enough information to make my topic clear to my readers?

☐ Do I give specific examples to support my opinion?

After you have revised your review, proofread it for spelling, grammar, and punctuation. Then copy it over neatly.

QUIZ

The following is a quiz for Section 2. Write the answers in complete sentences on your paper.

Reading Comprehension

1. Why did Cherdyakov introduce himself and his wife to General Brassilhov in "The Sneeze"?

2. How do you know the sneeze incident worried Cherdyakov more than it worried the General?

3. In "I Remember Mama," how did Miss Moorhead's attitude toward Mama change?

4. What was Miss Moorhead's advice to Katrin? How do you know the advice was good?

5. What caused Randy's death in the screenplay "Sudden Death"? When did this condition start? Why didn't the doctor stop Randy from playing?

Understanding Literature

6. What kind of man was Cherdyakov? Find an action in "The Sneeze" to support your answer.

7. How do you know that the General considered himself more important than Cherdyakov? Find dialogue from the play to support your answer.

8. How does Mama speak in the play "I Remember Mama"? How does her dialogue demonstrate that she was not born in the United States?

9. What is the setting at the beginning of "I Remember Mama"? How do you know the setting?

10. The action changed in "Sudden Death" more often and quickly than in the other two plays in this section. How do the stage directions help you follow the changes in setting and plot? What special term is used in the stage directions of a TV screenplay?

ACTIVITIES

Word Attack

1. The sentences below are from plays in this section. One word in each sentence is written in phonetics. Use the pronunciation key in the glossary to help you decode the words. Write the words on your paper.

   a. My (plĕzh′ər), General.
   b. I was humiliated in such (sŭt′əl) fashion.
   c. Sounds like *The (līt) That Failed.*
   d. . . . she would as soon turn out a good (sōō flā) as a short story. . . .
   e. Now, your (dô′ tər) wants to write, you say?
   f. I can show you what to do on the (kôrt).

2. Now use the pronunciation key to write the phonetic respelling for these words from the selections in this section.

clerk	trifle	curse
suite	sauce	local
coma	veins	gym

3. The words below are from the selections in this section. Use a dictionary to find out what language each word comes from and what it means in that language.

   faux pas   soufflé   goulash

Speaking and Listening

1. With a group of your classmates, act out the scene in "The Sneeze" where Cherdyakov introduces his wife and then sneezes and tries to apologize to the General. You will need people to play these characters: Cherdyakov, his wife, Madame Brassilhov, the General, and the Writer. Prepare to perform the scene for the entire class.

2. Plan a discussion or formal debate with your classmates about the following statement. Be prepared to give examples to support your opinion.

   "High school sports programs are too demanding."

Researching

1. Lutefisk was referred to in "I Remember Mama." Look for a recipe for Lutefisk in the library. Try to find recipes for other Norwegian dishes as well and share your recipes with the class. If you wish, follow the directions to make one of the recipes you have found.

2. Use an encyclopedia to find the difference between a *proscenium stage* and *theater-in-the-round.*

Creating

1. Get together with some classmates to pantomime the scene in "The Sneeze" when Cherdyakov plays back the incident in his mind. Try to make your pantomime as dramatic as possible.

2. Write a letter from Katrin to Miss Moorhead. Thank her for her advice. Also explain why you chose Mama as the subject of your story.

ADVENTURE

*My favorite thing is to go where I've
never been.*

— Diane Arbus

Breezy Day, Tugboats, N.Y. Harbor
William Glackens (1870–1938).
Milwaukee Art Museum Collection,
Gift of Mr. & Mrs. Donald B. Abert and Mrs. Barbara Abert Tooman.

Adventure

Throughout history, authors have told or written stories about adventures. Some of the adventures have been very dramatic. Cave people faced a world of savage animals and physical hardships. Explorers in the Middle Ages embarked on dangerous journeys across unknown seas. Twentieth-century adventurers have walked on the moon and opened up the world inside the atom.

Other adventures are on a smaller scale and are more personal. A person attempts to scale an "unclimbable" mountain. A child is trapped inside a house during a tornado. An injured person attempts to walk again. Someone pilots a raft down a series of rapids on a river.

Authors of adventures use short stories, dramas, novels, personal narratives, diaries, or other literary forms to tell true stories. Or they make up adventures that could be true or that explain the limits of human imagination.

Exciting and Popular

Adventure stories are popular because they are exciting. Readers can't put them down until they find out what happens to the characters. Will they succeed? What new problems will they face? Will the ending be happy or tragic? Adventure stories capture a reader's attention, build up the reader's excitement, and finally relieve the reader's tension when the problem is solved. While following other people's adventures, readers experience many of the same thrills, fears, and triumphs.

Adventure stories are also popular because of what they reveal about people. Adventure stories deal with the best and worst in people, their strengths and weaknesses.

In this section, you will observe the bravery and cowardice of a group of people confronting an army of millions of killer ants. Then you will read about a group of people trapped on a giant airplane. They have to overcome the life-threatening problems of disease and landing an out-of-control aircraft. You will also read the real-life adventure of a woman who battles the forces of nature and her own internal limitations to swim long distances. Then you will go with a young Indian man as he tries to befriend a remarkable wolf. Finally, you will read about a king who tries to recover his throne and his family after a 20-year absence. Three of the adventures you will read are made up, and two are true. All five selections provide readers with a clearer understanding of the capabilities and limitations of human beings.

Resolving Conflicts

Adventure stories always revolve around a problem, or *conflict*. A conflict occurs when a character faces a serious problem. The way the conflict is worked out in the end is called the *resolution*. The most common conflicts in adventure stories are those in which people confront (1) nature, (2) other people, (3) machines and technology, or (4) their own internal feelings. You will find examples of all four types of conflicts in the selections in Section 3. You will also find some exciting resolutions.

In "Leiningen Versus the Ants," a group of men battles a natural force, an army of killer ants. Both the men and the ants try to adapt other elements of nature—water, trees, fire—to aid their cause. Which side will triumph?

The conflict in "Flight Into Danger" arises when most of the passengers and both pilots on Flight 714 get food poisoning. Only one passenger, George Spencer, has ever flown a plane before. Can he fly this one? And can he land it safely, in time to save the sick passengers? Only Spencer can resolve these conflicts, and time is running out. . . .

In "Mind Over Water," Diana Nyad describes her own two-sided conflict. She has to battle nature as well as her own fears of failure. Long-distance swimming, she says, is the ultimate test of physical and mental strength.

"In the Shadow of a Rainbow" is the true story of a young Native American's closeness with nature and of his conflict with his own people. The wolves and other forces of nature are at ease with him. But this brings out jealousy and fear in the people he meets.

In "The Homecoming of Ulysses," Ulysses—a king and hero of Ancient Greece—has survived a war and the tests of the gods. But will he be able to survive a plot to keep him from his wife and son and from his throne?

Close, But Not Too Close

There is one more thing that adds to the popularity of adventure stories. Readers are nearly always glad that the adventures and conflicts are happening to someone else. Having an adventure can be scary, but reading about one is safe and exciting. So come along. Battle the killer ants with Leiningen. Try to bring in a giant airplane with George Spencer—without crashing. Swim Lake Ontario with Diana Nyad. Get to know the wilderness and the wolves in the special way that Gregory Tah-Kloma does. Learn how Ulysses took back his kingdom. An adventure is just a page away.

Leiningen Versus the Ants

by Carl Stephenson

*"Ten miles long, two miles wide—ants, nothing but ants!"
These ants can't be killed by a squirt of bug spray. Before
you can count to 10, they can strip a stag to the bone. But
Leiningen is sure he is more than a match for the
"unbeatable" ants. Dead sure. . . .*

"There is no reason why they should change course. They will reach your plantation in two days at the latest."

For a few seconds, Leiningen gazed at the District Commissioner without answering. Then he took the cigar from his lips. With his gray hair, hooked nose, and sharp eyes, he looked like a shabby, aging eagle.

"Nice of you to come all this way to tell me," he said. "But I won't get out. Even a herd of dinosaurs couldn't drive me from this plantation of mine."

The Brazilian officer threw up his arms. "Leiningen!" he shouted. "You're insane! They're not creatures you can fight. Ten miles long, two miles wide—ants, nothing but ants! Before you can spit three times, they'll eat a full-grown buffalo to the bones. I tell you, if you don't clear out now, there'll be nothing left of you but a skeleton. And your plantation will be picked just as clean."

Leiningen grinned. "I'm not the kind of fathead who tries to stop lightning with his fists. I've got a brain, man. I started this model farm and plantation three years ago. I thought of everything that could happen to it. And I'm ready for everything—including your ants."

The Brazilian rose. "I've done my best," he said. "You're not just putting yourself in danger. The lives of 400 workers are in danger, too. You don't know these ants!"

But Leiningen did know the enemy. He had lived long enough in the country to see for himself the fearful damage the hungry ants could do. Leiningen had defeated drought, flood, plague, and all the other terrors nature had flung against him. His brain had won every time. He was sure that he was more than a match for the "unbeatable" ants.

That night, though, Leiningen called his workers together. He wanted them to hear the news from him first. Most of them had been born in the district. The cry "The ants are coming!" would make them run for their lives. But their trust in Leiningen, his word, and his wisdom, was total. He gave his orders calmly, and they received them calmly. The ants were mighty, but not as mighty as the boss. Let them come!

They came at noon the second day. They were announced by the wild unrest of the horses, who scented horror from far off.

A water-filled ditch had been dug around three sides of the plantation. The fourth side faced the river. Shaped like a huge horseshoe, the ditch was 12 feet across, though not very deep. Leiningen had built a dam at the end nearer the house. Now, by opening the dam, he was able to fling a circle of water around the plantation. Unless the ants could build rafts, he was sure they could not cross it.

Even so, he took one more defense measure. The western section of the ditch ran along a wood. Branches of some great tamarind trees hung over the water. Leiningen had them lopped off, so the ants could not climb on them.

First the wives and children of the workmen were taken to the other side of the river. When they were safe, the cattle were driven over. Leiningen did not really believe they were in danger. But he wanted them out of the way when the battle began.

Another, smaller ditch had been dug around the ranch house, barns, and other buildings. Pipes from three great gasoline tanks could empty into it. Even if by some miracle the ants managed to cross the water, this ditch could not be passed. Leiningen was positive of it.

He stationed his men along the water ditch. Then he lay down in his hammock and smoked until a servant came to tell him the ants had been seen in the south.

Leiningen mounted his horse. He rode slowly in the direction of the threat. The southern stretch of the ditch was nearly three miles long. From its center one could see the advance of the enemy.

It was an unforgettable sight. Over the range of hills, as far as the eye could see, crept a darkening wave. The shadow spread from east to west, then down, down, faster and faster. All the green growth for 20 miles was being mown as if by a giant sickle. The vast, moving shadow grew wider and deeper—and rapidly nearer.

Leiningen's men screamed and cursed as they saw the ants come toward them. But as the distance between the insects and the water ditch narrowed, they were silent. As the terrible army advanced, their faith in Leiningen began to weaken.

Even Leiningen himself felt a surge of sickness. Had his brain taken on more than it could manage? What if the creatures rushed the ditch? If their corpses filled it to the brim, there would still be enough ants to destroy him. He straightened in the saddle. They hadn't got him yet, and he'd see to it that they never would.

The army approached in perfect formation. No human soldiers could ever march in such straight lines. They came closer and closer to the ditch. Then they learned from their scouts that the water blocked them. The two side wings of the army pulled away from the main body. They marched down the western and eastern sides of the ditch, seeking a crossing.

This movement took more than an hour. Leiningen's workers could look at the thumb-long, reddish-black, long-legged insects. Some of the men believed they could see bright, cold eyes and razor-edged jaws, watching and waiting. It seemed to them that every one of the creatures was sending out a single thought: Ditch or no ditch, we'll get to your flesh!

At four o'clock, by some secret means of mind-reading, all the ants learned that the ditch could not be crossed. Leiningen noticed that the news had the greatest ef-fect on the southern front of the army. A dark flood of ants about a hundred yards wide began to go down the far slope of the ditch. Thousands upon thousands drowned. Their comrades climbed upon their bodies, willingly dying to provide stepping-stones for the hordes that followed.

Leiningen ordered one of the men to dam the river more strongly. Another man went to summon more help. Ants struggled nearer and nearer to the inner bank.

Luckily, they were attacking in one place, not on the whole length of the bank. On Leiningen's orders, his men be-gan to dig up the edge of the ditch and throw clods of earth and sand at the in-vaders. Gasoline sprinklers were brought into action. Streams of evil-smelling oil

fell upon an enemy scattered by the bombing of earth and sand.

Leiningen felt like a champion in some new Olympic game, a thrilling contest that he was certain to win. His confidence was so great that the men forgot their fear of the gruesome death only a yard or two away.

Then the ants began to attack along a wider front. Dark ribbons were already mounting the inner bank. One man struck with his spade at an enemy clump. He did not draw it back quickly enough from the water. Instantly, the wooden handle swarmed with upward rushing insects. Cursing, he dropped the spade into the ditch. It was too late. They were already on his body. Wherever they found bare flesh, they bit deeply. A few, bigger than the rest, carried stings that injected a burning poison. Screaming with pain, the man danced and twirled.

Leiningen roared, "Douse your arms in the gasoline!" The man tore off his shirt and plunged his arm and the ants hanging on it into one of the vats of gasoline. Even then, the fierce jaws did not loosen. Another workman had to help him squash and pull off each separate insect.

Some of the defenders had turned away from the ditch to watch. The ants did not waste their chance, though only a few managed to get across. The men set to work again with bombs of earth and sand.

Leiningen thought, "The odds against us are a thousand to one." But he still had his brain.

The water in the ditch began to swirl

with more power—the stronger damming of the river was taking effect. Surging masses of water broke the dark pattern on its living surface. Millions of ants were carried away by the current.

The men shouted for joy, and hurled more earth and sand. Ants scurried back up the slope to safety. Thousands of drowned insects eddied in the water. A storm of clods drove the survivors around the bend toward the mouth of the ditch. They vanished into the river, leaving no trace.

The men celebrated wildly. But Leiningen was not sure. Twenty square miles of ants still stretched back to the hills. They would probably remain quiet until dawn. Still he ordered his men to camp along the bank overnight. Parties were to patrol the ditch in motor cars and shine headlights and torches onto the water. To defeat any attempt at a crossing, the flow of water through the ditch was strengthened still further.

Leiningen ate a hearty supper and slept well. He did not even dream of the millions of cold, cruel eyes watching and waiting on the opposite bank.

At dawn a refreshed Leiningen rode along the ditch. A motionless throng of ants coated the opposite bank. He was almost sorry the fight was over. But the strong current would sweep them away if they tried to cross again.

He rode along the eastern and southern sections of the ditch. Everything was in order. He reached the western section, opposite the tamarind wood. Here the enemy was very busy. Ants were gnawing through the branches of trees and the stalks of vines. A thick green shower of leaves was falling to the ground and being dragged away.

"Food gatherers for the army," Leiningen thought with respect. He knew that ants were intelligent, that some even used ants of other types as cows, watchdogs, and slaves. He was well aware of their sense of discipline and their talent for organization.

Suddenly he realized that the leaves were not being dragged to the troops as food. Each leaf, pulled or pushed by dozens of toiling insects, went straight to the edge of the ditch. The rain of green was a rain of rafts. Every leaf that rustled down the slope into the water carried two or three ants.

Leiningen galloped away yelling orders. "Bring gasoline pumps to the southwest front! Issue spades to every man facing the wood!"

He looked up at the slope of the hill. A strange being twisted toward him, reached the bank, and fell. Leiningen saw that it was a stag, covered over and over with ants. They had eaten its eyes first. With a shot from his rifle, Leiningen put it out of its misery. Then he took out his watch. He had to know how long the ants would take. In six minutes, the white, polished bones alone were left.

That, he knew, was how he himself would look unless. . . . He put spurs to his horse. It was no longer a sporting contest. He must send these bugs back to hell, where they belonged.

The number of floating leaves was increasing swiftly. Soon a mile of water would be covered by a green bridge. Ants could rush over it in millions.

Leiningen galloped to the wheel that controlled the dam. He ordered a man to lower the water in the ditch almost to nothing. "Next," he said, "wait a moment, then suddenly let the river in again. Repeat the same thing over and over again."

At first it worked. The water in the ditch sank, and with it the film of leaves. The troops on the bank swarmed down the slope to the ditch. Then a violent flow of water raced through the ditch, sweeping leaves and ants along.

The rapid current, off and on, kept most of the enemy from crossing the ditch. But it also flung a few squads, here and there, to the inner bank. The air rang with the curses of bitten men. They were able to crush the small number of attackers. But suddenly the lowered water failed to rise in its killing spiral. Something had stopped the machinery. A man rushed up to Leiningen:

"They're over!"

The line beyond the wood had become the theater of action. A throng of ants poured into the emptied water bed. The man at the wheel had seen himself surrounded by raging ants. He had run for his life.

Leiningen knew that the plantation was doomed. But human lives might still be saved. He fired three revolver shots into the air. It was the signal for his men to retreat inside the inner ditch. He rode toward the ranch house. The gasoline in the great tanks near the house must be emptied into the concrete trench.

By twos and threes, Leiningen's men joined him. They were trying to be calm. But their belief that they would win had been shaken.

The planter called them around him. "We've lost the first round," he said. "But we'll win yet. Anyone who doesn't think so can draw his pay here and now. There are rafts on the river and time to reach them."

Not a man stirred.

The bridges over the ditch were removed. Already, a few ants had reached the ditch. They looked at the gasoline and hurried away. At the moment, they did not care. They had the plantation. The trees, shrubs, and fields for miles around were soon filled with gobbling insects.

Night began to fall. Leiningen posted sentries. He knew that his losses were already great. But he was sure he could overcome them. He slept peacefully.

In the morning he rose with the sun. Climbing the flat roof of his house, he looked down on a scene from hell. For miles in every direction there was nothing but a black, glittering mob of ants. They were not satisfied with stripping the plantation. They were still greedy for human flesh, horses, and stored grain.

They sensed the danger in trying to swim through the gasoline. Everything green, from which to make rafts, had been eaten. Soon, though, a long procession could be seen bringing the tamarind leaves they had used the day before.

Leiningen had ordered no one to move or try to stop the ants. When the first few

had climbed the wall, he roared, "Everyone back from the ditch!" The men rushed away. He stepped forward and dropped a match into the gasoline. In a flash, a high wall of flame circled the farm.

The ants retreated. But as soon as the flames died down, they marched forward to attack again. Fresh gasoline flowed into the tank. Fresh flames rose to burn them. But each time the scene was repeated, the ants came back to try again. And the supply of gasoline was limited.

Some of the men fell to their knees and began to pray. Others, shrieking, fired their revolvers at the black masses of ants. Then the nerve of two men broke. One leaped over the north side of the gasoline trench. Another followed. They ran toward the river. But they were not fast enough. Before they could reach the rafts, the ants covered their bodies from head to foot.

In agony, both sprang into the river. Wild screams told Leiningen that other enemies had found them. Crocodiles and saber-toothed piranhas were as hungry as ants.

He flogged his brain. Was there nothing to do? Suddenly he had a terrible inspiration.

"Listen, men!" he shouted. "There's still a chance to save our lives. I am going to try to flood the plantation from the river. The moment I'm over the ditch, set fire to the gasoline. That will allow time for the flood to do the trick. Then just wait until I come back. For I *am* coming back."

He pulled on high leather boots and put on heavy gloves. He stuffed the spaces between pants and boots, gloves and arms, shirt and neck, with gasoline-soaked rags. With close-fitting goggles, he shielded his eyes. Finally, he plugged his nose and ears with cotton. The men poured gasoline over his clothes.

An old Indian came up to him. He had, he said, a salve with an odor that kept ants away. He smeared the boss's boots and gloves and face with the ointment. Then he gave him a gourd full of a bitter medicine—"For their poison," he said. Leiningen drank it down.

With a bound, he leaped over the trench. He was among the ants.

Behind him, the ring of flame blazed high again. Leiningen ran. He *must* get through.

Not until he reached the halfway point did he feel ants under his clothes. He struck at them, scarcely conscious of their bites. He reached the dam. The wheel was thick with ants. They flowed over his hands, arms, and shoulders. Before he had turned the wheel once, the swarm had covered his face. Straining madly, he turned and turned. In minutes, the river began to flood the plantation.

Leiningen let go of the wheel. He was coated from head to foot with a layer of ants. In spite of the gasoline, his clothes were full of them. He felt the pain raging over his flesh.

But he began to run the return journey. He knocked ants from his gloves and jacket, brushed them from his bloodied face, squashed them under his clothes.

One of them bit him below the rim of his goggles. He tore it away, but the acid drilled into the eye nerves. He saw now through circles of fire into a milky mist, and ran almost blinded. The old man's brew had weakened the poison a bit, but it was not enough.

Suddenly he could see again. But the burning ring of gasoline seemed far away.

Scenes from his past flashed through his mind. "The pictures one sees in the moment before death," he thought.

A stone in the path—he stumbled and fell. He tried to rise—he seemed pinned down. The dying stag, furred with ants, flared in his memory. In six minutes—gnawed to the bones. He *couldn't* die like that! Something outside him seemed to drag him to his feet. He began to stagger on.

Through the blazing ring leaped a weird creature. It touched ground on the other side and fell. For the first time in his life, Leiningen had lost consciousness.

The men rushed to him. They tore the ants from a body that seemed almost one open wound. In some places the bones were showing. They carried him to the ranch house.

Outside, the curtain of flames lowered.

Instead of a blanket of ants, one could see a stretch of water. The river had swept over the whole plantation, carrying with it the army of ants. They could not reach the house on the hill—the fire blocked them. Caught between fire and water, they were washed away forever by the freed river.

Leiningen lay on his bed, wrapped from head to foot in bandages. One question was on every face: would he live? "He won't die," said the old Indian, who had bandaged him, "if he doesn't want to."

Leiningen opened his eyes.

"They're gone," said his nurse. He held out a gourd full of sleeping medicine.

Leiningen grinned and drank.

"I told you I'd come back," he said. "Even if I am a bit streamlined." He shut his eyes and slept.

Note

You've just read "Leiningen Versus the Ants"—in which a stag is eaten alive by ants and a man barely escapes being reduced to "a polished skeleton." You've also read about a 20-mile swarm of ants that cuts down every bit of green growth on a huge plantation. Could it really happen?

"Never!" according to Dr. Harold Topoff, an animal behaviorist at the American Museum of Natural History in New York City. "A 20-mile ant swarm? Twenty feet *would be* more like it." Also, Dr. Topoff explained, unless a human being or animal were to lie down in an ant swarm, death wouldn't result. Even then, it would be from thousands of stings, not from being gnawed to the bone.

Scientists walk into ant swarms to study them and are rarely stung at all. And, unless someone happens to be violently allergic to them, a few stings cause about as much trouble as bee or wasp stings. They're unpleasant, but the poison doesn't "drill into the eye nerves."

As far as being eaten is concerned, the jaws of the swarming Brazilian army ant are just not equipped to tear flesh—much less pare a person down to a pile of bones in six minutes. The ants don't want to eat people, anyway, even if they could. They feed on arthropods—other insects—and don't even eat vegetation.

Other ants, called leaf-cutter ants, do eat vegetation, but only certain kinds. No ants known could, or would care to, strip a plantation down to the ground. Leaf-cutters can grow to about two inches—the size of a rather small thumb. But army ants are much smaller.

Dr. Topoff enjoyed reading "Leiningen Versus the Ants." He said, "It's great science fiction."

READING COMPREHENSION

Summarizing. Choose the best phrase to complete each sentence. Then write the complete statements on your paper.

1. Leiningen was determined not to leave his plantation because he was sure that _____ (the ants would not attack, he could outsmart the ants, the ants were not dangerous).

2. Leiningen and his men dug a ditch around only three sides of the plantation because _____ (they didn't have much time, the plantation was too big, the river formed the fourth side).

3. Thousands of ants drowned on purpose so that _____ (they wouldn't have to fight, others might use them as a bridge, Leiningen wouldn't be able to kill them).

4. Many of the ants began to gather green leaves to use _____ (as rafts, for food, to cure the sick ants).

5. The "Note" at the end of the story tells you that what happened _____ (could be true, could not be true, really occurred).

Interpreting. Write the answer to each question on your paper.

1. What did Leiningen finally do that defeated the ants?

2. Why were the ranch workers so loyal to Leiningen?

3. What qualities made Leiningen a tough enemy for the ants?

4. Leiningen was sure the ants wouldn't get across the ditch—but he was wrong. How did the ants prove to be more clever than Leiningen expected them to be?

5. What did Leiningen mean when he thought, "The odds against us are a thousand to one"?

6. How did thinking about the dying stag help to save Leiningen's life?

For Thinking and Discussing

1. When it seemed that the ants couldn't get across the ditch, Leiningen felt almost sorry. Why might he have been disappointed?

2. Dr. Topoff of the American Museum of Natural History said this story was "great science fiction." What details were too fantastic to be true?

3. Were there any ways in which the army of ants was similar to Leiningen's "army" of workers? If so, explain the similarities. In what ways were the army of ants and Leiningen's workers different?

UNDERSTANDING LITERATURE

Conflict and Resolution. In most stories, the main character comes face to face with some person, some force, or some problem. This confrontation is called the story's *conflict*. The way it ends is called the story's *resolution*.

The title of "Leiningen Versus the Ants" presents the conflict in this story. Leiningen's final victory over the ants is the story's resolution.

Here are five events from the story. On your paper, write each event. Then write C to indicate which events are part of the story's conflict, and write R to indicate which events are part of the resolution.

1. Leiningen's men lopped off tree branches that hung over the water.

2. The ants began climbing over each other to cross the ditch.

3. The ants used leaves as rafts.

4. The entire plantation became flooded, and the ants were washed away.

5. Leiningen woke up in his bed and learned that the ants were gone.

WRITING

Think about the following adventure story conflict: Two people are traveling on a raft down a river. As they approach some dangerous rapids, the raft begins to fall apart. How do you think the story will turn out? Write a paragraph in which you present the story's resolution.

Flight Into Danger

a teleplay by Arthur Hailey

Fasten your seat belts and get ready for adventure high in the sky. When the crew of Flight 714 takes a nose dive, a salesman becomes a pilot. Can the doctor on board keep the sick crew and passengers alive until they land? And can the salesman ever get them all safely on the ground again?

CHARACTERS

Aboard Flight 714:
George Spencer
Dr. Frank Baird
Four Male Passengers
Two Women Passengers   } Passengers
Captain
First Officer
Flight Attendant Janet Burns   } Crew

At Vancouver Airport:
Captain Martin Taylor
Airport Controller
Harry Burdick
Switchboard Operator
Radio Operator
Tower Controller

Act One

Fade in on a passenger cabin of a DC-4. The plane is on the ground at Winnipeg Airport, bound for Vancouver. There is one empty aisle seat. Seated next to it is Dr. Frank Baird, M.D. George Spencer enters, sees the empty seat, and goes toward it.

Spencer: Pardon me, is this anyone's seat?

Baird: No.

Spencer: Thanks. *(He sits.)*

Baird: I guess you're going to the big game like the rest of us.

Spencer: I hate to admit it, but I'd forgotten about the game.

Baird: I wouldn't say that too loudly if I were you. Some of the fans might tear you limb from limb.

Spencer *(laughing):* I'll keep my voice down. Matter of fact, I'm making a sales trip up the coast.

Baird: What do you sell?

Spencer: Trucks. Need any? How about 40? Give you a real good discount today.

Baird *(laughing):* I couldn't use that many, I'm afraid. Not in my line.
Spencer: Which is?
Baird: I'm a doctor. Can't buy one truck, let alone 40.
Spencer: Glad to hear it. Now I can relax.

(The plane's engines begin their roar.)

Baird: Do you think you can in this racket? I never could figure out why they make all this noise before they take off.
Spencer: It's the normal run of the engines. If they're okay and the motors are giving all the power they should—away you go!
Baird: You sound as if you know something about it.
Spencer: I'm pretty rusty now. But I used to fly fighters in the Air Force. Well, there we go. *(The sound of the motors increases. Both men look out the window to watch the takeoff.)*
Flight Attendant *(entering):* We were held up at Winnipeg, sir, and we haven't served dinner yet. Would you care for some?
Spencer: Yes, ma'am, please.
Attendant: And you, sir?
Baird: Thank you, yes. It'll pass the time away.
Attendant: There's lamb chops or grilled halibut.
Baird: I'll take the lamb.
Spencer: Yes, I'll have that, too.

(Dissolve to airplane galley. Attendant picks up phone.)

Voice of First Officer: Flight Deck.
Attendant: I'm finally serving the din-

ners. What'll you have? Lamb chops or grilled halibut?
Voice of First Officer: Skipper says he'll take the halibut. Make that two, Janet.
Attendant: Okay.

(Fade to Flight Deck. Captain and First Officer are at the controls.)

First Officer *(into radio mike):* Height 16,000 feet. Course 285 true. ETA Vancouver 0505 Pacific Standard. Over.
Voice on Radio: Flight 714. This is Winnipeg Control. Roger. Out.

(Attendant enters with meal tray.)

Attendant: Who's first?
Captain: You take yours, Harry. *(First Officer takes tray.)*
First Officer: Thanks.
Captain: Everything all right at the back, Janet? How are the football fans?
Attendant: They tired themselves out on the way back from Toronto. Looks like a peaceful night.
First Officer: Ah! Those are the sort of nights to beware of. It's in the quiet times that trouble brews.
Attendant: How's the weather?
Captain: Should be smooth all the way.
Attendant: Good. *(She exits.)*
Captain: How's the fish?
First Officer: Not bad. Not bad at all.

(Fade to passenger cabin, three hours later. Captain is seen strolling the cabin, greeting those who are awake. Spencer and Baird are sleeping. The Attendant can be seen in the rear of the cabin, bending over a woman. The Captain approaches them.)

Captain: Something wrong, Miss Burns?

Attendant: This lady is feeling a little unwell. I'm going to get her some aspirin. *(She exits.)*

Captain: Sorry to hear that. What seems to be the trouble?

First Woman Passenger *(speaking with effort):* It hit me all of a sudden . . . dizziness and nausea and a sharp pain *(Indicates abdomen)* . . . down here.

Captain: Well, I think the Attendant will be able to help you. *(Attendant returns with aspirin and water.)*

First Woman Passenger: Thank you very much.

Captain *(quietly to Attendant):* Is there a doctor on board, do you know?

Attendant: I'll see if I can find out.

(Spencer wakes to see Attendant leaning over another section of seats.)

Attendant *(to another passenger):* I'm sorry to disturb you, but we're trying to find out if there's a doctor on board.

Spencer: Ma'am, *(Pointing to Baird, who is still sleeping)* this man is a doctor.

Attendant: Thank you. I think we'd better wake him. I have a passenger who is quite sick.

Spencer: All right. Doctor! Doctor!

Baird *(sleepily):* Um. What is it?

Attendant: Doctor, I'm sorry to disturb you, but we have a passenger who is quite sick. I wonder if you'd take a look at her.

Baird: Yes, yes of course. *(He goes to the First Woman Passenger. She is shivering and gasping.)* Now, just relax. *(He makes a quick examination. To Attend-ant)* Please tell the Captain we must land at once. This woman has to be taken to the hospital.

Attendant: Do you know what's wrong, Doctor?

Baird: I can't tell. But it's serious enough to land at the nearest city with a hospital.

Attendant: Very well. While I'm gone, will you take a look at this gentleman here? He's also complaining of sickness and pains. *(Baird goes to a Male Passenger.)*

Baird: I'm a doctor. Will you put your head back, please? *(The man groans.)* What have you had to eat in the last 24 hours?

First Male Passenger: Just the usual meals . . . breakfast . . . bacon and eggs . . . salad for lunch . . . then dinner here.

(Attendant enters with Captain.)

Baird: How quickly can we land, Captain?

Captain: There's thick fog over the prairies. But it's clear at the coast, so we'll have to go through.

Baird: Then how soon do you expect to land?

Captain: Three hours and 45 minutes from now.

Baird: Then I'll have to do what I can for these people. Can my bag be reached? I checked it in Toronto.

Captain: We can get it.

(The plane suddenly lurches. The three are thrown sharply to one side. At that moment, the telephone in the galley rings. The Attendant picks it up, listens for a moment.)

Attendant: The First Officer is sick. He says to come quickly.

Captain *(to Baird):* You better come, too.

(Cut to the Flight Deck. The First Officer is at the controls, retching and shuddering. The Captain slides into the other seat and takes the controls.)

Captain: Get him out of here! *(Baird and the Attendant lower the First Officer to the floor and cover him with a blanket. Baird examines him. The Captain has steadied the plane and put it on automatic pilot.)* Doctor, what is it? What's happening?

Baird: These attacks have something in common. Most likely it's the food. *(To Attendant)* How long is it since we had dinner?

Attendant: Two-and-a-half to three hours.

Baird: Now, then, what did you serve?

Attendant: The main course was a choice of meat or fish.

Baird: I remember. What did he have? *(Points to First Officer.)*

Attendant *(with alarm):* Fish.

Baird: Find out what the other two passengers had, please. *(She exits. To First Officer)* Try to relax. You'll feel better if you stay warm.

Attendant *(returning):* Doctor, both those passengers had fish. And there are three more cases now. Can you come?

Baird: Yes. Have someone get my bag out of the luggage. *(Attendant exits.)*

Captain: Doctor, I'm going to get on the radio and report this to Vancouver.

Baird: Tell them we have three cases of

suspected food poisoning, and maybe others. When we land, we'll want medical help waiting.

Captain: Right. *(Reaches for the radio mike, but remembers something suddenly.)* Doctor, I just remembered . . . I ate fish.

Baird: When?

Captain: I'd say about a half hour after he did. *(He points to the First Officer.)*

Baird: You feel all right now?

swer it, the Doctor and the Attendant run to the Flight Deck door.)

(Cut to the Flight Deck. The Captain is in his seat. Sweat pours off his face. His right hand is on his stomach.)

Captain: I did what you said . . . guess it was too late. . . . You've got to give me something, Doctor . . . so I can hold out. . . . It'll fly itself on this course . . . but I've got to take it in. . . . (He collapses. Baird and the Attendant help the Captain to the floor.)

Baird: Get blankets over him. Keep him warm.

Attendant: Can you do what he said? Can you bring him around long enough to land?

Baird: Unless I can get him to a hospital quickly, I'm not sure I can even save his life. And that goes for the others, too.

Attendant: But . . .

Baird: I know what you're thinking, and I've thought of it, too. We have to hope that there's one person back there who is able to land this airplane, and didn't have fish for dinner tonight.

Attendant: Then I suppose I should begin to ask.

Baird: . . . Wait! The man who was sitting beside me! He said something about flying in the war. And we both ate meat. Get him first! (Attendant exits, and Baird begins to look after the First Officer and the Captain. Spencer enters.)

Spencer: The Attendant said. . . . Oh, no! Not both pilots!

Baird: Can you fly this plane . . . and land it?

Spencer: No! No! Not a chance!

Baird: But you told me you flew in the war.

Spencer: So I did. But those were little fighting planes, not a great ship like this. I flew planes that had one engine. This has four. And I haven't touched an airplane in 10 years!

Baird: Then let's hope there's someone else on board this plane who can do the job. . . . (Attendant enters.)

Attendant (quietly): There's no one.

Baird: Mr. Spencer, all I know is that of all the people on this plane, you are the only one who might be able to fly it.

(Pause.)

Spencer: Well, I guess I just got drafted. Let's take a look. (He starts to look at the controls.) Well, maybe we'd better tell the world about our problem. (To Attendant) Do you know how to work this radio?

Attendant: It's this panel up here, but I'm not sure which switches you have to set.

Spencer: Oh, here we are—"transmit." Now we're in business. (He picks up the headset and turns to the other two.) I'm going to need another pair of hands here. Doc, I guess you'll be needed back with the others, so I guess the best choice is our friend here. (He points to the Attendant.) How about it?

Attendant: But I know nothing about all this!

Spencer: Then that will make us a real good pair! Better get in that other seat and strap yourself in.

Baird: I'll take care of things in back. Good luck!

Spencer: Good luck to *you!* We're all going to need it. *(Baird exits.)*

Spencer: What's your first name?

Attendant: Janet.

Spencer: Okay, Janet. Let's see if I can remember how to send out a distress message. Better put on that headset. *(Into mike)* Mayday! Mayday! *(To Attendant)* What's our flight number?

Attendant: 714.

Spencer: This is Flight 714, Maple Leaf Charter, in distress. Come in, anyone. Over.

Voice on Radio: This is Vancouver, 714. Go ahead.

Spencer: Thank you, Vancouver. This aircraft is in distress. Both pilots and some passengers.... *(To Attendant)* How many passengers?

Attendant: It was seven a few minutes ago.

Spencer *(into mike):* At least seven people are sick with food poisoning. Both pilots are in serious condition. We have a doctor on board who says that neither pilot can be revived. *(Pause.)* Now we come to the interesting part. My name is George Spencer. I am a passenger on this airplane. I have a little flying experience, but all of it was on single-engine fighters. And that was over 10 years ago. Now, then, Vancouver, you'd better get someone on the radio who can help me fly this machine. Over.

(Cut to Control Room, Vancouver. The Controller gets a message from the Radio Operator, then steps to the mike.)

Controller: All right, 714, stand by, please. *(He turns to the Switchboard Operator.)* Get me Air Traffic Control—fast. *(Into phone)* Vancouver Controller here. The emergency we had—right now it looks like it's shaping up for a disaster! *(Fade out.)*

Act Three

Fade in on the Control Room, Vancouver. The room is alive with activity. Phones ring, people are typing. The Controller is on one phone; Harry Burdick, the local agent for Maple Leaf Charter, is on another.

Burdick *(into phone):* Is that Cross-Canadian Airlines? Who's on duty in Operations? ... Let me talk to him.... Mr. Gardner, it's Harry Burdick of Maple Leaf Charter. We have an incoming flight that's in bad trouble, and we need a good pilot to talk on the radio. Someone who's flown DC-4's.... Captain Taylor? Yes, I know him well. Can he come over to Control right away? Thank you very much.

Controller *(on another phone):* Hold everything taking off for the East. You've got 45 minutes to clear any traffic for South, West, or North. If you've any flights coming in from the Pacific, divert them to Seattle. Get that? *(A messenger enters, hands Controller a note. He looks at it, then says to messenger.)* Tell the security officer.

Switchboard Operator *(to Controller):* I've got the fire chief.

Controller (*switching to another line*): Chief, we have an emergency. It's Flight 714, due here at 0505. It may be a crash landing. Have everything you've got standing by. If you have any men off duty, call them in. (*To Switchboard Operator*) Now get me the police.

(*Captain Taylor enters. He walks quickly up to Burdick.*)

Burdick: Have you been given the facts?

Taylor: Yes. You realize, of course, that the chances of a man who has only flown fighter planes landing a four-engine passenger ship safely are about nine to one against.

Burdick: Of course I do! But do *you* have any other ideas?

Taylor: No, I just wanted to make sure you knew what you were getting into. All right, let's get started.

Controller: Over here. (*Burdick and Taylor cross to the radio panel.*)

Taylor (*speaking into the mike*): Hello, Flight 714. This is Vancouver and my name is Martin Taylor. I am a Cross-Canadian Airlines captain, and my job right now is to help fly this airplane in. Are you hearing me okay? Over.

Voice of Spencer: Yes, Captain, loud and clear.

Taylor (*looking at paper in front of him*): I see that I'm talking to George Spencer. Well, George, I don't think you're going to have too much trouble. These DC-4's handle easily.

(*During the following conversation, the scene switches back and forth between the Flight Deck and the Control Room.*)

Spencer: Hello, Vancouver, this is 714. Glad to have you along, Captain. But let's not kid each other, please. I haven't flown in over 10 years.

Taylor: Don't worry about that. It's like riding a bicycle. You never forget it. Are you still on automatic pilot? If so, look for the switch to release it. It's a push button that's plainly marked. Do you see it? Over.

Spencer: Yes, Vancouver, I see it. Over.

Taylor: Now, George, in a minute you can unlock the automatic pilot and get the feel of the controls. When you use the controls, they will seem heavy and sluggish compared with a fighter airplane. But don't worry, that's quite normal. You must take care to watch your speed. Don't let it get below 120 knots while the wheels and flaps are up. Keep it steady at 160.

Spencer: Okay, Vancouver. I'm turning off the automatic pilot now. Over.

Taylor: Now, George, you must avoid any quick movements of the controls, or you'll be in trouble. Is that understood? Over.

Spencer: Yes, I understand. Over. (*To Attendant*) Watch that airspeed, Janet. You'll have to call it off to me when we land, so you may as well start to practice.

Attendant: It's 200 now . . . 190 . . . 180 . . . 175 . . . 165. . . .

Spencer: I can't get used to this plane!

Attendant: 150 . . . 155 . . . 160. . . . It's steady on 160.

Taylor: All right, 714. The next thing to do is to put the wheels down. Try to keep your altitude and your speed at

140. Then when the wheels are down, take the speed to 120.

Spencer: Wheels down, Janet, and call off the airspeed.

Attendant (*pulling the lever to lower wheels*): 140 . . . 135 . . . 125 . . . 120 . . . 115. . . . The speed's too low!

Spencer: Keep calling it!!

Attendant: 115 . . . 120 . . . 120. . . . Steady on 120.

Taylor: Hello, George. Your wheels should be down now. Look for three green lights to show that they're locked. Over.

Spencer: I see them. Over.

Taylor: Good. Now I'm going to tell you how to hold your height and airspeed while you raise the landing gear. Then we'll run through the whole thing again.

Spencer: Again! I don't know if my nerves will stand it!

(*Fade to Control Room clock showing 2:55. Fade to clock showing 5:20. Cut back to Control Room.*)

Taylor: You are now 12 minutes flying time from Vancouver Airport. You should be able to see us at any minute. Do you see the airport beacon? Over.

Voice of Attendant: Yes, we see the beacon. Over.

Taylor: Okay, George, now you've practiced everything we need for a landing. Continue to approach at 2,000 feet and wait for instructions. Remember, we want you to do at least one dummy run, and then go around again, so you'll have practice in making the landing. Over.

(*Cut to Flight Deck.*)

Spencer: No dice, Captain. We're coming straight in. Dr. Baird is here. He says that some of the passengers are in critical condition, and we must land in the next few minutes.

(*Cut to Control Room.*)

Burdick: He mustn't! We need time!

Taylor: It's his decision. By all the rules, he's in command of the plane. (*Into mike*) 714, your message is understood. Good luck to us all. We're heading to the Control Tower now to watch your arrival.

(*Fade to Flight Deck.*)

Spencer: This is it, Doctor. You'd better go back now and make sure everybody's strapped in tight.

Baird: Right. Good luck.

Spencer: Thanks.

(*Fade to Control Room Tower. It is a glass-enclosed area with radio panels. The Tower Controller, Taylor, Burdick, and the Controller are looking at the sky. The Tower Controller has binoculars.*)

Tower Controller: There he is!

Taylor (*into mike*): Hello, 714. This is Taylor in Vancouver Tower. Do you read me? Over.

Voice of Spencer: Yes, Vancouver. Loud and clear.

Taylor: You are now ready to land. The runway for landing is zero eight. Begin to lose height to 1,000 feet. Let your airspeed come back to 160 knots and hold it steady there.

Controller (*into mike*): Runway is zero eight. All vehicles stand by near the south end. Is that clear?

(*Cut to film of fire trucks, police cars, and ambulances moving away with sirens wailing.*

(*Cut to Flight Deck.*)

Spencer: We are now at 1,000 feet and leveling off. Over.

(*Cut to Control Tower.*)

Taylor: Now bring your airspeed back slowly to 140 knots. Begin to make a left turn on the downwind leg. . . . Watch your height! Don't make that turn so steep! Get back that height! (*He turns to the others.*) He can't fly the bloody thing! You're watching 50 people about to die!

Burdick (*shouting*): Keep talking to him! Tell him what to do.

Taylor (*into mike*): Spencer, you can't come straight in! Stay up, man! Stay up!

(*Cut to Flight Deck.*)

Spencer: Listen, down there! I'm coming in! Do you hear me? There are people up here who will die in less than an hour! Now get on with the landing check. Wheels down, Janet!

Attendant: Wheels down.

(*Cut to Control Tower.*)

Burdick: He may not be able to fly, but he's sure got guts!

Taylor *(into mike):* Now check your propeller setting.

(Cut to Flight Deck.)

Spencer: Janet, let me hear that airspeed.

Attendant: 130 . . . 125 . . . 120 . . . 125 . . . 130. . . .

(Cut to Control Tower.)

Taylor: You can begin to make a left turn. Begin to lose height to 800 feet. *(He looks through the binoculars, then quickly puts them down.)* You're losing height too fast! Open up! Open! Hold your height!

(Cut to Flight Deck.)

Spencer: What a lousy wagon this is. It doesn't respond!

(Cut to Control Tower.)

Taylor: Start your turn now. Make it a gentle one. Begin losing height about 400 feet a minute. *(Turns to others.)* This is it. In 60 seconds we'll know.

(Cut to Flight Deck.)

Spencer: Janet, give me height and airspeed.

Attendant: 700 feet, speed 120 . . . 600 feet, speed 120. . . . We're going down too quickly!

Spencer: I know! I know! Keep watching it!

Attendant: 450 feet, speed 100. . . .

(Cut to Control Tower.)

Burdick: He's recovering.

Taylor: Now listen, George. Straighten up just before you touch down. All right, your approach is good. Get ready to round out. *(Pause.)* You're coming in too fast! Lift the nose up! Back on the throttle! Hold her off! Ease her down *now!*

(Cut to film of plane landing. As it lands, the picture rocks.

(Cut to Flight Deck. Spencer and Janet are jolted in their seats. Everything shakes.)

Spencer *(shouting):* Cut the switches! Cut the switches! *(Janet reaches up and pulls switches. Spencer stretches out and puts all of his force on the toe brakes. At the same time, he pulls back on the control column. There is a scream of rubber on cement. The two are thrown with great force to one side. Then there is silence as the airplane stops.)*

Spencer *(annoyed):* I ground looped! We're turned right around the way we came!

Attendant: But we're all right! You did it! You did it! *(She kisses him.)*

Voice of Taylor: Hello, George! That was probably the worst landing in history. But there are some people here who would like to shake your hand. Stay right where you are! We're coming over!

(Fade out.)

READING COMPREHENSION

Summarizing. Choose the best phrase to complete each sentence. Then write the complete statements on your paper.

1. People on the plane became sick after they _____ (drank poisoned water, ate fish for dinner, learned that the plane might crash).

2. The captain couldn't land the plane immediately after the first passenger became sick because _____ (there was heavy fog, the plane was behind schedule, there was no airport nearby).

3. Spencer was nervous about flying the plane because he _____ (didn't feel well, had once been in a crash, hadn't flown an airplane for 10 years).

4. When Spencer landed the plane, he was annoyed because _____ (Janet had not been helpful, the passengers were angry with him, he had not made a good landing).

Interpreting. Write the answer to each question on your paper.

1. How did Taylor and Burdick really feel about Spencer's chance of bringing the plane in for a safe landing?

2. In what ways did Taylor try to build Spencer's confidence?

3. Why did Spencer tell Baird to make sure everyone was strapped in tight?

4. How did Spencer's personality help him handle the emergency situation?

For Thinking and Discussing

1. How did the author try to build up the tension during the play? Was he successful?

2. Why are airplane dramas often so dramatic and exciting? Why are movies and television shows about airplane adventures so popular?

3. What do you think might have happened if Spencer had not overcome his feeling of being unable to handle the plane?

UNDERSTANDING LITERATURE

Types of Conflict. The conflict in an adventure story is usually one of four types: (1) person vs. person, (2) person vs. nature, (3) person vs. technology, or (4) person vs. self. In some stories, the conflict may be a combination of several types.

"Leiningen Versus the Ants" is an example of a *person vs. nature* conflict. The ants represent the forces of nature. Leiningen uses his intelligence and daring to defeat them.

"Flight Into Danger" involves two different conflict types: *person vs. technology* and *person vs. self*. The play is mainly about George Spencer's ability to master the technology of an airplane and land it safely. George's ability to overcome his self-doubt about flying the plane is also an important part of the play's conflict.

Below is a list of conflicts. Each one could be the conflict in a story. On your paper, write out each conflict. Then indicate which type or types of conflict fit each situation. Then write at least one or two sentences to explain each of your decisions.

1. A woman discovers that the brakes on the car she is driving down a hill do not work.

2. The members of a mountain-climbing party encounter a severe blizzard as they attempt to reach the top of a mountain.

3. A teenager gets a painful cramp in his leg during an important marathon running race.

4. Two boys who dislike each other learn that they are going to be on the same basketball team.

5. A soldier must travel through 10 miles of enemy territory in order to reach his regiment.

6. A teenager's boyfriend asks her to help him by cheating on an exam.

WRITING

Imagine that you were a passenger on Flight 714. You are being interviewed by a TV news reporter after the plane has landed. Write the dialogue of the interview. Describe the conflict within yourself about whether or not ever to fly again.

Mind Over Water

by Diana Nyad

On October 7th, 1974, Diana Nyad got a shot of gamma globulin and, at 11:35 a.m., climbed down into the chilly waters of Manhattan's East River, called to her friends, "Bye—see you all back here tonight," and began swimming. Twenty-five miles and less than eight hours later, she had kept her promise. She had swum completely around Manhattan Island, easily breaking the record set nearly 50 years earlier by a man. (He took 59 minutes longer.)

A competition swimmer from the age of 13, Diana Nyad became the world's first-ranked woman in the highly specialized sport of marathon swimming. Not long before she circumnavigated Manhattan in 1974, she wrote the following account of what her sport is all about.

I have been working on swimming since I was 10, four hours a day or more, every day. I skipped the greater part of my social life, not a huge sacrifice, but something. I have put more tiring hours into it than a tennis champ like Jimmy Connors will ever know in a lifetime. Not even he would be able to understand the work that goes into marathon swimming.

What I do is comparable to other long-distance competitions: running, cycling, rowing. In those sports, training time far exceeds actual competition time. But swimming burns more calories per minute than anything else. The lungs, heart, and muscles must all be working their best for the sport. You don't need brute strength for this but rather the strength of endurance.

I can do a thousand sit-ups in the wink of an eye. I've run the mile in 5:15, which is better than what most women can do. My lung capacity is 6.1 liters, which is greater than a lot of football players'. My heartbeat is 47 or 48 when I am at rest; this is compared to the normal 72 for other people. A conditioned athlete usually has a heartbeat of 60 plus. This is all due to swimming hour after hour, year after year.

My first marathon, the 10-miler at

Hamilton, Ontario, scared me to death. Judith De Nijs, the best in the world during the Sixties, was there. She said that if a woman ever beat her she would stop swimming. I swam the race and beat her by about 15 minutes. Judith De Nijs never swam again.

I'm interested in people who are involved in seeing how much they can do. Because of this, there is no one group I can respect more than marathon swimmers. For instance, once I was in a hospital bed after swimming in a 24-hour team race. I was weak and had almost frozen to death during the race. There was a guy in the hospital whom I had passed in the race at 3:00 in the morning. We looked at each other as if we were kings of the mountain. We had a love for each other, a close feeling.

There is a lot of anxiety before a swim. I don't know until the day of the race whether the wind will be whipping up 15-foot waves or whether the surface will be glass. On the morning of a swim, our trainers wake us at around 3:00 a.m. for breakfast. We see the press; we eat. Nobody talks. The tension in the room is amazing. I never look at the swimmers. I look out at the lake and wonder what it will do to me. I wonder if I'll be able to cross it. The race is more than me against a swimmer. There is always the risk that I may not conquer the water.

At breakfast I have five or six raw eggs, a lot of cereal, toast and jam, and juice. For my feedings during the race from the boat, I drink a hot powdered liquid. It provides me with 1,300 calories and more protein per tablespoon than a four-ounce steak. It gets my blood sugar back up. In a race, my blood sugar drops below level in three minutes. A cup of this stuff every hour barely helps. Before the hour's up, my sugar is way down. I can feel it. I feel low. But if my protein level stays high, I'm not really in trouble.

I would say that 80 percent of success in a race is due to mind. Once out there, it's a matter of mental guts. After 12 hours in cold water, my blood sugar is down. I'm 17 pounds lighter, and exhausted. It takes more than knowing I've trained hard for this. I have to dig down deep.

I've done some marathon running. I still think that the feeling of being alone in long-distance swimming is greater. I'm cut off from all communication. The water moving over my cap leaves me just about deaf. I wear tiny goggles that fit just over my eyes. They're always foggy, so I can't see very well. I turn my head to breathe on every stroke. That means 60 times a minute, 600 strokes every mile for hours and hours. As I turn my head, I see the blur of the boat and some people on it. During a long swim I'm left with my own thoughts. My mind drifts. It's hypnotic. It's dreaming for hours on end. All I hear is the water slapping and my arms whishing through water. All I see is fog. It is very lonely.

I'm strong at the beginning of a swim. Then I have low points. I know the pain in my shoulders will be bad all the way. I've rolled over on my back, thinking this

body will not do another stroke. Sometimes at a low point a swimmer will get out. In 10 minutes he's saying to himself, "Why didn't I stick it out? I could have made it. I could have come back around." That's happened to me, too, when I couldn't get back into it.

In rough ocean, I have thrown up from the beginning of the race to the end. I would do anything to stop this feeling. The only thing that will do it is to be on dry land. But I can put up with it—I have to. In my first year of marathon swimming, I got out because of

day for Europe. I thought, "Why waste the time? Why not swim for just an hour to loosen up?" I did a thousand strokes out. Then I stopped to turn around, empty my goggles, and get a sighting onshore. But I realized I hadn't been feeling my legs. I couldn't bring them to the surface. My skin was bright red. My breath stuck in my throat. I tried to scream to some boys onshore, but nothing came out. I started to swim a slow breaststroke. My hands were so cold I couldn't close my fingers.

People onshore finally saw I was in trouble. By now I was onto some rocks. A man came out and grabbed me under my arms. He lifted me out of the water. His hands, his 98.6-degree hands, burned my skin. They took me to the hospital and put me in a warmer. I had terrible burns all the way through the Capri-Naples race.

There are still a few bodies of water I want to conquer.

Marathon swimming will never be as popular as other sports because one can only watch the finish, not the whole race.

Some people do spend the whole day just waiting for you to finish. From a mile out I can hear clapping and screaming. They know I swam from a place they couldn't even see on the clearest day. They know I may faint when I arrive. They share with me the most extreme moment of all. After the pain, the cold, the hours, the distance, the tiredness, and the loneliness, I come out of the water. And this is what it's all about.

seasickness. Now I get just as seasick but I stick to it.

I can handle tiredness, pain, and huge waves. The hardest part is cold water.

My coldest time was training in Ontario for the Capri to Naples race in 1974. I was supposed to leave later that

READING COMPREHENSION

Summarizing. Choose the best phrase to complete each sentence. Then write the complete statements on your paper.

1. Before a race, marathon swimmers are usually _____ (happy and joking, not able to eat, very tense and anxious).

2. Diana Nyad believes that 80 percent of the success in a long-distance race depends on _____ (hard work and practice, the swimmer's state of mind, how good the competition is).

3. The hardest problem Diana Nyad has to overcome is the effects of _____ (tiredness, cold water, loneliness).

Interpreting. Write the answer to each question on your paper.

1. Why is there so much anxiety before a swim?

2. Why is it necessary for marathon swimmers to have great strength and endurance?

3. What makes marathon swimming such a lonely sport?

4. What are some of the obstacles that a marathon swimmer must face during a competition?

For Thinking and Discussing. What insights can people gain about themselves by participating in contests of great physical strength and endurance?

UNDERSTANDING LITERATURE

Person vs. Self Conflict. Many adventure stories involve characters struggling to achieve personal goals. The characters in the story may battle nature, machines, or other people, but their real conflict is *within* themselves.

Diana Nyad's "Mind Over Water" demonstrates the *person vs. self* type of conflict. The resolution is her ability to keep going and complete a race.

The following descriptions illustrate person vs. self conflicts. On your paper, write a resolution for each conflict.

1. Larry has accidentally seen the answers to an upcoming history test. He is not sure whether he should take the test anyway or tell his teacher.

2. Joan is an excellent diver who is also afraid of heights. More than anything else, she wants to be able to dive from the high board in the state meet.

3. Hector has always been shy and unsure of himself. A new girl has moved into the neighborhood. She seems to like him, but Hector is afraid to get to know her.

WRITING

A *monologue* is a speech in which a character reveals his or her inner thoughts to an audience. Imagine you are swimming a marathon race. Write a monologue in which you describe a conflict that develops within yourself as you swim the race.

138

In the Shadow of a Rainbow

by Robert Franklin Leslie

*Gregory Tah-Kloma is a lone wolf. That means that he likes
to be alone—when it comes to people. But when it comes to
wolves, he likes to run with the pack. This nonfiction
account tells of Gregory's relationship with the leader of the
pack—and their terrifying escape from the hunters into the
Canadian wilderness.*

In the summer of 1970, a young Indian beached his canoe near my camp in the backwoods of British Columbia, Canada. He told me he was Gregory Tah-Kloma. For several days, we hiked together. One night, he told me the following story.

Greg went looking for gold in the summer of 1964. Few people lived in the area where he camped. So he was surprised when a middle-aged Indian approached him one day.

"My name is Eugene Charley," the man said. "Have you seen Nahani?"

"Who is Nahani?" Greg said.

"A huge silver she-wolf and leader of a killer pack. There is a reward for her skin. Her pack will come here for the winter. If you stay, they'll eat you alive."

"Why should anybody fear wolves?"

"Nahani has taught her pack to steal animals from traps. Lately, people have disappeared. But I'll bring Nahani down!"

Greg was glad when the man left. He seemed too greedy for that reward money. He probably made up stories about Nahani so the reward would go up. Greg did not believe that wolves attack people—unless they are cornered or sick with rabies.

Three nights later a huge silver wolf stepped within the light of Greg's campfire. It had to be Nahani. She stared at Greg, then disappeared.

The next day members of her pack watched every move that Greg made. He did not want to scare them away. So he stayed in plain sight and moved on all fours.

That night he walked along the beach of the lake near his camp. When he walked back, he saw that many of his prints were covered by wolf prints. He had not been aware of being followed.

The wolves got used to seeing him walk along the beach at night. But they became tense whenever he stood up during the day.

One night Nahani came to his camp and sat down within 10 feet of him. She stared at the fire. Now and then, she stared at Greg. After an hour, she left.

The next night she came to his camp, wagging her tail. Eight male wolves paced nearby, whining. When she barked an order, they ran off. She sat next to Greg for several hours until the males came back. Then she led them up to their dens on a ridge above the lake.

The next day Greg saw several wolves sleeping on the beach. Their bellies were very full. The eight males must have gone hunting and brought back meat. When Nahani appeared on the beach, the wolves jumped to attention.

Later Greg wrote in his diary: "She is much larger than the other wolves. She has weight, speed, guts, and brains. That's why she's a leader. She doesn't follow any male. That means she either lost a mate or never had one."

After a while Greg started walking upright during the day. The wolves finally

got used to this. But Nahani was the first to accept his standing up.

One evening Greg cooked some fish for her. She ate one of the fish. She took the other to the dens—probably to a sick or injured wolf.

When she came back Greg was moving about on foot. Suddenly she jumped in front of him. She stood on her hind legs and put her forepaws on his shoulders, almost knocking him over. She licked his face, then backed away.

Greg did not try to pat Nahani until she started shedding hair. Then he tried combing out her loose hair with his fingers. After that, she let him scratch her head, back, and belly.

Nahani was the only wolf who came into Greg's camp. But several guards always stayed fairly close to their leader. At first they were nervous when Greg combed Nahani. Finally they seemed to realize that this would not harm her.

As the weeks passed, Greg noticed how Nahani ordered the pack around. She assigned guards for injured wolves. She ordered certain adults to help feed and protect the cubs of others. She drilled the pack in hunting skills. She formed hunting squads, then either led them or sent them toward the scent of game.

Greg learned to follow her orders, too. When she brought fish bones to him, he would catch and cook fish for her. When she barked to go for a walk, he would follow her.

In September it turned cold. One night the whole pack gathered around Greg's campfire and howled. Nahani licked Greg's face, then led her pack into the darkness.

By October the wolves had not come back. Greg realized they had gone to their winter quarters. It was time for him to go home.

Greg went back to the lake the next summer. He hoped to find more gold and to see Nahani again. He found gold, but not Nahani. Some north-woods Indians said she had been seen in the wilderness to the north.

Meanwhile, she had become a legend. Rumors about her robbing animal traps and killing people had spread. The price on her head was now up to $800.

In June, 1966, Greg got ready to look for the wolf in the northern wilderness. Two Indians heard what he planned to do. To prove he was crazy, they took him to Trapper Dan. Dan was one of the best trackers in the country. He also had a bad temper.

"I've heard that you made friends with Nahani," he growled at Greg. "Well, wolf-man, you can count her dead. A group of us trappers are going after her in July."

"How do you know where she is?" Greg asked.

"We'll find her before you do. There ain't no trails up where she is. But we know that country. You don't."

It took many days for Greg to hike deep into the wilderness. Along the way he saw many kinds of animals, but no wolves.

One morning a breeze carried to him the faint smell of coffee. Through his binoculars, he saw smoke about five miles away. He hiked to a ridge about a mile from the campsite. Again he looked through his binoculars. Trapper Dan, Eugene Charley, and three white strangers were sitting around the fire. A float plane was beached on the nearby lake.

Greg hurried back to his camp. He covered up the signs that he had camped there, and moved on. He walked on stones or in streams when he could. When he couldn't, he erased his footprints as he went.

Several days later he found wolf tracks on the shore of a lake. One set of prints was larger than the others. He set up camp and waited. But for two weeks he neither saw nor heard a wolf.

He feared that the wolf pack had gone in the direction he had come from. So he hiked back to his former camp. The wolves—and Trapper Dan—had been there. The wolves had dug up his fire pit. Boot prints and seven empty bullet shells showed that a running man had stopped to fire seven times.

Trapper Dan and his men must have found the wolves exploring the campsite. Wolf guards must have warned the pack to run before the shooting began. The pack must have been Nahani's. One set of wolf prints was larger than the others.

Greg followed the tracks northward for weeks. He came across the trails of different wolf packs. Often he lost Nahani's trail for hours at a time. Did she sense that she was being followed? Was her pack being careful not to leave tracks?

In September he lost the trail completely. His boots were worn out, so he headed home. He had not found Nahani, but at least she was still alive. If she came south this winter, though, the bounty hunters would get her.

Greg decided to rent a cabin in the north for the winter. If Nahani came south, he thought he knew which route she would take. And maybe he could stop her.

He found that the only cabin for rent belonged to Trapper Dan. He visited Dan, who was not at all friendly.

Greg said, "I want to spend the winter north of here if I can find a cabin."

"Are you really friendly with Nahani?"

"Maybe."

Dan's attitude suddenly changed. He said he owned a cabin which he'd rent to Greg. Then he did two things which made Greg suspicious. He helped Greg haul winter supplies to the cabin. Then he insisted on leaving a rifle with Greg. Greg knew that Dan was plotting something, but didn't know what.

During October Greg repaired the cabin. He chopped many logs for firewood. He caught and smoked fish for winter meals.

One day, a young Indian came to the cabin. He told Greg, "Trapper Dan thinks Nahani will find you here. He says you can talk to her. He'll keep an eye on this cabin. So will Eugene Charley. That's why Dan rented it to you. If Charley gets Nahani first, Dan will kill him and claim the reward. Don't trust either man."

About 10 days later, Eugene Charley came to the cabin. Greg decided to put him to the test.

"Tomorrow I'm heading for Swan Lake," Greg said. "You can keep me company. I think we'll meet some wolves. There are two cabins 15 miles apart. It's 60 miles round trip."

Charley grinned and said, "Okay."

They reached the first cabin without any trouble. After supper that evening, Charley drank some rum. Then he began to talk. He said that many of the Indians thought he was a liar and a coward. He was afraid that Trapper Dan was trying to get rid of him. Greg suddenly felt sorry for him, an Indian so little at peace with himself.

They reached the second cabin the next day. That evening Charley seemed nervous. About midnight wolves began howling outside. Charley ran to the door with his rifle.

"Nahani!" Greg yelled.

143

Charley panicked and fired seven times into the darkness. Then he did what Greg hoped he would do. He packed his gear and left.

When Greg woke up the next morning, a snowstorm was raging. It would be risky trying to make it back to the first cabin. But it would be worse if he became snowbound here without enough supplies. So he set off.

It was midnight when he reached the cabin. Candlelight shone through the window. Through the ice-covered glass, Greg saw the outlines of four men.

He knocked on the door. Finally, it opened a crack, and someone said, "Go away, wolf-man."

"I can't get through the mountain pass in this storm," Greg said. "Let me in."

"Go away." And the door slammed shut.

About 24 hours later, Greg arrived at Trapper Dan's cabin. He ate a huge meal, then slept soundly.

Two days later two policemen arrived on snowshoes. One of them said, "We heard that a wolf pack paid you a visit at the Swan Lake cabin. Was Nahani there?"

Greg said, "I don't know."

The other policeman said, "Four Indians are working for Trapper Dan. They knew about that wolf pack. They thought it might be Nahani's. They followed you and Eugene Charley and hid in the forest, hoping for a close-up shot. Charley blew their chances when he fired his rifle. Charley is dead. Trapper Dan, of course, wants us to believe you killed him."

While hiking a few days later, Greg found wolf tracks. They led to a bloody spot and a set of elk prints. Four different sets of boot prints led to and from the spot. But the men had visited the scene before the wolves. Wolf prints covered boot prints. None of the prints looked like Nahani's.

Soon the two policemen visited him again. One said, "A wolf pack killed an elk about five miles from here. Some loggers made the report. They said Nahani was one of the pack."

"I saw where the elk was killed. You'll find wolf tracks and the tracks of four hunters. The elk was gone before the wolves got there," Greg said.

In December and January pairs of wolves came down from the hills. After breeding, they went back to their packs.

During February Greg often heard a wolf pack howling. On clear evenings he followed them on his snowshoes. But they never let him get closer than 50 yards. And not once did he see Nahani.

Now he was restless for winter to end so he could search for her. He spent most of March and April with his maps, planning a day-by-day trip from June to September.

In late May he went home and got ready for the trip. A friend warned him, "Many of the Indians believe you killed Eugene Charley. That's why Dan left you a rifle at the cabin. He figured you hated Charley enough to kill him. The reward for Nahani is now $1,800. Dan and his men will follow you this summer. Be careful. They are dangerous men."

Greg started out—on a new route. He wore heavy moccasins over his boots, so he wouldn't leave boot prints. He was careful where he stepped. And he didn't build a fire for several days.

He hiked far into the wilderness. Now and then he found wolf tracks, but none of them were fresh.

In late July he found fresh tracks. And one set was larger than the others!

He followed the tracks for 60 miles. Then he lost them. The wolves must have known that somebody was trailing them.

Two days later Greg reached a large lake. A wolf runway led to dens on a hill near the beach. Fresh tracks suggested that the pack had been there about six hours before.

Greg set up camp near the lake. During the next week he didn't see a single wolf. But he felt as though he were being watched. And he feared that Trapper Dan and his men had found him.

He pretended to break camp. Then he backtracked. He searched for boot prints, but found none. Suddenly, he froze. A twig snapped about 20 yards behind him. He spun around—and saw four wolves staring through some bushes.

The wolves quickly disappeared. Greg realized they were acting as scouts for a pack. They—not Trapper Dan—had been watching him for a week.

Greg went back to the lake and set up camp again. For several days he sensed, but could not see, wolves nearby. Then one day he saw about 25 wolves sleeping on a cliff above the wolf dens. The scouts must have decided that Greg was no threat, so the pack had come back home.

That night, as Greg sat by his fire, he heard a growl. He turned and saw Na-hani watching him. Slowly, he moved toward her on all fours. He stopped when she snarled. He saw several wolves behind her. He began talking to her. But she backed away, then led the other wolves into the forest.

Greg feared that she hadn't recognized him—and never would. But she came back the next night. This time he sat quietly. She walked to within a yard of him, looked him in the eye, and wagged her tail. She did remember him.

It took several days for Nahani to get used to Greg again. Finally she licked his hands and let him scratch her.

Nahani visited him every night and stayed for several days. When the moon was bright, she often led him on walks along the beach. At times she also appeared in the afternoon or at sunrise. If she found him asleep, she waited for him to wake up. On sunny days, she led him on hikes into the hills.

In August the wolf parents began taking their cubs on training trips away from the pack. When all the families were away, Nahani never left Greg's side.

When the families came back, the cubs had learned how to track animals. Now Nahani taught them how to hunt as a team.

In late September it turned cold. But Greg did not want to leave. He decided to stay until he ran out of food—or the wolf pack left for the winter.

One night Nahani tugged at Greg's jeans. This meant she wanted to walk. He followed her along the beach. Then a strange thing happened. One by one, every member of the pack joined them.

Nahani trotted in front, with a bodyguard on either side. Greg came next, also with a bodyguard on either side. The rest of the pack trotted in formation behind them.

Later Greg wrote in his diary: "Nahani had the whole thing planned. When something strengthens a friendship, our people say the friends have walked in the shadow of a rainbow."

Every night after that the whole pack walked with Nahani and Greg along the beach. Greg wished that winter would never come.

One October morning Greg and Nahani were eating baked fish at his camp. Several wolves were playing tag on the beach. Suddenly a float plane landed on the lake. Every wolf faded into the forest.

The plane headed toward the beach in front of the campsite. Two hunters and the pilot came ashore. Greg recognized them. They were the three white men he had seen with Trapper Dan last summer.

They introduced themselves to Greg. Then one of the hunters said, "That was Nahani sitting around here. You must be the wolf-man. If I hadn't seen it, I wouldn't have believed it!"

Greg was silent.

The pilot explained that the two hunters wanted Nahani's skin. They didn't care about the reward. Last summer, they had hired Trapper Dan and Eugene Charley to lead them to the great wolf. Both Indians said that Greg would lead them to Nahani sooner or later.

He added, "Too bad about Dan."

"What do you mean?" Greg asked.

"He and two trappers were hunting

147

near Swan Lake this summer. Dan shot and wounded a silver wolf. The wolf rushed him and chewed him badly before the other men killed her. Dan claimed that the wolf was Nahani. Most people believed him. Later Dan died of rabies."

After a long pause Greg decided to tell his story. He spoke slowly and in great detail. He wanted to give Nahani plenty of time to hide.

When he finally finished, the three men looked at him with respect. One of them said, "The last time we spoke to Trapper Dan, he said, 'Nahani won't come south again. She'll head for the Yukon. No man will ever kill her.' "

The two hunters looked at each other, then nodded. One of them said to Greg, "We won't go after your wolf. If she goes to the Yukon, she'll be safe."

The three men left some canned food with Greg. Then they went back to the plane and flew off.

Three nights later Nahani walked into Greg's camp. As they shared some food, Greg told her, "Trapper Dan is dead. The hunt for you is over. We did walk in the shadow of a rainbow."

On the last of October it snowed. Nahani and Greg sat inside a shelter that Greg had built. Suddenly the whole pack came to the shelter, their heads and tails held high. Greg knew what this meant.

Nahani allowed him to hug her around the neck. She licked his face and hands. Then she leaped from the shelter and led her pack north. Trapper Dan had been right. Nahani was headed for the Yukon.

READING COMPREHENSION

Summarizing. Choose the best phrase to complete each sentence. Then write the complete statements on your paper.

1. Trapper Dan and Eugene Charley tried to capture Nahani because they _____ (thought she was dangerous, wanted her for a zoo, wanted the reward for her skin).

2. Greg believed that _____ (wolves attacked people, wolves were valuable for their skins, wolves did not attack people unless they were cornered or sick).

3. Eugene Charley made up stories about Nahani so that _____ (people would fear her, the reward for Nahani's skin would go up, he would be popular with the hunters).

4. Greg decided to rent a cabin during the winter because he _____ (wanted to capture Nahani and bring her back alive, wanted to stop Nahani from going south where the hunters were, had no other place to live).

5. When Nahani headed for the Yukon, Greg knew that _____ (she would be safe, the hunters would follow her there, the wolf pack would starve).

6. The story of Gregory Tah-Kloma and Nahani _____ (was made up by a writer, really happened, is an Indian legend).

Interpreting. Write the answer to each question on your paper.

1. Why did Greg stay in sight and walk on all fours the first time he saw the wolf pack?

2. Why did Greg search for Nahani the first time?

3. Why did Greg continue to search in the wilderness for Nahani over the next few years?

4. How did Nahani show her friendship toward Greg?

5. How did Greg feel when he knew that Nahani and the wolf pack were headed for the Yukon?

For Thinking and Discussing

1. What kind of person was Gregory Tah-Kloma? How did he show that he was sensitive to animals and understood how they acted?

2. What made Nahani a good leader? How did she lead the wolf pack?

3. What did Greg's people mean when they said that "friends have walked in the shadow of a rainbow"? Why did Greg tell Nahani, "We did walk in the shadow of a rainbow"?

UNDERSTANDING LITERATURE

Climax. The conflict in a story is a struggle, usually between the main character and opposing forces. The conflict usually builds until it reaches a high point, called the *climax*. Following the climax, the conflict becomes resolved.

You can often divide a story into three sections:

(1) the buildup of the conflict,
(2) the climax or turning point, and
(3) the resolution.

The diagram above illustrates this.

The following events from "In the Shadow of a Rainbow" are not in the correct sequence. On your paper, draw a "conflict-climax-resolution" diagram. Arrange the events in the right place on the diagram.

1. Nahani led the pack to the Yukon.

2. Greg found Nahani again.

3. Nahani and the other wolves walked with Greg along the beach.

4. Greg gained the wolves' trust and began walking upright around them.

WRITING

What might have happened if Trapper Dan had caught Nahani when Greg was there? Would Dan have killed the wolf? Would Greg have stopped him? Write a paragraph in which you present a climax and resolution different from those in the story.

The Homecoming of Ulysses

a radio play based on The Odyssey *by Homer*

A war was fought between the Trojans and the Greeks around 1200 B.C. According to legend, it started because Paris, a Trojan prince, ran off with Helen, the wife of Menelaus, King of Sparta. Menelaus and his brother, Agamemnon, declared war on Paris' country, Troy. Then they went to the many kingdoms in Greece, persuading the leaders to join their army.

One of these leaders was Ulysses, King of Ithaca. He did not want to go to war, so he pretended to be too crazy to fight. He hitched a horse and an ox to his plow, and he plowed a sandy beach, planting salt.

Agamemnon believed Ulysses was insane, but he tested him. Ulysses' baby son, Telemachus, was thrown in front of the sharp plow. Ulysses turned his plow aside to save his son. It was clear he was not crazy, after all, so he sailed to Troy with the Greeks.

Once he was in the war, Ulysses fought bravely, but he never stopped using his head. His clever tricks helped the Greeks win the war.

A famous poet, Homer, composed an epic poem about the Trojan war. It was called The Iliad. Then he chose a popular Greek hero of the war, Ulysses, and made him the main character of another epic poem, The Odyssey.

Homer composed this epic poem around 800 B.C., when the Trojan War was already ancient history. Many legends had grown up around it. Homer used those legends, since most of the facts had been forgotten. And he included the roles of the gods and goddesses of Greek mythology. So The Odyssey is a mixture of legend and myth.

CHARACTERS

Ulysses (Yoo-LIS-sees), King of Ithaca

Telemachus (Tel-LEH-mah-kus), Ulysses' son

Penelope (Peh-NELL-oh-pee), Ulysses' wife

Eumaeus (Yoo-MAY-us), the king's pigherder

Eurycleia (Yur-ih-KLAY-ah), the king's old nurse

Antinous (An-TIH-no-us), one of Penelope's suitors

Eurymachus (Yur-IH-mah-kus), another suitor

Athena (Ah-THEE-nah), goddess of war and wisdom

Menelaus (Men-uh-LAY-us), King of Sparta

Alcinous (Al-SIN-oh-us), King of Phaiacia

Narrator I

Narrator II

Narrator I: This is the story of a hero and a wanderer. He was King of Ithaca, Greece, many centuries ago, when gods and goddesses walked the earth. He fought bravely for 10 long years in the war between the Greeks and the Trojans. Then it took him 10 more years to sail home, for one of the gods became angry with him and made his return difficult. His entire crew lost their lives along the way. Only Ulysses survived, struggling against fate, hoping to see his wife and son again.

Narrator II: When Ulysses left for the Trojan War, his son Telemachus was a baby. Telemachus grew up without knowing his father. But he felt sure Ulysses would come home one day. There were other people in Ithaca, however, who believed King Ulysses was dead.

(Sounds of a feast: laughter and the clatter of dishes.)

Penelope: Telemachus, my son, why don't you join the feast?

Telemachus: I will not sit with those men, Mother. They all say they want to marry you, but they are greedy for the kingdom. They have been hanging around for four years now, and they will soon eat us out of house and home. Why don't you tell them to leave?

Penelope: Your father told me to marry again if he was killed in the Trojan War.

Telemachus: The stories say he survived as a hero.

Penelope: But it's been 10 years since then. Perhaps he's never coming home.

Telemachus: Then choose one man from among these suitors. And send the rest away.

Penelope: I said I'd wait until you were grown up.

Telemachus: I *am* grown up now.

Penelope *(after a pause)*: You are right. But none of these men is as clever or brave as my Ulysses. *(Her footsteps hurry away.)*

Telemachus *(to himself)*: If my father were here, he'd get rid of all these suitors in a second!

Antinous (*calling out*): Ho! Telemachus! Why don't you join us? The wine is delicious.

Telemachus: Antinous, you and your friends are drinking our wine cellars dry. You are eating up all our cows and pigs and sheep. Someday you will pay for this!

Antinous (*laughing*): Who will make us pay? You, boy?

Telemachus: I am not a boy. I am 20 years old.

Antinous: Pardon me! Anyway, it is your mother's fault. She said she'd marry when she finished weaving a burial cloth for her father-in-law. For three years we have watched her weave, day after day. But she is never finished. Now we know why. Every night she pulls apart her day's work. She is a clever woman, worthy of being the widow of a clever man like Ulysses.

Telemachus: He is still alive. And when he comes home, he will take care of you!

Antinous: If he were coming home, he would be here by now.

Telemachus: Perhaps not. I am going to visit King Menelaus in Sparta. He may know where my father is.

Antinous: Where do you think you will find a ship? (*He laughs cruelly.*)

(*Feast sounds fade out. Sea sounds rise.*)

Narrator II: Telemachus walked to the seashore and looked out over the sea, wondering where his father was. Then he noticed a stranger standing beside him.

Telemachus: Who are you? I didn't hear you walk up.

Athena: I am an old friend of Ulysses. You look a lot like him, Telemachus. You will make him very proud when he comes home.

Telemachus (*eagerly*): Do you believe he is coming home?

Athena: He is on his way now.

Telemachus: What has kept him so long?

Athena: Poseidon, the sea god, was angry at him. I tried to help Ulysses, but Zeus

would not let me. And Zeus has the final say about such things.

Telemachus: *You* tried to help? Then you must be—

Athena: Yes, I am Athena.

Telemachus: I know my father prayed to you. But it is hard to believe that you, a goddess, are speaking to me!

Athena: Your father is heading home, but he will need your help. You need a ship to visit Menelaus. Be here at dawn tomorrow, and a ship will be waiting.

(Sea sounds fade out.)

Narrator II: Telemachus woke early the next morning and ran to the shore. A fine ship and a good crew were waiting. Telemachus went aboard, and they sailed to Sparta. There, Telemachus was welcomed by King Menelaus, his father's old friend.

(Sounds of crackling fire.)

Menelaus: Your father was a hero in the Trojan War. He fought bravely, as many of us did. But he was very clever, too. Have you heard the story of the Trojan Horse?

Telemachus: Yes, sir.

Menelaus *(telling it anyway)*: The Greek army could not get past the walls of the city of Troy. So your father thought up a clever trick. He had us build a huge wooden horse on wheels. We filled it with soldiers, wheeled it to the gates of Troy, and left it there. The Trojans thought it was a gift, so they took it inside. At night, our soldiers climbed out and killed the gate guards. Then they opened the gates to our army, and we quickly captured the city. What a trick! Yes, your father is clever, all right.

Telemachus: *Is?* Then you believe he's still alive?

Menelaus: Yes. A few years ago, I traveled to Egypt, and I had a hard time getting home because the winds were against me. I prayed to one of Poseidon's sons. He told me news of my friends who survived the Trojan War. He said they had reached home safely, except for King Ulysses.

Telemachus: Did he say where my father is?

Menelaus: He said Ulysses is under a spell. He is trapped on an island by Calypso, a magician. He has lost both his ship and his crew. Every day he sits on the shore and longs to be home.

Telemachus: How will he ever get away?

Menelaus: The gods and goddesses hold his fate in their hands. Maybe Athena will help.

Narrator II: Telemachus sailed home with his heart filled with hope. But back in Ithaca, a plot was being hatched.

(Sounds of a feast.)

Antinous: Eurymachus, I have a plan.

Eurymachus: What is it, Antinous?

Antinous: Telemachus somehow found a ship and went to visit King Menelaus.

Eurymachus: What of it?

Antinous: Menelaus is powerful. If he helps the boy, it could be the end of our easy life here.

Eurymachus: I see. Then I would not get to marry Penelope.

Antinous: You mean that *I* would not get to marry her. And none of us would get free room and board anymore. We must get rid of Telemachus. When his ship returns, we must attack it before it enters the harbor here.

(Feast sounds fade. Soft music begins.)

Narrator I: Meanwhile, a stranger in ragged clothes appeared in the court of King Alcinous. His ship and crew had been lost in a storm, and King Alcinous welcomed him.

Alcinous: You must eat and drink with us tonight, stranger. Tomorrow we will see about getting you home. But first, please accept a bath and new clothes.

Narrator I: The stranger thanked Alcinous, but he would not tell his name. Alcinous was curious, but he asked no questions. Instead, he treated the proud stranger like a guest. He gave a fine feast that night. When a singer entertained them with a song about the Trojan War, Alcinous noticed that tears filled his guest's eyes.

Alcinous: Stranger, why does this song make you sad? Did you fight at Troy?
Ulysses *(after a pause):* Yes. I am Ulysses of Ithaca.
Alcinous *(surprised):* King Ulysses? The hero of the Greeks?
Ulysses: That was 10 years ago. I have been trying to get home ever since. But Poseidon, the sea god, is angry at me, and he has kept me from sailing home.

Alcinous: How did you make Poseidon angry?
Ulysses: After leaving Troy, my men and I landed on the island of the Cyclopes, the one-eyed giants. One of them trapped us in his cave. I stood helpless as he picked up two of my men and swallowed them—clothes and all. When he fell asleep, we stuck a sharp stake into his single eye and blinded him. Only then did we escape. But it turned out that he was Poseidon's son, and Poseidon swore revenge on us.
Alcinous: What did he do to you?
Ulysses: He sent us from one misfortune to another. We landed on the island of the keeper of the winds, who gave me a bag filled with east, west, north, and south winds. Only I was to handle it—to steer us home. But my men thought I was hiding something in it. When I wasn't looking, they opened it and let loose a wild storm, which swept us off our course.
Alcinous: Suspicion and greed cause nothing but trouble.
Ulysses: How true that is. After that, we landed on another island to hunt for food. There, a magician named Circe turned my men into hogs. I persuaded her to turn them back into men. But to leave that island, I had to agree to visit Hades.
Alcinous: The Land of the Dead? But no one returns from there.
Ulysses: We did, thanks to Athena. She let me visit the ghosts of my friends who were killed in the Trojan War. I also spoke to a prophet, who told me how to get home.
Alcinous: Did you follow his advice?
Ulysses: Yes, but the way was dangerous. We had to sail past the Sirens, the singing sisters. Their voices are so sweet that they

make sailors dive overboard to their deaths. I made my men plug their ears with wax, so they could not hear the Sirens' songs. I was curious to hear them, so I had myself tied to the mast. Their singing almost drove me mad, but the ropes kept me on board.

Alcinous: You are clever, Ulysses. What happened next?

Ulysses: My men and I soon became very hungry again. We landed on an island where we found no food, except for a herd of fat cattle. But they belonged to the sun god, so we knew we should not kill them. We had to starve while we watched them grazing.

Alcinous: Why didn't you sail on?

Ulysses: The winds were against us. One day I went off to pray to Zeus. When I came back, my men were roasting six of the cows.

Alcinous: Your men failed you again. What happened next?

Ulysses: As soon as we left the island, a storm sank our ship. I was the only one who was able to swim to land.

Alcinous: Surely the gods helped you then.

Ulysses: Yes and no. I landed on the island of Calypso, and she cast a spell on me. For seven years I was unable to leave. Finally, Athena forced Calypso to lift the spell. I built a raft and drifted here.

Alcinous: What an amazing story! My men will sail you home to Ithaca tomorrow.

Ulysses: Thank you, sir. Perhaps they should not take me straight into the harbor. It might be safer if I landed up the coast a bit.

(Sounds of the sea.)

Narrator I: The next morning Alcinous' men set sail for Ithaca with Ulysses. After staying up all night talking with Alcinous, Ulysses fell asleep. When he awoke, he was on a beach covered with mist.

Ulysses: Where am I?

Narrator I: Through the mist, he saw someone coming. Little did he know that it was Athena in disguise.

Ulysses: Hello there, stranger. What country is this?

Athena: This is Ithaca.

Narrator I: Athena caused the mist to rise. Then Ulysses recognized his homeland. Tears came to his eyes, but he blinked them back. He did not want to give himself away.

Ulysses: I have heard of Ithaca. I fought with King Ulysses in the Trojan War. I am from Crete, and I am on my way to Pylos. A ship just let me off here.

Athena *(laughing):* You always have a story ready, Ulysses.

Ulysses: How do you know who I am?

Athena: I will get rid of my disguise. Look at me now.

Ulysses: It is Athena, my goddess! What are you doing here?

Athena: I want to help you. Your palace is filled with greedy men who want to marry your wife. She has kept them at bay, but she is losing hope that you will return. Your son, however, knows you are alive.

Ulysses: My son . . . I do not even know him.

Athena: Do not let anyone know who you are at first. I will disguise you.

(Sea sounds fade.)

Narrator I: Athena disguised Ulysses as an old beggar. He went first to a pig farm where Eumaeus, a loyal old servant, lived.

(Sounds of pigs grunting.)

Ulysses: Hello, old man. Can you spare a bite of food?

Eumaeus: Why not? It is the fashion in Ithaca today to eat other people's food.

Ulysses: What do you mean?

Eumaeus: The palace is filled with lazy men who are eating up the wealth of King Ulysses. Every day I must take some pigs over for their dinner. I wish Ulysses would return. I loved him with all my heart.

Ulysses: He will return.

Eumaeus: Well, I have just about lost hope. Many people have gone to Queen Penelope with "news" about her king, but their stories are always lies, cooked up to get a piece of gold or a free meal.

(The sound of pigs fades. Sea sounds rise.)

Narrator II: Meanwhile, Athena found Telemachus standing alone on the deck of the ship that was carrying him home.

Athena: Be careful, Telemachus.

Telemachus: Athena!

Athena: Antinous and Eurymachus plan to attack you near the harbor. So land up the coast. And before you go home, visit Eumaeus.

Narrator II: Telemachus followed the advice of Athena. He landed where his father had landed earlier, and he reached Eumaeus' hut before sundown.

(Sound of pigs grunting.)

Eumaeus: Is that you, Telemachus? I've missed you, lad.

Telemachus: I've been away on a trip, Eumaeus. What's been going on?

Eumaeus: Not much. A stranger showed up, pretending to know your father. He's inside my hut.

Telemachus: Let me talk to him.

(The sound of pigs fades, as a door opens and closes.)

Telemachus: Hello, old man. Don't stand up. I can sit on the floor. My bones are not as stiff as yours.

Ulysses: But you are Telemachus, the king's son. I heard him say so.

Telemachus: That doesn't mean I'm not polite to strangers.

Narrator II: Athena looked into the hut. She lifted Ulysses' disguise. Now he looked strong and handsome.

Telemachus: This is magic! You must be one of the gods!

Ulysses: No, I am your father.

Telemachus: Is it really you? I've waited so long for my father to come home. Don't play a cruel trick on me.

Ulysses: I am truly your father. Athena helped me come home, but I hear that the palace is filled with suitors. You and I must send them away.

Telemachus: What can two do against so many?

Ulysses: Athena is on our side.

Narrator II: Telemachus spent the night making plans with his father. The next morning he went home, promising to keep his father's return a secret from Penelope.

Penelope: Telemachus, my son, what did you learn on your trip?

Telemachus: King Menelaus said that my father is held under a spell on Calypso's island. He's been there seven years.

Penelope: So he is alive! But maybe Calypso will never lift the spell. What shall I do? The suitors are demanding that I choose one of them now.

Telemachus: You must only marry a man who is worthy of you. Perhaps there is a test we could give them. *(Pause.)* Do you remember Father's great hunting bow? We will have an archery contest.

Penelope: No one but your father has ever been able to bend that bow.

Telemachus: I know, and that will make it a good test.

(Footsteps approach.)

Penelope: Good morning, Eurycleia.

Eurycleia: Good morning, my lady. Master Telemachus, I'm glad to see you back.

Telemachus: And I am glad to be back, Eurycleia.

Eurycleia: You seem taller and stronger since your trip. You hold your head higher. My lady, doesn't he remind you of his father, more and more?

Penelope: Indeed he does.

Narrator I: Meanwhile, Athena had once again disguised Ulysses as an old beggar. Now he and Eumaeus were driving some pigs to the palace to be roasted for dinner.

Eumaeus: Here is the palace, old fellow. I must take my pigs around to the back, but you might ask for some food in the dining hall.

Ulysses: Thank you.

(Sounds of a feast.)

Narrator II: Inside the dining hall, the noonday feast was beginning. Antinous and Eurymachus were surprised to see Telemachus walk in.

Antinous: How did he get here? Our men have been waiting to attack his ship.

Eurymachus: He's Ulysses' son, all right—full of tricks.

Narrator II: Telemachus announced the archery contest to be held that evening. Then he saw the old beggar standing in the doorway. Only he knew that it was Ulysses in disguise.

Telemachus *(calling out):* Come join us, stranger. Guests, share your food with this man. Let him go around and get something from each of you.

Ulysses: Thank you, young prince. You are very kind.

Narrator II: The old beggar walked around the tables, asking for bits of food and money. Some of the guests gave him something. Others pushed him away.

Ulysses: Sir, can you spare something for an old wanderer?

Antinous: Who is this old fool, Eurymachus?

Eurymachus: He's just a beggar, Antinous. Give him something to make him quiet.

Antinous: I'll give him a word or two. Hey, you old bag of bones! Aren't you ashamed of eating another man's food?

Ulysses: Why? I am old and weak. You are young and strong, yet you eat another man's food.

Antinous: How dare you speak to me that way, you old beggar!

Narrator II: Antinous picked up a chair and threw it at Ulysses. It hit Ulysses in the back, but he did not flinch. He turned and stared coldly at Antinous. Then he went and sat in a corner. Telemachus slipped over to talk to him.

Telemachus (whispering): Father, are you all right?

Ulysses: I'm fine. Now, do you see all those spears and swords hanging on the walls? This afternoon we must lock them away. If you are questioned, say that you're afraid they are getting rusty. We don't want any extra weapons handy at the contest tonight.

Eurycleia (approaching): Master Telemachus?

Telemachus: Yes, Eurycleia?

Eurycleia: Your mother wants to talk to this old man. She has heard that he saw King Ulysses during the Trojan War.

Ulysses: I would be honored to talk with her about him.

Eurycleia: I'll take you to her.

(Sounds of the feast fade as their footsteps move along a hallway, then stop.)

Eurycleia: Here is the man you wished to speak to, my lady.

Penelope: Sit down, stranger. I want to hear all you know about my husband, Ulysses.

Narrator I: Ulysses stared at his wife. She was even more beautiful than when he had left, 20 years ago. His heart was bursting with love for her, but he kept his feelings hidden.

Ulysses: I cannot tell you much, my lady. I saw him only once many years ago. That was in the Greek camp outside of Troy.

Penelope: How did he look? What was he wearing?

Ulysses: He was a fine figure of a man. He wore a purple cloak. It was fastened with a beautiful gold pin.

Penelope: I gave him that cloak and that pin when he left for the war. Oh, it was an evil day when he sailed off. I fear he will never come home again.

Ulysses: He will, my lady.

Penelope: I wish I could believe you. Well, thank you for your words. Eurycleia, take care of this man.

Eurycleia: This way, sir.

(Their footsteps go along a hallway. Then there's the sound of water being poured into a bowl.)

Eurycleia: Take your sandals off, and I will wash your feet.

Ulysses: I can do that.

Eurycleia: Look, I am used to waiting on people. (She gasps.) What's this?

Ulysses (nervously): It's just a scar.

Eurycleia: Master Ulysses had a scar like that on his leg. It was a hunting wound he got as a boy. Is it you, my master and king?

Ulysses: Yes, Eurycleia, but no one must know yet.

Eurycleia: But your wife and son should know!

Ulysses: Telemachus knows already. Penelope will know soon enough. But first, we must drive these suitors away.

Narrator II: Ulysses and Telemachus took the weapons from the dining hall. They hid two swords and two shields under the head table for themselves. Then Ulysses went outside to speak to Eumaeus.

Ulysses: Eumaeus, what would you do to help Ulysses if he came home?

Eumaeus: I'd fight to the death for him. But I fear he won't return.

Ulysses: He *has* returned. I am Ulysses.

Eumaeus: Can it be, sir? Have you changed so much?

Ulysses: No. Athena gave me this disguise. Look, here is the old hunting scar on my leg.

Eumaeus: I remember it well. Welcome home, my lord!

Ulysses: Now, here is my plan. When the contest begins tonight, be sure you are nearby and armed.

(His voice fades as the sound of many men's voices rises.)

Narrator I: When the suitors gathered in the hall that night, there were 12 battle-axes stuck into the floor in a straight line. Ulysses had once shot an arrow through the notches of 12 battle-axes lined up like this. No one else had ever been able to do such a thing. Now Penelope carried Ulysses' hunting bow into the hall. Eurymachus was the first to pick it up. He pulled on the string, but the bow didn't bend.

Eurymachus: This bow has gotten stiff with age.

Telemachus: It has always been the toughest bow in Ithaca. Only my father was strong enough to bend it.

Eurymachus: But if we cannot bend it, how can we take part in the contest?

Antinous: Stand aside, Eurymachus. Let a better man try.

Narrator II: Antinous tried. He also failed. One man after another tried to bend Ulysses' bow. Not one was strong enough.

Antinous *(angrily):* This is not a fair contest. It is a trick!

Narrator II: The old beggar stepped forward.

Ulysses: May I have a try?

Antinous: Get out of the way, you old fool!

Telemachus: Let him try. It is an open contest.

Narrator I: Ulysses picked up the bow gently. He raised it and pulled back the string. The bow bent easily.

(The crowd gasps.)

Narrator I: Ulysses put an arrow to the string and aimed it at the row of battle-axes. The arrow flew through all 12 notches of all 12 axes.

(The crowd murmurs angrily.)

Narrator I: Antinous pulled out a dagger and rushed at Ulysses. Ulysses stopped him with an arrow through the neck. Telemachus pulled the two swords and two shields from under the table. Eumaeus appeared with a sword and shield, and Eurymachus pulled out a dagger.

Eurymachus: Be prepared to die, old beggar!
Ulysses: Old beggar! You dogs thought I would not return from Troy. But now I'm here, and I want you gone!
Eurymachus: It's Ulysses! Get him!

(Sounds of clashing knives, fists, and shouts.)

Narrator II: Ulysses, Telemachus, and Eumaeus fought bravely against the mob. And Athena's magic helped them. One by one, the suitors fell dead among the tables where they had feasted for so long.

(Fighting sounds fade out.)

Ulysses: That's the last of them. Thank you, Eumaeus. Well done, my son.
Telemachus: I have never seen so much blood before.
Ulysses: I have—at Troy. And I do not want to see any more. Let the bloodstains in the hall be a warning that no one shall steal Ulysses' home from him. You fought well, Telemachus. I am proud of you.
Telemachus: Thank you, Father.
Ulysses: Eumaeus, call the servants. There is cleaning up to do.

Narrator II: Meanwhile, Athena had cast Penelope into a deep sleep in the royal bedroom. Eurycleia found her and woke her up.

Eurycleia: Wake up, my lady. Your prayers have come true. Your husband is home!

Penelope: You have gone crazy. Let me go back to sleep.

Eurycleia: But it's true. That old beggar you spoke to was King Ulysses in disguise. He's gotten rid of all the suitors. Your home is free again.

Narrator II: Penelope got out of bed, threw on a fine robe, and ran to the front hall. There she saw a man in bloody, torn clothes who looked like Ulysses. Athena had lifted the beggar disguise. Penelope's heart was bursting with love, yet numb with fear. She was so afraid that the man was merely a vision—a god disguised as her Ulysses. She stared at the man without saying a word.

Telemachus *(impatiently):* Mother, why don't you speak to Father?

Penelope: Can this really be Ulysses?

Ulysses: Give her time, Telemachus. I have been gone many years. And now, I am not looking my best, drenched with blood and sweat.

Penelope: You should rest, sir. I will have a bath prepared for you. Then you can take a nap in the guest bedroom. The old royal bed has been moved in there, and you will find it comfortable.

Ulysses: What do you mean? No one could have moved that bed from our bedroom. I built the room myself, and I left a tree growing up through the floor. Then I used the tree trunk for one of the bedposts. It was a fine piece of work.

Penelope *(with passion):* Now I know you are Ulysses for sure! No one else could have known how that bed was built. Welcome home, my husband!

Narrator I: She rushed into his arms, and Ulysses knew he was really home at last.

READING COMPREHENSION

Summarizing. Choose the best phrase to complete each sentence. Then write the complete statements on your paper.

1. Originally, Ulysses had left Ithaca _____ to (sail around the world, fight in the Trojan War, battle against the gods).

2. Ulysses couldn't return home to Ithaca after he landed on the island of Calypso because _____ (suitors had taken over his kingdom, he had no ship or crew, Calypso had cast a spell over him).

3. The goddess Athena disguised Ulysses as an old beggar so that Ulysses could _____ (take the suitors by surprise, get a free meal, test Penelope's loyalty).

Interpreting. Write the answer to each question on your paper.

1. Why did Telemachus go to visit King Menelaus?

2. How did Poseidon try to defeat Ulysses?

3. How did Penelope show her loyalty to Ulysses?

4. How did Athena help Ulysses?

For Thinking and Discussing. Which of the tricks Ulysses used to escape danger do you think was the most clever? What other qualities did Ulysses have in addition to cleverness?

UNDERSTANDING LITERATURE

Conflict. Most story plots are centered around a *conflict*, or struggle between two or more opposing forces. A character may be in conflict with an outside force such as another person, a group, society, nature, or fate. In a myth, the conflict may be against a god or goddess. A character may also be struggling within himself or herself. This is called *inner conflict*, or *person vs. self conflict.*

"The Homecoming of Ulysses" is based mainly around Ulysses' struggle to return to Ithaca, but it also contains several other conflicts. On your paper, use complete sentences to answer the following questions about conflict in "The Homecoming of Ulysses."

1. What was the person vs. person conflict between Penelope and the suitors in Ithaca? How did Penelope deal with the conflict between herself and the suitors? How would this conflict finally be resolved?

2. How did the conflict between Ulysses and Poseidon arise? What events resulted from this conflict?

3. What was the conflict between Ulysses and his crew?

WRITING

In a paragraph, take the part of one of the narrators and describe how Ulysses and Telemachus ultimately drove away the suitors.

Section Review

VOCABULARY

Experience Clues. Your experiences can act as a context clue. You can sometimes tell the meaning of a new word based upon experiences you have had or have read about.

Use your experience to help you define the italicized word in this sentence from "Leiningen Versus the Ants."

> Their comrades climbed upon their bodies, willingly dying to provide stepping-stones for the *hordes* that followed.

Since, from your experience, you know that ants travel in large groups, you can guess that *hordes* means "large groups."

On your paper, write a definition for each italicized word below. Then explain how you thought out the meanings.

1. "A few [ants], bigger than the rest, carried stings that *injected* a burning poison."

2. "If you've any flights coming in from the Pacific, *divert* them to Seattle."

3. "Dr. Baird . . . says that some of the patients are in *critical* condition, and we must land in the next few minutes."

4. "When he fell asleep, we stuck a sharp *stake* into his single eye and blinded him."

READING

Cause and Effect. Many events you read about follow a special pattern called *cause and effect*. In this pattern, something happens and *causes* something else to happen. The second event is the result, or *effect*, of the first.

You can often recognize a cause-and-effect pattern in your reading by noticing clue words such as: *since, because, as a result, due to, consequently, why, therefore,* and *so*.

For example: George Spencer was asked to take over the controls of Flight 714 because he was the only passenger who had flying experience.
Cause: Spencer was the only passenger who had flying experience.
Effect: He was asked to take over.
Clue word: because

The passages below come from selections in this section. Each contains a cause-and-effect pattern. On your paper, list the cause, effect, and reading clue word in each passage.

1. "'Many of the Indians believe you killed Eugene Charley. That's why Dan left you a rifle at the cabin. He figured you hated Charley enough to kill him.'"

2. "My heartbeat is 47 or 48 when I am at rest; this is compared to the normal 72 for other people. A conditioned athlete usually has a heartbeat of 60 plus. This is all due to swimming hour after hour, year after year."

164

WRITING

A Paragraph.   A paragraph is a group of sentences related to one main idea. A good paragraph contains a topic sentence which states the main idea and supporting sentences which give details about the main idea. The paragraph may also include a concluding sentence which summarizes or restates the paragraph's main idea. A popular speaker once told his formula for success: "First I tell my audience what I'm going to tell them. Then I tell them. Then I tell them what I told them." This is the same formula writers use for paragraphs.

Step 1: Set Your Goal

The first step in writing a paragraph is deciding what the topic will be. Choose a topic you know well and are interested in. The following is a list of general topics that may give you ideas:

a sport	an actor or actress	a hobby
a friend	your school	a TV show
a musical group	a current event	an animal

After you have selected a general topic, you must narrow it down. Your topic must be specific enough to be treated in a single paragraph. For example, the general topic "Cats" would be too broad to cover in a single paragraph. You might narrow the subject to the topic of "Why cats make good pets." Or you may narrow your topic down to "Differences between Siamese and Persian cats."

Step 2: Make a Plan

Now that you have narrowed down your topic, you should be able to write your topic sentence. The topic sentence states the main idea of your paragraph or what the paragraph is about. Write three possible topic sentences for your paragraph. Choose the one that expresses your topic most clearly and concisely. The topic sentence will be the first sentence in your paragraph, so it should grab the reader's attention. As you write your paragraph, remember that all the supporting sentences must relate to your topic sentence.

When you have decided on your topic sentence, you can begin to develop your paragraph. One way to do this is with *examples*. If your main idea was to show how a friend has helped you out again and again, you would include specific examples in your paragraph.

Another way to develop your paragraph is to use *facts*. If your main idea was to show how much damage leaf-cutter ants could do in the jungle, your paragraph would contain facts to prove that.

A third way to develop a paragraph is to give *reasons*. If you were writing about why cats make good pets, you would support your main idea by stating your reasons for believing as you do.

Step 3: Write a First Draft

Now that you have your main idea and have an idea of how to develop it, it is time to write a first draft. Begin with your topic sentence. Then develop the paragraph with sentences that give examples, facts, or reasons. Concentrate on getting everything you want to say down on paper. At this stage, don't worry about how your sentences sound or about your spelling or punctuation. You will have time to make changes in the next step.

Step 4: Revise

Read over your paragraph, looking for ways to make it clearer and more effective. You may want to change the order of your supporting sentences or add or take out certain details. To help you revise, ask yourself these questions:

☐ Does the paragraph have a main idea?

☐ Is the main idea stated clearly in a topic sentence at the beginning of the paragraph?

☐ Does the topic sentence make the reader want to read more?

☐ Does every other sentence relate to the topic sentence?

☐ Did I develop the paragraph in a way that suits the topic?

After you have revised your paragraph, proofread it for spelling, grammar, and punctuation errors. Finally, type your paragraph or copy it over neatly.

QUIZ

The following is a quiz for Section 3. Write the answers in complete sentences on your paper.

Reading Comprehension

1. In "Leiningen Versus the Ants," what defenses did Leiningen set up against the attack of the ants? In what ways did his defenses succeed? In what ways did they fail?

2. In "Flight Into Danger," what events led to Spencer's successful landing of Flight 714?

3. What are some of the problems that marathon swimmers such as Diana Nyad have to overcome?

4. What qualities did Gregory Tah-Kloma have that led to his being accepted by the wolves?

5. What qualities did Ulysses have that made him a hero?

Understanding Literature

6. "Leiningen Versus the Ants" is an example of a person vs. nature conflict. What human qualities did Leiningen bring to the conflict? What natural qualities did the ants bring?

7. What event marks the climax of Leiningen's conflict with the ants? How is the story finally resolved?

8. In what ways is "Flight Into Danger" an example of a person vs. self type of conflict? How is it resolved?

9. What forces of nature does Diana Nyad have to battle when she swims marathon races? What forces within herself does she have to overcome?

10. Describe Gregory's conflicts with nature and with other people in "In the Shadow of a Rainbow." How are these conflicts resolved?

ACTIVITIES

Word Attack

1. When you come across an unfamiliar word in your reading, you can sometimes figure out its meaning through context clues. But unless you have heard the word before, you cannot always figure out how it is pronounced. For example, if you had never heard the word *piranha*, how would you know whether the *h* was silent or not? You could find out by looking up the phonetic respelling of the word in a dictionary.

   Look up the following words in a dictionary and write their phonetic respellings. Use the pronunciation key to help you. Then write a sentence telling what all the words have in common.

   piranha   drought   plague
   gnawing   exhausted   discipline

2. The Tower Controller in "Flight Into Danger" and Greg in "In the Shadow of a Rainbow" used binoculars. In this word, the prefix *bi-* means "two." Binoculars are an optical device designed for use by both eyes. Use a dictionary to find the meanings of these other words beginning with the prefix *bi-*. Write them on your paper.

   bifocals   bicuspid   bicentennial
   bisect   biped   biannual

Speaking and Listening

1. Get together with classmates to act out the scene in "Flight Into Danger" where Spencer is landing the plane. Choose people to play these characters: the Tower Controller, Taylor, Spencer, Burdick, the Flight Attendant. Perform the scene for the class.

2. Pretend you are a newscaster. Prepare a "live" report of Diana Nyad's swim around Manhattan Island. Be prepared to deliver it to the class.

Researching

1. The only place in North America where wolves are found in any great numbers are in Alaska and Northern Canada. Some scientists fear that some species of wolves will soon be extinct in these areas because too many of them are being killed. Use the encyclopedia and periodic guide in the library to find out about this topic. Report your findings to the class.

2. Many words we use today have their origins in the myths and legends of ancient Greece. Homer named his story *The Odyssey* after its hero, Odysseus (known to the Romans as Ulysses). Today we use the word *odyssey* to mean "an extended adventurous wandering or series of travels." Find out the meanings and origins of the following words. Then choose one of the words and write a summary of the myth it came from.

   narcissism   hyacinth   tantalize
   herculean   arachnid   panic

Creating. In "Mind Over Water," Diana Nyad described how she prepared for marathon swimming. Make a list of training and performance tips for a sport or activity you participate in.

MYSTERIES

*Solving a mystery involves uncovering
secrets or hidden information. Sometimes
all the mysterious pieces fall into place.
Sometimes a detective is needed.
Sometimes a mystery is never solved. . . .*

The Questioner of the Sphinx
Elihu Vedder (1836–1923).
Museum of Fine Arts, Boston,
Bequest of Mrs. Martin Brimmer.

Mystery

A mystery is a story with a secret. The author conceals something from you, the reader. At the same time, the author gives you hints that keep you guessing. You keep turning the pages because there is something you have to find out. And you can't stop until you discover what it is.

A mystery writer gives you a feeling of increasing excitement. He or she keeps you in suspense. Perhaps a crime has been committed. Your curiosity is aroused. Who did it? Or maybe unusual events take place. Can they be explained? How? As you read a mystery, your curiosity becomes more and more intense. In a well-written mystery, the feeling of suspense continues until the very end.

Elements of a Mystery

One element that mystery writers often use is *surprise*. The most skillful writers introduce plot twists to scare readers, to shock them, or simply to confuse them a little bit. The surprise may make readers gasp or laugh. It may also provide the missing link to the mystery puzzle.

Hidden clues are another special tool mystery writers use to keep readers' eyes glued to the pages. An event occurs that provides a key to the solution of the mystery. A character may make a slip of the tongue or act in a strange way. Someone finds a crumpled piece of paper with a code word written on it. Attentive readers of a mystery story watch carefully for hidden clues. Like a detective, readers can use these clues to uncover the secrets of the mystery.

A third important element used by mystery writers is *mood*. Mood is the atmosphere or feeling that a writer creates in a work of literature. Skillful mystery writers use writing tricks to make readers shudder in fear or scratch their heads in confusion.

Two Kinds of Mysteries

One kind of mystery is the *detective story*, or "whodunit." A detective story follows a certain pattern: A crime is committed. A detective, usually *not* a police officer, is called in. The detective finds clues and puts them together to solve the crime. Writers of good detective stories are fair—they always give the readers the same clues as the ones the detective uses to solve the crime.

In this section you will read two detective stories: "The Adventure of the Copper Beeches" and "The President Regrets." In the first story, you will solve the mystery with Sherlock Holmes, the world's most famous fictional detective. In the second, you will meet another fictional detective—Ellery Queen.

Another kind of mystery story does not involve a crime. It usually centers around some event that seems impossible to explain. Sometimes, one of the characters finds a reasonable, natural explanation. "The Haunted Chess Set" is an example. At other times, the explanation involves the supernatural, as in "The Third Level."

Solving the Mysteries

You will have the opportunity to match wits with four mystery writers in this section. As you read each mystery, watch for clues the author provides. Try to solve the mystery before the writer presents the solution at the end of the story.

The title of the first selection, "The Haunted Chess Set," prepares you for a spooky story. The story starts off with a mysterious occurrence. In the middle of a dream about a horse, Angelica Ramos hears the noise of horse's hooves in her room, and is struck on the cheek by a falling object. Pay attention and look for hidden clues as Angelica solves this mystery. Soon after, she will have a more important mystery to unravel.

The second mystery, "The Adventure of the Copper Beeches," is a drama starring Sherlock Holmes. At first, there is no mystery at all. A young woman tells the bored detective a story that is a little unusual—

just a little. The suspense builds as the play progresses and strange, more sinister things begin to happen.

In the next selection, "The Third Level," the narrator gets lost in New York City's Grand Central Station. There, he finds an additional level—a third level—where no level is supposed to exist. On this third level, trains take people from the 20th century back to the 19th century. What could possibly explain such a thing? As you read, you will probably think that there must be a logical explanation for this mysterious occurrence. But is there? In reading a mystery, it is sometimes more exciting and intriguing not to know all of the answers.

In the last selection, "The President Regrets," the mystery never really happened! It is made up by Ellery Queen as a challenge to the members of an elite mystery fans' club—one that the President has been invited to join. The President, regretfully, is unable to attend the meeting. To entertain the disappointed members, Ellery Queen weaves a tale for them to unravel. How they go about solving Queen's mystery is a how-to lesson in using clues to make deductions. Follow their step-by-step method and see if you arrive at the solution along with the experts. After all, as Sherlock Holmes might say, it is "Elementary, my dear readers!"

The Haunted Chess Set

by Julia Remine Piggin

When her 17-year-old niece is accused of robbery, Angelica Ramos is forced to play amateur detective. She never dreamed she'd find herself in such a strange situation. After all, what does a retired architect know about the rules of the detective game?

Someone was riding a horse along the boardwalk. In her dream, Angelica Ramos could not see the shadowy rider's face. But she could hear the steady tap-tap-tap of the horse's hooves on the wooden planks. She could hear the waves breaking on the beach and the jingling metal of the harness.

Suddenly, something small and hard struck her on the cheek. She woke, alarmed. The dream of the horse and faceless rider dissolved. But she could still hear the waves, the tap-tap-tap-tapping noise, and the jingling. Beside her, on the pillow, lay a little bottle of her favorite "Silver Night" perfume.

Angelica laughed aloud as it all came together. Yesterday her next-door neighbor had carried a big painting into his apartment. He had bought it on the boardwalk. The tapping sound was made by his hammer as he drove a picture hook into the wall. Angelica's bureau had been pushed against her side of the

same wall. The vibration of the hammering was making objects on the bureau dance and jingle as they touched one another. The little perfume bottle had skidded across the polished surface and landed on her bed.

"After all the wonderful buildings I designed, I retire to one with walls like paper," Angelica thought to herself, sliding back down under the covers. But her apartment had features she liked, in spite of the less-than-solid construction. She had the best view of the ocean in Neptune City. The waves in her dream had been real—they crashed all day on the sand just outside the windows.

Retirement in Neptune City had other advantages, too. Since Angelica had closed her architect's office in New York four years ago, she had found a new circle of friends and a busy, active life.

She stretched her tall, slim body and looked at the clock on her night table. In an hour, she had an appointment to go

173

over plans for a new civic center with Emil Cooper, chairman of the committee.

The plans had been drawn up by a young local architect, but Cooper wouldn't approve them unless Angelica checked them first. He knew her fine reputation as an architect, and he gave her steady business as a consultant. Still, she always dreaded going to his office in the big, modern home from which he ran his many projects. He was a good friend, but his harsh, demanding manner annoyed her. She felt a little sorry for her 17-year-old niece, Iris, who had just started a summer job in Cooper's office.

"Oh, well," she thought, "it looks like a gorgeous day. The walk down the boardwalk to Emil's house will put me in a good mood—even for dealing with him."

The sun was warm, the sea breeze salty and cool. Swinging along the boardwalk, Angelica thought of her plans for the evening. Her friend, Colonel Robert Drummond, was to drive over from the army post he commanded and take her dancing. She would wear the silvery dress that matched her hair. Robert would be tall and trim in his uniform. The stars would arch down into the sea outside the ballroom on the pier.

"Life is really an adventure," she said to herself, smiling. Then she caught sight of a familiar head of dark curls. Iris was sitting on a bench, looking out at the sea. Angelica walked up behind her.

"Iris!" she said. The girl turned. Her face was pale and sad. She looked as if she might have been crying.

"I'm on my way to see your boss," her aunt said. "I thought I'd treat you to lunch. Is something wrong?"

"Oh, Aunt Angelica, it's so unfair," Iris said. "I've been fired. And it's going to be hard to get another job. Mr. Cooper will tell everybody, and nobody in Neptune City will hire me. He says I went into his private study and tried to find the box he keeps his money in. He says he can prove that I did it. But I didn't, Aunt Angelica! He told me never to go in there, and I never did. Honestly, I never, never went in there, not even once."

"I know you didn't, if you say so," Angelica said. "Now, sweetheart, don't worry. I'll talk to Emil Cooper about this. I'll make him see reason."

It was never easy to make Emil Cooper see reason, and this time it seemed impossible. Angelica found him in his office, banging angrily on a typewriter. When she presented Iris's case, he jumped up and began to storm around the room.

"I know Iris is your niece, Angelica," he shouted, "but no one else could have been in that study. It's right next door, and she knows I keep my cash there. I usually lock the room, but yesterday I forgot. I went out for a while. When I came back and went into my study, someone had been in there hunting for something. Iris herself said that no one else had been in the house. So who was it? I ask you."

"But was anything actually taken?" Cooper shook his head. "Then how do you know anyone had been in there?" Angelica asked.

"Nothing was missing—only because she couldn't find the cash box," Cooper snarled. "I know because I had set up a chess game on a table with a drawer in it. She must have been looking in the drawer for the money box, and knocked over some of the chess pieces. She didn't know how to put them back as they were, so she just placed them on the board anywhere. It happens that I had just begun to play a new game by mail with Anton Simonovich, the ex-champion. I always set up his game and mine on the board, make my move, and write him what it is. Of course, I remembered how the chess pieces should have been placed. I'd already started my letter to Simonovich. But they had been moved. Somebody had moved them, Angelica. I'm sorry, but that somebody had to be Iris. I see you don't believe me. Well, come into my study. I'll show you."

He strode ahead of her into the hall and unlocked the door to the next room. As he had said, a chess game was set up on a small table against the wall. The antique chess pieces, carved out of wood and painted in red, black, silver, and gold, stood on their squares like a medieval army.

"They're beautiful—" Angelica began to say. But Cooper's face stopped her. He had turned deathly pale.

"It's happened again," he said. "They've been moved again. No one could have been here since I set them up again this morning. Iris had no key. The door was locked—you saw that. The window is barred. Angelica, this chess set is over 300 years old. Who knows where it's been? Do—do you believe in ghosts?"

Angelica looked at the chess game. The gold-painted crowns of the kings and queens sparkled. The knights in silver armor sat on miniature horses, swords in their hands. She drew in her breath sharply.

"There are ghosts and ghosts," she said. "But a young woman's reputation and peace of mind should be more important to you than a ghost, Emil. I think I know who—what—moved those chess pieces. I can stop it, too. But first, I want you to go into your office and type a letter of apology to Iris."

Cooper looked amazed. "In the middle of all this—type a letter? Now? Angelica—"

"I will not help you unless you write it," Angelica said sternly. "And I *can* help you. I know how. But Iris comes first."

Cooper looked at the chess set. He picked up one of the bishops and set it on a square. Then he looked up, into Angelica's cold eyes. Meekly, he followed her into his office and sat down at the typewriter. With shaking hands, he rolled in a sheet of paper with the letterhead "Cooper Enterprises."

"What shall I say?" he asked.

"Dear Iris," Angelica began to dictate. Cooper typed the words as she said them. "I am very, very sorry for the false accusation I made against you. I know that I was wrong, and will be happy to have you back at work on Monday. The whole thing was an unfortunate misunderstanding. I hope you will forgive me. Most sincerely, Emil Cooper."

with a slipper—Slap! Smack! Smack!

Violet: Knocking—them—off?

Rucastle: Roaches, beetles, garter snakes —loves to finish them off.

Violet: Oh. (She laughs nervously.) And taking care of him would be all I had to do?

Rucastle: Well, now, my wife might give a few little commands from time to time. For example, suppose you were asked to wear a certain dress that we might give you. Or suppose we asked you to sit in a special place from time to time. You wouldn't mind, would you?

Violet: No, I don't think so.

Rucastle: And to cut your hair. Cut it quite short. You'd be willing to do that, of course, wouldn't you?

Violet: Cut my hair? Oh, no. My hair is—well, a very unusual shade of red, as you can see. Everyone has always admired it. I couldn't cut it!

Rucastle: I'm afraid it will be necessary. A little notion of my wife's. Not very important.

Violet: It *is* important to *me*. I'm sorry, but I could not cut my hair.

Rucastle: That's your final word?

Violet: Yes, it is.

Rucastle: Very well. Have you any other young ladies I might meet, Miss Stoper?

Violet (back in the present): I went back to my rooms, Mr. Holmes. I found two or three bills in my mail, and not much to eat in my cupboard. I began to think I had done a foolish thing. But the next day, a letter came. . . .

Rucastle's Voice: "My dear Miss Hunter: Miss Stoper has given me your address. My wife is very eager that you should come. We will pay you 120 pounds a year. All we ask is that you wear a dress of a certain shade of blue in the morning. My wife happens to like the color. We will give you one that belonged to our dear daughter, Alice, who is now in Philadelphia. Of course, you *must* cut your hair. But do think it over and come to work for us. Let me know what train you will be on, and I will meet it. Yours faithfully, Jephro Rucastle."

Violet (back in the present): I'm going to accept their offer, Mr. Holmes. But I would like to know what you think of it.

Holmes: Miss Hunter, if you were my sister, I should not like to see you take this position.

Violet: Why, Mr. Holmes? Do you think the wife may be crazy?

Holmes: That is one possibility. Why should they give you 120 pounds a year when they can hire any governess in England for 40? There must be a strong reason. Miss Hunter, your problem interests me very much. If you should find yourself in danger—

Violet: What danger could I be in?

Holmes: If I knew, it would no longer be a danger. At the moment, I can only guess. But, remember—at any time, day or night, a telegram will bring me to help you.

Watson (narrating): In the next two weeks, Holmes could not seem to get Miss Hunter out of his mind. He sat for hours on end, muttering and thumbing through books of poetry and essays. . . .

Holmes: Too much money—why? Why

the hair, why the dress? "Apparel oft proclaims the man." Might it not proclaim the woman, too? "Beauty draws us with a single hair." What if we did not wish to draw, but to drive away? Might we not adopt the opposite of those lines? But why? "Gold is the key." Gold is the key, Watson.

Watson: Holmes, I don't understand a single syllable you are saying.

Holmes: When one has no data, one must use one's imagination. But of one thing I am sure. We will soon hear from Miss Violet Hunter.

Watson (narrating): Holmes was right. The telegram came the next day. . . .

Violet's Voice: "Please be at the Black Swan Hotel in Winchester at noon tomorrow. Please do not fail me."

Watson (narrating): By 11 o'clock the next morning, we were on our way to Winchester. Violet Hunter met us at the door of the inn. . . .

Violet: I am so glad to see you. I've ordered lunch. In here—please sit down. I must be back at three.

Holmes: What has happened to you?

Violet: Nothing bad, really. But something *so* strange is going on.

Holmes: The insane woman?

Violet: No, Mrs. Rucastle isn't crazy. She's just quiet and pale and rather sad. Although she does love that cruel, ugly little boy. He's always trying to hurt something—birds, mice, anything small and weak. The daughter in Philadelphia is a child of Mr. Rucastle's first marriage. Mr. Rucastle told me privately that she left because she hated her stepmother.

Then there's the housekeeper, Mrs. Toller. I didn't know she existed until two days after I arrived at The Copper Beeches. I'd just had breakfast. . . .

Rucastle (in flashback): Ah, Miss Hunter. Did you enjoy your breakfast? Let me say, you are just as attractive with short hair as you were before you cut it. And now let's see how that electric blue dress will look. You'll find it on the bed in your room. If you'll go and put it on—

Violet (back in the present): The dress was an odd shade of blue, Mr. Holmes. It must have been expensive, but it wasn't new. It fit me perfectly. When I came into the drawing room wearing it, the Rucastles were more than pleased. Too pleased, I thought. . . .

Mrs. Rucastle (in flashback): It's wonderful! Jephro, look! It's absolutely perfect!

Rucastle: Couldn't fit her better if it had been made for her! Now, my dear Miss Hunter, come and sit over here. That's right, the chair with its back to the window. Very good. Now, I want to tell you a story. (Clears his throat.) There was an old farmer who thought his sheep were crocodiles. Every morning—

Violet (back in the present): He told one of the funniest stories I've ever heard, Mr. Holmes. (She laughs.) And then another, just as funny. He walked up and down, telling funny stories for more than an hour. I laughed until my sides ached. But Mrs. Rucastle just looked sadder and sadder. Then the door opened and Mrs. Toller came in with a tea tray. . . .

Mrs. Toller (in flashback): I've brought

Mrs. Toller: I'm sorry—I'm sorry—*(Door closes.)*

Rucastle: The woman's been dipping into my whiskey again. That will do for today, Miss Hunter. Go up and change your dress.

Violet *(back in the present):* Mrs. Toller had not seemed drunk to me. What had she meant—"You mustn't sit there"? And who was "he"? I began to wonder. If the blue dress belonged to Alice Rucastle—why would she wear a color just to please a stepmother she hated? And how could anyone like a color *that* much? I didn't understand any of it, Mr. Holmes. Two days later, Mr. Rucastle asked me to put on the dress again. But this time, after an hour of funny stories. . . .

Rucastle *(in flashback):* Here, Miss Hunter, take this book. Now, if you'll just stand up, I'll move your chair a little bit this way. Then you can get some sun on the pages. There, very good. Now, if you'll just sit down and read aloud to me. Start right where I've marked the page.

Violet *(back in the present):* I read for about 10 minutes. Suddenly, right in the middle of a sentence. . . .

Rucastle: That's enough. I'll take the book. Go and change your dress.

Violet *(back in the present):* It went on like that, day after day, Mr. Holmes. The jokes, the book, my face turned away from the window. I *had* to find out why. Then I thought of something. I hid one of the pieces of my broken hand mirror in a handkerchief. Next time, when I began to laugh at the funny stories, I put

your morning tea, mum—oh! Miss! You mustn't sit there! He'll—*(Sound of breaking dishes.)*

Rucastle: Mrs. Toller, you've been drinking again! You've spilled tea all over the rug!

Mrs. Rucastle: And broken two of our best cups!

Mrs. Toller: I'm sorry. I'll clean it up. But—you—Miss—

Rucastle: Miss Hunter. Miss Violet Hunter. She is our son's new governess. And what must she think of you?

the handkerchief up to my eyes. I could see what was outside the window. A man was standing in the road. A slender man with a beard, wearing a gray suit.

Holmes: "Apparel proclaims the woman." And a very clever woman, Miss Hunter.

Violet: But not so clever that Mrs. Rucastle didn't suspect. When I lowered my handkerchief, she was staring at me. I think she knew I had a mirror. . . .

Mrs. Rucastle *(in flashback)*: Jephro, there is a man outside in the road. He is staring in at Miss Hunter.

Rucastle: Indeed? A friend of yours, Miss Hunter?

Violet: No, Mr. Rucastle. I don't know anyone in this part of England.

Rucastle: Well, we can't have Peeping Toms about. Turn around and motion for him to go away.

Violet: Wouldn't it be better just to ignore him?

Rucastle: Kindly do as I say. Turn and wave for him to go away.

Violet *(back in the present)*: I did as I was told. Just as I waved, Mrs. Rucastle pulled down the blind. That was a week ago. From that time, I have never sat in the window or worn the blue dress. And I have not seen the man in the road.

Holmes: Go on, please. This is most interesting.

Violet: I'm afraid neither of you gentlemen will believe what I have to tell you now.

Watson: Try us, my dear.

Violet: Well, as you know, I'd had my hair cut off in London. I'd wound it into a coil, and put it in my trunk. I didn't finish unpacking until I'd been at The Copper Beeches for almost a week. There was a chest of drawers in my room. One of the drawers was locked, and I really needed the space. I called Mrs. Toller. . . . *(In flashback, calling)* Mrs. Toller!

Mrs. Toller: Yes, miss?

Violet: One of these drawers is locked. Might you have a key to fit it?

Mrs. Toller: Well—I'm not sure. *(Keys jingle.)* I think this one might fit. Yes, it does. Pull out the drawer.

Violet: Thank you. No! It can't be!

Mrs. Toller: What is it, miss?

Violet: My hair! In this drawer. My hair! My *hair* that I cut off in London!

Mrs. Toller: I'm leaving, miss! I shouldn't be here.

Violet: No—you must help me open my trunk. My hands are shaking so. . . . Look. My hair is in the trunk, too. The same shade, the same thickness. Two coils—exactly alike.

Mrs. Toller: Miss, I didn't see them. And take my advice—put that hair you found back in the drawer and lock it up again. And don't say a word to the Rucastles, or it won't go well with you.

Violet *(back in the present)*: What does it mean, Mr. Holmes?

Holmes: "Beauty draws us with a single hair."

Watson: Holmes, these quotations are maddening!

Holmes: Go on with your story, Miss Hunter.

Violet: The Copper Beeches is a large house, Mr. Holmes. One whole wing

READING COMPREHENSION

Summarizing. Choose the best phrase to complete each sentence. Then write the complete statements on your paper.

1. Violet Hunter came to see Holmes and Watson _____ (for advice about taking a job, for help in solving a crime, because they were old friends).

2. Mr. Rucastle demanded that Violet _____ (change the color of her hair, cut her hair, wear her hair in braids).

3. Mr. Rucastle didn't want his daughter to marry Mr. Fowler because he _____ (hated Fowler's family, hoped she would find a better husband, wanted to control her money).

Interpreting. Write the answer to each question on your paper.

1. Who was in the "deserted" wing of The Copper Beeches?

2. Why did Mr. Rucastle offer Violet Hunter such a high salary?

3. Why did Mr. Rucastle tell Violet funny stories while she sat in the drawing room of The Copper Beeches?

4. What did Holmes mean when he said, "Gold is the key"?

For Thinking and Discussing. Why did the Rucastles think Violet was a "perfect" choice to be governess?

UNDERSTANDING LITERATURE

Mood. Good mystery stories create a mood that attracts and holds a reader's attention. *Mood* is the feeling or atmosphere in a story.

Writers can create a mysterious mood by presenting incidents that put questions into a reader's mind. These questions remain unanswered until the mystery is solved.

Read the list of incidents below from "The Adventure of the Copper Beeches." On your paper, write a question that each incident made you ask yourself and the answer that Sherlock Holmes discovered.

1. Violet was offered too much money to become the Rucastles' governess.

2. Mr. Rucastle told Violet funny stories, but Mrs. Rucastle just looked sadder and sadder.

3. Mr. Rucastle accused Mrs. Toller of being drunk.

4. A man was standing in the road looking in the window.

5. Mr. Rucastle angrily left the "empty" wing of the house.

WRITING

Imagine that you are Violet Hunter and have not met with Sherlock Holmes. Write a letter to Miss Stoper at the employment agency describing the strange incidents you have encountered. Try to create a mysterious mood in your letter.

The Third Level

by Jack Finney

The modern world is full of fear, war, and worry. That's why Charley wants to escape to "the good old days" when life was less complicated and eggs cost 13 cents a dozen. His wife, Louisa, is worried about him. So is his psychiatrist friend. But Charley knows how to make his fantasy a reality. . . .

The presidents of the New York Central and the New York, New Haven, and Hartford railroads will swear on a stack of timetables that there are only two. But I say there are three, because I've *been* on the third level at Grand Central Station. Yes, I've taken the obvious step: I talked to a psychiatrist friend of mine about the third level at Grand Central Station. He said it was a waking-dream. He said I was unhappy. That made my wife kind of mad. But he explained that he meant the modern world is full of fear, war, worry, and all the rest of it, and that I just want to escape. Well, who doesn't? Everybody I know wants to escape. But they don't wander down into any third level at Grand Central Station.

But that's the reason, he said, and my friends all agreed. Everything points to it, they claimed. My stamp collecting, for example. That's an "escape from reality." Well, maybe, but my grandfather didn't need any escape from reality. Things were pretty nice and peaceful in his day, from all I hear. And he started my collection. It's a nice collection, too—blocks of four of almost every U.S. issue, first-day covers, and so on. President Roosevelt collected stamps, too, you know.

Anyway, here's what happened at Grand Central. One night last summer I worked late at the office. I was in a hurry to get uptown to my apartment. I decided to subway from Grand Central because it's faster than the bus.

Now, I don't know why this should have happened to me. I'm just an ordinary guy named Charley, 31 years old. I was wearing a tan suit and a straw hat with a fancy band. I passed a dozen men who looked just like me. And I wasn't trying to escape from anything. I just wanted to get home to Louisa, my wife.

I turned into Grand Central and went down the steps to the first level. There you take trains like the Twentieth Century. Then I walked down another flight to the second level. There you get the suburban trains. I ducked into a doorway heading for the subway—and got lost. That's easy to do. I've been in and out of Grand Central hundreds of times, but I'm always bumping into new doorways and stairs. Once I got into a tunnel about a mile long. I came out in the lobby of the Roosevelt Hotel. Another time I came up in an office building on 46th Street, three blocks away.

Sometimes I think Grand Central is growing like a tree, pushing out new corridors and staircases like roots. There's probably a long tunnel that nobody knows about under the city right now, on its way to Times Square. Maybe there's another to Central Park. And maybe—because for so many people Grand Central *has* been a way of escape—maybe that's how the tunnel I got into . . . . But I never told my psychiatrist about that idea.

The corridor I was in slanted downward. I thought that was wrong, but I kept on walking. All I could hear was the empty sound of my own footsteps. I didn't pass a soul. Then I heard that sort of hollow roar ahead that means open space. The tunnel turned sharp left. I went down a short flight of stairs and came out on the third level at Grand Central Station. For just a moment I thought I was back on the second level, but I saw the room was smaller. There were fewer ticket windows and train gates. The information booth in the center was wood and old-looking. And the man in the booth wore a green eyeshade and long, black, sleeve protectors. The lights were dim and sort of flickering. Then I saw why. They were open-flame gaslights.

There were brass spittoons on the floor. Across the station a glint of light caught my eye. A man was pulling a gold watch from his vest pocket. He wore a dirty hat, a black four-button suit with tiny lapels. He had a big, black handlebar mustache. Then I looked around. Everyone in the station was dressed like the 1890's. I never saw so many beards, sideburns, and fancy mustaches in my life. A woman walked in through the train gate. She wore a dress with leg-of-mutton sleeves and her skirt came to the top of her high-buttoned shoes. Back of her, out on the tracks, I saw a locomotive. It was a very small Currier & Ives locomotive with a tunnel-shaped stack. And then I knew.

To make sure, I walked over to a newsboy. I glanced at the stack of papers at his feet. It was the *World*. The *World* hasn't been published for years. The lead story said something about President Cleveland. I've found that front page since in the Public Library files. It was printed June 11, 1894.

I turned toward the ticket windows. I knew that here—on the third level at Grand Central—I could buy tickets that would take Louisa and me anywhere in the United States—in the year 1894. And I wanted two tickets to Galesburg, Illinois.

Have you ever been there? It's a wonderful town still, with big old frame houses, huge lawns, and tremendous trees. And in 1894, summer evenings were twice as long. People sat on their lawns, the men smoking cigars and talking quietly, the women waving palm-leaf fans, in a peaceful world. I longed with all my heart to be back in that world. To be back there with the First World War still 20 years off, and World War II over 40 years in the future. I wanted two tickets for that.

The clerk figured the fare. I had enough for two coach tickets, one way. But when I counted out the money and looked up, the clerk was staring at me. He nodded at the bills. "That ain't money, mister," he said, "and if you're trying to skin me you won't get very far." He glanced at the cash drawer beside him. Of course the money was old-style bills. They were half again as big as the money we use nowadays and different looking. I turned away and got out fast. There's nothing nice about jail, even in 1894.

And that was that. I left the same way I came, I suppose. Next day, during lunch hour, I drew 300 dollars out of the bank. It was nearly all we had. I bought old-style money (that really worried my psychiatrist friend). You can buy old money at almost any coin dealer's, but you have to pay a premium. My 300 dollars bought less than 200 dollars in old-style bills. I didn't care. Eggs were 13 cents a dozen in 1894.

But I've never again found the corridor that leads to the third level at Grand Central Station, although I've tried often enough.

Louisa was pretty worried when I told her all this. She didn't want me to look for the third level anymore. After a while I stopped. I went back to my stamps. But now we're both looking, every weekend, because now we have proof that the third level is still there. My friend Sam Weiner disappeared! Nobody knew where, but I sort of think that Sam went to Galesburg. He always said he liked the sound of the place when I talked about it. And that's where he is, all right—in 1894.

Because one night, I found—well, do you know what a first-day cover is? When a new stamp comes out, stamp collectors buy some. They use them to mail envelopes to themselves on the very first day of sale. The postmark proves the date. The envelope is called a first-day cover. They're never opened. You just put blank paper in the envelope.

That night, among my oldest first-day covers, I found one that shouldn't have been there. But there it was. It was there because someone had mailed it to my grandfather at his home in Galesburg. That's what the address on the envelope said. And it had been there since July 18, 1894. The postmark showed that. Yet I didn't remember it at all. The stamp was a six-cent, dull brown, with a picture of President Garfield. Naturally, when the envelope came to Granddad in the mail, it went right into his collection. It stayed there—till I took it out and opened it.

The paper inside wasn't blank. It read:

941 Willard Street
Galesburg, Illinois
July 18, 1894

Charley:

I got to wishing that you were right. Then I got to *believing* you were right. And, Charley, it's true. I found the third level! I've been here two weeks. Right now down the street at the Daly's someone is playing a piano. They're all out on the front porch singing "Seeing Nellie Home." And I'm invited over for lemonade. Come on back, Charley and Louisa. Keep looking till you find the third level! It's worth it, believe me!

The note is signed Sam.

At the stamp and coin store I go to, I found out that Sam bought 800 dollars worth of old-style money. That ought to set him up in a nice little hay, feed, and grain business. He always said that's what he really wished he could do. He certainly can't go back to his old business. Not in Galesburg, Illinois, in 1894. His old business? Why, Sam was my psychiatrist.

READING COMPREHENSION

Summarizing. Choose the best phrase to complete each sentence. Then write the complete statements on your paper.

1. When Charley found the third level in Grand Central Station, he discovered a way to _____ (go to the suburbs, escape to the past, learn about the future).

2. According to Charley, he and everyone he knew wanted to _____ (retire, escape, work overtime).

3. Charley collected _____ (coins, marbles, stamps).

4. Charley knew he had returned to the year 1894 because he _____ (talked to his psychiatrist, asked the ticket seller, saw a newspaper's front page).

5. Another thing that showed Charley he was in the past when he found the third level was the way people _____ (talked, dressed, acted toward each other).

6. Charley wanted to go back to Galesburg, Illinois, in 1894 because _____ (he was searching for his roots, he thought he could be rich there, it was a peaceful time and place).

7. The clerk on the third level _____ (sold Charley a ticket to Galesburg, called the police, would not take Charley's money).

8. Charley was convinced about the existence of the third level when _____ (he read Sam's letter, he found the corridor again, his wife told him she was worried about his health).

Interpreting. Write the answer to each question on your paper.

1. How many levels do most people think there are at Grand Central Station?

2. Why was Charley dissatisfied with modern life?

3. What things showed Charley that he was in the past when he found the third level?

4. What kind of life did Sam discover people lived in Galesburg in 1894?

5. Did Sam like his life in 1894 better?

6. Why couldn't Sam have gone back to his old business in 1894?

7. How did the discovery of the note from Sam add to the mysteriousness of the story?

For Thinking and Discussing

1. Why didn't Louisa want Charley to look for the third level at first? Why did she change her mind and start looking with him?

2. How do you think Sam would react if he met Charley and Louisa in Galesburg in 1894? Explain your answer.

3. If Charley lived in Galesburg in 1894, how might he earn his living?

4. What does the phrase "escape from reality" mean? What did Charley do that was called an escape from reality?

5. What are some of the positive things you might do to escape from reality?

UNDERSTANDING LITERATURE

Mood and Setting. One of the ways writers create a mood is through their descriptions of the setting in a story or play. A description of a creaking house filled with cobwebs can create a mood of fear or uncertainty. A description of a murder scene can create a mood of horror or disgust.

Often when a story setting changes, the mood will also change. One story can have several different settings and create several different moods.

Match the following descriptions from "The Third Level" with the appropriate mood words listed below the descriptions. Then write your answers.

1. "Sometimes I think Grand Central Station is growing like a tree, pushing out new corridors and staircases like roots. There's probably a long tunnel that nobody knows about under the city right now, on its way to Times Square."

2. "The corridor I was in slanted downward. I thought that was wrong, but I kept on walking. All I could hear was the empty sound of my own footsteps. I didn't pass a soul."

3. "Have you ever been there? It's a wonderful town still, with big old frame houses, huge lawns, and tremendous trees."

   a. eerie   **b.** peaceful   **c.** joking

WRITING

In what kind of setting would you expect the mood to be scary? Pick a setting and write a brief description of it in which you establish a scary mood.

The President Regrets

by Ellery Queen

In this story, the tables are turned when Ellery Queen is asked not to solve, but to create, a crime to challenge the esteemed members of The Puzzle Club. See if your powers of observation would win you membership.

The Puzzle Club is a group of very important people drawn together by unimportant purpose but common interest— to mystify one another. Their pleasure, in short, is puzzles.

Application is by invitation only, and membership must be won. The applicant has to submit to the Ordeal by Puzzle. If he survives the test, it earns him automatic admission.

Shortly after Ellery became The Puzzle Club's sixth regular member, it was proposed and unanimously voted to invite the President of the United States to apply for membership.

This was no frivolous motion. The members took their puzzles seriously, and the President was known to be a fan of mysteries in all lawful forms. Besides, the Club's Founder and First Member, multimillionaire oil man Syres, had been buddy-buddy with the occupant of the White House since their youthful days as riggers in the Texas oil fields.

The invitation went to Washington, and rather to Ellery's surprise the President promptly accepted the challenge. In deference to affairs of state, he was urged to name his own date, which he did. But when Ellery arrived at Syres's Park Avenue penthouse on the appointed evening to find the membership assembled, he was greeted with gloomy news. The President regretted that he could not make it after all. A Secret Service man had brought the message that a new crisis in the Middle East had caused a last-minute cancellation of the President's flight to New York.

"What shall we do now?" asked Darnell, the famous criminal lawyer.

"There's no point in wasting the puzzle we've prepared for the President," said Dr. Vreeland, the well-known psychiatrist. "Let's save it for whenever he can get here."

"It's too bad Dr. Arkavy is still attending that meeting in Moscow," said wispy little Emmy Wandermere, the poet. Dr.

Arkavy was the Nobel Prize-winning bio-chemist. "He has such a fertile mind, he can always come up with something on the spur of the moment."

"Maybe our newest member can help us out," said their Texan host. "What do you say, Queen? You must have a hundred problems at your fingers' ends, from your long experience as a writer and a detective."

"Let me think," Ellery said. Then he chuckled. "All right. Give me a few minutes to work out the details . . ." It took him far less. "I'm ready. I suggest we work together, to begin with. Since this is going to be a murder mystery, we will require a victim. Any suggestions?"

"A woman, of course," the lady poet said at once.

"Reeking of glamour," said the psychiatrist.

"That," said the criminal lawyer, "would seem to call for a Hollywood movie star."

"Good enough," Ellery said. "And a glamourous star of the screen calls for a glamourous name. Let's call her . . . oh, Valetta Van Buren. Agreed?"

"Valetta Van Buren." Miss Wandermere considered. "Yes."

"Well, Valetta is in New York to attend the premiere of her latest picture and to do a round of TV appearances in promotion of it," Ellery went on. "But this hasn't proved an ordinary publicity tour. In fact, Valetta has had a frightening experience. It so shook her up that she wrote me an agitated letter about it which, by the magic of coincidence, I received just this morning."

"In which," Dr. Vreeland pressed, "she said—"

"That during this New York visit she permitted herself to be escorted about town by four men—"

"Who are all, naturally, in love with her?" asked the lady poet.

"You guessed it, Miss Wandermere. She identified the four in her letter. One is the man-about-town and playboy, John Thrushbottom Taylor the Third—and if you haven't heard of Mr. Taylor, it's because I just made him up. The second is that wolf of Wall Street, named . . . well, let's call him A. Palmer Harrison. The third, of course, is the latest rage among society Pop Art painters, Leonardo Price. And the last of the quartet is—let's see—Biff Wilson, the professional football player."

"A likely story," grinned Oil Man Syres.

"Now." Ellery made a professional bridge of his fingers. "Having named the four men for me, Valetta went on to say that yesterday all four proposed marriage to her—each of them, on the same day. Unhappily, Valetta felt nothing for any of them—nothing permanent, at any rate. She rejected all four impartially. It was a busy day for Miss Van Buren, and she would have enjoyed it except for one thing."

"One of them," said the criminal lawyer, "turned ugly."

"Exactly, Darnell. Valetta wrote me that three of them took their turndowns with grace. But the fourth flew into a rage and threatened to kill her. She was terrified that he would try to carry out his threat and asked me to get in touch with her at once. She felt reluctant to go to the police, she wrote, because of the bad publicity it would bring her."

"What happened then?" asked Syres.

"I phoned, of course," Ellery replied, "as soon as I finished reading her letter. Would you believe it? I was too late. She was murdered last night, a short time after she must have mailed the letter. So the screen has lost a star and millions of Americans at this very moment are mourning the sheer waste of it all."

"How," asked Darnell, "was the foul deed done?"

"I could tell you," Ellery said, "that she was done in by a Tasmanian yoyo, but I won't be unfair—the nature of the weapon is irrelevant. However, I will say this, to avoid complications: Valetta was murdered by the suitor who threatened her life."

"And is that all?" asked the tycoon.

"No, I've saved the kicker for last. Valetta's letter gave me one clue. In writing about the four men, she said that she'd noticed *she had something in common with three of the four,* and that the fourth was the one who had threatened her."

"Oh," said Dr. Vreeland. "Then all we have to establish is the nature of the common denominator. The three sharing it with Valetta would be innocent. By elimination, therefore, the one left over has to be the guilty man."

Ellery nodded. "And now—if my initiation at the last meeting was a criterion—the floor is open. Any questions?"

"I take it," the lady poet murmured, "that we may disregard the obvious possibilities of connection—that Valetta and three of the men were of the same age, or had the same color hair, or the same religious affiliation, or came from the same town or state, or attended the same college, or were investors or board members in the same corporation—that sort of thing?"

Ellery laughed. "Yes, you may disregard those."

"Social position?" the multimillionaire asked. "Three of the men you described—Playboy John Something Taylor, Wall Street man A. Palmer Harrison, Pop Art Painter Price—did they all come from high society? That probably wouldn't be true of the pro football player, What's-His-Name."

"It just happened," Ellery mourned, "that Pop Art Painter Price was born in a Greenwich Village pad. And Valetta, of course, hailed from the slums of Chicago."

They pondered.

"Had three of the four men ever served with Valetta," asked Darnell suddenly, "on the same jury?"

"No."

"On a TV panel show?" asked the poet.

"No, Miss Wandermere."

"Don't tell me," said Dr. Vreeland, smiling, "that Valetta Van Buren and three of her suitors at one point in their lives went to consult the same psychiatrist?"

"That's a good solution, Doctor. But it's not the solution I have in mind."

"Politics," the oil man said. "Valetta and three of the suitors are registered in the same party."

"My information, Mr. Syres," said Ellery, "is that Valetta was Democrat, the playboy and the Wall Street man are conservative Republicans, and Price and Biff Wilson never voted in their lives."

Miss Wandermere suddenly said, "It isn't anything like that. Am I right, Mr. Queen, in assuming that all the relevant facts were in the body of your story?"

"I wondered when someone was going to ask that," Ellery chuckled. "That's exactly so, Miss Wandermere. There's really no need to ask questions at all."

"Then I for one need more time," said the tycoon. "What about the rest of you?" At their nods their host rose. "I suggest we

make an exception tonight and eat dinner before we crack Queen's puzzle."

Miss Wandermere's shocking blue eyes sparkled with understanding over the appetizer. Darnell's mustache-sized brows lifted with elation during the sipping of the soup. Dr. Vreeland uttered his self-congratulatory exclamation at the serving of the roast beef. And their host, Syres, achieved sweet victory over his chocolate dessert. But no one uttered a word until they were seated about the drawing room again over coffee and brandy.

"I detect from this and that," Ellery said, "that none of you encountered any real difficulty with my little puzzle."

"It's too bad the President had to miss this," Syres roared. "It was made to order, Queen, for his type of mind! Are you all quite ready?"

There was a universal nod.

"In that case," Ellery said, with resignation, "which of Valetta's four suitors murdered her?"

"Females first, always," said Dr. Vreeland with a gallant nod to Miss Wandermere.

"The key to the answer," said the lady poet promptly, "consists in the fact, Mr. Queen, that you really told us just one thing about Valetta *and* her four suitors. It follows that whatever she and three of the four men had in common must relate to that thing."

"A logic I can't dispute," murmured Ellery. "And that thing was?"

Darnell grinned. "What the anticipation of the President's visit here tonight suggested to you when we asked for an impromptu puzzle. Their names."

"You named the movie star Valetta Van Buren," said Syres. *"Van Buren—the name of a President of the United States."*

"Then Playboy John Thrushbottom Taylor the Third," said the psychiatrist. "You buried that one, Queen! But of course Taylor is the name of a President of the United States, too—Zachary Taylor."

"And the Wall Street man, A. Palmer Harrison," the lawyer said. "Harrison—William Henry. Also Benjamin."

"And professional football player Biff Wilson," Miss Wandermere twinkled. "That 'Biff' was masterly, Mr. Queen. But—of course, Wilson, for Woodrow Wilson."

"And that leaves one character whose name," said the oil man, "bears no cross-reference to a President's name—Leonardo Price. So Price, the Pop Art painter, murdered Valetta. You almost had me fooled, Queen. Taylor, Van Buren, Harrison! That was tricky, picking the more obscure Presidents."

"You could hardly expect me to name one of my characters Eisenhower," Ellery grinned. "Which reminds me." He raised his brandy snifter. "Here's to our absent President—and may he turn out to be the next member of The Puzzle Club!"

READING COMPREHENSION

Summarizing. Choose the best phrase to complete each sentence. Then write the complete statements on your paper.

1. After the President sent his regrets, the members of The Puzzle Club _____ (solved the puzzle they had prepared for the President, called off their meeting, asked Ellery Queen to come up with a puzzle).

2. The plot of Queen's puzzle involved _____ (the murder of a movie star, a jealous boyfriend's threats, the trials of three innocent men).

3. Valetta and the three innocent men _____ (had a President's name for a last name, came from high society, had the same initials).

Interpreting. Write the answer to each question on your paper.

1. Why did the members of The Puzzle Club invite the President to apply for membership?

2. Why were the questions the members of the club first asked about Valetta's murderer a waste of time?

3. How did the members of the club figure out that the key to the puzzle was in the characters' names?

For Thinking and Discussing. Did you solve the puzzle with the members of The Puzzle Club? How did you feel when the answer was revealed?

UNDERSTANDING LITERATURE

Plot. Sometimes a story has more than one plot. A writer can achieve this by writing a story within a story. In "The President Regrets," the main plot involves a group of people who get together, solve a puzzle, and share a meal. The story within the story is a mystery told by one of the characters—Ellery Queen.

One of the elements of a good mystery is the use of *foreshadowing*, or providing clues about the ending. The members of The Puzzle Club used these clues to solve the crime Ellery Queen gave them.

On your paper, write the facts from the list that are clues about the story within the story in "The President Regrets."

a. Everyone expected to see the President.

b. Queen was a writer and a detective.

c. Valetta was murdered by the suitor who threatened her life.

d. Ellery Queen said that all of the relevant facts were given in the story.

e. Ellery Queen paused in his story when he was naming the characters.

WRITING

Imagine that you are stuck in an elevator with a group of children. To calm them, you tell them a story. Write two paragraphs. In the first, describe the situation in the elevator. Make the second paragraph the story within the story.

Section Review

VOCABULARY

Multiple Meanings. Many words have *multiple meanings*—two or more different meanings. When you read a word with multiple meanings, you have to decide which meaning fits the way the word is used in the passage.

Each of the italicized words below has more than one meaning. For each italicized word, write the meaning that applies in the sentence. Then use each word to write a sentence in which you present the other meaning listed.

1. "When she presented Iris's case, he jumped up and began to *storm* around the room."
   a. rain heavily
   b. rush around angrily

2. "'I should say so! *Capital*! I could not ask for anything better!'"
   a. excellent
   b. money used in business

3. "You can buy old money at almost any coin dealer's, but you have to pay a *premium*."
   a. something offered free
   b. additional amount above the usual

4. "'That,' said the criminal lawyer, 'would seem to call for a Hollywood movie *star*.'"
   a. a heavenly body
   b. a leading actor or actress

READING

Drawing Conclusions. An important part of understanding what you read involves getting the facts, putting them together, and then making logical guesses based on the facts. This process is called *drawing conclusions*. Detectives are experts at putting facts together and drawing conclusions.

Do your own detective work. Read each of the following situations. Then draw your own conclusions to answer the questions. Write your answers on your paper.

1. The child could barely lift the bowling ball. He started it rolling down the center of the alley, but it slowly began edging toward the side.

   How many pins did the ball probably knock down?

2. Helen is a cashier at a supermarket. One customer pays her with two $10 bills. Helen notices that both bills have the same serial number. She tells her boss to stop the customer.

   Why does Helen want the customer to be stopped?

3. A murder is committed during a heavy rainstorm. Muddy footprints on the carpet lead toward the body. A police officer says, "I want to know which people now in the house have been outside the building in the past hour."

   Why does the police officer want this information?

WRITING

An Objective Firsthand Report. A first-hand report is an eyewitness account of an event. It is written or told by someone who was on the scene and carefully observed the people and events. Newspaper articles and radio and TV newscasts are examples of firsthand reports.

There are two kinds of firsthand reports. In an *objective* firsthand report, the writer uses only facts to describe an event or a person. In a *subjective*, or personal, firsthand report, the writer includes his or her feelings and opinions. You will be writing an objective firsthand report.

Step 1: Set Your Goal
When you decide on a topic, remember that it has to be something that you can actually witness firsthand. Here are some topics that you might like to consider.

- ☐ a sporting event you can attend
- ☐ a school play or assembly
- ☐ a class outing
- ☐ a person in your town whom you can interview
- ☐ a meeting of a club to which you belong

Step 2: Make a Plan
The next step is to gather information for your report. For other kinds of writing, you might do research in the library to find information. For a firsthand report, however, you will collect all your information on the scene of the event you will write about. You may collect information in two ways:

1. observing what is taking place

2. interviewing people

Later, when you write your report, you may not be able to remember everything you saw and heard. Therefore, while you are observing, take notes. Jot down all of the important details. Don't worry about spelling out all the words or writing complete sentences. Use abbreviations whenever possible. Your notes should include answers to these questions: *Who? What? When? Where? Why? How?*

If you are interviewing someone, prepare a list of questions to ask. Avoid questions that require a "Yes" or "No" answer. Include the *Who? What? When? Where? Why?* and *How?* questions in planning your interview. For example, if you were interviewing a local artist about his or her work, you might ask the following questions:

1. When did you become interested in painting?

2. Who had the greatest influence on your choice of career?

3. Where did you receive your training?

4. How long did it take for you to become recognized?

5. What are some of the difficulties or problems of your work?

6. Why do you like your work?

Step 3: Write a First Draft
Use your notes to write the first draft of your objective firsthand report. Answer the major *Who? What? When? Where?*

Why? and *How?* questions in the first paragraph. For example, suppose you were writing about a basketball game that just took place at your school. Your first paragraph might read something like this:

> On Friday night, March 14, Wakefield High's Blazers held out for a victory against the visiting Reds from Terrace Park in the closest game this basketball season. Center John Jones led the Blazers in a 10-point comeback and scored the winning play. The score was 62–60.

After the first paragraph, add others in which you provide supporting information that fills out your report of the event. Additional paragraphs about the basketball game might describe the spectators, the coaches, and the reactions of the players. When you write your report, remember to be objective.

Step 4: Revise
When you revise your objective firsthand report, ask yourself these questions:

1. Have I answered the most important questions in the first paragraph?

2. Have I presented supporting information in the paragraphs that follow?

3. Have I included only facts?

When you are satisfied with the content of your report, proofread it for errors, and copy it neatly.

QUIZ

The following is a quiz for Section 4. Write the answers in complete sentences on your paper.

Reading Comprehension

1. In "The Haunted Chess Set," why did Emil Cooper suspect that ghosts were haunting his chess set?

2. In "The Adventure of the Copper Beeches," why was Violet Hunter nervous about taking the job?

3. In "The Third Level," why did Charley do his searching at Grand Central Station?

4. Why is it surprising that Sam Weiner turned out to be the person who found and used the third level?

5. In "The President Regrets," what was Ellery's inspiration for the puzzle?

Understanding Literature

6. At the beginning of "The Haunted Chess Set," Angelica's dream was interrupted when something small and hard hit her on the cheek. What mood does this incident create?

7. How did Emil Cooper's excitability add to the mysterious mood of "The Haunted Chess Set"?

8. How did Violet Hunter feel when she discovered the coil of red hair in the locked drawer? How does this incident add to the suspense of "The Adventure of the Copper Beeches"?

9. Why is it important that Charley found the third level once but not a second time?

10. In "The Third Level," what unan-

swered questions does the finding of Sam's letter raise?

ACTIVITIES

Word Attack

1. In "The Adventure of the Copper Beeches," Violet went to an employment agency for a job. The word *employment* is made of the suffix *-ment* added to the base word *employ*.

   Below are some words from the stories in this section. Each one is a base word to which a prefix or suffix has been added. Find each base word. Then write a short paragraph explaining Mr. Rucastle's motives for doing what he did. Use all the base words.

retirement	construction
insane	exactly
seriously	governess

2. The words *universal* and *united* appear in "The President Regrets." These words begin with the prefix *uni-*, which means "only one; single." Use a dictionary to find five other words that begin with the prefix *uni-*. Be careful not to choose words that start with the prefix *un-*, meaning "not," followed by a base word beginning with *i*, such as *unimportant* and *uninvited*. Use each word you find in a sentence that demonstrates the word's meaning.

Speaking and Listening

1. With a partner, prepare a dialogue that might take place between Angelica and Iris or Iris and Mr. Cooper after the mystery of the haunted chess set has been solved.

2. Get together with some classmates to act out the scene where Holmes and Watson meet Violet Hunter at The Copper Beeches. You will need people to play these characters: Sherlock Holmes, Dr. Watson, Mrs. Toller, Violet, and Mr. Rucastle.

Researching

1. "The Third Level" included many details that tell what life was like in 1894. For example, you learned that gas lights were used, instead of electric ones, bills were larger and different looking, and women wore long skirts with high-buttoned shoes. Use the library to learn more about day-to-day life in the 1890's. Use the card catalog to find a book with photographs.

2. Find out more about stamp collecting in the library or at your local post office. Take notes on the different types of stamps people collect and what kinds of things make a stamp valuable.

Creating

In this section, you met two famous detectives—Sherlock Holmes and Ellery Queen. Invent a detective of your own. Think about and jot down notes on your detective's looks, age, hobbies, and background. Does your detective work for a police department or have a private agency? What methods does your detective use to solve a case? What trademark does your detective have that makes him or her distinctive? Write a paragraph or two describing your detective.

SECTION 5

POETRY

WHEN I READ POETRY
    Sometimes
when I read
    poetry—I get
    hurt
because somebody stole
    my idea —
but I think
    it's mostly that
I realize
    that
sometimes
    I have to hear
    other people's
words
    to realize
        what
    I feel.

    —Lauri London (student)

Sunlight and Shadow
Winslow Homer (1836–1910).
Cooper-Hewitt Museum, The Smithsonian Institution,
Gift of Charles Savage Homer.

Poetry

Poetry began with the first music and dance. As people danced, they sang words that expressed their feelings. Today, poetry is not usually sung; it is written down. But most poems are still meant to be read aloud. Poetry is a special, intense way of expressing thoughts and feelings.

Poetry is intense because a poet tries to get the most out of every word. Even a short poem can say a lot, because the poet chooses each word with great care. To understand the poet's ideas and emotions, it is important to read a poem with equal care.

As you read, think about each word. What is the exact meaning of the word? What does the word make you think of? How does it make you feel?

The way the words of a poem are arranged is also very important. Does the poem have a regular beat, like a song? Or is the beat irregular and unpredictable? Does the poet repeat certain words or phrases over and over again? Do any words rhyme? Answering these questions can help you understand what the poet is saying.

Telling a Story

Like a short story or play, a poem can have characters, a setting, and a plot. Poems that tell stories are called *narrative poems*. Narrative poems don't look like short stories or plays, however. They are usually written in lines of varying lengths. The words in each line create a rhythm and establish a mood. Narrative poems are divided into groups of lines called *stanzas*. Often, a word, phrase, line, or group of lines is repeated throughout a narrative poem, usually at the ends of stanzas. The use of repetition is one way a poet can build emotion when telling a story.

Narrative poems are different from short stories and plays in another way. They usually focus on just one part of a story, telling about a few key events. The poem "Frankenstein" doesn't tell the whole story of the monster from beginning to end. Instead, it focuses on the monster's escape from the dungeon and the time he spends with an old man.

Describing Something

Poets often write poems that describe. Descriptive poems are called *lyric poems*. They convey feelings about a person, place, object, or moment in time. Lyric poets use words to create *images,* or pictures, in a reader's mind. Images allow readers to see things in the same way the poet sees them. Often poets choose words that do more than tell readers what something looks like. If you read the words carefully, they will also tell you how the poet feels about the subject of the poem.

Sometimes poets describe their feelings about one thing by comparing it to something else. In one of the lyric poems you will read in this section, "Butterfly," Donald James Solomon compares his love for someone to a butterfly. His love is beautiful and delicate. Another poet uses a different comparison to express a different idea about love. To Robert Burns, love is "like a red, red rose"—fresh and sweet.

The *sounds* of a poem can also create pictures in your mind. Look at these lines from "Player Piano."

> At times I'm a jumble of rumbles,
> At others I'm light like the moon,
> But never my numb plunker fumbles,
> Misstrums me, or tries a new tune.

The sounds and rhythm in the lines let you hear that fast, jingly music of a player piano.

Getting a Point Across

Poets also write poems to give *messages*. Perhaps they want you to change your mind about something. Or maybe they just want the world to know what they think. In this type of poem, the message is the most important element.

To explain their views, poets often use *symbols*, objects or actions that, in the poem, really stand for something else. The writer of "A Work of Artifice" describes a small bonsai tree in a pot. A gardener cuts off a bit of the tree every day to prevent it from growing too large for the pot. The poet is really writing about women, not trees. She feels that society can keep women from growing and becoming strong. Try to figure out what the writer is saying in the other message poems you read in this section.

Another Look

All poets try to create mental pictures. Some poets also use words and symbols to create meaningful *visual* images.

Sometimes poets take lines or phrases they did not write and put them together in a *found poem*, such as "Right of Way" in this section. They may have seen the words on road signs or in advertisements. They arrange the words in a new way. They are asking you to look at these words again to find a new meaning in them.

Other poets sometimes create *concrete poems*, such as "Urban Landscape." They make pictures on the page with words or letters. In poems like these, how the words look on the page is more important than how they sound or what they mean.

Poetry expresses feelings and usually makes you think. And sometimes a poem can be more than you think!

Narrative Poems

Ghosts *by Sandra Gardner*

On Sunday mornings, my father and my
    uncle,
both widowed, in their 70's and feeling
    their age,
would sit together for hours, over coffee
    and bagels
and the Sunday papers, in the sunny
    room
that had been my aunt's sewing room.

They talked of their children, their
    children's
children, their youth, past scandals,
cold winters, getting old.

Sometimes they sat silent, thinking of
    the one
who had bound them together, made
    them put aside
differences, made them become friends
for her sake, the sister, the wife.

They sat silent, her ghost between them,
never saying her name aloud, pushing
    away
the angel of death, refusing to give her
    up.

My uncle died in his sleep
one cold black night last winter.
Now my father sits alone with two
    ghosts,
hugging them tight to him,
never saying their names.

1. You never met the speaker's aunt, yet you can tell things about her from the poem. What kind of woman was she?

2. What is the mood or feeling in the first stanza (section)? What is the mood in the last stanza? How are they different from each other?

3. Why did the characters not say the name of the dead? How would it have made them feel to mention her name?

Frankenstein

by Edward Field

The monster has escaped from the dungeon
where he was kept by the Baron,
who made him with knobs sticking out from each side of his neck
where the head was attached to the body
and stitching all over
where parts of cadavers were sewed together.

He is pursued by the ignorant villagers,
who think he is evil and dangerous because he is ugly
and makes ugly noises.
They wave firebrands at him and cudgels and rakes,
but he escapes and comes to the thatched cottage
of an old blind man playing on the violin Mendelssohn's "Spring Song."

Hearing him approach, the blind man welcomes him:
"Come in, my friend," and takes him by the arm.
"You must be weary," and sits him down inside the house.
For the blind man has long dreamed of having a friend
to share his lonely life.

The monster has never known kindness—the Baron was cruel—
but somehow he is able to accept it now,
and he really has no instincts to harm the old man,
for in spite of his awful looks he has a tender heart:
Who knows what cadaver that part of him came from?

The old man seats him at table, offers him bread,
and says, "Eat, my friend." The monster
rears back roaring in terror.
"No, my friend, it is good. Eat—gooood"
and the old man shows him how to eat,
and reassured, the monster eats
and says, "Eat—gooood,"
trying out the words and finding them good, too.

Lyric Poems

Hector the Collector

by Shel Silverstein

Hector the Collector
Collected bits of string.
Collected dolls with broken heads
And rusty bells that would not ring.
Pieces out of picture puzzles,
Bent-up nails and ice cream sticks,
Twists of wires, worn-out tires,
Paper bags and broken bricks.
Old chipped vases, half shoelaces,
Gatlin' guns that wouldn't shoot,
Leaky boats that wouldn't float,
And stopped-up horns that wouldn't toot.
Butter knives that had no handles,
Copper keys that fit no locks,
Rings that were too small for fingers,
Dried-up leaves and patched-up socks.
Worn-out belts that had no buckles,
'Lectric trains that had no tracks,
Airplane models, broken bottles,
Three-legged chairs and cups with cracks.
Hector the Collector
Loved these things with all his soul—
Loved them more than shining diamonds,
Loved them more than glistenin' gold.
Hector called to all the people,
"Come and share my treasure trunk!"
And all the silly sightless people
Came and looked . . . and called it junk.

---

1. What happened when Hector let other people see his collection? Why do you think he decided to share his "treasure trunk"?

2. Read the poem aloud. Do the rhythm and rhymes make it sound a little like a children's song? In what ways?

Of Kings and Things

by Lillian Morrison

What happened to Joey on our block
Who could hit a spaldeen four sewers
And wore his invisible crown
With easy grace, leaning, body-haloed
In the street-lamp night?

He was better than Babe Ruth
Because we could actually see him hit
Every Saturday morning,
With a mop handle thinner than any
    baseball bat,
That small ball which flew forever.
Whack! straight out at first, then
Rising, rising unbelievably soaring in a

Tremendous heart-bursting trajectory
To come down finally, blocks away,
Bouncing off a parked car's
Fender, eluding the lone outfielder.

Did he get a good job?
Is he married now, with kids?
Is he famous in another constellation?
I saw him with my own eyes in those
    days
The god of stickball
Disappearing down the street
Skinny and shining in the nightfall light.

1. What kind of game is stickball? What do you learn about the game in the poem?
2. How does the speaker feel about Joey?

What images does she use to describe him?
3. Babe Ruth was a great baseball player. Why was Joey "better than Babe Ruth"?

Still

by Andrés Purificasion

It has been six years
Six long revolutions round the sun
And she still haunts me.
The memory is gray, like an October
    New York City day.
Forgotten is the reason why it stopped
Hazy is the memory of how it began
Lost forever is the magic of it all;
And she still haunts me.

1. Who is the "she" of the poem?
2. "She" is not a ghost. What does the poet mean when he says, "And she still haunts me"?

Medicine

by Alice Walker

Grandma sleeps with
my sick
    grand-
pa so she
can get him
during the night
medicine
to stop
  the pain

    In
  the morning
    clumsily
      I
  wake
   them

Her eyes
look at me
from under-
       neath
his withered
arm

   The
  medicine
   is all
    in
  her long
    un-
     braided
       hair.

1. How is Grandma's long unbraided hair a kind of medicine for Grandpa?

2. In what ways does the poem itself look like "long unbraided hair"?

Could Be

by Langston Hughes

Could be Hastings Street,
Or Lenox Avenue.
Could be 18th and Vine
And still be true.

Could be 5th and Mound,
Could be Rampart:
When you pawned my watch
You pawned my heart.

Could be you love me
Could be that you don't.
Might be that you'll come back
Like as not you won't.

Hastings Street is weary,
Also Lenox Avenue.
Any place is dreary
Without my watch and you.

---

1. What are some of the ways in which this poem is like a song? What effect do the rhymes and repetition have?

2. What does the speaker mean by saying, "When you pawned my watch / You pawned my heart"?

Butterfly

by Donald James Solomon (student)

You took my love
Gently in your hands
Like a butterfly;
Then you plucked off
One of the wings
And laughed as it flopped
Upon the ground.

1. In this poem love is compared to a butterfly. What do the two have in common?

2. What type of poem do you expect from reading the first three lines? But then what happens? Does the contrast make the ending seem even harsher?

A Red, Red Rose   *by Robert Burns*

O, my luve is like a red, red rose,
    That's newly sprung in June.
O, my luve is like the melodie,
    That's sweetly play'd in tune.

As fair art thou, my bonie lass,
    So deep in luve am I,
And I will luve thee still, my dear,
    Till a' the seas gang dry.

Till a' the seas gang dry, my dear,
    And the rocks melt wi' the sun!
And I will luve thee still, my dear,
    While the sands o' life shall run.

And fare thee weel, my only luve,
    And fare thee weel a while!
And I will come again, my luve,
    Tho' it were ten thousand mile!

1. Robert Burns lived in the 18th century in Scotland. He wrote in the Scottish dialect of that time. In this poem, *luve* means love; *bonie* : beautiful; *a'* : all; *gang* : go; and *weel* : well.

2. In stanzas 1 and 2, to what does Robert Burns compare his love?
3. In stanzas 3 and 4, Robert Burns declares that his love will last. How does he make this point?

Starting at Dawn

by Sun Yün-feng (translated by Kenneth Rexroth & Ling Chung)

Under the waning moon
In the dawn—
A frosty bell.
My horse's hooves
Tramp through the yellow leaves.
As the sun rises
Not a human being is visible,
Only the sound of a stream
Through the misty trees.

1. In what season does this poem take place? What details tell you this?
2. What is the overall mood of the poem? Does it seem sad or cheerful? What are the phrases that create the mood?

Player Piano

by John Updike

My stick fingers click with a snicker
And, chuckling, they knuckle the keys;
Light-footed, my steel feelers flicker
And pluck from these keys melodies.

My paper can caper; abandon
Is broadcast by dint of my din,
And no man or band has a hand in
The tones I turn on from within.

At times I'm a jumble of rumbles,
At others I'm light like the moon,
But never my numb plunker fumbles,
Misstrums me, or tries a new tune.

---

1. A player piano is a mechanical instrument. A paper roll with holes in it makes the keys move as if someone were playing the instrument. What lines describe how a player piano works? Which words and lines suggest the *sounds* a player piano makes?

2. Who is the speaker of this poem? What words or phrases make the piano seem almost human?
3. This poem rhymes. But not just at the end of the lines. "My paper can caper" is an example. What are some others?

The Earth's a Baked Apple

by Michael Colgrass

The earth's a baked apple
Circling on a stick
Of sunlight
For best results
Add patience and let cool
    Serves 3½ billion

---

1. Why does the speaker call the earth a "baked apple"? What mental pictures does this image make you see?

2. Why does the speaker suggest adding patience and letting the earth cool? Who are the 3½ billion to be served?

READING COMPREHENSION

Summarizing. Choose the best phrase to complete each sentence. Then write the complete statements on your paper.

1. Hector the Collector collected _____ (stamps and coins, valuable treasures, things no one else wanted).

2. In "Of Kings and Things," Joey was a "king" of _____ (stickball, basketball, football).

3. Two images of love that are used in the poems are _____ (a baked apple and a frosty bell, a butterfly and a rose, an October day and an oak tree).

Interpreting. Write the answer to each question on your paper.

1. What imagery in "Butterfly" tells the reader that the poet's love was rejected?

2. How do the poems "Still" and "Medicine" show the power of love?

3. What mood does Langston Hughes create by repeating "Could Be" over and over again?

For Thinking and Discussing

1. Do you think the poet of "Could Be" is in love or not?

2. Do you think "A Red, Red Rose," which was written over a hundred years ago, can still talk to us about love in a way we understand?

UNDERSTANDING LITERATURE

Images, Similes, and Metaphors. Poets describe things carefully. They want readers to create a mental picture, or *image*, of how something looks, sounds, smells, tastes, or feels.

Two special kinds of images are *similes* and *metaphors*. A simile is an image in which a poet compares two different things by using the word *like* or *as*. For example: *The hard rain was like a curtain at my window.* A metaphor is a comparison that doesn't use *like* or *as*. One thing becomes another thing. For example: *The rain was a gray wall blocking my view.*

Here are some images from the lyric poems in this section. On your paper, indicate which images are *similes* and which are *metaphors*. Then briefly explain the mental picture you "see" in each image.

1. "The memory is gray, like an October New York City day."

2. "O, my luve is like the melodie, That's sweetly play'd in tune."

3. "The earth's a baked apple"

4. "At times I'm a jumble of rumbles"

WRITING

Create your own images. Write similes for 1–3 and metaphors for 4–6.

1. a winter storm
2. a kitten's fur
3. a sunny day
4. happiness
5. fear
6. love

Message Poems

Thief

by Tom Whitecloud

We knew of war
For we were warriors
The winner takes all.

We knew of lies
For we were diplomats
in a small way.

We knew of politics,
for we were democrats:
a man was a man.

You took the land
We tried to understand;
You live on it; not with it.

But, my friends,
(And you were often good friends
As you understand friendship):

Why did you steal the smiles
From our children?

1. Who are the "we" of this poem? Who are the "you"? What happened between "we" and "you"?

2. According to the poem, how do Native Americans feel about nature and the land? What does the speaker mean by "You live on it; not with it"?

A Work of Artifice

by Marge Piercy

The bonsai tree
in the attractive pot
could have grown eighty feet tall
on the side of a mountain
till split by lightning.
But a gardener
carefully pruned it.
It is nine inches high.
Every day as he
whittles back the branches
the gardener croons,
It is your nature
to be small and cozy,
domestic and weak;
how lucky, little tree,
to have a pot to grow in.
With living creatures
one must begin very early
to dwarf their growth:
the bound feet,
the crippled brain,
the hair in curlers,
the hands you
love to touch.

---

1. What is a bonsai tree? What special care does it require? Why?

2. Why does the speaker feel women are like bonsai trees? According to the poet, what special care do women receive? Why?

3. What is the mood of the poem? Sad? Happy? Angry? Calm? How do you know?

Telephone Conversation

by Susan Keady

Half a mile of copper wire
separates us, yet brings us
this close
in protective anonymity
and privacy from each other
that eases our shyness
and fearful reserve.
But when I see you tomorrow
I know we'll regret
the impulse to confide.
Our faces will be closed
and our speech awkward,
but that will end in time.
The first time we talk this way
face to face
without fears of our vulnerability,
Then we'll have something
even more precious
than this first honest conversation
with the armor
of half a mile of copper wire
between us.

1. How does a telephone help bring people together? How does it keep them apart at the same time? Why does the speaker call a phone "armor"?

2. Do you think there are some things that people should only tell each other face to face? Why or why not?

Where the Rainbow Ends

by Richard Rive

Where the rainbow ends
There's going to be a place, brother,
Where the world can sing all sorts of
    songs,
And we're going to sing together, brother,
You and I, though you're white and I'm
    not.
It's going to be a sad song, brother,

Because we don't know the tune,
And it's a difficult tune to learn.
But we can learn, brother, you and I.
There's no such tune as a black tune.
There's no such tune as a white tune.
There's only music, brother,
And it's music we're going to sing
Where the rainbow ends.

1. The writer of this poem comes from South Africa where there is strict separation between white and black people. How does the speaker feel about this separation?

2. Who is the speaker calling "brother"?
3. Why is the song "sad"? According to the speaker, what could make the song a happier one?

Memo to the 21st Century

by Philip Appleman

It was like this once: sprinklers mixed
our marigolds with someone else's phlox,
and the sidewalks under maple trees
were lacy with August shade,
and whistles called at eight and fathers
    walked
to work, and when they blew again,
men in tired blue shirts followed
their shadows home to grass.
That is how it was in Indiana.

Towns fingered out to country once,
where brown-eyed daisies waved a fringe
    on orchards
and cattle munched at clover, and
fishermen sat in rowboats and were
    silent,
and on gravel roads, boys and girls
stopped their cars and felt the moon and
    touched,
and the quiet moments ringed and
    focused
lakes   moon   flowers.

That is how it was
in Indiana.

But we are moving out now,
scraping the world smooth where apples
    blossomed,
paving it over for cars. In the spring
before the cover goes purple,
we mean to scrape the hayfield, and
next year the hickory woods:
we are pushing on, our giant diesels
    snarling,
and I think of you, the billions of you,
    wrapped
in your twenty-first century concrete,
and I want to call to you, to let you
    know
that if you dig down,
down past wires and pipes
and sewers and subways, you will find
a crumbly stuff called earth. Listen:
in Indiana once, things grew in it.

---

1. A *memo* is a note or reminder. What is the memo reminding the 21st century of? Did the poet really write the message for the people of the future, or for the people of today?

2. Is the picture the poet paints of Indiana something that you are familiar with? Is it anything like where you live?

3. Does the poet believe there is hope for the 21st century? Does he think it will ever again be the way it once was in Indiana?

236

Do Not Go Gentle Into That Good Night

by Dylan Thomas

Do not go gentle into that good night,
Old age should burn and rave at close
of day;
Rage, rage against the dying of the light.

Though wise men at their end know
dark is right,
Because their words have forked no
lightning they
Do not go gentle into that good night.

Good men, the last wave by, crying how
bright
Their frail deeds might have danced in a
green bay,
Rage, rage against the dying of the light.

Wild men who caught and sang the sun
in flight,
And learn, too late, they grieved it on
its way,
Do not go gentle into that good night.

Grave men, near death, who see with
blinding sight
Blind eyes could blaze like meteors and
be gay,
Rage, rage against the dying of the light.

And you, my father, there on the sad
height,
Curse, bless, me now with your fierce
tears, I pray,
Do not go gentle into that good night.
Rage, rage against the dying of the light.

1. What is "that good night" another name
for? What does "rage against the dying light"
mean? Does the poet think we should give in
to death?

2. To whom is the speaker addressing the
poem? How do you think he feels about that
person?

READING COMPREHENSION

Summarizing. Choose the best phrase to complete each sentence. Then write the complete statements on your paper.

1. In "Thief," the speaker says the white man has stolen the Native Americans' _____ (land, future hopes, land and future hopes).

2. In "Memo to the 21st Century," the speaker believes that someday there will be no _____ (fertile soil, quiet moments, parking lots).

3. The message of the poem by Dylan Thomas is that people should _____ (accept death willingly, fight against death, be gentle).

Interpreting. Write the answer to each question on your paper.

1. Who is the poet referring to in the title, "Thief"?

2. According to the author of the "Telephone Conversation," why do people confide things on the phone rather than in person?

3. What does the speaker in "Where the Rainbow Ends" hope to persuade people to do?

For Thinking and Discussing. Why are the poets of "Thief" and "A Work of Artifice" angry? How are they using sarcasm in their poems?

UNDERSTANDING LITERATURE

Symbols and Mood. Poems with a message seek to persuade the reader to think or feel a certain way about something. Sometimes the poet uses a symbol to help the reader see things in a new way, or to create a specific mood.

The passages below are from the poems in this section. On your paper, indicate whether the symbols used in each passage were chosen to make you feel *sad, angry, happy, worried,* or *guilty.*

1. "Why did you steal the smiles
   From our children?"

2. "The bonsai tree . . .
   could have grown eighty feet tall . . .
   But a gardener
   carefully pruned it."

3. "There's only music, brother,
   And it's music we're going to sing
   Where the rainbow ends."

4. "and I think of you, the billions of you,
   wrapped / in your twenty-first century
   concrete,"

5. "Rage, rage against the dying of the light."

WRITING

Think of an issue that you feel strongly about. Write a short poem to persuade others to feel the way you do about the issue. Think about a mood you would like to create. Try to use a symbol in your poem that will help to create the mood.

Found Poems and Concrete Poems

Right of Way

by Marjorie Burns

No | parking

standing | passing

lane-switching | horn-blowing

U-Turn | right turn

left turn | exit.

---

1. A *found poem* is made up of lines or phrases the poet has found written or printed somewhere. Where do you think the poet found the words for this poem?

2. Why has the poet drawn two parallel lines down the middle of "Right of Way"?

Food Processor

by Marjorie Burns

with this compact
counter-top appliance,
you will handle in a flash
all those
   slicing,
      mincing,
         and chopping chores.
in a flash you will
slice and mince,

mince and chop,
chop and beat,
beat and puree,
puree and shred,
shred and grate,
grate and grind,
grind and crush,
crush and crinkle-cut,
crinkle-cut and crumble.

1. Where do you think the poet found the words for this poem?

2. What effect does the repetition of words have in creating a mood?

Urban Landscape

by Spike St. Croix

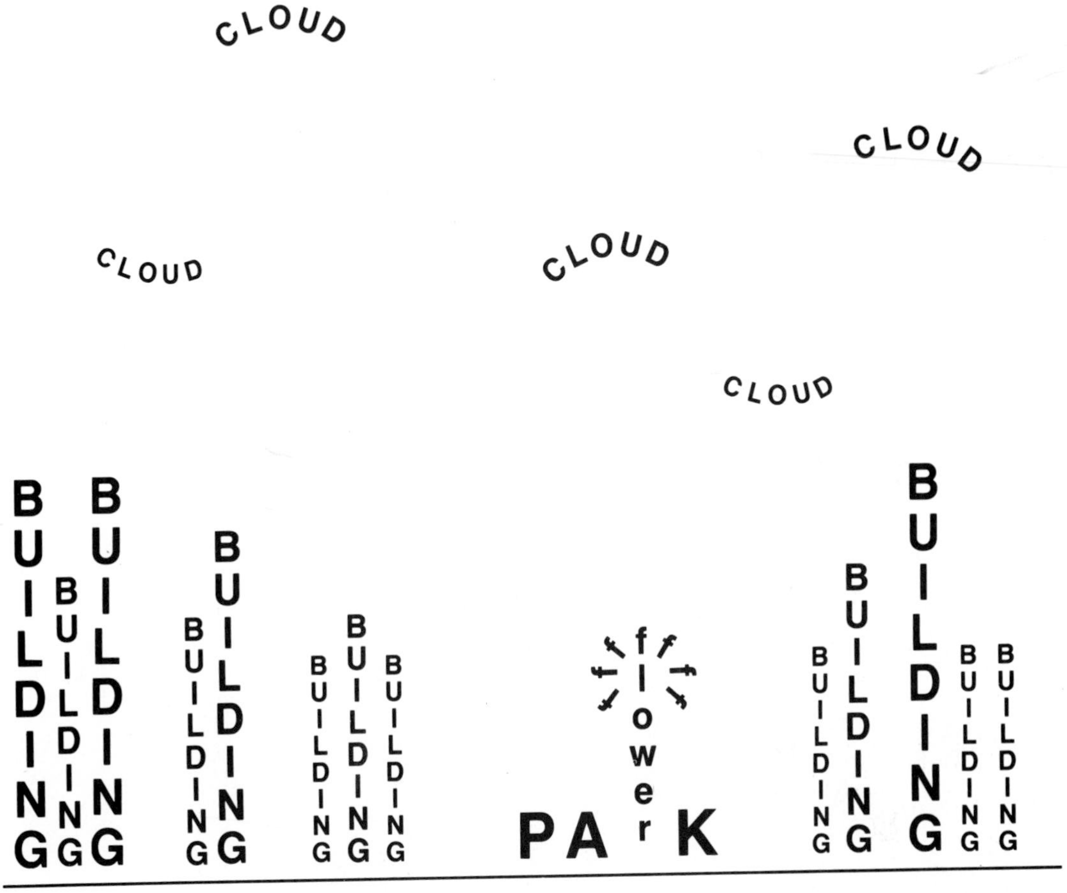
CLOUD
CLOUD
CLOUD
CLOUD
CLOUD
BUILDING
BUILDING
BUILDING
BUILDING
BUILDING
BUILDING
BUILDING
BUILDING
flower
PARK
BUILDING
BUILDING
BUILDING
BUILDING
BUILDING

1. This poem presents a picture of a city. Is the single flower too important in the picture? Why do you think the poet made it appear so large and important in the picture?
2. What are some other details of the view of a city that could have been included?

Tribute to Henry Ford—3

by Richard Kostelanetz

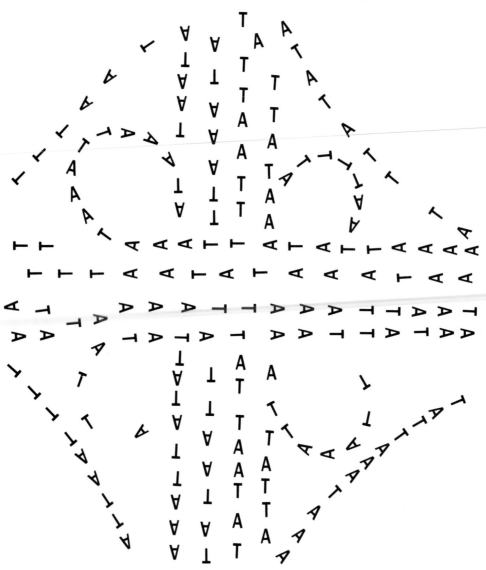

1. What do the letters in this poem symbolize? Clue: Two of the early cars designed by Henry Ford were the Model T and the Model A.

2. Why are the letters arranged the way they are in the poem? What is the poet trying to show about American society from Henry Ford's time to our own time?

READING COMPREHENSION

Summarizing. Choose the best phrase to complete each sentence. Then write the complete statements on your paper.

1. The poem "Food Processor" describes _____ (how to cook, how to operate a food processor, the different functions of a food processor).

2. Marjorie Burns found the words she used in "Right of Way" _____ (in a magazine, on street signs, in a book she had read).

3. In "Tribute to Henry Ford—3," the poet describes _____ (early cars, the importance of cars today, the future role of cars).

Interpreting. Write the answer to each question on your paper.

1. In "Urban Landscape," what does the cloud over the flower mean?

2. Why is the cloverleaf traffic arrangement of the letters in "Tribute to Henry Ford—3" presented from an aerial view?

3. The mood of the poem "Right of Way" is mostly negative. What other street signs might be used to create a poem with a more positive message?

For Thinking and Discussing. Do you think that concrete and found poems are "true" poems? Do they present intense feelings the way other kinds of poems do?

UNDERSTANDING LITERATURE

Physical Symbols. In found poems and concrete poems, the way the words and letters are arranged *physically* on the page helps to convey the meaning. The shape of the poem is as important as the words and helps to illustrate them.

Each of the following questions is about a physical symbol in a poem in this section. Select the best answer and write the entire sentence on your paper.

1. Two of the poets use physical symbols related to _____.
   a. buildings
   b. highways
   c. kitchen appliances

2. The double line in "Right of Way" symbolizes how road signs _____.
   a. help people
   b. make life easier
   c. control people

3. Richard Kostelanetz uses a clover leaf pattern to symbolize _____.
   a. the confusion of traffic on many roads today
   b. how well cars are built today
   c. how cities are growing

WRITING

Think of something from everyday life. Then create your own concrete poem. Arrange the words on the page to make a physical symbol. The shape of the poems should illustrate what you are saying in the poem.

Section Review

VOCABULARY

Denotation and Connotation. Every word has a dictionary meaning. That meaning is called its *denotation*. Sometimes a word will suggest other meanings not listed in a dictionary. These meanings relate to the feelings readers have when they read the word. These additional meanings are called *connotations*.

For example, the denotation of the word *spring* is "a season that comes between winter and summer." When you read the word *spring*, you may also think of such connotations as: "birth," "greenness," "beauty," or "softness."

Here are some words from the poems in this section. Find each word. Then, on your paper, write the connotation you think the poet was trying to bring out.

scandals ("Ghosts," p. 211)
monster ("Frankenstein," p. 212)
piano ("Last Day at the Job," p. 215)
constellation ("Of Kings and Things," p. 219)
withered ("Medicine," p. 221)
dreary ("Could Be," p. 223)
rose ("A Red, Red Rose," p. 225)
smiles ("Thief," p. 231)
pruned ("A Work of Artifice," p. 233)
armor ("Telephone Conversation," p. 234)
night ("Do Not Go Gentle Into That Good Night," p. 238)

READING

Figurative Language. Writers use words and expressions to create images. Often these words take on special connotations from their context. The exact meaning of an expression is called its *literal* meaning. The meaning the writer is trying to convey is called the *figurative* meaning.

The sentences below contain figurative expressions you may have heard. What does each one mean literally and figuratively? Write the answers on your paper.

1. The young girl blossomed into a beautiful young woman.

2. The building decayed during the ebb and flow of time.

Poets often use figurative language. Here is part of a poem that you will read in the next section of this book. Write what you think the poet means by each expression listed below the passage.

The road has another hand,
   palm out
   to the north.
Caresses a forest floor.
Sprinkles sand in the moss.
The wind is gentle there
and rain sounds are violet voices
speaking past the sea.

1. road has another hand

2. palm out

3. caresses a forest floor

4. rain sounds are violet voices

246

WRITING

A Poem. Poetry is a special way of expressing thoughts and feelings. A poet's purpose is to stimulate the reader's senses, emotions, thoughts, and imagination. The poet chooses and arranges words carefully to create a special sound. Rhyme, rhythm, sound words, and repetition are some of the things that create the "music" of a poem. The special language of poetry—imagery and figurative language—appeals to the senses and helps you experience what is being described in new ways.

Step 1: Set Your Goal

Writing poetry may seem difficult, but it doesn't have to be. The four-step writing process can help you get started. First, think about a subject you would like to write about. The following list of ideas may help you decide on a subject:

a person	a scene
an animal	an event
an object	an emotion

Choose a subject that creates a striking image in your mind or evokes a strong feeling. If you choose to write about a scene, for example, your subject may be a park on the first day of spring.

Step 2: Make a Plan

After you choose your subject, close your eyes and try to picture it in detail. What do you see, hear, taste, smell, and touch when you think of your subject? Write down specific images that appeal to the senses. The writer of a poem about a park on the first day of spring might list images:

- shoots of grass sprouting in the dirt
- children laughing and shouting
- the warm sun on my face

Now write several examples of figurative language to use in your poem. You can write similes, in which you compare two things using the words *like* or *as*. You can write metaphors, in which you compare two things without using *like* or *as*. Or you can use personification, in which you give human traits to an object, animal, or idea. Here are some examples:

Simile   The air was as fresh as a daisy.
Metaphor   The field was a blanket of people.
Personification   The crocuses bowed their heads to the sun.

Next, think of how you can add sound to your poem. One technique poets use is choosing words that imitate sounds. For example: Bicyclists *whizzed* by. Another device poets use is alliteration, which is the repetition of sounds at the beginning of words: *Pigeons pecking at peanuts.* You might also write a line or phrase that you will repeat in your poem.

Step 3: Write a First Draft

Before you begin to write, think about the form of your poem. Your poem can have a regular rhythm and rhyme, or it can be free verse, having no strict form. Begin your poem by identifying your subject. If you were writing a poem in free verse about the first day of spring, your first line might be something like this:

Spring begins. People flood to the park.

In the lines that follow, use your list of images and your examples of figurative

247

language and sound devices. Use one or two of these details per line. The last line of your poem should leave the reader with a striking image. This image should convey your feelings about the subject, or repeat an important phrase from the poem.

Step 4: Revise
Ask yourself the following questions as you read your poem aloud.

☐ Did I use images that appeal to the senses?

☐ Did I include an example of figurative language?

☐ Did I use devices to give the poem sound?

☐ Does the poem convey the mood or feeling I want it to?

☐ Does the poem flow naturally?

Check your poem for any errors in spelling, grammar, and punctuation, and copy it over neatly.

QUIZ

The following is a quiz for Section 5. Write the answers in complete sentences on your paper.

Reading Comprehension

1. In "Frankenstein," the monster goes into an old man's house to find safety. What else does he find there?

2. Why has the mother in "Last Day at the Job" decided to retire?

3. In "Of Kings and Things," what does the poet remember about Joey? What does she wonder about him?

4. Why is the speaker in "Thief" angry? At whom is he angry?

5. What is the "half a mile of copper wire" in "Telephone Conversation"?

Understanding Literature

6. Find one metaphor and one simile in the lyric poems in this section. What is being compared in each one?

7. What technique is used in "Player Piano" to help readers "hear" how a player piano sounds?

8. In "A Work of Artifice," how is a bonsai tree used to describe the way society treats many women?

9. What is the message of "Where the Rainbow Ends"?

10. What are found poems and concrete poems? How do writers create them?

ACTIVITIES

Word Attack

1. The following words from the poems in this section imitate sounds:

click   snicker   whack
toot   pluck   grind

Write a word for each sound described below. You can use sound words you know or make up your own.
a. a book dropping on the floor

b. a new piece of chalk on a black-board
c. the school PA system turning on
d. a rusty door closing
e. students rushing down the stairs
f. a smoke alarm going off

Use your sound words and others you think of in a poem or story about school.

2. In "Player Piano," the poet made up the word *misstrums* to mean "strums badly." The prefix *mis-* can mean "bad or wrong," as in *misconduct;* "badly or wrongly," as in *miscast;* or "lack of," as in *mistrust*. Write the meaning of the following words with the prefix *mis-*. Then write three additional words with *mis-* in them:

misbehave   mislead
misquote   misunderstanding
misjudge   mistreatment

Speaking and Listening. Choose one of the poems from this section to read aloud. Practice reading the poem until you have mastered the rhythm of the lines. Be sure your reading creates the proper mood. Then read the poem aloud to the class.

Researching

1. *Frankenstein* is the name of a novel by Mary Shelley, an English author. Research to find out more about Mary Shelley and the monster she created. Find the answers to these questions:

a. Who was Frankenstein?
b. When was *Frankenstein* published?
c. What happens to the monster at the end of the novel?

You may wish to read *Frankenstein* and write a report about it to share with the class.

2. Review the poems in this section written by the following authors: Alice Walker, Langston Hughes, Robert Burns, Dylan Thomas, and Shel Silverstein. Choose the one you like best, and find a collection of the author's poems in the library. Pick a favorite among the poems you read, and copy it. Then write a paragraph describing the poem and what you like about it. You may want to compare the poem with the one in this section by the same author. Share the poem and your reaction to it with the class.

Creating

1. Write the words to a song that you know. Decide whether the words make a good poem. Do the words tell a story? Did the songwriter use special images or symbols? Change some of the words or write some of the lines differently to create your own song/poem.

2. Think of someone you know well and would like to describe in a poem. Write your own lyric poem about the person. You might like to use the letters of the person's name as the first letter of each line in the poem. For example:

TONY
Taking the time
Out of your day
Never a frown from
You.

RELATIONSHIPS

Love one another, but make not a bond
of love:
Let it rather be a moving sea between
the shores of your souls....
Sing and dance together and be joyous,
but let each of you be alone,
Even as the strings of a lute are alone
though they quiver with the same music.

— Kahlil Gibran

Madame Charpentier and Her Children
Pierre Auguste Renoir (1841–1919).
Metropolitan Museum of Art, Wolfe Fund.
Catherine Lorillard Wolfe Collection.

Relationships

A relationship may last forever, or only for the moment it takes to smile at a stranger. But sharing experiences with others is an important part of everyone's life.

Writers often write about their own relationships or about other people's relationships. Some writers have told unusual stories about these experiences. Others have found new ways to describe emotions or experiences that almost everyone has had.

Families

In this section you will first explore family relationships. Some families are close and some are not, but most people have strong feelings about their families. You may love all the people in your family, or you may not get along with some of them. Reading what writers have to say about family relationships can help you understand your own experiences more clearly.

In "Very Special Shoes," the author uses a pair of shoes as a symbol of love between family members. Mary's mother lets her buy a pair of red shoes that the family really can't afford. Her mother understands how important the shoes are to Mary. She helps the rest of the family understand too. Later, Mary's shoes provide a constant reminder of her mother's love.

Bob Teague, in "Letter to a Black Boy," writes a true story about his own family relationships. He addresses the story to his young son in the form of a letter. Teague tells his son about his Aunt Letty and the other members of his family. He wants his son to learn the important lessons that Aunt Letty taught him and the rest of the family.

Belonging

"Letter to a Black Boy" is not only concerned with the personal relationships between family members. It also describes Teague's sense of belonging to two groups. One group is his whole family. The second group is a larger one—all black Americans. He wants his son to take pride in belonging to both groups.

Relationships to groups are important in everyone's life. Most people feel part of a family group. People may also feel strongly about belonging to a school, a country, an ethnic group—even about belonging to the human race.

The poem "Celebration" is about the joy of being part of a group. The Native American poet speaks of dancing, feasting, and laughing with his people. For him, just being part of "my people" is a good reason for celebrating.

A Special Relationship

Love is an emotion everyone has shared. Everyone knows how it feels to care deeply for someone or something. Many people also know the emptiness of not feeling loved. "The Troublemaker" is a true story about a boy's search for love. Until he adopts a dog, the boy seems to care for no one. Then his love for the dog changes him. But what might happen to the boy if the dog dies? That is the problem that faces the author, veterinarian James Herriot.

Writers often wish to express feelings about one person they care for very much. Millions of people have written about love, but each love relationship is unique. So every writer must find an original way of saying exactly what he or she feels.

In "Since You Left," a poet wants to say, "I miss you." The poet uses a comparison to express that feeling in a special way. When the lover is gone, the poet says, "I fade like the waning moon."

In the poem "Road," the poet never speaks of love. But the intense way he asks someone to stay with him reveals deep emotion. The poet wants someone to walk down a road with him. In the poem, the road may be a symbol for life. The poet is really saying, "Please let me share my life with you."

Kurt Vonnegut also writes about a walk that is more than a walk. In "Long Walk to Forever," a young woman and man take a walk through the woods. During the walk, they learn something new about their feelings for one another. Is the walk the beginning of a more important journey together—into the future?

Guadalupe de Saavedra writes a poem to tell someone, "I will always love you." Millions have said those words, but Saavedra finds a different way to say them. In fact, Saavedra thinks of six new ways to express his eternal love.

A Lifesaving Relationship

"Take Over, Bos'n!" is about a relationship that develops in a life-threatening situation. A group of sailors is stranded in a lifeboat. They are dying of thirst and have only one canteen of water left to share between them. One of the men understands that they must ration the water to stay alive, and he guards the canteen with a pistol. The other men hate him. But the man on guard is showing that he really cares for the others by trying to keep them alive for as long as possible.

In reading the selections in this section, you will find that there are as many ways to say "I love you" or "I care about you" as there are people to say it.

Very Special Shoes

by Morley Callaghan

Mary Johnson finally saves up enough money to buy the wonderful red shoes. But because of those shoes, her relationship with her father, her sisters, and most of all, with her mother, will never be the same.

The shoes are not practical. By the end of the story, they are no longer even red. But for Mary, they will always be the most important shoes in the world.

All that winter and into the spring, the Johnson family waited for the doctor to decide what was really the matter with Mrs. Johnson. Mary, who was 11 years old, had only been told that her mother was troubled with pains in the legs from varicose veins. She stayed home from school to help with the housework and dreamed of a pair of red leather shoes. The shoes had been in a shoestore window over on the avenue. Mary had seen them one day in the winter when she had been walking along with her mother, doing the shopping.

All winter she had dreamed of the shoes. Now she could hardly believe that the day she had been waiting for had come at last. Every Saturday she got 25 cents for doing the housework all by herself. Today it finally added up to the six dollars which was the price of the shoes. Mary finished up the last of the dusting in the living room. She moved quietly so she would not wake her mother. She hurried to the window and looked out. She had been afraid it might rain, but the street was bright with sunlight. Then she went quickly into the bedroom where her mother slept.

"Mother, wake up," she whispered excitedly.

Mrs. Johnson was a handsome woman of 50 with a plump figure. She was breathing so softly Mary could hardly hear her. Every day now she seemed to need more sleep. This fact worried Mary's older sisters, Barbara and Helen. It was the subject of long whispering talks in their bedroom at night. It seemed to trouble Mr. Johnson, too. He had started taking long walks by himself and he came home with his breath smelling of whiskey. But to Mary, her mother looked as lovely and as healthy as ever. "Mother," she called again. She reached over and gave her shoulder a little shake. Then she

254

watched her mother's face eagerly when she opened her eyes to see if she had remembered about the shoes.

Her mother, still half asleep, only murmured, "Bring me my purse, Mary, and we'll have our little treat." Mary was not disappointed. She gleefully kept her secret. She took the dime her mother gave her and went up to the store to get the two ice cream cones, just as she did on other days. But she was still dreaming of the red leather shoes. By the time she got back to the house, she had eaten most of her own cone. But then she sat down at the end of the kitchen table to enjoy herself watching her mother eat her share of the ice cream. When she was finished and was wiping her fingers with her apron, Mary blurted out, "Are we going to get my shoes now, Mother?"

"Shoes? What shoes?" Mrs. Johnson asked.

"The red leather shoes I've been saving for," Mary said, looking puzzled. "The ones we saw in the window that we talked about."

"Oh. Oh, I see," Mrs. Johnson said slowly, as if she hadn't thought of those shoes since that day months ago. "Why, Mary, have you been thinking of those shoes all this time? I told you at the time, child, that your father was in debt and we couldn't afford such shoes."

"I've got the six dollars saved, haven't I?"

"Well, your father. . . ."

"It's my six dollars, isn't it?"

"Mary, darling, listen. Those shoes are far too old for a little girl like you."

"I'm 12 next month. You know I am."

"Shoes like that are no good for running around, Mary. A pair of good, sensible shoes is what you need, Mary."

"I can wear them on Sunday, can't I?"

"Look, Mary," her mother tried to reason with her, "I know I said I'd get you a pair of shoes. But a good pair of shoes. Proper shoes. Your father is going to have a lot more expenses soon. Why, he'd drop dead if he found I'd paid six dollars for red leather shoes for you."

"You promised I could save the money," Mary whispered. Then she saw that worried expression on her mother's face and knew she was not going to get the shoes. She ran into the bedroom and threw herself on the bed and started to cry. Never in her life had she wanted anything as much as she wanted the red shoes. She felt she had been cheated.

It began to get dark and she was still crying. She heard her mother's slow step coming toward the bedroom. "Mary, listen to me," she said. "Get up and wipe your face, do you hear?" She had her own hat and coat on. "We're going to get those shoes right now," she said.

"You said I couldn't get them," Mary said.

"Don't argue with me," her mother said, sounding somehow far away. "I want you to get them. I say you're going to. Come on."

Mary got up and wiped her face. On the way to the store, her mother's grim, silent way made her feel lonely and guilty. They bought a pair of red leather shoes. As Mary walked up and down in them on the store carpet, her mother

SALE!
UPTO 40% OFF!

William
$5 49
0326300

256

watched, unsmiling. Coming back home, Mary longed for her mother to speak to her. Mrs. Johnson held Mary's hand and walked along, looking straight ahead.

"Now, if only your father doesn't make a fuss," Mrs. Johnson said when they were standing together in the hall, listening. They heard Mr. Johnson in the living room. In the last few months, Mary had grown afraid of her father. She did not understand why he had become so moody and short-tempered. Mary began to get scared. "Go on into the bedroom," Mrs. Johnson whispered to her. She followed Mary into the bedroom and put the red shoes on her feet. It was a strangely quiet, secret little ceremony. Mrs. Johnson's breathing was heavy. "Now, don't you come in until I call you," she warned Mary.

For a while she heard only the sound of her mother's quiet voice, and then suddenly her father cried angrily, "Are you serious? Money for that at a time like this! You'll take them back, do you hear?" But her mother's voice flowed on, the one quiet voice, slow and even. Then there was a long and strange silence. "Mary, come here," her father suddenly called.

"Come on and show your father your shoes, Mary," her mother urged her.

The new shoes squeaked as Mary went into the living room. They felt like heavy weights that might not let her escape her father's anger. Her father was sitting at the little table by the light and Mary watched his face.

Her father did not seem to be looking at the shoes. With a kind of pain in his

257

eyes he was looking at her. It was as if he saw her for the very first time. "They're fine shoes, aren't they?"

"Can I keep them? Can I really?" Mary asked breathlessly.

"Why, sure you can," he said quietly.

Mary intended to wear the shoes to church that Sunday, but it rained. She put them back in the box and decided to wait a week. But in the middle of the week her father told her that her mother was going to the hospital for an operation.

"Is it for the pains in her legs?" Mary asked.

"Well, you see, Mary, if everything comes off all right," her father answered, "she may not have any pains at all."

It was to be an operation for cancer. The doctor said the operation was successful, but Mrs. Johnson died under the anaesthetic. The two older sisters and Mr. Johnson kept saying, "But she looked all right. She looked fine." They all went home. They seemed to huddle first in one room and then in another. They took turns trying to comfort Mary, but no one could console her.

On the night when they were arranging things for the funeral, Mary blurted out, "I'm going to wear my red shoes."

"Have some sense, Mary. That would be terrible," Helen said.

"You can't wear red shoes," Barbara said crossly.

"Yes, I can," Mary said stubbornly. "Mother wanted me to wear them. I know she did. I know why she bought them."

Mr. Johnson looked at Mary with the same puzzled, gentle expression he had on his face the night his wife had talked to him about the shoes. "I kind of think Mary's right," he said.

"Red shoes. That would be terrible," said Helen, now outraged.

"Well, I guess that's right. All the relatives will be there," Mr. Johnson said. Then he turned hopefully to Mary. "Look Mary," he began. "If you get the shoes dyed, you can wear them to the funeral and then you'll be able to wear them to school every day. How about it?"

Mary didn't like to think that anyone might say she hadn't shown the proper respect for her mother. She got the red shoes and handed them to her father. "It's just what people might say. Do you see, Mary?" he said.

When the shoes were returned to Mary the next day, she put them on slowly. Then she put her feet together and looked at the shoes a long time. They were no longer the beautiful red shoes. Yet she stared at them and felt a strange kind of secret joy. She felt certain that her mother had gotten her the shoes so that she might understand at this time that she still had her special blessing and protection.

At the funeral the shoes hurt Mary's feet. They were new and hadn't been worn. Yet she was glad she had them on. After that she wore them every day. She was careful with them. Every night she polished them and looked at them and was touched again by that secret joy. She wanted them to last a long time.

READING COMPREHENSION

Summarizing. Choose the best phrase to complete each sentence. Then write the complete statements on your paper.

1. Mary did the housework because her mother was _____ (busy with other children, too sick, busy at her job).

2. When Mary's mother told her she couldn't have the red shoes, Mary _____ (went shopping, didn't care, went to her room and cried).

3. Mary's family wanted her to dye her shoes black because _____ (red was not proper for a funeral, the shoes were scuffed, they didn't match her dress).

4. Mary agreed to dye her shoes black because she _____ (thought they would look prettier, didn't like the color red anymore, didn't want people to say she was not respectful).

Interpreting. Write the answer to each question on your paper.

1. What reasons did Mrs. Johnson give Mary for not getting the new red shoes?

2. Why had Mary's father changed and become so moody and short-tempered?

3. Why did Mary want the shoes to last a long time?

For Thinking and Discussing. Why do you think Mrs. Johnson changed her mind and allowed Mary to buy the red shoes?

UNDERSTANDING LITERATURE

Theme. In every story, the author tries to convey a central thought, or message. This message is called the *theme* of the story. The theme is developed throughout the story but is seldom stated directly.

Sometimes authors use a symbol to help develop the theme in a story. Here is a list of what the red shoes might stand for in "Very Special Shoes." On your paper, write those things you believe the red shoes symbolize.

a. the need to buy practical things

b. a promise that must not be broken

c. Mary's mother's love and protection

d. the death of Mary's mother

e. parents' understanding of their children

Use your understanding of the symbolism of the red shoes to help you choose the more appropriate theme of "Very Special Shoes" from the pair below. Explain your choice briefly.

1. Children should honor parents.

2. The love between parents and children is developed through understanding and compromise.

WRITING

Choose one theme from the pair above. Then outline the plot of a very short story that would convey this new theme. Include some information about the characters and the setting.

Letter to a Black Boy

by Bob Teague

Bob Teague is a well-known television newscaster. After his son Adam was born, Teague began writing him a series of letters. The letters describe Teague's childhood memories and his feelings about growing up black in America. Through these letters, Teague hoped to give his son an understanding of family roots and relationships.

The following is one of the letters Teague wrote. In it, he describes his Aunt Letty, who raised Teague after his mother died.

Dear Adam,

I was a bit miffed today by your response to me when the Tall Lady went shopping and left us alone. ("Tall Lady" is the name you call your mother.) No matter what games I devised, you made it clear that you would not be satisfied till she returned.

Every five minutes, it seemed, you would break off whatever you were doing and crawl to the front door. "Taw Lady? Taw Lady?" was the only question you could phrase. You would remain at the door—a questioning look on your face—until I opened it to prove that she was not just beyond it in the hallway. I also tried to explain that she had gone to the supermarket. But you had no idea what your daddy was driving at. You must have repeated that routine a dozen times.

Anyway, new fathers are sensitive about things like that. It makes them feel useless.

Not that I don't fully understand your point of view. Daddies are seldom there when you need them. Mothers, on the other hand, are dependable. Furthermore, they have the patience for the hundred tiny details so important to your sense of well-being. I felt exactly the same way about the only mother I ever knew, Aunt Letty.

When my real mother died giving birth to me, Aunt Letty, her sister, dropped whatever she was doing in Detroit, and came to live with me and my daddy in Milwaukee. I never did find out what it was she left behind. Her reasoning, I gathered years later, was that to know might have given me a feeling of guilt. Or of being in her debt.

Whatever it was, Aunt Letty seemed to have no regrets. She plunged into the job of helping a squalling black infant to grow up. She stayed with us until I went away to college at 17.

By then she had taught me what I still regard as the most important lesson a black boy has to learn. She convinced me that life was much larger than the limits imposed on us for the color of our skins; that I must keep in mind that my world is bigger than the boundaries of the ghetto; that it is a world of different pains and pleasures, beauty and ugliness, victories and defeats that all people, everywhere, come to know. She taught me to dream beyond my blackness.

Years later, she taught the entire family how to make a common dream come true.

During the Thanksgiving Day recess of my sophomore year in college, she invited—no, she ordered—the whole clan to dinner. By then, she had won her master's degree and was teaching at a small teachers' college. My daddy and I drove 300 miles in his 1937 Chevrolet to see her in Detroit.

When we arrived at Aunt Letty's four-room apartment on Twelfth Street in the ghetto, the others were already there. I met 14 strangers—relatives I had never seen. But I felt our kinship immediately. Three of the men and two of the women —my daddy's brothers and sisters—reminded me of him. There was also something in their features—eyes, noses, and chins—that looked like me. Two other women—my mother's sisters—who were standing next to their husbands, showed

a resemblance to the pictures of her my daddy kept. Aunt Kathleen and Aunt Thelma. My daddy's sisters were Aunt Sally and Aunt Minnie, both with husbands. My daddy's brothers, with their wives, were Uncle Mark, Uncle James, and Uncle Claybourn Junior.

Although all of them had children, I

was the only non-adult present. Aunt Letty had told the others to leave their kids at home; that this was an important meeting. I was flattered that she regarded me, at 18, as a man.

Aunt Letty had stuffed three turkeys for the occasion, but her dining room was not big enough for the herd she had invited. We served ourselves from the table, then filled the chairs, the stools, and the couch in the living room. Some of us wound up sitting on the floor.

During the meal, there was much reminiscing among my daddy and his brothers, who had not seen one another for nearly 20 years. I gathered from their

263

as Western movies on Saturday mornings at the Princess Theater.

Finally, when we began eating dessert—sweet potato pie—Aunt Letty made a little speech.

"This is the first time we've been together as a family, but I hope it won't be the last. The thing that prompted me to call you all together was a letter I received a few months ago from James there. He wanted to know if there was anything I could do to help his boy Raymond get to college. In case you haven't heard, Raymond wants to be an airline pilot."

She paused as some of her sisters and brothers-in-law caught their breaths and groaned sympathetically.

"I know what you're thinking," Aunt Letty went on. "It's a terribly big dream for a black boy to have in Tennessee. But I say why not? I say Raymond ought to have his chance to follow his dream. I say that's what living is all about. I say chances are that boy will wind up in a foundry just like his father unless he gets that chance. Now none of us at this moment can afford to send anybody to college. It's terribly expensive. But if we stick together as a family, we can send them all, one or two at a time."

She went on to explain her idea of a fund that each branch of the family would contribute to every year to guarantee college for every child who dreamed of going. She didn't bother asking for a vote. She could tell from the looks on our faces — and from the tears in the women's eyes — that she was providing the answer to many prayers.

talk that their daddy — my grandfather Claybourn—had been a tough old codger when they were boys together in Tennessee. Almost every story ended with "and then Poppa Claybourn whupped me till I couldn't sit down." Laughter. I was glad that my daddy remembered those "whuppings." It explained why he had spanked me less than a dozen times when I was a boy. As a rule, he had punished me instead by denying privileges—such

READING COMPREHENSION

Summarizing. Choose the best phrase to complete each sentence. Then write the complete statements on your paper.

1. Aunt Letty came to take care of Bob Teague, the author, when his mother _____ (died giving birth to him, went to work, went on vacation).

2. The most important lesson that Aunt Letty taught the author was that _____ (he should be satisfied with what he had, he should not allow himself to be limited by the color of his skin, his family was important).

3. The "common dream" that Aunt Letty helped to come true was _____ (sending the author to college, setting up a college fund for the younger members of the family, establishing annual family reunions).

Interpreting. Write the answer to each question on your paper.

1. Why didn't Aunt Letty tell Bob what she had left behind in order to come look after him?

2. What did the author mean when he said mothers are dependable?

3. Why did all the family members agree to contribute to a college fund if money was scarce?

For Thinking and Discussing. What lesson do you think Bob Teague hopes his son will learn from Aunt Letty?

UNDERSTANDING LITERATURE

Theme and Main Idea. You learned earlier in this book about main ideas and details. Every paragraph is developed around a main idea which is supported by details presented in the paragraph. In the same way, every article or story is built around an overall theme. The main ideas and details in the different paragraphs support and illustrate this overall theme.

The theme of "Letter to a Black Boy" is closely related to the lessons that Aunt Letty taught the author. These lessons are the main ideas of the piece.

Below are some of the ideas that Aunt Letty believed in. Find and write details from the letter that support each of the ideas. Then use your list of main ideas and details to write a brief explanation of the story's theme.

a. You are not owed anything in return for kindness.

b. You must work hard to get what you want in life.

c. Families should stick together.

d. There are no limits to what you can do or become.

WRITING

Imagine that you have a child of your own. Think about a lesson you learned from someone when you were younger. Write a letter to your child about this lesson so the child can learn from it.

Celebration

by Alonzo Lopez

I shall dance tonight.
When the dusk comes crawling,
There will be dancing
   and feasting.
I shall dance with the others
   in circles,
     in leaps,
       in stomps.
Laughter and talk
   will weave into the night,
Among the fires
   of my people.
Games will be played
And I shall be
   a part of it.

1. What is the overall feeling of the poem?
What words does the speaker use to help you
feel this mood?

2. Why is dancing an important part of the
celebration? What kinds of emotions can
people show when they dance?

266

The Troublemaker

from All Things Wise and Wonderful *by James Herriot*

Wesley Binks is a troublemaker. One of his victims is Dr. James Herriot, a veterinarian. But a remarkable change comes over Wesley when his dog, Duke, gets sick. Wes's relationship with Duke is the best one in his life. Can a sick little dog change a troublemaker? And can Dr. Herriot, the writer of this true account, save Duke?

Wesley Binks, 10 years old, liked to play tricks on me. He'd put firecrackers through our mail slot in the door, ring the doorbell, and run away. When I'd answer the door, the firecracker would explode at my feet.

Sometimes he put garbage through the mail slot. Sometimes he tore the flowers out of our garden. Sometimes he chalked rude messages on my car.

I wasn't his only victim. He stole food from the grocer. He skipped school. He made nasty remarks to adults.

His greatest triumph must have been the time he took the grating from the coal cellar beside our front steps. There was going to be a parade through town that day. Members of the parade were lining up in front of our house. Spectators were on the sidewalks.

My wife and I went outside to watch the parade. I waved to several people. Then I happened to move to the left, where the grating should have been—and slid into the cellar.

I wish I had slid *all* the way into the cellar. But I got stuck, so that my shoulders and head were still in view.

One or two people looked alarmed. But most people couldn't help laughing. I was helpless and very embarrassed.

It took two men to pull me out. Then I saw Wesley Binks grinning wickedly at me. It was now clear who had taken the grating.

I learned from my wife that Wesley's father had left home when the boy was six. His mother had married again. Wesley lived with her and his stepfather in the poorest part of town.

It was about a week later when I saw Wesley sitting all alone in the waiting room of the animal hospital. Alone, that is, except for a skinny black dog in his lap.

I pulled on a white coat and went in.

"Well, what can I do for you?" I asked coldly.

The boy stood up. The look on his face showed it wasn't easy for him to

come here. I led the way along the passage to the consulting room.

"Put him on the table, please," I said. As he lifted the little animal, I thought now was my chance to discuss recent events. Nothing nasty. I would just say something like, "What's the idea of all those tricks you play on me?" But when I took my first look at the dog, everything else left my mind.

He was a big puppy and a mongrel. He had a friendly face.

But I could see he had distemper. Yellow fluid was in the corners of his eyes. His nose was running, too. He blinked painfully at the light.

"I didn't know you had a dog," I said. "How long have you had him?"

"A month. A feller got him from the dog-and-cat home. Sold him to me."

"I see." I took the temperature and was not surprised to find it was 104° F.

"How old is he?"

"Nine months."

That was just about the worst age for a dog to get distemper. I asked all the usual questions but I knew the answers already.

Yes, the dog had been slightly sick for a week or two. No, he wasn't really ill, but weak and sometimes he coughed. When the eyes and nose began to run, the boy brought him here. That was when we usually saw these cases—when it was too late.

As Wesley answered my questions, he looked as though he expected me to hit him at any moment. But as I looked at

269

him, any angry feelings I may have had left me quickly. I saw how neglected he was. His elbows stuck out through holes in his shirt. His trousers were ragged and dirty. He smelled as though he hadn't washed for months.

When he had answered my questions he asked, "What's the matter with him?"

I hesitated. "He's got distemper."

"What's that?"

"Well, it's a serious disease. He must have gotten it from another sick dog."

"Will he get better?"

"I hope so. I'll do the best I can for him." I didn't want to tell him that his pet was probably going to die.

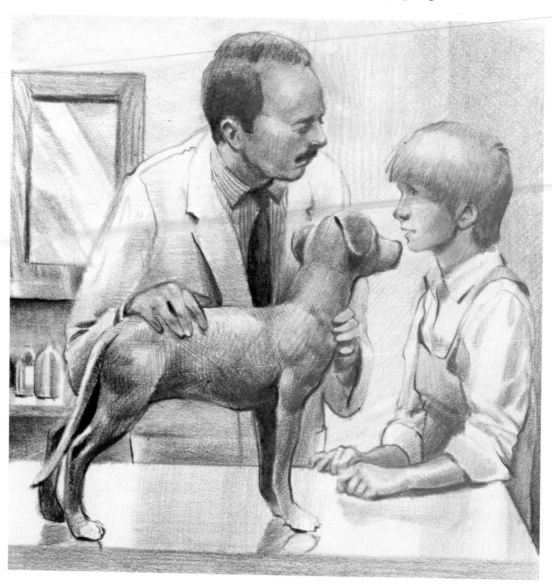

I filled a needle and gave the dog a shot. The dog whimpered a little. Wesley patted him gently.

"It's all right, Duke," he said.

"Is that his name—Duke?"

"Yes." He rubbed the dog's ears and the dog turned, wagged his tail, and licked the boy's hand. Wes smiled and looked up at me. For a moment his tough look was gone. His dark eyes glowed with delight.

I handed him some medicine. "Use this to keep his eyes and nose clean. You can make him a lot more comfortable."

He dropped some money on the table. It was my average charge.

"When should I bring him back?" he asked.

I looked at him doubtfully for a moment. All I could do was repeat the shots but it wasn't going to make the slightest difference.

The boy misread my hesitation.

"I can pay!" he burst out. "I can get the money!"

"Oh, I didn't mean that, Wes. I was just wondering when you should bring him back. How about Thursday?"

The next three weeks saw an incredible change in Wesley Binks. He had been known as an idle troublemaker. But now he was working at all kinds of jobs. He delivered papers in the mornings. He dug people's gardens. I was perhaps the only one who knew he was doing it for Duke.

He brought the dog in every two or three days and paid when he came. I charged him as little as possible. The money he earned went for fresh meat from the butcher and extra milk. These things were for Duke.

"Duke's looking very smart today," I said on one of the visits. "I see you got him a new collar and leash."

The boy nodded shyly, then looked up at me. "Is he any better?"

"Well, he's about the same, Wes. That's how it goes—dragging on without much change."

"When . . . will you know?"

I thought for a moment. Maybe he would worry less if he understood the situation. "The thing is this. Duke will get better if he can avoid getting chorea. That's something that makes the muscles twitch."

"What if he gets it?"

"It's bad in that case. But not all dogs develop it." I tried to smile. "And there's one thing in Duke's favor—he's not a purebred. Crossbred dogs have a thing called hybrid vigor which helps them to fight disease. After all, he's eating fairly well and he's quite lively, isn't he?"

"Yes."

"Well, then, we'll carry on. I'll give him another shot now."

The boy was back in three days and I knew by his face he had some news.

"Duke's a lot better. His eyes and nose have dried up and he's eating like a horse."

I lifted the dog onto the table. There was no doubt he was greatly improved. I did my best to join in the excitement!

"That's great, Wes," I said. But a warning bell was tinkling in my mind. If nervous symptoms were going to develop, this was the time.

I forced myself to be cheerful. "There's no need to come back anymore. Watch him carefully. If you see anything unusual, bring him in."

Wes was overjoyed. He almost pranced along with his pet. I hoped that I would not see them here again.

That was on Friday evening. By Monday I had put the whole thing out of my head until the boy came in with Duke.

"What is it, Wes?"

"He's trembling."

I studied the dog intently. At first I saw nothing. Then as I watched I could see its head nodding. I placed my hand on the top of the skull and waited. And it was there: the slight but regular twitching of the muscles.

"I'm afraid he's got chorea, Wes," I said. "I was hoping it wouldn't happen."

The boy looked suddenly small. He stood there silent, twisting the new leather leash between his fingers. It was so hard for him to speak that he almost closed his eyes.

"Will he die?"

"Some dogs do get over it, Wes." I didn't tell him that I had seen it happen only once. "I've got some pills which might help him. I'll get you some."

During the next two weeks Duke got worse and worse. The twitching spread from his head to his legs. Then he swayed as he walked.

Wes brought him in again and again. I did what I could to make it clear that it was hopeless. But the boy wouldn't give up. He continued with his paper deliveries and his other jobs. He insisted on paying, even though I didn't want his money. Then one afternoon he came in alone.

"I couldn't bring Duke," he muttered. "He can't walk now. Will you come and see him?"

We got into my car. It was a Sunday at about three o'clock. The streets were quiet. He led me up the cobbled yard and opened the door of one of the houses.

The place was filthy. Mrs. Binks was slumped over the kitchen table, reading a magazine. The table was covered with dirty dishes. The sink was filled with them, too.

On a couch under the window, her husband was asleep. Clothes, newspapers, and beer bottles were all over the floor. A radio was playing very loudly.

The only clean, new thing was the dog basket in the corner. I went over and looked at the little animal. Duke was now helpless. His body was very thin and it twitched all over. The sunken eyes had filled up again with yellow fluid.

"Wes," I said, "you've got to let me put him to sleep."

He didn't answer. As I tried to explain, the loud radio drowned my words. I looked over at his mother.

"Do you mind turning the radio down?" I asked.

She jerked her head at Wes. He went over and turned the radio down.

"It's the only thing. Believe me. You can't let him die slowly like this."

He didn't look at me. All his attention was fixed on his dog. Then he raised a hand and I heard his whisper, "All right."

"I promise you he'll feel no pain," I said as I filled the needle. The little dog just sighed before he stopped twitching at last.

"Do you want me to take him away, Wes?"

He looked at me, confused. His mother spoke up. "Yes. Get him out. I never wanted the thing here in the first place." Then she went back to her reading.

I quickly lifted the little dog and went out. Wes followed me and watched as I opened the trunk and laid Duke gently on top of my working coat.

As I closed the trunk he put his hands up to his eyes. His whole body shook. I put my arm across his shoulders. He leaned against me for a moment and sobbed. I wondered if he had ever been able to cry like this—with somebody to comfort him.

But soon he stood back. He wiped the tears from his face.

"Are you going back into the house, Wes?" I asked.

He blinked and looked at me with his old tough look.

"No!" he said and turned and walked away. He didn't look back and I watched him cross the road, climb a wall, and trail away across the fields toward the river.

It seemed to me that at that moment Wes walked back into his old life. He stopped delivering papers and doing other odd jobs. He never played any more tricks on me. Instead, he started breaking the law. He set barns on fire. By the time he was 13, he was stealing cars.

Finally he left town. Nobody knew where he went. Most people forgot him. But one person who didn't was the police sergeant.

"That young Wesley Binks," he said to me, "was a bad one if ever I saw one. You know, I don't think he ever cared for anybody or anything in his life."

"I know how you feel, sergeant," I replied, "but you're not entirely right. There was one living thing . . ."

READING COMPREHENSION

Summarizing. Choose the best phrase to complete each sentence. Then write the complete statements on your paper.

1. When Wesley was 10, he was already known as a troublemaker because he _____ (played mean tricks on people, stole cars, broke into people's homes).

2. Mr. Herriot knew that Wesley's dog had distemper _____ (after he took Duke's temperature, when Wesley answered his questions, as soon as he saw Duke's eyes and nose).

3. When Duke began to tremble, Mr. Herriot knew that he _____ (was getting better, would probably die soon, could still get well with care and medicine).

4. Wesley's mother said that _____ (she was sorry the dog had died, they should get another dog to replace Duke, she never wanted the dog in the house in the first place).

5. After Duke was put to sleep, Wesley _____ (began playing mean tricks again, decided to be good to others, began breaking the law).

Interpreting. Write the answer to each question on your paper.

1. What were some of the tricks Wesley played on Mr. Herriot?

2. Why did Mr. Herriot decide not to say anything to Wesley about the tricks he played?

3. Why didn't Duke have a very good chance of surviving distemper?

4. How did Wesley prove that he could be a responsible person?

5. Why did Wesley change after Duke died?

For Thinking and Discussing

1. How do you think Wesley's home and family life contributed to his becoming a troublemaker?

2. What do you think Wesley found in his relationship with Duke that was missing from the rest of his life?

UNDERSTANDING LITERATURE

Theme and Characterization. The theme of a story is sometimes a message about how people live or should live. The theme is seldom stated directly in the story. Instead, it is revealed indirectly by the way the characters act and think.

Through their thoughts and actions, the characters in "The Troublemaker" illustrate the theme: *When individuals feel love and respect, they will act in a loving and respectful way.*

Below are lists of characters and actions from "The Troublemaker." On your paper, match each character and action. Then write a sentence or two explaining how the actions help illustrate the theme.

Characters
1. Wesley
2. Wesley's mother
3. Wesley's dog
4. Mr. Herriot
5. Police sergeant

Actions
a. tried never to show that the situation was hopeless
b. ignored Wesley's feelings
c. showed real affection for Wesley
d. said the boy was a hopeless case
e. tried to change his way of life

WRITING

Suppose that Wesley became Mr. Herriot's assistant. Write a new ending for the account based upon this change.

Since You Left

by Ch'ang Ch'u Ling

Since you left, my lover,
I can't take care of myself.
I do nothing but think of you.
I fade like the waning moon.

1. A waning moon marks the end of a month or a season. How does the image of the waning moon fit the meaning of this poem?

2. What are some other images from nature that could convey the same idea as the waning moon?

Road

by Larry Libby

Don't leave.
Tomorrow I'll show you a road.
It touches the ocean on one end.
    Reaches like a hand.
    Sand fingers to the water.
    It's a walking beach and the sky
    is good.
The road has another hand,
    palm out
    to the north.
    Caresses a forest floor.
    Sprinkles sand in the moss.
    The wind is gentle there
    and rain sounds are violet voices
    speaking past the sea.

It's a barefoot road, but you have to
    walk slow.
There are rocks,
    anyway it's not the sort of road
    for hurrying.
The wind is there
    and it smells like sea-sky
    and sounds warm and cold
    altogether.
After we've walked to the ocean end
    we could go back to the other.
We could spend all day
    or
    as long as you like.
Stay.

1. Does the speaker of this poem make the place he describes sound like a pleasant place to be? What are some of the descriptions that make it sound inviting?

2. How does the speaker of this poem sound? Sad? Lonely? Happy? Like someone in love? Does this poem sound like an invitation for anyone, or for someone special?

Long Walk to Forever

by Kurt Vonnegut, Jr.

A young man invites a young woman to go for a walk—an innocent beginning. But the young man is Absent Without Leave from the Army. The woman is engaged to be married—to someone else. Newt and Catharine haven't seen each other for a year. But their relationship goes back much longer than that. Maybe their long walk is the beginning of an even longer journey.

They had grown up next door to each other. Now they were 20 and had not seen each other for nearly a year. There had always been a warm feeling between them. But there never had been any talk of love.

His name was Newt. Her name was Catharine. In the early afternoon, Newt knocked on Catharine's front door.

Catharine came to the door, carrying a bride magazine. "Newt!" she said. She was surprised to see him.

"Could you come for a walk?" he said. He always talked as though he weren't very interested in what he was saying. It was a way to cover his shyness.

"A walk?" said Catharine.

"One foot in front of the other," Newt said. "Through leaves, over bridges—"

"I didn't know you were in town," she said.

"Just got in this minute," he said.

"Still in the Army, I see," she said, looking at his wrinkled uniform. "I'm getting married, Newt."

"I know," he said. "Let's go for a walk."

"I'm very busy, Newt," she said. "The wedding is only a week away."

"If we go for a walk," he said, "it will make you look rosy. Like the brides in that magazine. That will be my present to Henry Stewart Chasens. By taking you for a walk, I'll be giving him a rosy bride."

"Can—can you come to the wedding, Newt?" she said.

"I doubt it," he said.

"Isn't your leave long enough?" she said.

"I'm what they call A.W.O.L.—Absent Without Leave."

"Oh, Newt!" she said. "Why?"

277

"I had to find out what kind of silverware you were getting," he said. "I plan to give you and your husband a spoon."

"Newt," she said, "tell me really why you came."

"I want to go for a walk," he said.

"Oh, Newt!" she said. "Are you really A.W.O.L.? How did you manage to get here?"

"I hitchhiked," he said. "Two days."

"Does your mother know?" she said.

"I didn't come to see my mother," he said.

"Who did you come to see?" she said.

"You," he said.

"Why me?" she said.

"Because I love you," he said. "Now can we take a walk? One foot in front of the other. Through leaves, over bridges—"

They were taking the walk now, in a woods with a brown leaf floor. Catharine was angry and close to tears.

"What a crazy time to tell me you love me," she said. "You never talked that way before." She stopped walking.

"Let's keep walking," he said.

"No," she said. "I shouldn't have come with you at all."

"But you did," he said.

"To get you out of the house," she said. "If somebody heard you talking this way, a week before the wedding—"

"What would they think?" he said.

"They'd think you were crazy," she said.

"Why?" he said.

Catharine took a deep breath and made a speech. "I'm deeply honored by this crazy thing you did. I'm very fond of you as a friend, Newt. But it's just too late. You've never even kissed me. I don't mean you should do it now. I just mean this is all so unexpected. I don't even know how to react."

"Just walk some more," he said. "Have a nice time."

They started walking again. "How did you expect me to react?" she said.

"I don't know," he said. "I've never done anything like this before."

"Did you think I would throw myself into your arms?" she said.

"Maybe," he said. "But I wasn't counting on it. This is very nice, just walking."

Catharine stopped again. "You know what happens next?" she said. "We shake hands and part friends."

Newt nodded. "All right," he said. "Remember how much I loved you."

Catharine started crying. She turned her back to Newt.

"Why are you crying?" said Newt.

"Anger!" Catharine said. "You have no right—"

"I had to find out," he said.

"If I'd loved you," she said, "I would have let you know before now."

"You would?" he said.

"Yes," she said. "You would have seen it. Women aren't very clever at hiding it."

Newt looked closely at her face. Catharine felt troubled. She realized that what she had said was true. A woman couldn't hide love.

Newt was seeing love now. He kissed her.

"You shouldn't have done that," she said.

"You didn't like it?" he said.

"What did you expect?" Catharine said. "Wild passion?"

"I keep telling you," he said. "I don't know what's going to happen next."

"We say good-bye," she said.

He frowned. "All right," he said.

She made another speech. "I'm not sorry we kissed. That was sweet. We should have kissed. We've been so close. I'll always remember you, Newt. Good luck."

"Thirty days," he said.

"What?" she said.

"Thirty days in the stockade," he said. "That's what one kiss will cost me."

"I'm sorry," she said. "I didn't ask you to go A.W.O.L. You don't deserve a hero's reward for doing something that foolish."

"Must be nice to be a hero," said Newt. "Is Henry Stewart Chasens a hero?"

"He might be, if he got the chance," said Catharine. She noticed that they had begun to walk again. The farewell had been forgotten.

"You really love him?" he said.

"Certainly I love him!" she said. "I wouldn't marry him if I didn't love him!"

"What's good about him?" said Newt.

"Honestly!" she cried, stopping again. "Do you know how rude you're being? Many things are good about Henry! Yes, and many, many, many things are probably bad, too. But that isn't any of your business. I love Henry, and I don't have to defend him to you!"

"Sorry," said Newt. He kissed her again. This time, she wanted him to.

They were in a large orchard now.

"How did we get so far from home?" said Catharine.

"One foot in front of the other," said Newt. "Through leaves, over bridges—"

"I've got to go back now," she said.

"Say good-bye," said Newt.

"Every time I do," said Catharine, "I seem to get kissed."

Newt sat on the grass under an apple tree. "Sit down," he said.

"I won't touch you," he said.

"I don't believe you," she said.

She sat down under another tree. She closed her eyes.

"Dream of Henry Stewart Chasens," he said. "Dream of your wonderful husband-to-be."

"All right, I will," she said. She closed her eyes tighter. Newt yawned.

Catharine almost fell asleep. When she opened her eyes, she saw that Newt really was asleep. He began to snore softly.

Catharine let Newt sleep for an hour. While he slept, she adored him with all her heart.

She came out from under her tree and knelt by Newt.

"Newt?" she said.

"Hm?" he said. He opened his eyes.

"It's late," she said.

"Hello, Catharine," he said.

"Hello, Newt," she said.

"I love you," he said.

"I know," she said.

"Too late," he said.

"Too late," she said.

He stood up and stretched. "A very nice walk," he said.

"I thought so," she said.

"Do we part company here?" he said.

"Where will you go?" she said.

"Hitch into town," he said. "Turn myself in."

"Good luck," she said.

"You, too," he said. "Marry me, Catharine?"

"No," she said.

He smiled and stared at her for a moment. Then he walked away quickly.

Catharine watched him go. She knew that if he stopped and turned, if he called to her, she would run to him. She would have no choice.

Newt did stop. He did turn. He did call.

"Catharine," he called.

She ran to him and put her arms around him. She could not speak.

READING COMPREHENSION

Summarizing. Choose the best phrase to complete each sentence. Then write the complete statements on your paper.

1. Catharine was surprised to see Newt because _____ (she didn't know he was in town, she was getting married in a week, she had told him to stay away).

2. At first, Catharine reacted to Newt's declaration of love with _____ (joy, sadness, confusion and anger).

3. While Newt was asleep, Catharine realized that she _____ (should go home right away, adored him with all her heart, was lost).

4. At the end of the story, Catharine let Newt know that _____ (she loved him, they could never see each other again, she loved Henry Chasens).

Interpreting. Write the answer to each question on your paper.

1. What will happen to Newt when he returns to the army?

2. Why did Catharine continue walking with Newt even though she was angry with him?

3. What would have happened if Newt had not come to see Catharine and taken her on the walk?

For Thinking and Discussing. If Catharine really loved Newt, why do you think she was going to marry someone else?

UNDERSTANDING LITERATURE

Theme and Plot. The theme of a story is developed as the plot develops. In other words, the various events all play a part in revealing the theme. "Long Walk to Forever" is a story about love. But what does the story help readers to understand about love? The theme is that true love can conquer any obstacles put in its way. The love between Newt and Catharine grew as their walk continued. Each step of their walk, each event showed another obstacle to love being conquered.

Here is a list of incidents from the story. On your paper, explain how each incident shows true love conquering an obstacle in its way.

1. Newt convinced Catharine to go for a walk with him.

2. Newt studied Catharine's face.

3. Newt kissed Catharine for the first time.

4. Newt slept under the tree while Catharine watched him.

5. Newt turned and called to Catharine.

WRITING

Newt went A.W.O.L. because he wanted to talk to Catharine face to face. Suppose that they had written letters to each other instead. Write two letters. In the first, have Newt reveal his love and ask Catharine to change her wedding plans. In the second, present her response.

If You Hear That a Thousand People Love You

by Guadalupe de Saavedra

If you hear that a thousand people love
    you
remember . . . saavedra is among them.

If you hear that a hundred people love
    you
remember . . . saavedra is either in the
    first
             or very last row

If you hear that seven people love you
remember . . . saavedra is among them,
like a wednesday in the middle of the
    week

If you hear that two people love you
remember . . . one of them is saavedra

If you hear that only one person loves
    you
remember . . . he is saavedra

And when you see no one else around
    you,
   and you find out
   that no one loves you anymore,
   then you will know for certain
   that . . . saavedra is dead

1. How would you feel if someone you love sent you this poem? Why? How do people hear that other people love them? Do you think people count the number of people who love them?

2. Why do you think the poet speaks of himself in the third person (*saavedra*) instead of in the first person (*I*)? What effect does the repetition of the poet's name have on the mood of the poem?

Take Over, Bos'n!

by Oscar Schisgall

The survivors of the wrecked Montala *are half-crazed
from too much sun and not enough drinking water. But
they would never have lasted this long without the man
they hate—the man with the gun. . . .*

Hour after hour I kept the gun
pointed at the other nine men. From the
lifeboat's stern, where I'd sat most of the
twenty days of our drifting, I could keep
them all covered. If I *had* to shoot at such
close quarters, I wouldn't miss. They realized that. Nobody jumped at me. But in
the way they all glared I could see how
they'd come to hate my guts.

Especially Barrett, who'd been bos'n's
mate; Barrett said in his harsh, cracked
voice, "You're a dope, Snyder. Y-you
can't hold out forever! You're half asleep
now!"

I didn't answer. He was right. How
long can a man stay awake? I hadn't
dared shut my eyes in maybe seventy-two
hours. Very soon now I'd doze off, and
the instant that happened they'd pounce
on the little water that was left.

The last canteen lay under my legs.
There wasn't much in it after twenty days.
Maybe a pint. Enough to give each of
them a few drops. Yet I could see in their
bloodshot eyes that they'd gladly kill me
for those few drops. As a man I didn't

count anymore. I was no longer third officer of the wrecked *Montala*. I was just a
gun that kept them away from the water
they craved. And with their tongues
swollen and their cheeks sunken, they
were half crazy. . . .

The way I judged it, we must be some
two hundred miles east of Ascension.
Now that the storms were over, the Atlantic swells were long and easy, and the
morning sun was hot—so hot it scorched
your skin. My own tongue was thick
enough to clog my throat. I'd have given
the rest of my life for a single gulp of
water.

But I was the man with the gun—the
only authority in the boat—and I knew
this: once the water was gone we'd have
nothing to look forward to but death. As
long as we could look forward to getting a
drink later, there was something to live
for. We had to make it last as long as possible. If I'd given in to the curses and
growls, if I hadn't brandished the gun,
we'd have emptied the last canteen days
ago. By now we'd all be dead.

The men weren't pulling on the oars. They'd stopped that long ago, too weak to go on. The nine of them facing me were a pack of bearded, ragged, half-naked animals, and I probably looked as bad as the rest. Some sprawled over the gunwales, dozing. The rest watched me as Barrett did, ready to spring the instant I relaxed.

When they weren't looking at my face, they looked at the canteen under my legs.

Jeff Barrett was the nearest one. A constant threat. The bos'n's mate was a heavy man, bald, with a scarred and brutal face. He'd been in a hundred fights, and they'd left their marks on him. Barrett had been able to sleep—in fact, he'd slept through most of the night—and I envied him that. *His* eyes wouldn't close. They kept watching me, narrow and dangerous.

Every now and then he taunted me in that hoarse, broken voice:

"Why don't you quit? You can't hold out!"

"Tonight," I said. "We'll ration the rest of the water tonight."

"By tonight some of us'll be dead! We want it now!"

"Tonight," I said.

Couldn't he understand that if we waited until night the few drops wouldn't be sweated out of us so fast? But Barrett was beyond all reasoning. His mind had already cracked with thirst. I saw him begin to rise, a calculating look in his eyes. I aimed the gun at his chest—and he sat down again.

I'd grabbed my Luger on instinct, twenty days ago, just before running for

the lifeboat. Nothing else would have kept Barrett and the rest away from the water.

These fools—couldn't they see I wanted a drink as badly as any of them? But I was in command here—that was the difference. I was the man with the gun, the man who had to think. Each of the others could afford to think only of himself; I had to think of them all.

Barrett's eyes kept watching me, waiting. I hated him. I hated him all the more because he'd slept. He had the advantage now. He wouldn't keel over.

And long before noon I knew I couldn't fight anymore. My eyelids were too heavy to lift. As the boat rose and fell on the long swells, I could feel sleep creeping over me like paralysis. It bent my head. It filled my brain like a cloud. I was going, going . . .

Barrett stood over me, and I couldn't even lift the gun. In a vague way I could guess what would happen. He'd grab the water first and take his gulp. By that time the others would be screaming and tearing at him, and he'd have to yield the canteen. Well, there was nothing more I could do about it.

I whispered, "Take over, bos'n."

Then I fell face down in the bottom of the boat. I was asleep before I stopped moving. . . .

When a hand shook my shoulder, I could hardly raise my head. Jeff Barrett's hoarse voice said, "Here! Take your share o' the water!"

Somehow I propped myself up on my arms, dizzy and weak. I looked at the men, and I thought my eyes were going. Their figures were dim, shadowy; but

then I realized it wasn't because of my eyes. It was night. The sea was black; there were stars overhead. I'd slept the day away.

So we were in our twenty-first night adrift—the night in which the tramp *Groton* finally picked us up—but now, as I turned my head to Barrett, there was no sign of any ship. He knelt beside me, holding out the canteen, his other hand with the gun steady on the men.

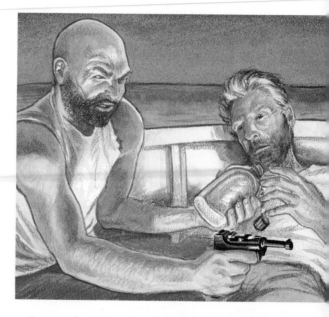

I stared at the canteen as if it were a mirage. Hadn't they finished that pint of water this morning? When I looked up at Barrett's ugly face, it was grim. He must have guessed my thoughts.

"You said, 'Take over, bos'n,' didn't you?" he growled. "I been holdin' off these apes all day." He hefted the Luger in his hand. "When you're boss-man," he added, "in command and responsible for the rest—you—you sure get to see things different, don't you?"

READING COMPREHENSION

Summarizing. Choose the best phrase to complete each sentence. Then write the complete statements on your paper.

1. Snyder held a gun on the men because _____ (they were his prisoners, he wanted to kill them, he was protecting their last canteen of water).

2. Barrett had an advantage over Snyder because _____ (he was the bos'n's mate, he had been able to get some sleep, he had been in over a hundred fights).

3. When Snyder woke up, he learned that _____ (Barrett had taken over Snyder's command, the remaining water had been finished that morning, the *Groton* had finally come to pick them up).

Interpreting. Write the answer to each question on your paper.

1. Why were the men drifting in the lifeboat?

2. According to Snyder, how did the gun save their lives?

3. Why did Snyder want to wait until night to give out the last ration of water?

4. Why was Snyder shocked when Barrett handed him the canteen?

For Thinking and Discussing. What do you think would have happened if Snyder hadn't said "Take over, bos'n"?

UNDERSTANDING LITERATURE

Theme. The central idea, or theme, in a literary work is the message the author is trying to communicate. The theme is usually a general truth or observation about some aspect of life, such as nature, society, or human behavior. Sometimes the theme of a story is directly stated by the author or by one of the characters. Details and events in the story support the theme.

The following questions are about the theme of "Take Over, Bos'n!" Write the answer to each question on your paper. Refer to the story if you need to.

1. How did Snyder use his authority to take responsibility for the other men?

2. Snyder states the theme of the story directly when he says, "But I was in command here—that was the difference. I was the man with the gun, the man who had to think. Each of the others could afford to think only of himself; I had to think of them all." What does this theme mean?

3. Barrett's point of view changed when he took over for Snyder. How did Barrett restate the theme of the story?

WRITING

Think of a time when you were in a position of authority, such as when you babysat. How did your added responsibilities affect the way you acted? Write a paragraph describing your experience.

Section Review

Word Parts. Many English words are made up of several parts. Every word starts with a central part, called the *base word*. Word parts added before the base word are called *prefixes*. Word parts added after the base word are called *suffixes*. Prefixes and suffixes add to or change the meaning of the base word. For example, the word *doubtfully* was used in "The Troublemaker." The word *doubtfully* contains the base word *doubt*, which means "not believing," and the suffixes *-ful* and *-ly*. So *doubtfully* means "in a manner that is full of doubt or not believing."

Look at the italicized word in each sentence below from the selections in this section. On your paper, list the base word of each italicized word and its meaning. Then write the meaning of the whole word.

1. ". . . she watched her mother's face *eagerly*. . . ."

2. "Mothers, on the other hand, are *dependable*."

3. "The boy *misread* my hesitation."

4. "Wes was *overjoyed*. He almost pranced along with his pet."

5. "I just mean this is all so *unexpected*."

Making Inferences. Sometimes when you read, you have to make a logical guess about what a writer means or about what seems to be true. Your guess will be based upon the facts you read and your own experience. Making logical guesses is called "reading between the lines" or *making inferences*.

For example, at the beginning of "Very Special Shoes," you learn that every day Mrs. Johnson seemed to need more sleep. You can infer that she is sick and becoming sicker.

For each question below, choose the best inference to explain why the characters act the way they do. Write the entire statement on your paper.

1. In "Very Special Shoes," Mary's mother was silent when they went to buy the shoes because she _____.
   a. thought the whole idea was silly
   b. knew they couldn't afford them
   c. was angry with Mary

2. Wesley's decision not to go back into his house after the dog died in "The Troublemaker" showed that he _____.
   a. loved his family very much
   b. wanted to get to work quickly
   c. didn't feel loved in his house

3. Barrett guarded the canteen after Snyder fell asleep because he _____.
   a. owed Snyder a favor
   b. felt responsible for the rest
   c. wanted to keep the water for himself

WRITING

A Social Letter. There are a number of reasons you might write a social letter. You might write to say thank you or to invite someone to a party. Or you might simply want to share your experiences with someone who is far away.

Social letters can be very informal. Even so, the four-step writing process can help you make your letters clear and informative. It will also help you write letters that create a good impression.

Step 1: Set Your Goal

Choose one of the following topics for a social letter:

1. Pretend you are Newt in "Long Walk to Forever," back at the Army base to complete your duty. Write a letter to Catherine telling her how happy you are and describing what kind of future you hope to have with her.

2. Pretend you are Wesley in "The Troublemaker." You have been away for some time, and you want to return to town and mend your ways. Write a letter to Mr. Herriot thanking him for helping Duke and asking him for a job.

Step 2: Make a Plan

Think about what you want to say in your letter and jot down your ideas. Then organize your ideas, placing those on the same topic together.

Suppose the narrator of "Take Over, Bos'n!" were to write a letter to a friend about his ordeal at sea. He might come up with the ideas shown below and organize them in these three groups:

☐ Storm wrecked the *Montala*
storm sudden and violent
escaped in lifeboat with nine other men
took my Luger

☐ Spent twenty-one days in lifeboat
suffered from thirst and heat
guarded water and rationed it
men got too weak to row
Barrett threatened my hold on canteen
fell asleep after 72 hours
whispered "Take Over, Bos'n!"

☐ Was rescued
woke to find Barrett had guarded water supply
rescued by *Groton*
recovered

Review your list of the facts and ideas you want to cover in your letter. Add any details you can. Make sure the items are arranged according to topic.

Step 3: Write the First Draft

When you write your letter, each topic that you want to cover should be given a separate paragraph. Each paragraph should have a topic sentence. Other sentences should state the specific points you want to make.

Step 4: Revise

Check your letter to be sure it is well organized and clear. Did you stick to one topic in each paragraph? Will your reader know what you think and how you feel about the topics you covered? Correct any errors in grammar, spelling, and punctuation you find. When you copy your letter over, include all these parts:

Heading: Three lines at the upper right-hand corner with your address and the date.

Salutation: A greeting—usually "Dear"—followed by the name of the person you are writing to.

Body: The actual text of the letter.

Closing: Words such as "Yours," "With love," or "Fondly," followed by your signature.

QUIZ

The following is a quiz for Section 6. Write the answers in complete sentences on your paper.

Reading Comprehension

1. In "Very Special Shoes," why did Mary's mother change her mind and let Mary buy the red shoes?

2. What brought the family together in "Letter to a Black Boy"?

3. In "Celebration," why does the poet feel so happy?

4. What was the one successful relationship that Wesley Binks had in "The Troublemaker"? How did this relationship change the way he acted?

5. In "Long Walk to Forever," why was Catharine reluctant at first to go for a walk with Newt?

Understanding Literature

6. What did the red leather shoes symbolize for Mary Johnson at the beginning of "Very Special Shoes"? What did they symbolize at the end?

7. The theme of "Long Walk to Forever" is that love can conquer all obstacles. In what ways does that theme also apply to "Letter to a Black Boy"?

8. List several incidents from "The Troublemaker" that illustrate that Wesley Binks's actions were affected by how others treated him.

9. In the poem "Road," the road represents love. According to the speaker, how long does it take to develop a strong relationship? What must two people do to develop such a relationship?

10. "Take Over, Bos'n!" has a surprise ending. What in the story led you to believe that the bos'n's mate would not act the way he did?

ACTIVITIES

Word Attack

1. In "Very Special Shoes," Helen felt *outraged* at the idea of Mary wearing red shoes to their mother's funeral. In this word, the prefix *out-* means "more than." *Outraged* means "more than ordinarily angry" or "greatly enraged." Sometimes the prefix *out-* means "better than" or "outside or outward."

Write the meaning of the following words with the prefix *out-*. Use a dictionary to check your answers.

outbid   outcast   outlying

outshine   outfield   outguess

outrank   outrun   outline

outgrow   outdo   outsmart

2. The words below all appear in Section 6. Find and write the base word in each one. Then write a few sentences telling what you think might have happened to Wes in "The Troublemaker" if Duke had recovered from his bout with distemper. Use as many of the base words as you can in your sentences.

relationship   shyness

sympathetically   blackness

eagerly   dependable

overjoyed   helpless

unsmiling   entirely

Speaking and Listening

1. Pretend that like Mary in "Very Special Shoes," you want to convince your parents to let you buy something you don't think they will approve of. Think of the most convincing arguments you can, and present them to a small group in class. Find out from your classmates which arguments they found most convincing.

2. Talk to one of the adults in your family about an interesting family experience that may have happened before you were born or when you were very young. If you want, take notes that will help you remember. Then practice retelling the story, so that you can share it with your classmates.

Researching

1. Find out more about the work of a veterinarian. Go to the library and try to find the answers to these questions:
   a. What kind of schooling must a veterinarian have?
   b. What qualifications must a veterinarian have?
   c. What are some of the areas a veterinarian can specialize in?

2. Look in your library for another survival story such as "Take Over, Bos'n!" Write a report about it to share with the class.

Creating. Write a few sentences to describe the kind of person you think would make an ideal companion for you. What kinds of things would this person like to do? What kinds of things would this person know? Perhaps you think your ideal companion would not be a person but an animal. Describe the animal and tell your reasons for choosing it.

BIOGRAPHY

A biography is like a time machine. It transports you from your own time and place to the world of another person. You experience that person's actions, thoughts, and feelings. You may also learn about your own history and feelings at the same time.

Washington Crossing the Delaware
Emanuel Gottlieb Leutze (1816–1868).
Metropolitan Museum of Art,
Gift of John Stewart Kennedy.

Personal Narrative

A personal narrative is a piece of writing that gives a writer's views about a real person or event. One kind of personal narrative is a biography—the story of someone's life written by another person. The word *biography* comes from the Greek words for "life" and "writing." Usually a biography is the story of a famous person. In reading biographies, you may discover, however, that the lives of famous people are not so different from your own. Even the most successful person has the same kinds of hopes and difficulties that nearly everyone else has.

Biographies often provide readers with a new way of looking at famous people. Readers may decide that the most important aspect of a person's life was not the ability or success that made the person famous. Millions cheered Roberto Clemente because he was a great baseball player. But Clemente's biography shows that his skill at baseball was not the only reason for his greatness.

Biographies may also be written about people who are not famous. Anyone's life story can be interesting if the writer tells the story in a way that makes readers care about the person.

Looking Back

Many biographies are written about people who lived many years or even centuries ago. In "The Story of Little Sure-Shot," Fiona Greenbank tells the story of someone she never knew—Annie Oakley, the sharpshooter who never missed a target. She also writes about a time in which she never lived—100 years ago.

John Dos Passos also looks back in time to describe the events in the life of Thomas Edison. In "The Electrical Wizard," Dos Passos captures the feeling of the era in which the inventor lived.

Biographers must do research to learn about the people they want to write about. In a good biography, the important facts about a person's life are always carefully researched.

Sometimes, however, a writer may guess at small details. Fiona Greenbank describes one of Annie Oakley's amazing shooting performances through dialogue.

> "I didn't think any woman could ever shoot a gun like that," a farmer in the audience marveled. "Nor," he added, "no man either."

Did the author really find an account of what the farmer had said? Probably not. It is likely that she invented his words to give you an idea of how people reacted when they saw Annie shoot. The use of small, invented details like this can create a more vivid picture of the person written about in a biography.

The biographer who writes about a person who lived many years ago has a hard job in some ways. Yet, there are advantages, too. The writer can tell what effect the person's ideas or actions have had on history and explain why or if the person is still remembered.

A Closer Look

Many biographies are written by people living at the same time as their subjects. Even if they have never met the person they are writing about, they are able to talk to people who have and find out important details from them.

Jerry Izenberg was not a close friend of Roberto Clemente, the great baseball player, but he knew how the public felt about Clemente. He had seen him play baseball, and he certainly admired him. In "Clemente—A Bittersweet Story," Izenberg lets you see Clemente through the eyes of his friends. Their love and respect for Clemente as an athlete and a humanitarian are clearly shown in Izenberg's use of quotations in the biography.

An Inside Look

Nikki Giovanni's "400 Mulvaney Street" and "Growing Up" by Russell Baker are a special type of personal narrative—*autobiography*. *Auto* is the Latin word for "self." An autobiography is about the writer's own life. It gives you an inside look at the writer. You share his or her thoughts and emotions. You discover exactly how the writer feels about the events of his or her life. And the writer of an autobiography never has to guess or do research.

Giovanni describes two different times in her life. She tells about going back, as a successful poet, to the place where she grew up. And in a flashback, she recalls her childhood in the same small town.

Reading this account, you learn how Giovanni feels about being invited to her hometown to make a speech. She is flattered. She is also a little nervous. And above all, she is excited to be going home again.

In another selection you will read, Nikki Giovanni writes about her childhood in another way. "Knoxville, Tennessee" is a poem that expresses some of the same feelings as "400 Mulvaney Street." Poetry can be a very intense, personal form of autobiography.

The final selection, "Growing Up," is a humorous account of Russell Baker's boyhood. Baker tells of his mother's ambitions for him. Was there a way his talent could be used to make something of himself? If there was, his mother would find it! And, eventually, so would Baker.

In this section, you will learn about the lives of a sharpshooter, an inventor, a baseball player, a poet, and a humorist. And you may learn a little more about your own life, too.

The Story of Little Sure-Shot

by Fiona Greenbank

Shooting a pistol backward over her shoulder, she could hit a playing card held thin edge out 30 paces behind her. From the back of a galloping horse, she could hit 999 out of a thousand glass targets tossed into the air. She was an Ohio farm girl, an Indian princess, and a legend in her own time. Her picture was on billboards all over Europe and North America. Everyone knew her name. Everyone wanted to meet her.

Fiona Greenbank never met Annie Oakley. But she read books and articles written about her over the last 100 years. From that research, she tells Annie's story once again.

"**L**adies and gentlemen, here she is! The lovely lass of the Western plains! Little Sure-Shot! The one, the only, the unbeatable—Annie Oakley!"

Into the arena of the Wild West Show rode a pretty young woman on a calico pony. She wore a tan deerskin jacket and a skirt trimmed with fringe. Her chestnut hair flowed over shoulders under a broad-brimmed hat. Ahead of her galloped a cowboy on a fast horse. As he rode, he threw targets into the air. The young woman hit every one of them with a bullet from her long rifle.

Then she slipped out of the saddle. A tall, blond young man stepped into the spotlight about 30 paces away from her. A drum rolled, and a bugle-call rang out.

"Now, ladies and gentlemen, the amazing Annie Oakley will shoot a cigarette from her husband's lips!"

The tall man put a cigarette in his mouth and lighted it. The young woman lifted the gun. Crack! The split cigarette fell at the man's feet.

"I didn't think any woman could ever shoot a gun like that," a farmer in the audience marveled. "Nor," he added, "no man, either."

Annie Oakley was the biggest star of her time. There were no films or TV in the late 1800's. But posters and newspaper pictures made her face familiar to fans all over the world. She was pretty, bright, and courageous. But the 19th century was a man's world. Marksmanship was a man's game. And Annie Oakley could outshoot any man who ever dared compete with her. It was a period when women were supposed to be dependent and domestic. Annie Oakley was neither. But instead of resenting her, men loved and respected her for her skill.

Annie was not really a "lass of the Western plains." She had never been west of the Mississippi until she went there to do a show. She was born on a farm in Darke County, Ohio. In the same year, 1860, a man from Illinois was elected President. His name was Abraham Lincoln.

A war was brewing, but it didn't much concern the hard-working Quaker parents of newborn Phoebe Ann Moses. They already had a brood of children to feed. Life was hard, but there were woods to walk in and unpolluted air to breathe. There was love and laughter.

Then Jake Moses caught a fever and died. Besides the land, he left his family one inheritance—a fine long-barrelled rifle. It hung over the fireplace, and it fascinated little Phoebe Ann. When she was four, she tried to lift it. It was taller than she was.

But when she was nine, a neighbor showed her how to load and aim. The little girl was able, now, to lift the gun to her shoulder.

"I'm going to hit that walnut on that bare branch there," she said.

She pulled the trigger. The shattered nut fell to the ground. As the man gasped in wonder, a tiny quail ran across the grass. Phoebe Ann lifted the rifle again. The bird fell, killed with a single shot through the head. The child had hit a moving target less than an inch wide.

From that time on, the Moses family never lacked fresh meat. No animal or bird ever suffered because Phoebe Ann failed to kill it with one quick, perfectly placed shot. The rifle seemed to be a part of the young girl. It sent the bullets precisely where her mind told them to go. Years later, Annie Oakley explained, "You have to feel the target. You can't always see it—you just feel where it is." It was a special, mysterious instinct.

Even with Phoebe Ann's help, Susan Moses found it too hard to raise her children on the farm. She had to take a job, and the family scattered. Some of the children went to live with friends. Phoebe Ann agreed to go with the Edingtons, who managed a county home for orphans. She wasn't an orphan, but it was a long-hoped-for chance to learn to read. Like many pioneer children, Phoebe Ann had never been to school.

The real orphans, hurt by loss and sadness, lashed out at her. They liked to make fun of her name. "Moses-Poses" they would chant, dancing around her. When a Frenchman she met later pronounced it "Mozee," Phoebe Ann began to write and say it that way, too.

One day, a pleasant, well-dressed man and woman drove up to the home. They asked Mrs. Edington to choose a girl to work for them. All she would have to do,

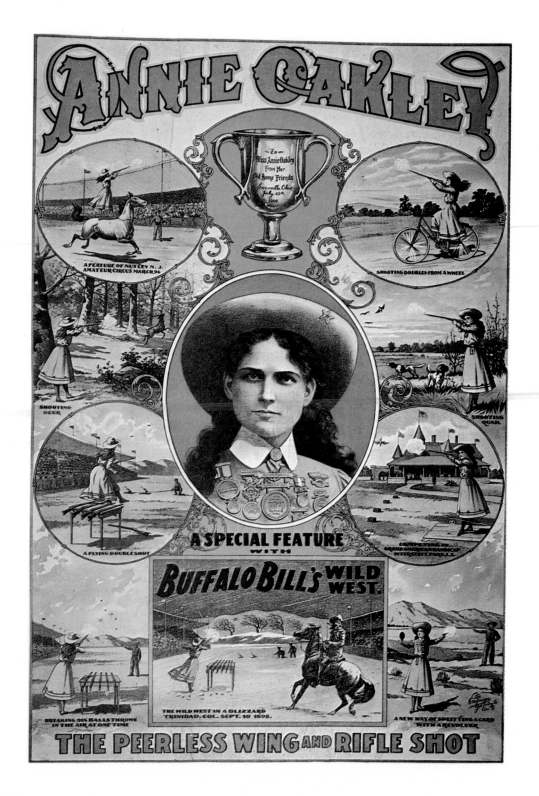

they said, was help take care of their baby. In return, she would live in their lovely tree-shaded farmhouse, and go to the fine school nearby. Unhappy at the taunts of the other children, and hungry for a better education, Phoebe Ann offered to go. She went, smiling, into slavery.

It was Christmas Eve, two years after Phoebe Ann Moses had left the county home. Somewhere, people were singing carols and lighting candles. But Phoebe Ann lay on her face on a rough straw mattress, stifling sobs. She could not lie on her back. It was covered with welts from a brutal beating.

The smooth-talking farmer and his wife seemed to have turned into wild animals. She was their prisoner. The Christmas beating was not the first. They had once even locked her out of the house to spend a night in the snow. She took care of their baby, as she had agreed to do. But she also cooked their meals, scrubbed their floors, hoed corn in their fields, and sewed their clothes. She was given only scraps to eat. Every morning she was forced to get up at four to work in the dark. She had never been near the school they had described. But they wrote letters to her mother telling how happy Phoebe Ann was. Her mother wrote back. Phoebe Ann never saw the letters.

One lucky day the vicious farmer piled his wife and children into his wagon and drove away. Phoebe Ann was alone on the farm. She did not have a cent to her name, or even a coat. But it was now or never. She ran. Gasping for breath, she reached the railroad station. A kind-looking man stood on the platform.

"Please help me!" she cried out to him. Tears streaming down her bruised cheeks, she told him about her life with the "wild animals."

"Where do you want to go?" he asked. "I'll buy your ticket." Phoebe Ann Moses was on her way home.

A lot had changed during her two years in bondage. She had a new stepfather, Joseph Shaw. Though the family was back together, her older sisters had married and moved away. Phoebe Ann was now the oldest child at home.

The rifle still hung over the mantelpiece. By the time she was 15, Phoebe Ann's skill with the gun was the talk of the county. And it was the source of a thriving little business.

She did a brisk trade in fur pelts with a local storekeeper, but quail were her main source of income. The tiny birds were much in demand in the dining rooms of big Cincinnati hotels. But most hunters scattered their shots. When the birds were cooked, diners sometimes broke their teeth on the pellets.

Phoebe Ann Moses could shoot a quail through the head with one clean shot. John Frost, owner of the Bevis House hotel, bought a few of her birds. After that, he would serve quail shot by no other hunter. Soon Phoebe Ann was able to help pay off the mortgage on the family farm.

Though her birds went regularly to Cincinnati, Phoebe Ann had never seen the city. Her sister Lyda lived there with her husband, Joseph Stein. They invited the young girl to visit them.

Phoebe Ann was thrilled by the colorful, growing town. As a special treat the Steins took her to dinner at the Bevis House, where she saw her own quail on the menu. Someone told Frost that his country marksman was in the dining room. He could hardly believe it when the crack shot turned out to be a pretty, gray-eyed girl just 15 years old.

It gave him an idea. Frank Butler, a native of Ireland, but one of the most famous marksmen in America, was in town. He was slated to give a demonstration of his skill. And he also liked to compete against local marksmen. Butler had advertised for someone to shoot against him, but no one had dared to take up his challenge. "How about Phoebe Ann Moses?" Frost asked.

On Thanksgiving Day, Phoebe Ann Moses arrived at Shooter's Hill in Fairmont, Ohio. Frost introduced her to Frank Butler. The handsome, 25-year-old Irishman took off his hat and asked, "Did you come to watch me shoot, Missy?" When he learned that she was his opponent, he laughed with delight. Of course, she couldn't win. But shooting against a pretty young girl would be a real crowd-pleaser.

The targets were clay pigeons, tossed into the air for the marksmen to hit. Annie matched Butler bird for bird. Finally he missed. The next pigeon would decide the match. Annie hit it. She had beaten Frank Butler.

And she had hit him in the heart. Butler went back on the road with his rifle. But he couldn't forget "the little girl with the raindrops in her eyes," as he came to call her. Letters poured into the Moses farmhouse. A year later Phoebe Ann signed her name "Moses" for the last time—on her marriage certificate.

Legally, she was Mrs. Frank Butler. But as a performer she needed her own identity. She had always liked the name of a Cincinnati suburb near her sister's home. She lengthened Ann to Annie and added "Oakley."

On theater programs all over the Middle West, the marvelous marksmen "Butler and Oakley" were featured. It was a hectic life, but they loved it. Riding dusty trains from city to city, staying in shabby actors' hotels, shooting at targets to the applause of all kinds of people—they wanted nothing else. Annie and Frank planned to perform in vaudeville until they were old and gray, with plenty of money and plenty of memories. Between shows Frank helped Annie catch up on her neglected schoolwork.

After a matinée in 1884, a man came backstage with an offer. Would they like to appear in the Sells Brothers Circus, the biggest show in America? Frank and Annie looked at each other and nodded. But the man was saying more. There would have to be some changes in the act. Butler was good, but male marksmen were a dime a dozen. Annie was the attraction. Could she ride into the ring on a horse? Could she shoot from horseback?

And would Frank Butler be willing to load her guns, hold her targets—take second place?

Some men of the 1880's would have shouted "No!" and dragged their wives away. But Frank Butler was secure. He knew he was a top marksman. He also knew his wife was a better shot than he was. Professionally, he never shot a gun again. He became the manager of the famous Annie Oakley.

In the circus, jugglers tossed colored balls, tumblers turned somersaults, clowns did crazy stunts. There was even a performing hippopotamus. Annie's display of super-shooting was just one of the acts. But another kind of show was growing popular in America. A famous buffalo hunter and soldier, William "Buffalo Bill" Cody, had started something new. His Wild West Show was not just entertainment. It was a slice of living history. It recreated an exciting yesterday that some people in the audience had lived through. Everyone else wished they had.

Out in the arena, Indians fought real-looking battles with U.S. soldiers. Stagecoaches and wagon trains were attacked by outlaws and saved by good guys. Cowboys roped steers. Indians did rain dances.

Frank Butler went to Cody's second-in-command. "My wife is the best markswoman in the world," he said. "We'd like to join your show."

Annie Oakley was in her 20's, but she looked 16. She was just five feet tall and weighed 98 pounds. She was sweet-faced and feminine. Her gray eyes were fearless, but her speech was soft. All her life, she was to seem like a modest, good-hearted sister or mother—who was also, somehow, a superstar.

Before Cody's men saw Annie shoot, they doubted. Afterward they cheered. Buffalo Bill took off his wide-brimmed hat. His long hair tumbled to his shoulders as he cried, "Sharp shooting, Missy!"

Annie Oakley appeared in Buffalo Bill's Wild West Show for 17 years. She traveled 170,000 miles. In that time, she missed exactly four performances—when she was at death's door from blood poisoning.

Her act was always the same. No one wanted it different, even after seeing it a dozen times. She rode in on horseback, shooting targets thrown into the air. She shot from the saddle and on foot. There was no gun she could not use, no object she could not hit. Shooting the cigarette from Butler's lips was one example. Another was her playing-card shot. Butler would stand, holding a playing-card, *thin edge* out. Annie would stand 30 paces away, her back to him. In one hand, she held a gun. In the other, she held a polished knife. Sighting the almost invisible edge of the playing card in the narrow knife blade, she would shoot backward over her shoulder. The card would split in half.

The miles stretched across America. They stretched across the Atlantic—to England, to Germany, to Paris, to Rome, to Spain. The Wild West Show became a world-wide sensation. And so did "Missy."

Annie performed for Queen Victoria, who pinned a medal on her blouse and told her, "You're a clever little girl." Victoria's grandson, Kaiser Wilhelm of Germany, insisted on taking Frank Butler's place. He lit a cigarette, put it in his mouth, and Annie shot it away.

Later, when World War I broke out, the German Emperor became America's arch-enemy. It was rumored that Annie wrote him a letter, saying she wished she had aimed an inch to the right.

An African king was supposed to have offered Buffalo Bill 100,000 French francs to borrow Annie. He wanted her to kill off the man-eating leopards that pestered his lands. A Russian grand duke, famed for marksmanship, challenged her to a contest. Annie won easily. Gossip said that one of Queen Victoria's daughters might have married him if he had beaten Annie Oakley.

A great Indian chief and warrior had been persuaded to join the other Indians in Cody's show. Sitting Bull had defeated the U.S. Army at the famous battle of Little Big Horn. General George Custer had lost his life at this "last stand." Many people thought the Wild West Show was a shameful comedown for a great man. But the chief didn't see it that way. He needed money, and here was money to be made. Even so, he was not much pleased when the audience jeered him as Custer's murderer. He sat still and stiff-faced among his Sioux warriors until Annie Oakley galloped out and be-

gan to shoot. Thrilled, the chief cried out in the Sioux language, "Wan-tan-yeya Ci-sci-la!" It means, "Little Sure-Shot." It became one of Annie's most famous nicknames. And Annie became Sitting Bull's adopted daughter. Phoebe Ann Moses of Darke County, Ohio, was now a princess of the Sioux nation. It was not just publicity. The old chief loved her. He thought of her as his true daughter until he died, five years later.

In 1893, Annie and Frank Butler decided it was time to build a home. They had performed many times in New York City, which had amusing memories for them. One was a sleigh ride down snowy Fifth Avenue on a winter day. Instead of a horse, they had harnessed Jerry, the show's tame moose, to the sleigh. A moose does not moo—it trumpets. Jerry had lifted his huge head with its yard-wide antlers and trumpeted loudly. Then he had broken into a fast run. Shoppers had also run—for cover. Horses had neighed, children had screamed with joy. Fifth Avenue did not forget Annie Oakley's sleigh ride for a long time.

Nutley, New Jersey, was a town only 12 miles from New York. In that year, it was still surrounded by a thick forest. It reminded the Butlers of Darke County. They sank their savings into building a corner house on Grant Avenue.

Annie was 33 and still looked 17. She had no plan to retire from the Wild West Show. But, during vacations, she planted flowers, polished silver, and cooked. She and Frank became popular members of Nutley's small artists' colony. She also gave exhibitions of marksmanship to help local charities.

Just before Halloween, 1901, the Wild West Show was finishing its annual season. In Charlotte, North Carolina, the performers boarded the show train a little after midnight. Only one more stop, one more show. Then home. Annie and Frank, in their stateroom, talked dreamily of Nutley. Frank had to talk a bit louder than he once had. Daily gunfire had left Annie, now 41, a little deaf.

The Butlers drifted off to sleep. The train pulled out into the cold, fall night, headed for Virginia. Two-and-a-half hours later, there was a crash of iron, and a terrible hissing sound. Frank, jolted awake, cried, "Annie!"

"I'm all right," she said, weakly. Frank helped her out of the wrecked stateroom.

On the track, staring at the tangled metal of the shattered cars, stood Buffalo Bill. Steam hissed and swirled around him. His white hair was wild. He wore a purple dressing gown and held a rifle. One of the star horses of the show lay writhing in pain. Cody lifted the gun to end the animal's suffering. Annie Oakley swayed against her husband and fainted as the shot rang out.

Two engines had met head on on the track. No one was killed. But Annie Oakley spent months in the hospital. She left with a leg stiff in a steel brace, leaning on a cane. Her chestnut hair had turned as white as Buffalo Bill's. Her left side was half-paralyzed.

Spring and summer slipped away. One day, in the autumn, Annie took a walk

through the fallen leaves on Nutley's streets. She stopped at the gun club. A young attendant watched nervously as she lifted a rifle for the first time since the wreck. Could she balance on her braced leg? Would her numb shoulder support the gun? He threw a target into the air. Annie Oakley hit it, dead center.

Her Wild West Show days were over. But ahead was a starring role in a stage play, *The Western Girl*. Playing a markswoman, she proved that she was still the best in the world. Ahead, too, were exhibitions of shooting to make money for the Red Cross during World War I. Just ahead was a battle of another kind.

In 1903, a Chicago drug addict was arrested for theft. She claimed to be Annie Oakley.

Annie exploded. In all her years of fame, her name had been free of scandal. She sued every newspaper that had printed the story. Nearly 50 papers were found guilty of libel, and Annie collected many thousands of dollars.

Her victory was not winning the money. It was the effect it had on American journalism. Newspapers at that time were careless in checking the facts they printed. After the Oakley case, reporters were ordered to find proof of what they wrote. Many innocent people were saved pain and shame by Annie Oakley's strong sense of justice.

Past 60, Annie Oakley shot a rattlesnake through the head with one shot during a vacation in Florida. She went on proving her uncanny skill until her hip was broken in a car accident in 1922.

Frank took her home to Ohio. There doctors found that she was suffering from a blood disease that could not be cured. The great and famous visited her, wrote to her, and wrote about her. Will Rogers called her "a greater character than she is a rifle shot. . . . Annie Oakley's name, her lovable traits, her thoughtful consideration of others, will live as a mark for any woman to shoot at."

Annie was proud of such tributes. But she was more pleased by letters and visits from her "children"—18 orphaned girls whom she had loved and put through school.

On a November day in 1926, Annie died in her sleep. Frank followed her, 20 days later. In another November, 51 years before, they had met on Shooter's Hill.

In the 1940's, Ethel Merman starred in a hit musical on the Broadway stage. *Annie Get Your Gun* was about Annie Oakley and Frank Butler. It was tuneful and dramatic. But it was not entirely true to the facts. In the show, Annie deliberately missed a shot, and lost a shooting match, to let Frank win and save his pride. In real life, Frank would not have been proud of that. He loved Annie just as she was—a winner, honest, a straight-shooter all the way. And so did the world.

READING COMPREHENSION

Summarizing. Choose the best phrase to complete each sentence. Then write the complete statements on your paper.

1. Annie first learned to shoot when she was _____ (four years old, nine years old, 15 years old).

2. During her childhood, Annie spent two years working for _____ (a minister and his wife, her uncle, a cruel farmer and his wife).

3. Annie stopped traveling with the Wild West Show because she _____ (had made enough money, was tired of the work, was hurt in a train crash).

4. After Annie stopped performing in the Wild West Show, she _____ (starred in *The Western Girl*, wrote *Annie Get Your Gun*, ran the Wild West Show).

Interpreting. Write the answer to each question on your paper.

1. What did Annie's father leave his family when he died?

2. What was unusual about Frank Butler becoming Annie's manager?

3. Why was "Little Sure-Shot" such a good nickname for Annie Oakley?

4. Why did Annie sue the newspapers that printed the story about the drug addict claiming to be Annie?

5. What does the author think Frank Butler would have objected to in the musical *Annie Get Your Gun*?

For Thinking and Discussing

1. In what ways do you think Annie Oakley seemed like a modern woman, even though she was born in 1860?

2. Why do you think people in the late 1800's liked Wild West shows so much?

UNDERSTANDING LITERATURE

Point of View. The *point of view* of a story is the angle from which it is told. A story can be narrated from either a *first-person* (inside) or *third-person* (outside) point of view.

Read the following statements from "The Story of Little Sure-Shot." On your paper, tell whether Annie Oakley could have made the comment herself in a *first-person* autobiography, or whether it could only have been made by someone else for a *third-person* biography. Explain why the information could or couldn't have come from Annie Oakley herself.

1. "But instead of resenting her, men loved and respected her for her skill."

2. "Unhappy at the taunts of the other children and hungry for a better education, Phoebe Ann offered to go."

3. "Some men of the 1880's would have shouted 'No!' and dragged their wives away. But Frank Butler was secure."

4. "Queen Victoria . . . told her, 'You're a clever little girl.'"

5. "In the 1940's, Ethel Merman starred in a hit musical . . . *Annie Get Your Gun*. . . ."

WRITING

Rewrite one incident from the biography as if Annie Oakley were telling it from a first-person point of view.

The Electrical Wizard

by John Dos Passos

Thomas A. Edison was the greatest inventor of all time. His inventions ranged from a stock tickertape machine, to the incandescent lamp, to the phonograph, to the movie projector, to the manhole. He was always experimenting, always trying something new.

In this unusual biographical sketch of Edison, John Dos Passos tries to capture some of the excitement and special qualities of the "Wizard of Menlo Park."

Edison was born in Milan, Ohio, in 1847.

Milan was a little town on the Huron River that for a while was the wheat shipping port for the whole Western Reserve. The railroads took away the carrying trade. So the Edison family went up to Port Huron in Michigan to grow up with the country.

His father was a shinglemaker who puttered round with various speculations. He dealt in grain and feed and lumber and built a wooden tower a hundred feet high. Tourists and excursionists paid a quarter each to go up the tower and look at the view over Lake Huron and the St. Clair River. And Sam Edison became a solid and respected citizen of Port Huron.

Thomas Edison went to school for only three months because the teacher thought he wasn't very bright. His mother taught him what she knew at home and read 18th century writers with him— Gibbon and Hume and Newton, and let him rig up a laboratory in the cellar.

Whenever he read about anything, he went down in the cellar and tried it out.

When he was 12 he needed money to buy books and chemicals; he got a concession as news-butcher (seller) on the daily train from Detroit to Port Huron. In Detroit there was a public library and he read it.

He rigged up a laboratory on the train and whenever he read about anything, he tried it out. He rigged up a printing press and printed a paper called *The Herald*. When the Civil War broke out he organized a news service and cashed in on the

big battles. Then he dropped a stick of phosphorus and set the car on fire and was thrown off the train.

By that time he had considerable fame in the country as the boy editor of the first newspaper to be published on a moving train. The London *Times* wrote him up.

He learned about telegraphy and got a job as night operator at Stratford Junction in Canada, but one day he let a freight train get past a switch and had to move on.

(During the Civil War a man that knew telegraphy could get a job anywhere.)

Edison traveled round the country taking jobs and dropping them and moving on, reading all the books he could lay his hands on. Whenever he read about a scientific experiment he tried it out; whenever he could get near an engine he'd tinker with it; whenever they left him alone in a telegraph office he'd do tricks

with the wires. That often lost him the job and he had to move on.

He was a tramp operator (traveling from place to place) through the whole Middle West: Detroit, Cincinnati, Indianapolis, Louisville, New Orleans; always broke, his clothes stained with chemicals, always trying tricks with the telegraph.

He worked for the Western Union in Boston.

In Boston he made a dummy model of his first patent, an automatic vote recorder for use in Congress, but they didn't want an automatic vote recorder in Congress. So Edison had the trip to Washington and made some debts and that was all he got out of that. He worked on a stock ticker and burglar alarms and burned all the skin off his face with nitric acid.

But New York was already the big market for stocks and ideas and gold and greenbacks.

When Edison got to New York he was stony broke and had debts in Boston and Rochester. This was when gold was at a premium and Jay Gould was trying to corner the gold market. Wall Street was crazy. A man named Law had rigged up an electric indicator (Callahan's invention) that indicated the price of gold in brokers' offices. Edison, looking for a job, broke and with no place to go, had been hanging around the central office passing the time of day with the operators, when the general transmitter stopped with a crash in the middle of a rush day of nervous trading. Everybody in the office lost his head. Edison stepped up and fixed the machine and landed a job at $300 a month.

In 1869, the year of Black Friday, he started an electrical engineering firm with a man named Pope.

From then on he was on his own. He invented a stock ticker and it sold. He had a machine shop and a laboratory; whenever he thought of a device he tried it out. He made $40,000 out of the Universal Stock Ticker.

He rented a shop in Newark and worked on an automatic telegraph and on devices for sending two and four messages at the same time over the same wire.

In Newark, he and a man named Sholes tinkered on the first typewriter, and invented the mimeograph, the carbon rheostat, and first made paraffin paper.

He worked all day and all night tinkering with cogwheels and bits of copper wire and chemicals in bottles. Whenever he thought of a device he tried it out. He made things work. He wasn't a mathematician. I can hire mathematicians but mathematicians can't hire me, he said.

In 1876 he moved to Menlo Park where he invented the carbon transmitter that made the telephone a commercial proposition and made the microphone possible

he worked all day and all night and
produced
the phonograph
the incandescent electric lamp
and systems of generation, distribution, regulation and measurement of electric sockets, switches, insulators, manholes. Edison worked out the first systems of electric light using the direct current and small unit lamps and the multiple arc that were installed in London, Paris, New York, and Sunbury, Pa.,

the three wire system
the magnetic ore separator,
an electric railway.

He kept them busy at the Patent Office filing patents.

To find a filament for his electric lamp that would work, that would be a sound commercial proposition, he tried all kinds of paper and cloth, thread, fishline, fiber, celluloid, boxwood, cocoanut-shells, spruce, hickory, bay, maple shavings, rosewood, punk, cork, flax, bamboo, and the hair of a red-headed Scotchman's beard. Whenever he got a hunch he tried it out.

In 1887 he moved to the huge laboratories at West Orange.

He invented rock crushers and the fluoroscope and the reeled film for movie cameras and the alkaline storage battery and the long kiln for burning out portland cement and the kinetophone that was the first talking movie and the poured cement house that is to furnish cheap, artistic, identical sanitary homes for the workers in the electrical age.

Thomas A. Edison at 82 worked 16 hours a day. He never worried about mathematics or the social system. He worked 16 hours a day trying to find a substitute for rubber. Whenever he read about anything he tried it out; whenever he got a hunch he went to the laboratory and tried it out.

READING COMPREHENSION

Summarizing. Choose the best phrase to complete each sentence. Then write the complete statements on your paper.

1. Thomas Edison went to school for only three months because _____ (his mother didn't like the school, his family moved, the teacher didn't think he was smart).

2. Whenever Edison read about something, he _____ (wanted to read more, tried out what he had read, wrote down notes in a journal).

3. When Edison was 82 years old, he worked 16 hours a day _____ (for the Patent Office, inventing the Universal Stock Ticker, trying to find a substitute for rubber).

Interpreting. Write the answer to each question on your paper.

1. What was Thomas Edison's first patent for?

2. What does Edison's work in finding a filament for his electric lamp show about his technique as an inventor?

3. What were two instances in which Thomas Edison's curiosity got him into trouble?

For Thinking and Discussing. Edison spent most of his life inventing things that were both practical and commercial. What do *practical* and *commercial* mean? In what ways do his inventions demonstrate both of these qualities?

UNDERSTANDING LITERATURE

Point of View and Character Motivation. First-person narrators can reveal their own thoughts but cannot tell what other characters are definitely thinking. *Third-person* narrators can reveal the thoughts and motivation of all the characters in the story.

In "The Electrical Wizard," John Dos Passos reveals the motivation of Edison and of other people who played a part in his life.

Based upon your reading of "The Electrical Wizard," who do you think might have made each statement below? Write your answers on your paper.

1. I'll try to teach you all I can, and I'll let you set up a laboratory in the cellar.

2. I'm sorry I have to fire you. You're a fine telegraph operator, but you just do too many tricks with the wires.

3. Can you believe it, that guy Edison has applied for a patent on another invention!

4. Why am I still working at age 82? There are still lots of things to try out, that's why.

WRITING

Imagine you are working with Edison in his Menlo Park laboratory. Write a first-person narrative about the experiments to find a filament for the electric light bulb.

Clemente— A Bittersweet Story

by Jerry Izenberg

What makes a man a hero? Strong arms? The ability to leap over tall buildings in a single bound? In the case of Roberto Clemente, physical strength was only part of what made him great. Certainly, he was a great baseball player. But that fact didn't make him a hero. What did? His capacity to give.

The record book will tell you that Roberto Clemente got 3,000 hits during his major-league career. It will say that he came to bat 9,454 times, that he drove in 1,305 runs, and played in 2,433 games over an 18-year span.

But these cold numbers won't begin to describe who the man Roberto Clemente was. To begin to understand what this wonderful athlete was all about, you have to work backward. The search begins at the site of its ending.

The car moves easily through the early-morning streets of San Juan. A heavy all-night rain has now begun, and there is that sweetness in the air that holds the promise of a new, fresh, clear dawn. This is a journey to the site of one of Puerto Rico's deepest tragedies.

Shortly before the first rays of sunlight, the car turns down a bumpy smaller road and moves past small houses where already the sounds of children begin to drift on the morning air. You can sense the nearness of the ocean. You can hear its waves. You can smell its saltiness. The car noses to a stop, and the driver says: "From here you must walk. There is no other way.

"This is the nearest place. This is where they came by the thousands on that New Year's Eve and New Year's Day. Out there," he continues, pointing with his right hand, "out there, perhaps a mile and a half from where we stand. That's where we think the plane went down."

The final hours of Roberto Clemente were like this: Just a month or so before, he had agreed to take a junior-league baseball team to Nicaragua and manage it in an all-star game in Managua. He had met people and made friends. He was not a man who made friends casually. He had always said that when people gave you their friendship, you had to

312

be willing to give something in return—no matter what the price.

Two weeks after he returned from that trip, Managua, Nicaragua, exploded into flames. The earth trembled and people died. It was the worst earthquake anywhere in the Western Hemisphere in a long, long time.

Back in Puerto Rico, a television personality named Louis Vigereaux heard the news and was moved to try to help the victims. He needed someone to whom the people would listen.

"I knew," Louis Vigereaux said, "that Roberto was such a man. Perhaps he was the only such man who would be willing to help."

And so the mercy project began. Roberto appeared on television. But he needed a staging area. The city agreed to give him Sixto Escobar Stadium.

"Bring what you can," he told the Puerto Rican people. "Bring medicine . . . bring clothes . . . bring food . . . bring shoes . . . bring yourself to help us. We need so much."

And the people of San Juan came. They walked through the heat and they drove old cars. The mound of supplies grew and grew. Within two days, the first mercy planes left for Nicaragua.

Unhappy stories began to drift back from Nicaragua. Not all of the supplies that had been flown in, it was said, were getting through. Nicaragua was in a state of panic.

"We have people there who must be protected. There are black-market types who must not be allowed to get their

hands on these supplies," Clemente told Vigereaux. "Someone must make sure—I'm going on the next plane."

The plane they had rented was an old DC-7. It was scheduled to take off at 4 p.m. on December 31, 1972. Long before takeoff time, it was clear that the plane needed more work.

The departure time was delayed an hour, and then two, and then three. But at 9 p.m., as the New Year's Eve celebration was beginning in downtown San Juan, the DC-7 taxied onto the runway, received clearance, rumbled down the narrow concrete strip, and pulled away from the earth. It headed out over the Atlantic, banked toward Nicaragua, and its tiny lights disappeared on the horizon.

Just 90 seconds later, the tower at San Juan International Airport received this message from the pilot: "We are coming back around."

Just that.

Nothing more.

And then there was a great silence.

Rudy Hernandez, a former teammate of Roberto's when they were both in the Puerto Rican League, recalls: "It was almost midnight, and somebody turned on the radio and the announcer was saying that Roberto's plane was feared missing."

Drawn by a common sadness, the people of San Juan began to make their way toward the beach. A cold rain had begun to fall. They came by the thousands, and they watched for three days. Towering waves boiled up and made the search almost impossible. Midway through the week, the pilot's body was found in the swift-moving currents to the north. On Saturday, bits of the cockpit were sighted.

And then—nothing else.

"I was born in the Dominican Republic," Rudy Hernandez said, "but I've lived on this island for more than 20 years. I've never seen a time or a sadness like that. All of us cried. All of us who knew him, and even those who didn't, wept that week. There will never be another like Roberto."

Who was he . . . really?

He was born in the small town of Carolina, Puerto Rico, in 1934.

Maria Isabella Casares is a schoolteacher there. She recalls: "His father was an overseer on a sugar plantation. He did not make much money. But then there are no rich children here. Roberto was typical of them. I had known him when he was a small boy because my father had run a grocery store in Carolina and Roberto's parents used to shop there.

"Each year," she said, "I let my students choose the seat they want to sit in. I remember the first time I saw Roberto. He was a very shy boy, and he went straight to the back of the room and chose the very last seat. Most of the time he would sit with his eyes down. He was an average student. But there was something very special about him. He wanted to be an engineer, you know, and perhaps he could have been. But then he began to play softball, and one day he came to me and said, 'Teacher, I have a problem.'

"He told me that Pedron Zarrilla, who was one of our most prominent baseball people, had seen him play and that Pedron wanted him to sign a professional contract with the Santurce Crabbers. He asked me what he should do.

"I told him: 'This is your chance, Roberto. But if in your heart you prefer not to try, then, Roberto, that will be your problem—and your decision.' "

There would always be a bond between Roberto and his teacher.

"Once, a few years ago, I was sick with a very bad back, and Roberto, not knowing this, had driven over to see me."

"Where is the teacher?" Roberto asked Mrs. Casares' stepdaughter that afternoon.

"Teacher is sick, Roberto. She is in bed."

"Teacher," Roberto said, pounding on the bedroom door, "get up and put on your clothes. We are going to the doctor, whether you want to or not."

"I got dressed," Mrs. Casares said, "and he picked me up like a baby and carried me in his arms to the car. He came every day for 15 days, and most days he had to carry me, but I went to the doctor and he treated me. Afterward I said to the doctor that I wanted to pay the bill.

" 'Mrs. Casares,' he told me, 'Clemente has paid all your bills. But don't you dare tell him I have told you.' "

On the night Roberto Clemente's plane disappeared, Mrs. Casares was at home. A delivery boy from the pharmacy stopped by and told her to turn on the radio, and then he sat down. "I think something has happened to someone who is very close with you, teacher, and I want to be here in case you need help."

Maria Isabella Casares heard the news. She is a brave woman, and months later, standing in front of the empty crypt in the cemetery at Carolina where Roberto Clemente was to have been buried, she said: "He was like a son to me. He was like my son, and he is all our sons in a way. We must make sure that the chil-dren never forget how beautiful a man he was."

The next person to touch Roberto Clemente was Pedron Zarrilla, who owned the Santurce club. He was the man who discovered Clemente on the country softball team.

"He was a skinny kid," Zarrilla recalls, "but even then he had those large, powerful hands. He joined us, and he was nervous. But I watched him, and I said to myself, 'This kid can throw and this kid can run and this kid can hit. We will be patient with him.' "

Luis Olme, who had been a major-league outfielder with the Brooklyn Dodgers, remembers the first time Roberto Clemente stepped up to bat.

"I was managing the other team," he says. "They had a man on base and this skinny kid comes out and, well, we had never seen him, so we really didn't know how to pitch to him. I decided to throw him a few bad balls and see if he'd bite.

"He hit the first pitch. It was an outside fastball, and he never should have been able to reach it. But he hit it down the line for a double. He was the best bad-ball hitter I have ever seen."

Once Pedron Zarrilla turned him loose, there was no stopping Roberto Clemente. As his confidence grew, he began to get better and better. The major-league scouts began to make their moves. Many teams wanted him, but it was the Pittsburgh Pirates who drafted him. He was the finest prospect the club had had in a long, long time. But the Pirates in

brush with bigotry and intolerance. He was arrested for violating the racial restrictions that were then in practice throughout the South concerning waiting rooms and rest rooms and other facilities. Today, that seems incredible. But back then it was a shameful part of American life.

He never forgot that. Also, there were few Latin ballplayers on the team for him to talk to that year. He was lonely and homesick, but he showed he could swing a bat.

The first winning year was 1960, when the Pirates won the pennant and went on to beat the Yankees in the seventh game of the World Series. Roberto Clemente had hit safely in every World Series game. He had batted over .300. He had been a superstar. But when they announced the Most Valuable Player Award voting, Roberto had finished a distant third.

"I really don't think he resented the fact that he didn't win it," Bob Friend continues. "What hurt—and in this he was right—was how few votes he got. He felt that he simply wasn't being accepted. I think his attitude became one of 'Well, I'm going to show them from now on so that they will never forget.'

"And you know, he sure did."

Roberto Clemente went home and married Vera, a childhood sweetheart. He felt less alone. Now he could go on and prove what it was he had to prove.

His moment finally came. It took 11 years for the Pirates to win a World Series berth again, and when they did in

those days were spectacular losers, and even Roberto Clemente couldn't turn them around overnight.

"We were bad, all right," recalls Bob Friend, who later became a great Pirate pitcher. "We lost over a hundred games, and it certainly wasn't fun to go to the ballpark under those conditions."

It was that year in spring training in Florida that Clemente ran into his first

1971, it was Roberto Clemente who led the way against the Orioles. It was a Series that the Pirates figured to lose. In fact, they dropped two games in Baltimore.

When they got back to Pittsburgh for the middle slice of the tournament, Roberto Clemente went to work and led his team. He was a superhero during the five games that followed. He was the Most Valuable Player. He was everything he had ever dreamed of being on a ball field.

The following year, Clemente ended the season by collecting his 3,000th hit. Only 10 other men had ever done that in the entire history of baseball.

Willie Stargell, his closest friend on the team, talks about Clemente: "When I think of Roberto now, I think of the kind of man he was. There was nothing phony about him. He was a man who chose his friends carefully. I don't think many people took the time to try to understand him, and I'll admit it wasn't easy. But he was worth it.

"The way he died, you know, I mean on that plane carrying supplies to Nicaraguans who'd been dying in that earthquake—well, I wasn't surprised he'd go out and do something like that. I just never thought what happened could happen to him.

"But I know this. He lived a full life. And if he knew at that moment what the Lord had decided, well, I really believe he would have said, 'I'm ready.' "

He was 38 years old when he died. He touched the hearts of Puerto Rico in a way that few men ever could. He touched a lot of other hearts, too.

READING COMPREHENSION

Summarizing. Choose the best phrase to complete each sentence. Then write the complete statements on your paper.

1. In 1972, Roberto Clemente died while he was flying to Nicaragua to _____ (manage an all-star baseball team, take supplies to earthquake victims, take a vacation).

2. Clemente had been asked to make a speech for aid to the Nicaraguans because _____ (he was famous for being a good speaker, no one else wanted to speak to the crowd, people respected him and would respond to his plea).

3. When Roberto Clemente was a boy, he _____ (was very shy, was a class leader, wanted to be a farmer when he grew up).

4. Roberto Clemente developed a special bond with his _____ (coach, brother, teacher).

5. Roberto was still in school when Pedron Zarrilla, who had seen Roberto play baseball, asked him to join _____ (the Santurce Crabbers, the Pittsburgh Pirates, the Baltimore Orioles).

6. When Clemente first joined the major-league Pittsburgh Pirates, the team was _____ (winning almost all of its games, in the process of moving to a new location, on a spectacular losing streak).

7. Clemente felt he hadn't received many votes for the Most Valuable Player of 1960 because he _____ (had not played well enough, wasn't being accepted, was too shy).

8. In 1971, the Pittsburgh Pirates _____ (traded Clemente to another team, were in a World Series again, moved to Los Angeles).

9. After Clemente's death, one of his closest friends said that Roberto _____ (had lived a full life, was an unhappy person, was a fine baseball player).

Interpreting. Write the answer to each question on your paper.

1. How was the year 1971 special for Roberto Clemente?

2. How did Roberto show concern for his teacher, Mrs. Casares?

3. During his early years with the Pirates, even Clemente couldn't turn the losing team around overnight. Why not?

4. After being passed over for the Most Valuable Player Award, what did Clemente mean when he said, "I'm going to show them from now on so that they will never forget"?

For Thinking and Discussing

1. What does the word *bittersweet* mean? Why do you think the author called this biography "Clemente—A Bittersweet Story"?

2. Do you think Roberto Clemente was a hero? Why or why not?

UNDERSTANDING LITERATURE

Changing Points of View. Sometimes a biographer depends on the words of several people to tell the story of one person's life. Each person adds to the story or presents a different way of looking at the subject's life.

In "Clemente—A Bittersweet Story," you learn about Roberto Clemente through the words of the author and several people who knew him.

Read each statement below. On your paper, indicate whether the statement represents the author's point of view. If not, write whose point of view the statement represents.

1. "He was not a man who made friends casually."

2. "All of us who knew him, and even those who didn't, wept that week."

3. "He was a very shy boy, and he went straight to the back of the room and chose the very last seat."

4. "This kid can throw and this kid can run and this kid can hit. We will be patient with him."

5. "I think his attitude became one of 'Well, I'm going to show them from now on so they will never forget.'"

WRITING

Imagine that you are Roberto Clemente. Write about your teacher, your baseball career, or why you help people, from a first-person point of view.

400 Mulvaney Street

by Nikki Giovanni

Nikki Giovanni grew up in Knoxville, Tennessee, and later became an accomplished poet. The following selection is from her autobiography, Gemini. *Ms. Giovanni begins her account at a time when, after becoming famous, she returned to her hometown as a guest speaker. Later in the article, the author goes even further back in time, and describes her childhood in Knoxville. Toward the end of the selection, the flashback ends, and the writer continues to describe her speech back home.*

I was going to Knoxville, Tennessee. I was going other places first. But mostly, to me, I was going home—to Knoxville. I had been asked to speak there. Running late, as usual, I hurried to the airport just in time.

The whole thing about going to Knoxville appealed to my vanity. Artists are seldom asked to come back home and say, "I think I've done you proud." People back home may be insecure or jealous or think so little of themselves that they don't think you would be honored to speak in your hometown or in your old high school. And some artists hate their hometowns so much that they don't want to go back. So artists and their homes don't get together often.

I was excited about going to Knoxville, but I didn't want to get my hopes up. What if the invitation was canceled? What if they didn't like me? What if nobody came to hear me? I decided to forget about the trip for a while.

Now, I was rushing to the airport, and they were calling my flight to Knoxville. I was heading home.

When we were growing up, Knoxville didn't have television, let alone an airport. It finally got TV, but the airport is located in Alcoa. It's now called Tyson Field. Small towns are funny. Knoxville even has a zip code and seven-digit phone numbers. All these changes seem strange to me.

What I mostly remember is Mrs. Flora Ford's white cake with white icing and Miss Delaney's blue furs and Armetine Picket's being the sharpest woman in town and Miss Brooks's wearing tight sweaters. And I remember the jukebox at

Carter-Roberts Drug Store sending out the sounds of the Modern Jazz Quartet playing "Fontessa" or of Nina Simone singing "Porgy" when you dropped in a nickel.

I remember Vine Street on which I was not allowed to walk to get to school. Grandmother didn't want me walking on Paine Street either because Jay Manning lived on it, and he was very beautiful with his black face and two dimples.

The Gem Theatre was on Vine, and for 10 cents you could sit all day and see a double feature, five cartoons, and two serials, plus previews for the next two weeks. And I remember Frankie Lennon would come in with her gang and sit behind me. I wanted to say, "Hi, can I sit with you?" But I thought they were too snooty. I found out later that they thought I was too Northern and stuck up.

All that is gone now. Something called "Progress" changed everything.

And I remember Mulvaney Street where I grew up. Mulvaney Street looked like a camel's back with both humps bulging— up and down. We lived in the down part. At the top of the left hill a lady made ice balls and would mix the flavors for just a nickel. Across the street from her was the Negro center, where the guys played indoor basketball and the little kids went for stories and nap time. Down in the valley part were the tennis courts, the creek, most of the park, and the beginning of the right hill. The houses started on the side of the left hill. In the middle, people got regular flat front lawns. Then the right hill started. On it was a big

apartment building that didn't have a yard at all.

Grandmother and Grandpapa had lived at 400 Mulvaney Street since they'd left Georgia. Mommy had been a baby there. My uncle and aunt were born there. They dated there and sat on the swing on the front porch and fussed there. Our good and our bad were recorded there.

That little frame house was duplicated twice more by the houses beside it. Edith and Clarence White lived next door. The grass wouldn't grow between our house and the Whites'. Mr. and Mrs. Ector's house rounded off the trio. Mr. Ector always wore a stocking cap until his hair was fixed and he looked dapper. He was in love with the various automobiles he owned. All summer he parked his car at the bottom of the hill and polished it twice a day and delighted in it. Grandmother would call across the porches to him, "Ector, you a fool about that car, ain't cha?" And he would smile back. "Yes, ma'am." We were always polite with the Ectors because they had neither children nor grandchildren so there were no grounds for familiarity. I never knew Nellie Ector very well at all. He was laughs, though.

I don't know when the Ectors passed away, but Mr. White was the first to die. After he died, I would play three-hand canasta with Grandmother and Mrs. White. I considered myself a hot-shot canasta player, but I would drag the game on and on so Mrs. White wouldn't have to rush back to her lonely house.

You always think the ones you love

will always be there to love you. It's hard to learn that that isn't so.

I moved with my parents to Cincinnati. I went on to my grandfather's alma mater, Fisk University in Nashville. I got kicked out in my first year, however. Fisk and I had trouble adjusting to each other. So Thanksgiving I rushed home to Grandmother's without the dean of women's permission. Somehow I knew what the future would hold. I'm glad I went because Grandmother and Grandpapa would have had dinner alone and I would have had dinner alone. And the next Thanksgiving Grandpapa would be gone, and Grandmother and I would be alone by ourselves.

My grandparents were surprised to see me in my brown slacks and beige sweater, nervous and so glad to touch base again. And she, who knew everything, never once asked me about school. And he was old so I lied to him. And I went to Mount Zion Baptist with them that Sunday and saw he was going to die. He just had to. And I didn't want that because I didn't know what to do about my Grandmother Louvenia who had never been alone in her life.

I left Sunday night and saw the dean Monday morning. She asked where I had been. I said home. She asked if I had permission to go home. She said, "Miss Giovanni," in a way I've been hearing all my life, and shook her head. I was released from the school February 1st because my "attitudes did not fit those of a Fisk woman." Grandpapa died in April. I was glad it was warm because he hated the cold so badly. Mommy and I drove to Knoxville with my nephew Chris. I was brave and didn't cry and made decisions. We stayed on until Mommy had to go back to work. And Grandmother never once asked me about Fisk.

We got up early Saturday morning, and Grandmother made fried chicken for us. Nobody said we were leaving, but we were. We walked down the hill to the car. We kissed. I looked at Grandmother standing there so bravely trying not to think what I was trying not to feel. I got in on the driver's side and looked at her standing there in her plaid apron and her hair in a bun, her feet hanging loosely out of her slippers. She was 63 years old. She was waving good-bye, and for the first time having to go into 400 Mulvaney Street without John Brown Watson.

I felt powerless. If I couldn't protect this magnificent woman, my grandmother, from loneliness, what could I ever do? I have always hated death. It is unacceptable to kill the young and distasteful to watch the old expire. There must be a better way.

A few years later, Knoxville decided to become a model city. A new mall was built to replace the marketplace, and they were talking about convention centers and expressways. Mulvaney Street was part of all this "Progress." Soon, it too was going to be replaced.

I remember us finding Grandmother the house on Linden Avenue and constantly reminding her it was as good as or better than the little old house. It had a bigger yard and no steps to climb. But I knew what grandmother knew. There

was no familiar smell in that house. No coal ashes from the fireplace. Nowhere that you could touch and say, "Yolanda threw her doll against this wall" or "Agnes fell down these steps." There was no smell or taste of biscuits Grandpapa had eaten with the Alaga syrup he loved so much. There was no sound of the old record player on which Billy Eckstine sang "What's My Name?" so many times that Grandmother said, "Lord! Any fool know his name!" There was no pain in my knuckles where Grandmother had rapped them because she was determined that I would play the piano. There was no echo of me being the only person in the history of the family to curse. And there was no Grandpapa saying, "Oh my, we can't have this." Linden Avenue was pretty, but it had no life.

And I took Grandmother one summer to Lookout Mountain in Chattanooga. She said I was the only grandchild who would take her riding. That was the summer I noticed her left leg was shriveling. She said I didn't have to hold her hand, and I said I liked to. And I made ice cream the way Grandpapa used to almost every Sunday. I churned butter in the hand churner.

I knew, and she knew, there was nothing I could do. "I just want to see you graduate," she said. I didn't know she meant it. I graduated February 4th. She died March 8th.

I came back to Knoxville for the funeral and to look for the Gem Theatre and Carter-Roberts Drug Store, but they were all gone. I went to 400 Mulvaney Street, but it was being torn down. And Grandmother was dead.

I was sick throughout the funeral. I had driven down from Cincinnati with my mother, my sister, and my nephew. From the moment my father had called my apartment I had been sick because I knew before they told me that she was dead. I had a cold. I ran the heat the entire trip, despite the sun coming directly down on us. I couldn't get warm. I drove on. My sister was supposed to relieve me, but she was crying too hard. The car was too hot, and it all seemed so unnecessary. She died because she didn't know where she was and didn't like it. There was no one around to add a touch or smell or feel. I should have been there.

At her funeral they said, "It is well," and I knew she would have agreed. It was peaceful in Mount Zion Baptist Church that afternoon. And I hope when I die that people will say all is well with my soul.

Now I was going back to Knoxville for my speech. They took me up what would have been Vine Street, past what would have been Mulvaney Street. And I was taken out to the beautiful homes on Brooks Road where we considered the folks "so swell, don't cha know." I was exhausted but feeling quite happy from being in a place where, no matter what, I belong. And Knoxville belongs to me. I was born there in old Knoxville General, and I am buried there with Louvenia.

As the time neared for my speech, I was nervous and afraid. I spoke, and they gave me a standing ovation. I wanted to say, "Thank you," but that wasn't enough. Mommy's old bridge club gave me beads. That's the kind of thing that happens in small towns where people aren't afraid to be warm.

I saw Mrs. Delaney in her blue furs in the audience, and I was reminded that life goes on. And I saw the young brothers and sisters who never even knew me or my family. I saw my grandmother's friends who shouldn't have even been out that late at night. They had come to say, "Welcome Home."

I thought Tommy, my son, must know about this. He must know we come from somewhere. He must know that we belong.

READING COMPREHENSION

Summarizing. Choose the best phrase to complete each sentence. Then write the complete statements on your paper.

1. 400 Mulvaney Street was the address of the _____ (author's grandparents, Gem Theatre, Whites' house).

2. The author, Nikki Giovanni, was going to Knoxville to _____ (visit her grandmother, make a speech, visit friends).

3. It didn't matter to Nikki that Knoxville had changed, because she _____ (had always hated it, would always feel at home there, knew she would never go back).

Interpreting. Write the answer to each question on your paper.

1. What did Nikki Giovanni's grandmother hope she would live long enough to see?

2. What were some of the changes in Knoxville that the author describes as "Progress"?

3. Why didn't Nikki's grandmother like her new home on Linden Avenue?

4. Why did Nikki feel sick and guilty when she drove to her grandmother's funeral?

For Thinking and Discussing. Do you feel the same way about your hometown as Nikki Giovanni feels about Knoxville?

UNDERSTANDING LITERATURE

First-Person Point of View. An autobiography is an example of first-person narration. The author writes about himself or herself and uses the words *I* and *me*.

A first-person narrator not only tells a story but also reveals a lot about the way he or she thinks. After reading "400 Mulvaney Street," you probably know a lot about the kind of person Nikki Giovanni is and about what is important to her.

Read each statement below. On your paper, indicate whether Nikki Giovanni would probably *agree* or *disagree* with each statement. Then write a sentence or two explaining each answer.

1. Your birthplace is a part of you.

2. Older people deserve respect.

3. You should always follow the rules.

4. Memories only get in the way of the present.

5. Houses have a life of their own.

6. Parents should pass their memories on to their children.

WRITING

Think of a place you know that has changed. Write a list of words that describe how the place used to look, smell, and feel. Write another list to describe the way the place is now. Use your lists to write a short, *first-person* account about how the place has changed.

Knoxville, Tennessee

by Nikki Giovanni

I always liked summer
best
you can eat fresh corn
from daddy's garden
and okra
and greens
and cabbage
and lots of
barbecue
and buttermilk
and homemade ice-cream
at the church picnic
and listen to
gospel music
outside
at the church
homecoming
and go to the mountains with
your grandmother
and go barefooted
and be warm
all the time
not only when you go to bed
and sleep

1. What is so special about summer? How is summer different from the other seasons?

2. What does the poet mean by "and be warm/all the time"? What mood do these lines give the poem?

& Rita" written in the snow.

Two old men playing, and six supervising, a checkers game.

The Michael Friedsam Foundation Merry-Go-Round, nearly empty of children but overflowing with calliope music.

A man on a bench near the carousel reading, through sunglasses, a book on economics.

Crews of shinglers repairing the roof of the Tavern-on-the-Green.

A woman dropping a camera she was trying to load, the film unrolling in the slush and exposing itself.

A little boy in aviator goggles rubbing his ears and saying, "He really hurt me." "No, he didn't," his nursemaid told him.

The green head of Giuseppe Mazzini staring across the white softball field, unblinking, though the sun was in its eyes.

Water murmuring down walks and rocks and steps. A grown man trying to block one rivulet with snow.

Things like brown sticks nosing through a plot of cleared soil.

A tire track in a piece of mud far removed from where any automobiles could be.

Footprints around a KEEP OFF sign.

Two pigeons feeding each other.

Two showgirls, whose faces had not yet thawed the frost of their makeup, treading indignantly through the slush.

A plump old man saying, "Chick, chick," and feeding peanuts to squirrels.

Many solitary men throwing snowballs at tree trunks.

Many birds calling to each other about

how little the Ramble has changed.

One red mitten lying lost under a poplar tree.

An airplane, very bright and distant, slowly moving through the branches of a sycamore.

READING COMPREHENSION

Summarizing. Choose the best phrase to complete each sentence. Then write the complete statements on your paper.

1. The author describes what he saw in Central Park in _____ (a week, an afternoon, a day).

2. It was a good day to go to Central Park because _____ (the park was so quiet, the weather was perfect for jogging, spring brought the park to life).

Interpreting. Write the answer to each question on your paper.

1. What were the men listening to on their car radio?

2. What are some of the signs of spring that the author saw?

For Thinking and Discussing. How does the author help you "see" what he saw?

UNDERSTANDING LITERATURE

Tone. Writers often show how they feel about a subject by the way they write. They may write in a serious way, a playful way, an angry way, a sarcastic way, or a sad way. The way authors write to show their feelings is called *tone*.

The writer's tone affects the way readers feel about the subject, too. For example, most people who read "Central Park" feel happy about what the author saw. They feel happy because John Updike used a very playful tone.

Suppose Updike had used a different tone. Would that make you feel different?

Here is one scene written in four different tones. On your paper, indicate which description has a *playful*, a *sad*, an *angry*, or a *sarcastic* tone.

1. The merry-go-round was nearly empty of children, but overflowing with calliope music.

2. No one dared come near the merry-go-round, with its dangerously broken-down horses and blaring calliope music.

3. The once-beautiful merry-go-round was now nearly empty except for the faint notes of the calliope.

4. The merry-go-round was nearly empty, unless you wanted to count the loud calliope music that filled the place.

WRITING

Close your eyes and think about a place. Write three or four sentences describing different sights and sounds there. Be sure to show how you feel about the place by the tone you use.

346

Steelworker: Mike Lefevre

from Working *by Studs Terkel*

Working, by Studs Terkel, is a book of interviews with people in different lines of work. "Steelworker" is Mike Lefevre's job description. What does a steelworker do? What is his opinion of his job? Studs Terkel asked Mike Lefevre a number of questions. He edited his tapes so that all you read are Mike's own words.

*I*t is a two-story dwelling, somewhere in Cicero, on the outskirts of Chicago. He is 37. He works in a steel mill. On occasion, his wife, Carol, works as a waitress in a neighborhood restaurant; otherwise, she is at home, caring for their two small children, a girl and a boy.

I'm a dying breed. A laborer. Muscle work . . . pick it up, put it down, pick it up, put it down. We handle between 40 and 50 thousand pounds of steel a day. (*Laughs.*) I know this is hard to believe— from four hundred pounds to three- and four-pound pieces. It's dying.

You can't take pride anymore. You re- member when a guy could point to a house he built, how many logs he stacked. He built it and he was proud of it. I don't really think I could be proud if a contractor built a home for me. I would

want to get in there and take the saw away from him. 'Cause I would have to be part of it, you know.

It's hard to take pride in a bridge you're never gonna cross, in a door you're never gonna open. You're mass-producing things and you never see the end result of it. (*Muses.*) I worked for a trucker one time. And I got this tiny sat- isfaction when I loaded a truck. At least I could see the truck depart loaded. In a steel mill, forget it. You don't see where nothing goes.

It's not just the work. Somebody built the pyramids. Somebody's going to build something. Pyramids. Empire State Build- ing—these things don't just happen. There's hard work behind it. I would like to see a building, say the Empire State, I would like to see on one side of it a foot- wide strip from top to bottom with the name of every bricklayer, the name of every electrician. So when a guy walked by, he could take his son and say, "See, that's me over there on the 45th floor. I put the steel beam in." Picasso can point to a painting. What can I point to? A writer can point to a book. Everybody should have something to point to.

It's the non-recognition by other people. To say a woman is *just* a housewife is degrading, right? Okay. *Just* a housewife. It's also degrading to say just a laborer.

You're doing this manual labor and you know that technology can do it. (*Laughs.*) Let's face it, a machine can do the work of a man; otherwise they wouldn't have space probes. Why can we send a rocket ship that's unmanned and yet send a man in a steel mill to do a mule's work?

Automation? Depends how it's applied. It frightens me if it puts me out on the street. It doesn't frighten me if it shortens my workweek. You read that little thing: What are you going to do when this computer replaces you? Blow up computers. (*Laughs.*) Really. Blow up computers. I'll be darned if a computer is gonna eat before I do! I want milk for my kids. Machines can either liberate man or enslave 'im, because they're pretty neutral.

If I had a 20-hour workweek, I'd get to know my kids better, my wife better. Some kid invited me to go on a college campus. On a Saturday. It was summertime. If I have a choice of taking my wife and kids to a picnic or going to a college campus, it's gonna be the picnic. But if I

worked a 20-hour week, I could go do both. Don't you think with that extra 20 hours people could really expand? Who's to say? There are some people in factories just by force of circumstance. . . .

It isn't that the average working guy is dumb. He's tired, that's all. I picked up a book on chess one time. That thing lay in the drawer for two or three weeks; you're too tired. During the weekends you want to take your kids out. You don't want to sit there and the kid comes up: "Daddy, can I go to the park?" You got your nose in a book? Forget it.

I know a guy 57 years old. Know what he tells me? "Mike, I'm old and tired *all* the time." The first thing happens at work: When the arms start moving, the brain stops. I punch in about 10 minutes to seven in the morning. I say hello to a couple of guys I like, I kid around with them. I put on my hard hat, change into my safety shoes, put on my safety glasses, go to the bonderizer. It's the thing I work on. They take the metal, they wash it, they dip it in a paint solution, and we take it off. Put it on, take it off, put it on, take it off, put it on, take it off. . . .

I say hello to everybody but my boss. At seven it starts. My arms get tired about the first half-hour. After that, they don't get tired anymore until maybe the last half-hour at the end of the day. I work from seven to three-thirty. My arms are tired at seven-thirty and they're tired at three o'clock. I hope I never get broke in, because I always want my arms to be tired at seven-thirty and three o'clock. (*Laughs.*) 'Cause that's when I know that there's a beginning and there's

an end. That I'm not brainwashed. In between, I don't even try to think.

When I come home, know what I do for the first 20 minutes? Fake it. I put on a smile. I got a kid three years old. Sometimes she says, "Daddy, where've you been?" I say, "Work." I could have told her I'd been in Disneyland. What's work to a three-year-old kid? If I feel bad, I can't take it out on the kids. Kids are born innocent of everything but birth. You can't take it out on your wife either.

If I were hiring people to work, I'd try naturally to pay them a decent wage. I'd try to find out their first names, their last names, keep the company as small as possible, so I could personalize the whole thing. All I would ask a man is a handshake, see you in the morning. No applications, nothing. I wouldn't be interested in the guy's past. Nobody ever checks the pedigree on a mule, do they? But they do on a man. Can you picture walking up to a mule and saying, "I'd like to know who your granddaddy was?"

I would like to have a place where college kids came and a steelworker could sit down and talk. Where a workingman could not be ashamed of Walt Whitman and a college professor could not be ashamed that he painted his house over the weekend.

If a carpenter built a cabin for poets, I think the least the poets owe the car-

penter is just three or four one-liners on the wall. A little plaque: "Though we labor with our minds, this place we can relax in was built by someone who can work with his hands. And his work is as noble as ours." I think the poet owes something to the guy who builds the cabin for him.

I don't know who the guy is who said there is nothing sweeter than an unfinished symphony. Like an unfinished painting and an unfinished poem. If he creates this thing one day—let's say, Michelangelo's Sistine Chapel. It took him a long time to do this, this beautiful work of art. But what if he had to create this Sistine Chapel a thousand times a year? Don't you think that would even dull Michelangelo's mind? Or if da Vinci had to draw his anatomical charts 30, 40, 50, 60, 80, 90, a hundred times a day? Don't you think that would even bore da Vinci?

READING COMPREHENSION

Summarizing. Choose the best phrase to complete each sentence. Then write the complete statements on your paper.

1. When Lefevre said, "I'm a dying breed," he meant that _____ (he was feeling very sick because of his work, his job was to dye fabric, his kind of job would soon be a thing of the past).

2. Mike Lefevre's job required him to do _____ (new things every day, the same thing over and over, a lot of reading and writing).

3. Lefevre believed that some working-class people don't fulfill themselves because they _____ (are physically exhausted, have no interests, are not smart enough).

351

4. By *automation*, Lefevre meant _____ (driving an automobile to work, setting up a plant by himself, machines taking the place of human workers).

5. Lefevre said that if he had a 20-hour work week, he would _____ (work overtime to make more money, get to know his wife and kids better, retire earlier).

Interpreting. Write the answer to each question on your paper.

1. Why was Mike Lefevre's job in the steel mill so boring?

2. How did Lefevre feel about computers and the way they could affect his life?

3. How did Lefevre feel when he got home from work?

4. What did Lefevre think were the positive and the negative effects of automation?

5. Why did Lefevre say that when he was working at his job he always wanted his arms to be tired at seven-thirty and at three o'clock?

For Thinking and Discussing. Why did Mike Lefevre feel that workers should get more credit for what they do? Do you agree?

UNDERSTANDING LITERATURE

Varying Tone. Writers or speakers show how they feel about a topic by the tone they use. They may vary their tone when dealing with different topics.

In his interview, Mike Lefevre talked about many different aspects of his work life and personal life. His tone changed depending on his topic.

Below are four descriptions of tone and four passages from Mike Lefevre's interview. On your paper, match each tone description with the proper passage.

bitter
sarcastic
angry
thoughtful

1. "It's hard to take pride in a bridge you're never gonna cross, in a door you're never gonna open. You're mass-producing things and you never see the end result of it."

2. "I'll be darned if a computer is gonna eat before I do! I want milk for my kids."

3. "If I were hiring people to work, I'd try naturally to pay them a decent wage. I'd try to find out their first names, their last names, keep the company as small as possible. . . ."

4. "Can you picture walking up to a mule and saying, 'I'd like to know who your granddaddy was'?"

WRITING

Write one more question that Studs Terkel might have asked Mike Lefevre about his job. Then write what you think the steelworker's answer would be in a tone that seems appropriate.

The Acorn People

from an account by Ron Jones

*Being handicapped doesn't mean you have to give up. That's
what Ron Jones learned from his summer job as a camp
counselor. And that's what his handicapped campers learned,
too.*

Children came out of cars and buses.
It was an eerie sight. Parents carefully
picked up children and placed them in
wheelchairs. There was an open-mouthed
silence. The woods and paths of Camp
Wiggin were used to troops of running
feet and the noise of children at play.
With these wheelchair children, there
was only silence. All life seemed to stop.

I was a counselor, and like the others
I did not know what to say. What do
you say to young people who move toward you only because their parents
push them? What do you say to young
people who seem to have no spirit? What
do you say to young people who are covered with blankets to hide their handicaps?

There were two men counselors for
each cabin of five boys and two women
counselors for each cabin of five girls.

Dominic Cavelli would be my partner.
You could tell he liked kids. He was
planning on working with handicapped
children as a career.

Sometimes I liked to think that I had
taken this job "to serve others." But to

be truthful, I wanted a good-paying job
for a few weeks, and I liked the idea of
playing with kids, swimming, and hiking.

When I saw these kids, I knew I
wouldn't be playing sports with them.
We'd be lucky, I thought, if we took a
few steps together.

I wondered what the boys and girls
were thinking. What were they feeling?
Did they have hopes for the future? But
I didn't have time to think about that because there was work to do.

It took 20 minutes to get each child
into a cabin. Some were pushed in wheelchairs, and some were carried. Others
simply had to be guided.

The camp wasn't set up for handicapped children. It was usually used as a
Boy Scout camp. Each cabin had three
steps, and you can't wheel a chair up a
set of stairs.

What would seem simple to most people was a struggle. Getting in and out of
a chair was a struggle. Getting to and
from a bathroom was a struggle, and
changing clothes was a struggle.

I looked forward to dinner. At last, I would be able to sit down and rest. Dominic and I got our five campers to the dining hall. I started to eat, and then I realized that half the kids couldn't feed themselves. I started spooning peas and potatoes into open mouths.

By evening, I was tired and angry. I thought I'd never get close to those kids, and I wanted to quit.

The next morning, a recording over a loudspeaker hurried everyone to breakfast. It was noisy in the dining hall. For the first time, I saw our five campers as individuals. Each one was staring at Dominic and me. Maybe they were seeing us for the first time, too. Maybe they were wondering if we would stay.

The youngest was eight-year-old Benny B. He was very small, and his legs were crippled by polio. But he was the most active kid at camp. Benny's "thing" was going fast, and he wore a crash helmet on his head. He could make his wheelchair go amazingly fast and could even perform "wheelies," as if on a bike.

Spider, 10, was another kid in our cabin. Spider was a weird name for a kid who had no arms or legs. He was as bright and alert as Benny B. His "thing" was talking, and he hardly ever stopped. Even when you fed him, he didn't stop. He talked, swallowed, and talked some more.

Thomas Stewart wasn't active and didn't talk much. He was 15, and he had muscular dystrophy. Benny B. and Spider looked their age, but Thomas Stewart didn't. He weighed 55 pounds, and pick-

ing him up was like holding a folding tent. His bones didn't seem to be connected. He had had his disease for 11 years, and he didn't seem to have the will to fight it anymore.

Martin, 14, was blind, but able-bodied. He was tall with red hair, and I was surprised at how straight he walked. He seemed to know when something on the ground—like a tree branch—was in his way.

Aaron Gerwalski was the fifth boy in our cabin. He didn't have a bladder. His body wastes went into a plastic bag, which was strapped to one leg. The bag

had to be emptied every hour. This condition is terrible for anyone to have. It must have been especially hard for a teenager to have.

I thought maybe I could deal with one of these kids, but I was sure I couldn't handle all five. I was afraid I would fail, but I was also afraid to quit. I didn't want to face the thought that "I couldn't take it." So I stayed on.

After breakfast, I took the boys to the craft room. The table was full of Boy Scout projects. There were things like whistles, Indian headdresses, and book-ends. I started making an acorn necklace. It showed how I felt—crazy.

Spider kept asking what the necklace was for. Finally, I said, "I feel a little weird being here, so I've made myself a necklace of nuts."

Spider laughed and said, "We all feel the same way. We're all a little nutty here."

"You might call us the nut people," Benny said. "Yeah, that's a good name for us."

"Can we make a necklace like yours?" Spider asked.

"Sure," I said.

When Dominic joined us, we had a surprise for him. The boys had made him an acorn necklace, as well as necklaces for themselves.

Next it was time for swimming and as we went to the pool, other kids noticed our necklaces. Spider kept saying, "We're the Acorn People."

Now our group had a name, and we had something special in common. This drew us together, and I was glad I had stayed.

The swimming pool was a new world for everyone. Each kid took to it differently.

Aaron paddled slowly around in an inner tube, and Benny B. became the inner tube speed king. Thomas Stewart was like a cruise ship. He sat on three inner tubes and quietly rode the waves the rest of us made.

Martin was a submarine and for some reason, he liked to take off his safety belt and sink to the bottom of the pool. It was a good thing he had red hair. I could easily spot him and lift him out of the water.

Spider was amazing in water. Even though he had no arms or legs, he could swim. He pulled himself through the water like a dolphin. He would dive forward, arch his back out, and then in. Then his head would come up before he'd dive forward again. When he swam the whole length of the pool, everyone cheered.

The next day, I still had on my necklace, and so did Dominic. We all did. The Acorn People were "on the move."

It was probably good that Mr. Bradshaw didn't know this. He was the head of Camp Wiggin, and he ran the camp as though it were an army. He believed in keeping kids busy—with one activity after another. But it took us a long time to get from place to place, so we had little time for each activity. The schedule also kept kids in one cabin from meeting kids from other cabins.

Dominic and I decided to change the schedule. We were supposed to go to crafts first, but we went to swimming first instead. When we got to the pool, some girls were using it. At first the boys and girls were shy—and kept apart. But soon they were splashing and chasing one another. By the end of the hour, they were teaching one another water tricks.

When we left the pool, I noticed that Mary, a blind girl, was wearing an acorn necklace. I wondered where she had gotten it. I found out when Aaron said, "I lost my necklace. Can we stop and make another one?"

"Let's make a bunch of necklaces," Martin said.

"Yeah, we can give them to our girl friends," Benny said.

By the end of the afternoon, there wasn't an acorn left on the camp grounds. Soon everyone at the camp—even Mrs. Nelson, the nurse—joined the Acorn Society. Well, Mr. Bradshaw didn't join, because he was away raising money.

The recordings that came over the loudspeaker were meant for Boy Scouts. One evening, the Boy Scout pledge was

followed by this announcement: A merit badge will be given to anyone who climbed Lookout Mountain. Benny B. asked, "If Boy Scouts can climb that mountain, can't we?"

Dominic and I looked at each other. We weren't sure. Aaron didn't like the idea, and Thomas was silent. But Spider and Martin liked Benny's idea. We decided to give it a try.

We left early the next morning. It was a six-mile hike round trip, and we didn't know what the trail would be like. We took along some fruit, water, and three kitchen knives.

Dominic led the way, pushing Spider. Next came Benny B. wheeling himself, and Martin followed pushing Aaron. I was last, pushing Thomas Stewart.

We didn't talk much. We were more afraid than excited. Every curve in the path was a problem, and the bushes kept getting caught in the wheels. The path kept getting narrower.

I felt Thomas shift his weight in the wheelchair. He was making it easier for me to push him. In fact, he was pulling his body as hard as I was pushing. It was the first time I'd seen him make such an effort. I could see that Aaron and Spider were doing the same thing.

The trail started upward, and we had to turn around and pull the chairs from behind. Each time Benny pulled his wheels, he had to brake them. It was pull, stop. Pull, stop.

We were sweating and gasping for breath, but I didn't want to turn back. My mind started to wander. Why are we doing this? Is it the climb that's important? Is it the top? Or is it the strength we find in trying something very hard?

Benny got so tired, he had to stop. He just stopped and didn't say a word. We all stopped, and Spider spoke up. "I name this place Benny's Landing, and I claim it for the Acorn Society!"

His speech gave us a chance to see what we had done. We looked around for the first time during the trip. Here we were in a forest in wheelchairs and until now, the wheelchairs had been only on streets and ramps. We passed around the food, and we rested. Then we moved on.

After several more rests, we reached the steepest part of the climb. We had gone over two and a half miles and the final half mile seemed to go straight up. The trail stopped, and it became a steep hill of rock and loose stones. There didn't seem to be any way to push or pull the chairs up that. Dominic suggested that we try to carry everyone. Thomas didn't like the idea, and Aaron didn't either.

Suddenly, Martin said, "Hey, it's easy."

He was sitting down, facing downhill, and he pulled his legs toward him. Then, with his hands, he pushed himself backward—up the hill.

Benny liked the plan, and Spider did, too. Thomas and Aaron were unsure. To take part, they would have to leave their wheelchairs. This would not be easy for them to do. Finally, we decided to try it. Dominic sat facing downhill, and I strapped Spider onto his lap, using straps from the wheelchairs. Dominic tried pushing himself backward. It worked!

Benny wanted to try it himself, so we tied a pillow from one of the chairs around him. He was ready.

Now Martin sat on the ground. I put Aaron on his lap and tied them together. Finally, I put Thomas on my lap and we tied ourselves together. Then we started off. Martin's idea was great. Who would have thought of going up a mountain backward?

At two o'clock we reached the top of Lookout Mountain. Spider gave one of his necklaces to the mountain. We had made it up there—together!

The trip back to camp seemed to take only half the time, but we got to the dining hall late. It was very quiet—too quiet. It didn't take long to find out what had happened. Mr. Bradshaw was angry at some of the counselors because they weren't following his schedule and because they were teaching boys and girls how to cook. Most of the kids had never held a knife before, and Dominic was teaching them how to make delicious meals. Mr. Bradshaw did not approve.

Several women counselors had brought some bows and arrows, and they were teaching kids to shoot the arrows. It was a thrill to watch them. But Mr. Bradshaw did not approve.

Mr. Bradshaw was especially angry at old Mrs. Nelson, the nurse. She wore bright red lipstick and a lot of eye makeup, and the girls wanted to know how she put on her makeup. So she gave them makeup lessons. Soon, half the girls had bright red lips. They thought they looked beautiful, but Mr. Bradshaw thought they did not look proper. Many of us didn't agree with him. We knew the kids were learning, and most important, they were happy. Able-bodied kids could shoot arrows, cook meals, and take hikes, so why shouldn't handicapped kids be allowed to, also?

Mr. Bradshaw warned us about Parents' Visiting Day. It would be on the next day, and he wanted to show the parents how smoothly the camp was being run. Everyone was given a job to do. Our cabin's job was to make a name tag for each of the 120 kids in camp.

We made the name tags the next morning. There were a lot of tags left over, and Aaron had an amusing idea. He printed "Indian headdress" on a tag and put the tag on the headdress. Then he printed "bookend" on another tag and put it on a bookend. Benny, Thomas, and I caught on and soon we had tags that said: "tree," "wheelchair," "rock," "door,"—even "handicapped child." Within an hour, almost everything in camp had a label.

When the parents arrived, Aaron kept writing. He wrote a label for every car and every visitor.

Mr. Bradshaw was pleased. The campers had been busy, and everyone and everything had a label. The camp was a model of order. That evening, he showed the kids and their parents a movie about water safety. They watched able-bodied kids swimming and diving into the water. The film ended with a water ballet, and when it was over, no one clapped.

Camp was quiet that night. During the day, the labels on everything had seemed funny. Now they were spying eyes. They reminded me of who we were and where we belonged. Late at night, a noise outside woke me up. I got out of bed and left the cabin. I was afraid a kid had gone outside and was in trouble. It wasn't a kid. It was Mrs. Nelson, the nurse. She held a flashlight in one hand and a bunch of labels in the other.

At breakfast, the kids wondered who had taken down the labels, and I pointed at Mrs. Nelson. She was sitting in a corner. "Not Mrs. Nelson," Benny B. said.

"Yes, Mrs. Nelson," I said.

Mrs. Nelson became the camp heroine. From then on, she couldn't keep the kids away from her. They seemed to think she had some kind of magic. Well, maybe she did. She had taken all those labels off us and she had given us back the chance to dream and play.

And we did play. The girls planned a dance, and we all dressed up. Both the boys and the girls spent a long time fixing their hair.

The dance started like any other dance. The boys were on one side of the dining hall, and the girls were on the other side. Three records played, and no one moved.

Janie, a counselor, put on a country music record and began calling directions for a square dance: "Circle left. Circle right. Turn around. Then say good night." Pretty soon, everyone was moving. We weren't moving together, but we were moving.

We danced all different kinds of dances, including the Bunny Hop. Then Janie announced the crowning of the King and Queen of Camp Wiggin. The girl campers had voted for the King and Queen beforehand. I thought I knew who their choices would be. I was wrong. Mrs. Nelson was elected, and she smiled and threw kisses to everyone. Then Janie said, "We name the King of Camp Wiggin to be . . . Aaron Gerwalski!"

Aaron was a perfect choice. We wheeled him to his throne and his Queen. She gave him a big kiss on the forehead. Then the crowd gave three cheers for the King and Queen of Camp Wiggin. Aaron was both amazed and thrilled.

Later, as I wheeled him back to our cabin, he started to cry. He turned his face away from the other campers because he was embarrassed.

"I'm so happy," he said. "I've never been a king before."

The days were going by quickly, and each day seemed shorter than the one before. Kids began to ask, "How many days are left?"

I noticed that some of them were starting to act the way they did at the beginning of camp. Thomas became silent again and slumped in his chair. Benny B. raced around more than ever. He said that if he stopped, camp would end. Kids who had stopped taking medicine wanted the medicine again.

Mr. Bradshaw didn't help anyone feel better. The pool was the thing we enjoyed the most, and he said that it was to be cleaned out now—three days before camp ended. I was supposed to clean it out, so I asked Mr. Bradshaw if we could keep the pool open until the last day. Then the parents could see how well their kids had learned to swim.

"The pool is your job," he said. "Just be sure it's clean by the time camp closes."

Both the campers and the counselors were feeling very sad, when Mrs. Nelson came up with an idea. "Why don't we put on a water show for the parents?" she said. "We'll make costumes, and everyone can take part." No one spoke. How could we put on a good show with only two days to get ready?

Mrs. Nelson said, "Do we want to sit around feeling sorry for ourselves, or do we want to put on a show? I'll get some TV reporters, and they can film us."

That did it! The boys and the girls had never been news. They had been watchers, but now they could be actors!

We went right to work. Mrs. Nelson would write and direct the show and tell us what to do. It would be called "Acorn Pirate," and we would begin by "setting

361

the stage." Then we would learn our parts.

We got materials from the craft center, and we painted the changing rooms by the pool to look like a pirate ship. The flagpole became the mast, and a sail was made with sheets. The ship was named the U.S.S. Acorn. The pool was a lagoon next to a South Pacific island. Inner tubes became islands of flowers.

Next we made costumes. Safety belts became ballet skirts and pirate belts.

The day before the show, Mrs. Nelson called everyone together and divided us into "good guys" and "bad guys." The good guys were the islanders, and the bad guys were the pirates.

Then we had a choice of doing one of three things. We could dive, race, or dance. During the show, Mrs. Nelson would read a story. She would signal when each group should take part. Meanwhile, we practiced our separate parts.

On the last day of camp, the campers' families arrived. They were given necklaces of flowers and invited to the show. The parents were delighted that their children were so excited. Brothers and sisters of the campers looked as though they wished they could be in the show.

The visitors took seats around the pool. Mr. Bradshaw arrived late. He had been away for a few days. He did not know about the show, so the only thing he could do was join the audience.

Mrs. Nelson began reading a story over a microphone. It was about pirates who wanted the treasures from the water.

They challenged the islanders. Which group could collect the most treasure?

Mrs. Nelson pulled a box to the edge of the pool. She emptied the "treasure" into the water. It was the camp silverware—every fork, spoon, and knife.

The divers, both pirates and islanders, entered the pool. There were sinkers like Martin, and there were kids who went down headfirst. Each time someone came up with some silver, the audience cheered.

The treasure was taken to the islanders' home. It was to be blessed by their god. First, to please the god, there would be a water ballet.

Boys and girls were placed in inner tubes, and they formed a large circle in the middle of the pool. They moved the circle around in one direction; then they moved it in the other direction. Then they formed a floating star.

The audience cheered. They knew how hard it was for the swimmers to do this. Kids like Benny B. wanted to go fast, and kids like Aaron and Thomas were doing their best just to keep floating. Each kid had to be very patient.

Mrs. Nelson announced the last part of the show. "The treasure will be given to the winner of the race," she said. "The race will be between a pirate and an islander. The captain of the pirates, Mr. Jones, will swim for them. Spider the Undefeated, the best islander swimmer, will swim for his team. It's an old custom to let the islander start first. This is because the captain of the pirates is known to cheat by using the gangplank as a diving board."

The audience booed at me, the captain

of the pirates. They cheered Spider, the good guy. "On your mark," Mrs. Nelson said. "Get set. Go!"

Spider started off. I knew that if I took a running dive, I would end up ahead of him. I also knew that this was a real race to Spider, and it would not be right for me not to try to win. I gave a pirate yell and dove into the pool.

"Come on, Spider!" the crowd yelled.

I caught up with Spider about halfway down the pool, but suddenly he went past me. He was going faster and faster. I started swimming as fast as I could, but he left me behind.

Then I saw what was going on. Some of the islanders had tied a rope around Spider's waist. When I had caught up with him, they started pulling him through the water. I thought they were going to pull him right through the side of the pool, but they let go at the last minute.

Spider won! The crowd went wild!

Summer camp was now over. It was very quiet, and it reminded me of the first day of camp. Benny rolled slowly out of my sight, and Spider was passed from a counselor's arms to his parents' arms. Martin led me to his parents, walking. Thomas had to be carried. Aaron wanted to push himself so he could show his parents how strong he was.

I didn't make a big deal over their leaving. I think they didn't want to say good-bye. I think they knew I would remember them forever. We were mountain climbers, pirates, and kings. We were the Acorn People.

READING COMPREHENSION

Summarizing. Choose the best phrase to complete each sentence. Then write the complete statements on your paper.

1. The real reason Ron Jones took the job as a counselor at Camp Wiggin was because he _____ (wanted to serve others, couldn't get any other job, wanted a good-paying job for a few weeks).

2. The author's first thought, that he wouldn't be playing with the campers, turned out to be _____ (true, false, nearly true).

3. Camp Wiggin had originally been set up for _____ (handicapped children, Boy Scouts, camp counselors).

4. In the craft room, Ron and the boys in his cabin made _____ (bookends, acorn necklaces, Indian headdresses).

5. Spider, the boy with no arms or legs, _____ (couldn't swim, swam like a dolphin, liked to sink to the bottom of the pool).

6. When they attempted to climb Lookout Mountain, Ron, Dominic, and the boys _____ (were successful, had to call off the hike near the beginning of the trail, decided to turn back just before they reached the top).

7. On the last day of camp, the campers _____ (made acorn necklaces, put on a water show, hiked to the top of Lookout Mountain).

Interpreting.   Write the answer to each question on your paper.

1. How did Aaron feel when he was elected the King of Camp Wiggin?

2. How did the acorn necklaces draw Ron and his campers together?

3. Why was Mrs. Wiggin elected the Queen of Camp Wiggin?

4. What things did the counselors and Mrs. Nelson, the nurse, do that helped the handicapped campers to be happy?

5. Why did most of the handicapped children at Camp Wiggin feel better about their ability to succeed by the end of the camp session?

6. What were the reactions of the campers' families when they arrived on the last day of camp?

For Thinking and Discussing

1. Why was climbing the mountain so important to the members of the Acorn Society? What did climbing the mountain represent to them?

2. What did Ron Jones learn from his experiences at the camp? How was he different by the end of camp?

3. Why do you think Ron Jones decided to write about what happened with the Acorn People?

4. In what ways could you describe Mr. Bradshaw as being the one who was "handicapped"?

UNDERSTANDING LITERATURE

Tone and Changing Attitude.   You have already learned that writers sometimes change their tone when writing about different topics. Writers may also change their tone when writing about only one topic. The change of tone reflects the writer's changing attitude.

Ron Jones changed his tone several times during the telling of "The Acorn People." The tone changes illustrate that Ron's attitude toward his job at Camp Wiggin was changing.

Read each of the statements below about Ron's changing attitude. Find a passage within the story that matches the tone and attitude of the statement. Write the passages on your paper.

1. At first, Ron's attitude seemed *solemn*.

2. Then, he seemed to have an *angry* attitude.

3. Next, he seemed very *serious*.

4. Later, he seemed *excited*.

5. Finally, he seemed *sad*.

WRITING

Think about an experience you had in which your attitude changed over time. Make a list of facts about the experience, and also list some of your different feelings. Use your lists to describe your experience and your changing attitude. Try to use different tones in your description to show your changing attitude.

Dolphins

by Alice Herman Lehrer

Dolphins are beautiful, playful, and intelligent. Scientists are trying to learn more about this fascinating sea mammal. But they are likely to make their reports in language most people would find hard to follow. This article was based on research into history and science—but it's aimed at the person who wants information and entertainment at the same time.

A dolphin looks like a big fish with a built-in smile. Actually, dolphins belong to the same group of living creatures that humans do: mammals. They grow larger than we do—up to 10 feet long. They live in water but must come to the surface to breathe. And though humans consider themselves the most intelligent of all mammals, dolphins may not be too far behind. Scientific studies made of them in recent years prove that they have a lot in common with their human "cousins."

A measure of a mammal's intelligence is the ability to communicate. Humans are able to pass detailed information to one another. And, scientists find, so are dolphins. They don't use words in our sense, of course. Dolphin talk is a variety of whistles, squeaks, chirps, clicks, and creaking sounds. But it works. In one experiment, Dolphin A was able to tell Dolphin B which lever to press if he wanted a reward of fish. Only Dolphin A knew the secret. There was no way for Dolphin B to find out unless Dolphin A told him.

We don't know that dolphins call one another by name, as people do, but something similar seems to be true. Each dolphin has a whistling signature, different in tone and pattern from the signatures of other dolphins. When a baby is born, its mother whistles almost constantly for several days. The baby learns to know its mother's voice pattern, and comes when she calls.

A human listener might not hear the call. Some dolphin sounds are too high for humans to pick up. They are probably not heard by other creatures in the ocean, either. So a sick or elderly dolphin can call for help from his own species without danger.

Most humans aren't much interested in whistling and squeaking in dolphin language. But dolphins like to mimic ours. Dolphins who have come in con-

tact with human beings can imitate words, laughter, and even the tones of different voices. Dr. John Lilly, a dolphin researcher, has made records of dolphins doing imitations of their human friends. He, himself, once displeased a dolphin he was working with. The dolphin scolded him angrily in his own voice—copied very clearly.

People who work with dolphins have found that they like to be stroked, too. They are very sensitive to touch. A dolphin has a dorsal fin on top of its body. If the fin is touched, the dolphin jumps just as a human would if touched by someone unseen.

Humans are convinced that they are superior to dolphins. Dolphin scientists studying *us* might not be so sure.

"Where is their sonar?" they would ask. "How can they get along without echo-location? They've got ears outside, but what good are they?"

Like most creatures that spend most of their time in water, the dolphin has no outer ear. Pinpoints behind each eye serve as ear openings. Yet the dolphin can size up its environment even when blindfolded, through its sense of hearing alone. Most dolphins *do* see well. But a sightless type called the Ganges River dolphin has no trouble traveling and locating food. A dolphin with its eyes covered by suction cups can weave smoothly through an underwater metal maze. A dolphin can find its mate, or its mother, even in murky water—by listening. A dolphin has been known to find a vita-min capsule dropped into the other end of a large pool.

Dr. Kenneth S. Norris, an authority on the species, believes that dolphins form sonic images. They can "hear" the objects around them, and tell them apart.

It's done by "echo-location." Scientists conducting the tests usually hear no sounds. But the dolphin is sending them out, too high for human ears. The sound waves bounce off objects and create sonar—a sort of echo in the water—so the dolphin knows exactly what is there. Dolphins have a mental picture of everything around them. They can find fish in the dark sea. They can slip around rocks and floating objects.

Performing dolphins in oceanariums use sonar in their acts. They communicate with one another through sonar before leaving the water. That's how they jump out of the tank together at precisely the same second, and jump through hoops as a perfect team. Acrobats take years to learn tricks that dolphins do perfectly after a few hours. Sonic images tell them the size, width, speed, direction, and everything else about objects—and other dolphins.

Our present electronic equipment cannot begin to match a dolphin's sonic ability. The Navy is trying, though. Scientists have copied high-pitched dolphin sounds and lowered the echoes so humans can hear them. That way, blindfolded divers will be able to choose between two targets as easily as a dolphin. Such a bionic sonar system would help divers to travel by night. It is the first step toward a foolproof torpedo-guidance program.

Like porpoises and whales, dolphins are part of the animal family called *Cetaceans*. Most of the dolphins we see in shows and on TV are bottle-nosed dolphins—in Latin a mouth-filling *Tursiops truncatus*. They're the ones with the curved mouths that make them look as if they're smiling at us.

Inside, dolphins are more like cows, goats, and sheep than they are like us. They have several stomachs. Mostly they're filled with fish or squid. An adult bottle-nosed dolphin can keep 20 pounds of fish inside his body and go without eating again for about a week.

The dolphin is often confused, even by scientists and fishermen, with its look-alike, the porpoise. But a close look shows important differences. The dolphin's teeth are cone-like and pointed, rather than spade-shaped like the porpoise's. A dolphin's dorsal fin is curved toward the tail, while most porpoises have triangular fins. And the dolphin has a much larger brain than its porpoise relative. That is where the intelligence that so interests its other relative, humankind, is stored.

For thousands of years humans have written about the dolphins who live in large bodies of water all over the world. The ancient Greeks called the dolphin "Euphrosyne," which means joyfulness. They admired its high, graceful leaps out of the water, and its love of play. Dolphins have, traditionally, been friendly to humans. For centuries stories have been told about dolphins who nudged tired swimmers to shore. It is not certain whether the dolphins meant to help or were just playing. But they saved lives. They are also credited with driving sharks away from threatened swimmers.

Fishermen of the past thought it was good luck when dolphins swam alongside their boats. If a dolphin got tangled in a fishing net, it was always freed.

But today, in some parts of the world, the dolphin has become an enemy. They often swim in the same waters as tuna. When dolphins get tangled in the nets, tuna escape—taking the fishermen's living with them. Thousands of dolphins have been killed by fishermen who feel they must protect their business.

The Marine Mammal Protection Act has made it illegal for a United States citizen to "harrass, hunt, capture, or kill" a dolphin. But the law is not binding everywhere, and dolphins die every year.

Someday we may be able to communicate with the dolphin and explain all this. Someday we may understand their language and learn, firsthand, about their attitudes and way of life. Or, perhaps, they will be asking *us* the questions.

READING COMPREHENSION

Summarizing. Choose the best phrase to complete each sentence. Then write the complete statements on your paper.

1. Dolphins have shown that they can imitate the way _____ (people swim, birds sing, people talk).

2. An experiment showed that dolphins are able to communicate with one another because _____ (one dolphin told another one how to get a reward of fish, scientists heard the dolphins squealing, dolphins have learned to write).

3. Humans cannot hear dolphin sonar because the sounds are too _____ (soft, high in pitch, low in pitch).

4. Scientists consider dolphins to be _____ (highly intelligent, very shy, not very smart).

Interpreting. Write the answer to each question on your paper.

1. What group of living creatures do dolphins belong to?

2. In what ways are dolphin's methods of communicating well suited to their environments?

3. Why can a dolphin with its eyes covered by suction cups still weave smoothly through an underwater metal maze?

For Thinking and Discussing

1. Do you think humans should capture dolphins to study how they act, or should dolphins be left alone in their natural environment?

2. Do you think all the information the author has presented about dolphins is true? What techniques does the author use to assure you of the accuracy of her information?

UNDERSTANDING LITERATURE

Serious, Formal Tone. "Dolphins" is a research article based on historical and scientific facts. To show that the information is important and factual, the author uses a tone that is *serious, formal.* The serious tone helps readers trust the accuracy of the author's information.

Look at the two passages below. One passage comes from "Dolphins." The other presents the same information, but uses a different tone. On your paper, indicate the tone of the second passage. Then briefly explain which passage gets across the ideas more effectively.

1. "It's done by 'echo-location.' Scientists conducting the tests usually hear no sounds. But the dolphin is sending them out, too high for human ears. The sound waves bounce off objects and create sonar—a sort of echo in the water—so the dolphin knows exactly what is there."

2. Dolphins use a really wild technique called "echo-location." They make sounds too high for humans to hear. The sound waves bump into things and then come zooming back, letting the dolphins in on the big secret of what is there.

WRITING

According to this article, dolphins are similar to porpoises. Look up *porpoise* in an encyclopedia. In a serious, formal tone, write two paragraphs about porpoises.

Emotion Twists Issues— Stick to the Facts

by Kevin E. Steele

You are about to read two articles about gun-control laws. Both articles are examples of nonfiction written to persuade the reader. The first is from Gun Magazine. *Kevin E. Steele is against gun control, and he wants to persuade the reader to agree with him. He uses facts to back up his opinions. Keep his arguments in mind when you read the second article.*

"**O**n the night of October 4, 1976, my grandson was sitting in a restaurant waiting for his order with his back to the door. This man came in, shot Michael twice in the head, put the gun back in his belt, and walked out. He did not know my grandson, but wanted to use the gun. He gave no reason for this murder, except one day, he said, some boys had teased him and wanted to ride his motorcycle. Thank you for listening to my sorrow. I am a lonesome grandmother, because of a handgun."

Peter Giron was alone in his Bronx, N.Y., dry-cleaning shop one evening when two youths armed with .38 pistols entered and demanded that Giron open his safe. Giron's response was to pull a li- censed *.38 of his own from his waistband and open fire, fatally wounding one of the would-be robbers. The other fled empty-handed.*

The preceding vignettes illustrate a point that I shall try to make in this month's column. The first is reprinted from a virulently anti-handgun fund-raising letter sent out by Handgun Control, Inc., headed by Nelson T. Shields, III, whose son was a victim in the San Francisco "Zebra" killings.

The second is taken from the Armed Citizen column that appears each month in the *American Rifleman.*

Obviously there are two sides to the coin. However, the side that Handgun Control, Inc., chooses to display is de-

SALE
PRICE
34 50-
046890

signed to grab noncommitted citizens by the heart and squeeze it for all the pity and guilt it contains.

The *American Rifleman* tries not to elicit emotions; they state it as it happened and allow the reader to objectively judge the advantages and disadvantages of being armed with a handgun—legally.

Currently, Handgun Control, Inc., is involved in a national campaign to build membership in their organization. According to the fund letter itself, this organization hopes to fill its ranks with victims of handgun crime. They hope to rival the membership of the NRA, and with that membership it is hoped that legislation banning the handgun will eventually come from Capitol Hill.

But has Handgun Control, Inc., done all its homework? They state in their letter that a victim is murdered every hour of every day with a handgun. In that context it does indeed sound appalling. However, simple multiplication reveals that the exact number of violent deaths caused by handguns is 8,760 a year. Is the illegal use of handguns of such magnitude that federal legislation is required to curb it? Let's take a look strictly at the numbers.

In the year ending December 31, 1979, a total of 51,900 people were killed in automobile accidents. The figures, according to the National Safety Council, show a direct parallel to those killed or involved with accidents while under the influence of alcohol. The figure 51,900 represents a number that is almost 500% over the number of Americans who are fatally injured with a handgun during a violent crime.

Guns are licensed, recorded, and re-stricted. Automobiles are also licensed, recorded, and restricted. Alcoholics, unfortunately, are not. Yet these figures strongly represent that the automobile is a more serious threat to the citizen of the United States than is the handgun. Yet victims of auto-related accidents are not clamoring and organizing for legislation to "ban the car."

Death is an accepted fact of life. While no person, pro-gun or anti-, wishes death or emotional anguish upon another human being, we will not end violent crime by banning handguns. In fact, all this would accomplish would be the disarming of the honest, law-abiding citizen who may require a handgun at one point in his life to defend life, either his own or that of an innocent party.

When asked, the police themselves will admit they cannot prevent violent crime, and they cannot protect every citizen of the United States from becoming involved in it. The handgun in the hands of a licensed, law-abiding citizen is a strong deterrent to crime. Let all those who expound the virtues of Handgun Control, Inc., post signs on their front doors advertising that "no handguns are in this house." Let *them* rely solely on police protection and we will see just how long it takes them to realize their error.

Handgun Control, Inc., should also do some research on how many lives each year are *saved* because of the handgun. This is a point that they neglect, and in their neglect they are condemning countless lives to death and anguish that could have been avoided had the victim been armed.

Less than one percent of all handguns produced in the United States each year are involved with violent crime. Compare that to the number of cars produced that become involved in fatal accidents. Compare that to the number of knives produced that inflict fatal wounds. Compare that to the number of baseball bats that bash the brains out of innocent people. Compare that to the number of tire irons that messily dissect the human skull.

Criminals who resort to the use of lethal weapons in the commission of a crime are animals, pure and simple. They forfeit the right to life when their insidious decision is made. These people, particularly second offenders who have made the wrong decision twice and have instigated the loss of innocent human life, should be executed—*immediately!*

I agree with Nelson Shields that the loss of innocent life in violent crime is a travesty that should not be tolerated. Shields makes his mistake in blaming the loss of life on the weapon used, instead of on the criminal using it.

Banning the handgun will not end violent crime. Those who believe it will are being naive in their assumptions and are being led down the rosy path by the "social reformers." We cannot allow our right of self-defense to be taken from us and we must all work to allay the fear of living in a day when only the *criminals* own guns.

Pro-gunners should fight back. Perhaps an organization should be formed composed of victims of violent crime whose lives were *saved* because of the handgun. You know, that's not a bad idea!

READING COMPREHENSION

Summarizing. Choose the best phrase to complete each sentence. Then write the complete statements on your paper.

1. Kevin E. Steele said the *American Rifleman* presents _____ (facts and not emotional appeals, many emotional appeals, national advertisement campaigns for guns).

2. Handgun Control, Inc., would like to have laws passed to _____ (allow people to own guns, ban the sale of handguns, reduce the price of handguns).

3. In the year 1979, fewer people were killed with guns than _____ (with knives, in airplane crashes, in automobile accidents).

4. Steele felt that banning handguns would _____ (end violent crime, not put an end to violent crime, save thousands of lives each year).

5. According to this article, of all the guns produced in the United States each year, the number used in violent crimes is _____ (greater than 10 percent, nearly 50 percent, less than one percent).

Interpreting. Write the answer to each question on your paper.

1. What is the name of the organization that is involved in a national campaign in favor of gun control?

2. What is the goal of the publication *American Rifleman*?

3. How does the author say handguns help save lives?

For Thinking and Discussing

1. In his article, did Steele always stick to the facts, or did he sometimes appeal to the readers' emotions?

2. According to the author, cars are more dangerous than guns. Do you agree? Why or why not?

UNDERSTANDING LITERATURE

Argumentative Tone. In some articles, writers take a strong stand on an issue. In this type of article, the writers often use an *argumentative,* or arguing, tone. They make strong statements for their side of the issue. They also try to challenge the opposite side.

Look at the following argumentative statements from "Emotion Twists Issues— Stick to the Facts." On your paper, indicate in which statements Kevin Steele argues *for* his side and in which statements he argues *against* the opposite side.

1. "But has Handgun Control, Inc., done all its homework?"

2. "Automobiles are . . . licensed, recorded, and restricted. Alcoholics, unfortunately, are not."

3. "Yet victims of auto-related accidents are not clamoring and organizing for legislation to 'ban the car.'"

4. "The handgun in the hands of a licensed, law-abiding citizen is a strong deterrent to crime."

5. "Shields makes his mistake in blaming the loss of life on the weapon used, instead of on the criminal using it."

6. "We cannot allow our right of self-defense to be taken from us. . . ."

WRITING

The gun-control problem is just one of the many controversial issues that are often in the news. Choose another topic (such as nuclear energy, the draft, equal rights for women). Take one side of the issue, and make a list of statements arguing for your side and against the other side.

Guns: A Serious Problem

by Ann Landers

In this article, Ann Landers tells the pro-gun-control story. Like Kevin E. Steele, she uses facts to support her opinion, and she tries to persuade the reader to agree with her. As you read, try to decide whether you agree with the Landers (pro-gun-control) or the Steele (anti-gun-control) argument.

DEAR ANN: Tonight at 9:55 p.m. our phone rang. Dad answered. We could tell from his responses that it was bad news.

It was the mother of a dear friend who had just died. The week before, *her* phone had rung. It was the sheriff asking her to come to the hospital. Her son had been shot in the head while driving down one of the main streets in Omaha.

He was only 33—a wonderful person, no enemies, no reason why anyone would wish him dead. But someone took a shot at him—and now he is gone forever. The agony of this man's parents is unbearable. He was their only child.

There are no clues as to who committed this senseless murder. They will probably never find the killer. It makes me sick to know that whoever did this awful thing is out there somewhere—walking around with that gun. God knows who will be next. **AMERICA, WHAT'S HAPPENING TO YOU?**

DEAR AMERICA: That's a good question. One of the answers is this: There are at least 90 million guns out there and many are in the hands of crazy, irresponsible people. Again I am asking all concerned citizens to urge their Congressmen and Senators to pass a strong federal gun law. Every poll taken shows that the vast majority of Americans want it. Are the gun manufacturers and lobbies in Washington stronger than the voice of the people? Let us make ourselves heard.

Do you have a handgun in your home or in the glove compartment of your car to protect yourself against assault or robbery? If the answer is yes, here are a few facts that deserve your consideration.

In 1976 approximately 25,000 Americans were killed by guns. To put that figure in its proper context, here's another way to look at it. During our 10-year involvement in the Vietnam War, over

375

twice as many Americans were killed by guns at home as were killed in that war.

So much for the heartbreak that goes hand in hand with loss of life. Here are some financial facts:

Gun killings and wounds cost the United States taxpayer at least $4 billion a year, according to the U.S. Department of Justice. Crimes committed with guns account for a large share of the cost of law enforcement, justice, prison upkeep, welfare to dependents, insurance premiums, medical expenses, recuperation time, losses in talent and experience, permanent disability, workmen's compensation, and property losses.

How do we compare with other countries in this regard? I don't want to burden you with statistics, but this one will give you a fairly good idea. From 1946 through 1967, 19 policemen were killed by guns in England, as compared with

1,014 policemen killed in the United States. No country in the world approaches us when it comes to shooting one another to death. We are the gun-happiest people in the world.

Why? Because guns are available almost anywhere, to anyone who wants them. This means minors, idiots, and people with criminal records. Anybody who wants a gun can walk into a store and buy one (or 10). In fact, you don't even have to go out of your own home. Guns are available through mail-order house catalogues. (The gun that killed John F. Kennedy was purchased from a Chicago mail-order house.)

In Japan the private ownership of pistols is forbidden to everyone except the police, military, and a few competitive marksmen. In France all guns must be registered and their owners licensed. In Sweden applicants for gun-ownership licenses must prove their need for a gun and their knowledge of the weapon.

Guns are big business in the United States. Many powerful interests would hate to see them go. Those who are fighting gun-control legislation have for years been bankrolling a powerful lobby in Washington. Their motto is: "Guns don't kill people—people kill people." Whenever I print a letter urging gun-control laws, that motto pops up in my mail at least 25,000 times. My response to these people is, "Yes, of course people kill people, but it's a lot easier if a person has a gun."

Part of the gun problem exists because we are afraid—and we have a right to be. Man can now walk on the craters of the moon, but he cannot walk safely after dark two blocks from his home. Many people insist they need a gun for protection. They say if guns are outlawed, only the criminals will have them. The response to that statement is, "Yes, the criminals—and the police." The war against crime would then be waged by those best equipped to do the job. And the police would win.

Citizens who keep guns in their homes to protect themselves against intruders would do well to keep these facts in mind: 98 percent of burglaries are committed when no one is at home. The burglar often adds insult to injury by making off with the handgun—along with the silverware.

A Chicago study showed that citizens who resisted being robbed by brandishing a weapon were eight times as likely to be killed. The average person is not adept at handling a gun. He is slower on the draw and more easily rattled than an experienced thug (U.S. Mayors' Conference, 1976).

If you wish to protect your home there are several things you can do:

(1) Install a security system.

(2) Get a dog. It doesn't have to be a large dog. If he barks and calls neighborhood attention to the fact that something is "wrong," he'll serve a very useful purpose.

Ordinary, everyday citizens like you and me must keep in mind this important fact. Almost 70 percent of the people

who are shot to death in the United States year after year are *not* killed by robbers or rapists. The murders are committed by husbands, wives, in-laws, brothers, sisters, lovers, neighbors, friends, employees, and other acquaintances. They are crimes of passion resulting from old grudges, new arguments, lost tempers. Often booze or drugs are involved.

If there were no gun handy, the victim would have been clobbered by a fist, a club, a piece of pipe, or stabbed by a kitchen knife. His chances for survival would have been infinitely better.

In addition to crimes of passion, approximately 14,000 Americans shoot themselves to death intentionally. Some psychiatrists argue that if a person wants to commit suicide he will do it— somehow. This may be true, but when a deeply depressed individual has a gun in his bedside table, it is easy to pull the trigger while in a state of anxiety. Often a suicide attempt is a cry for help. If pills are taken, the stomach can be pumped and the person may be saved, but when a bullet blows off a head or pierces the heart, no second chance is possible.

Accidental gun deaths are another tragedy. Last year nearly 4,000 people lost their lives in the United States because they "didn't know it was loaded." Can you imagine the excruciating guilt of a parent whose preschool youngster found a loaded gun on a shelf and accidentally killed his four-year-old playmate? This occurred in Chicago recently.

Every poll taken in the United States has shown that the American people are strongly in favor of handgun registration or an outright ban against their sale or possession. It's up to us to let our Representatives and Senators in Washington know how we feel about this vital issue.

Checked for accuracy by Nelson Shields, Executive Director, National Council to Control Handguns, Inc.; James Sullivan, National Committee for a Responsible Firearms Policy.

READING COMPREHENSION

Summarizing. Choose the best phrase to complete each sentence. Then write the complete statements on your paper.

1. Ann Landers knows that most Americans want gun control because _____ (polls show this to be true, people she talks to tell her so, most of her letters state this idea).

2. According to Landers, most people who are killed by guns are shot by _____ (criminals, the police, relatives or people they know).

3. Landers believes that banning guns would _____ (increase crime, save lives, upset most Americans).

Interpreting. Write the answer to each question on your paper.

1. How does Ann Landers feel about the availability of guns to anyone who wants them?

2. Why does Landers feel that guns are not very useful in the prevention of burglaries?

3. What obstacles does Landers see facing the passage of gun-control laws?

For Thinking and Discussing. What are some of the facts that Ann Landers presented? How do her facts compare with those presented by Kevin Steele in "Emotion Twists Issues—Stick to the Facts"? With whom do you agree?

UNDERSTANDING LITERATURE

Emotional vs. Factual Tone. In developing an argument, writers sometimes like to appeal to readers' feelings as well as to their minds. To reach readers' minds, writers use a serious, *factual* tone. To appeal to readers' feelings, writers use an *emotional* tone.

Read each of the following statements from Ann Landers' article "Guns: A Serious Problem." On your paper, indicate which statements are written in an emotional tone and which ones are written in a factual tone.

1. "It makes me sick to know that whoever did this awful thing is out there somewhere—walking around with that gun."

2. "There are at least 90 million guns out there and many are in the hands of crazy, irresponsible people."

3. "Are the gun manufacturers and lobbies in Washington stronger than the voice of the people?"

4. "Gun killings and wounds cost the United States taxpayer at least $4 billion a year, according to the U.S. Department of Justice."

WRITING

Choose one side of a controversial issue. Write one paragraph in which you make an emotional appeal for your side. Write another paragraph in which you make a factual appeal for your side.

A Kitten for Mrs. Ainsworth

by James Herriot

*James Herriot is famous for his series of books on the life
of a country veterinarian. They include* All Creatures Great
and Small, All Things Bright and Beautiful, *and* All Things
Wise and Wonderful. *These autobiographical works were
drawn largely from his own experiences as an animal
doctor in Yorkshire, a rural area in northern England.*

*In this story, Herriot paints a touching picture of a lit-
tle stray cat and the woman who cares for her.*

My strongest memory of Christmas will always be bound up with a certain little cat. I first saw her when I was called to see one of Mrs. Ainsworth's dogs. I looked in some surprise at the furry black creature sitting before the fire.

"I didn't know you had a cat," I said.

The lady smiled. "We haven't. This is Debbie."

"Debbie?"

"Yes, at least that's what we call her. She's a stray. Comes here two or three times a week and we give her some food. I don't know where she lives but I believe she spends a lot of her time around one of the farms along the road."

"Do you ever get the feeling that she wants to stay with you?"

"No." Mrs. Ainsworth shook her head. "She's a timid little thing. Just creeps in, has some food, then flits away. There's something so appealing about her, but she doesn't seem to want to let me or anybody into her life."

I looked at the little cat. "But she just isn't having food today."

"That's right. It's a funny thing but every now and again she slips through here into the lounge and sits by the fire for a few minutes. It's as though she was giving herself a treat."

"Yes . . . I see what you mean." There was no doubt there was something unusual in the attitude of the little animal. She was sitting bolt upright on the thick rug which lay before the fireplace. The coals glowed and flamed. She made no effort to curl up or wash herself or do anything other than gaze quietly ahead.

And there was something in the dusty black of her coat, the half-wild scrawny look of her, that gave me a clue. This was a special event in her life, a rare and wonderful thing. She was lapping up a comfort undreamed of in her daily existence.

As I watched, she turned, crept soundlessly from the room, and was gone.

"That's always the way with Debbie," Mrs. Ainsworth laughed. "She never stays more than ten minutes, then she's off."

Mrs. Ainsworth was a plumpish, pleasant-faced woman in her forties. She was the kind of client veterinary surgeons dream of; well off, generous, and the owner of three Basset hounds. It only needed the usual mournful expressions of one of the dogs to deepen a little and I was sent for post-haste. Today one of the Bassets had raised its paw and scratched its ear a couple of times. That was enough to send its mistress running to the phone in great alarm.

My visits to the Ainsworth home were frequent but undemanding. I had ample opportunity to look out for the little cat which had intrigued me. On one occasion I spotted her nibbling daintily from a saucer at the kitchen door. As I watched, she turned and almost floated on light footsteps into the hall, then through the lounge door.

The three Bassets were already in residence, draped snoring on the fireside rug. They seemed to be used to Debbie, because two of them sniffed her in a bored manner and the third merely cocked a sleepy eye at her before flopping back on the rich carpet.

Debbie sat among them in her usual posture: upright, intent, gazing absorbedly into the glowing coals. This time I tried to make friends with her. I approached her carefully, but she leaned away as I stretched out my hand. However, by patient wheedling and soft talk I managed to touch her and gently stroked her cheek with one finger. There was a moment when she responded by putting her head on one side and rubbing back against my hand, but soon she was ready to leave. Once outside the house she darted quickly along the road, then through a gap in a hedge. The last I saw was the little black figure flitting over the rainswept grass of a field.

"I wonder where she goes," I murmured half to myself.

Mrs. Ainsworth appeared at my elbow. "That's something we've never been able to find out."

It must have been nearly three months before I heard from Mrs. Ainsworth.

It was Christmas morning and she was apologetic. "Mr. Herriot, I'm so sorry to bother you today of all days. I should think you want a rest at Christmas like anybody else." But her natural politeness could not hide the distress in her voice.

"Please don't worry about that," I said. "Which one is it this time?"

"It's not one of the dogs. It's Debbie."

"Debbie? She's at your house now?"

"Yes . . . but there's something wrong. Please come quickly."

I drove through the marketplace of Darrowby on Christmas Day. The snow lay thick on the cobbles and hung from the eaves of roofs. The shops were closed. The colored lights of the Christmas trees winked at the windows of the clustering houses. They were warmly inviting against the cold white bulk of the fells behind.

Mrs. Ainsworth's home was lavishly decorated with tinsel and holly. Rows of drinks stood on the sideboard. The rich aroma of turkey and sage and onion stuffing floated through to the lounge.

Debbie was there all right, but this time everything was different. She wasn't sitting upright in her usual position. She was stretched quite motionless on her side, and huddled close to her lay a tiny black kitten.

I looked down in bewilderment. "What's happened here?"

"It's the strangest thing," Mrs. Ainsworth replied. "I hadn't seen her for several weeks, then she came in about two hours ago—sort of staggered into the kitchen, and she was carrying the kitten in her mouth. She took it through to the lounge and laid it on the rug. At first I was amused. But I could see all was not well because she sat as she usually does, but for a long time—over an hour—then she lay down like this and she hasn't moved."

I knelt on the rug and passed my hand over Debbie's neck and ribs. She was thinner than ever. Her fur was dirty and mud-caked. She did not resist as I gently opened her mouth. The tongue and mucous membranes were abnormally pale. The lips were ice-cold against my fingers. When I pulled down her eyelid and saw the dead white conjunctiva, a knell sounded in my mind.

I examined the abdomen with a grim certainty as to what I would find. There was no surprise, only a dull sadness as my fingers closed around a hard mass deep among the organs. Massive lymphosarcoma. Terminal and hopeless. I put my stethoscope on her heart and listened to the increasingly faint, rapid beat. Then I straightened up and sat on the rug, looking sightlessly into the fireplace, feeling the warmth of the flames on my face.

Mrs. Ainsworth's voice seemed to come from afar. "Is she ill, Mr. Herriot?"

I hesitated. "Yes, I'm afraid so. She has a fatal growth." I stood up. "There's absolutely nothing I can do. I'm sorry."

"Oh!" Her hand went to her mouth and she looked at me wide-eyed. When at last she spoke her voice trembled. "Well, you must put her to sleep immediately. It's the only thing to do. We can't let her suffer."

"Mrs. Ainsworth," I said. "There's no need. She's dying now—in a coma—far beyond suffering."

She turned quickly away from me. She was very still as she fought with her emotions. Then she gave up the struggle and dropped on her knees beside Debbie.

"Oh, poor little thing!" she sobbed, and stroked the cat's head again and again as the tears fell unchecked on the matted fur. "What she must have come through. I feel I ought to have done more for her."

For a few moments I was silent, feeling her sorrow, so out of place among the bright seasonal colors of this festive room. Then I spoke gently.

"Nobody could have done more than you," I said. "Nobody could have been kinder."

"But I'd have kept her here—in comfort. It must have been terrible out there in the cold when she was so desperately ill—I daren't think about it. And having kittens, too—I . . . I wonder how many she did have?"

I shrugged. "I don't suppose we'll ever know. Maybe just this one. It happens sometimes. And she brought it to you, didn't she?"

"Yes . . . that's right . . . she did . . . she did." Mrs. Ainsworth reached out and lifted the bedraggled black morsel. She smoothed her finger along the muddy fur. The tiny mouth opened in a soundless miaow.

"Isn't it strange? She was dying and she brought her kitten here. And on Christmas Day."

I bent and put my hand on Debbie's heart. There was no beat.

I looked up. "I'm afraid she's gone." I lifted the small body, almost feather-light, wrapped it in the sheet which had been spread on the rug, and took it out to the car.

When I came back Mrs. Ainsworth was still stroking the kitten. The tears had dried on her cheeks and she was bright-eyed as she looked at me.

"I've never had a cat before," she said.

I smiled. "Well, it looks as though you've got one now."

READING COMPREHENSION

Summarizing. Choose the best phrase to complete each sentence. Then write the complete statements on your paper.

1. Debbie was _____ (Mrs. Ainsworth's cat, one of Mrs. Ainsworth's dogs, a stray cat who visited Mrs. Ainsworth).

2. Mrs. Ainsworth called Mr. Herriot on Christmas because _____ (Debbie was sick, her dogs seemed sad, she wanted him to come for dinner).

3. After Debbie died, Mrs. Ainsworth was comforted because _____ (Debbie hadn't suffered, Debbie had brought her kitten to her, she had given Debbie a permanent home).

Interpreting. Write the answer to each question on your paper.

1. How did Debbie's behavior show that she was a stray?

2. Why did Mr. Herriot like having Mrs. Ainsworth as a client?

3. How would you describe Mrs. Ainsworth's attitude toward animals?

4. How did Mrs. Ainsworth react to Debbie's death?

5. Why do you think Debbie brought her kitten to Mrs. Ainsworth?

For Thinking and Discussing. What would you do if you found a stray cat or dog?

UNDERSTANDING LITERATURE

Tone and Imagery. Imagery is the descriptive language a writer uses to make characters, places, objects, and experiences come alive for the reader. Imagery appeals to the five senses of sight, sound, smell, taste, and touch.

In "A Kitten for Mrs. Ainsworth," James Herriot uses imagery to help create a warm, sensitive tone. This influences the way the reader feels, too.

Read the following passages. On your paper, identify the sense or senses each one appeals to. Then, in a word or phrase, tell how each passage makes you feel.

1. "She was sitting bolt upright on the thick rug which lay before the fireplace. The coals glowed and flamed."

2. "The lips were ice-cold against my fingers."

3. "Mrs. Ainsworth reached out and lifted the bedraggled black morsel. She smoothed her finger along the muddy fur. The tiny mouth opened in a soundless miaow."

WRITING

Imagine that you are James Herriot. Several weeks after Debbie's death, you visit Mrs. Ainsworth. Write a paragraph describing Debbie's kitten, who has begun to settle into her new home. Use images that appeal to the five senses to make your description vivid and alive.

Section Review

VOCABULARY

Technical Terms. People who study a subject area or work in any job field use certain specific terms to communicate important ideas. These terms are meaningful to the students and workers using them, but may be unfamiliar to other people. Words that are used in a specific subject area or job field are called *technical terms.*

Nonfiction writers often use technical terms in their articles. By using technical language, writers can show that they are knowledgeable in the subjects they are writing about. The use of technical language can also help readers understand important concepts.

Here are some technical terms that appeared in this section. Most of the terms were defined in the context of the selections. Find each term in the selections, and write its definition on your paper.

Hemitragus jemlaicus ("Central Park")
bonderizer ("Steelworker: Mike Lefevre")
muscular dystrophy ("The Acorn People")
echo-location ("Dolphins")
sonar ("Dolphins")
oceanariums ("Dolphins")
workmen's compensation ("Guns: A Serious Problem")
massive lymphosarcoma ("A Kitten for Mrs. Ainsworth")

Separating Facts and Opinions. A *fact* is a statement about something that exists or has happened. An *opinion* is a statement that tells how someone feels about something. Writers often try to convince readers that opinions are facts. But careful readers can separate facts and opinions.

Some ways to recognize facts are to look for specific dates, statistics, or other researched information. Writers often use words that signal an opinion. Some ways to recognize opinions are to look for clue words such as *feel, think, believe, seem, good, bad,* or words that express strong feelings.

Read each of the following statements from the selections in this section. On your paper, indicate whether each statement is a *fact* or an *opinion*.

1. "If I had a 20-hour workweek, I'd get to know my kids better, my wife better."

2. "I think the poet owes something to the guy who builds the cabin for him."

3. "He was very small, and his legs were crippled by polio."

4. "An adult bottle-nosed dolphin can keep 20 pounds of fish inside his body. . . ."

5. "Criminals who resort to the use of lethal weapons . . . are animals, pure and simple."

6. ". . . 98 percent of burglaries are committed when no one is at home."

Razzmatazz
Roy Lichtenstein (1923–).
Graham Gund Collection/Courtesy Art Resource.

Humor

A man who was carrying a penguin walked up to a policeman.

"I just found this penguin wandering in the street," he said. "What should I do with it?"

"Take it to the zoo," the policeman suggested.

"Thanks, I'll do that," the man replied.

The next day, the policeman saw the same man, still carrying the penguin.

"I thought you were going to take the penguin to the zoo," he said.

"I did," said the man, "and we had such a good time that today I'm taking it to the movies."

What's So Funny?

Are you laughing? Or at least smiling, just a little? How do you know the penguin story is a joke and is not to be taken seriously? What makes jokes or other forms of humor funny enough to make you laugh?

People have been making other people laugh and analyzing humor for thousands of years. One idea they have discovered is that people laugh at things that are *incongruous*. In an incongruous situation, things seem out of place. They may seem too big—like the red nose or enormous shoes of a clown. They may seem too small—like a small sports car filled with 30 people. They may seem impossible—like an elephant climbing a tree. They may seem unexpected—like a custard pie in the face. They may seem silly—like the mistake a newspaper reporter made when she wrote that "an enormous *crow* watched the game in the stadium," instead of writing *crowd*.

In the penguin joke, incongruity enters in when a few simple words fail to get across a simple idea. The policeman means that the man should take the penguin to the zoo and leave it there. The man assumes that he should take the penguin to the zoo to entertain it. To most of us, the idea of chumming around with a penguin is strange or incongruous. So we think it's funny.

Satire—Laughing and Thinking

There are many different kinds of humorous writing. You will read examples of several different kinds in this section.

The first type of humor you will read is called *satire*. Satire involves taking a serious situation and turning it into a joke. For example: An old Indian chief is asked what a peace treaty is. He answers, "A *peace* treaty is what is drawn up when the white man wants another *piece* of our land." The play on words makes us laugh, but it also makes us think. There is a bitter truth in the joke.

In "Fresh Air Will Kill You," Art Buchwald treats a serious situation in a funny way. The narrator has become so used to polluted air that fresh air smells strange to him. He's worried about breathing it. Buchwald could have handled the issue of air pollution in a more serious way, but he chose to use satire instead. He wants readers to laugh at the incongruous situation he's described, and then think seriously about the truth behind it. Sometimes people think best when they are laughing. That is the principle behind satire.

John Ciardi also uses satire in "And They Lived Happily Ever After for a While." The young couple thinks gasping and coughing are natural parts of life. The poem is funny—but only because the couple doesn't realize it would be more "natural" to breathe fresh air.

Satire is often used to explore important political and social issues. Sometimes writers develop satires to make fun of the way people act, look, or talk. In "The Cow Who Liked to Kick," Ambrose Bierce shows readers how foolishly some people can act. He exaggerates all the unusual habits of the people and animals in the story. Bierce's humor is funny, but also unkind.

Playing With Words

Another type of humor involves *puns,* or plays on words. Puns can be used to make a satiric point—as in the joke about the peace treaty—but usually they just make you laugh (or groan). Here's a pun to make you groan: What is the best way for a football player to get by defense? To go through *de gate.*

In "Who's on First?" Abbott and Costello present one pun after another to create craziness and confusion. The comedy routine is nonsensical and strictly for laughs. If there's a serious "message," it is that people often have trouble communicating with each other.

Everyday Humor

Relating events just the way they happened can also make people laugh. Sometimes everyday life can be funnier than a comedy skit. In "How Beautiful With Mud," Hildegarde Dolson describes what happened to her when she was a teenager trying hard to become a beautiful woman.

You'll probably laugh at Dolson's story for two reasons. For one thing, she takes even the strangest events so seriously. For another, the problems are hers, not yours.

Authors use humor to make points, expose problems, create confusion, or to make fun of themselves or other people. Most of all, they create humor to make readers laugh. To find out what makes you laugh, turn the page.

Fresh Air Will Kill You

by Art Buchwald

Up there in the mountains, something smelled terrible. What could it be? Art Buchwald often writes satire based on accepting the unacceptable. He turns things around so that bad seems to be good.

Smog, which was once the big attraction of Los Angeles, can now be found all over the country from Butte, Montana, to New York City, and people are getting so used to polluted air that it's very difficult for them to breathe anything else.

I was lecturing recently, and one of my stops was Flagstaff, Arizona, which is about 7,000 feet above sea level.

As soon as I got out of the plane, I smelled something peculiar.

"What's that smell?" I asked the man who met me at the plane.

"I don't smell anything," he replied.

"There's a definite odor that I'm not familiar with," I said.

"Oh, you must be talking about the fresh air. A lot of people come out here who have never smelled fresh air before."

"What's it supposed to do?" I asked suspiciously.

"Nothing. You just breathe it like any other kind of air. It's supposed to be good for your lungs."

"I've heard that story before," I said. "How come if it's air, my eyes aren't watering?"

"Your eyes don't water with fresh air. That's the advantage of it. Saves you a lot in paper tissues."

I looked around and everything appeared crystal clear. It was a strange sensation and made me feel very uncomfortable.

My host, sensing this, tried to be reassuring. "Please don't worry about it. Tests have proved that you can breathe fresh air day and night without its doing any harm to the body."

"You're just saying that because you don't want me to leave," I said. "Nobody who has lived in a major city can stand fresh air for a very long time. He has no tolerance for it."

"Well, if the fresh air bothers you, why don't you put a handkerchief over your nose and breathe through your mouth?"

"Okay, I'll try it. If I'd known I was coming to a place that had nothing but fresh air, I would have brought a surgical mask."

We drove in silence. About 15 minutes later he asked, "How do you feel now?"

"Okay, I guess, but I sure miss sneezing."

"We don't sneeze too much here," the man admitted. "Do they sneeze a lot where you come from?"

"All the time. There are some days when that's all you do."

"Do you enjoy it?"

"Not necessarily, but if you don't sneeze, you'll die. Let me ask you something. How come there's no air pollution around here?"

"Flagstaff can't seem to attract industry. I guess we're really behind the times."

The fresh air was making me feel dizzy. "Isn't there a diesel bus around here that I could breathe into for a couple of hours?"

"Not at this time of day. I might be able to find a truck for you."

We found a truck driver, and slipped him a five-dollar bill, and he let me put my head near his exhaust pipe for a half hour. I was immediately revived and able to give my speech.

Nobody was as happy to leave Flagstaff as I was. My next stop was Los Angeles, and when I got off the plane, I took one big deep breath of the smog-filled air, my eyes started to water, I began to sneeze, and I felt like a new man again.

READING COMPREHENSION

Summarizing. Choose the best phrase to complete each sentence. Then write the complete statements on your paper.

1. Art Buchwald suspected that something was wrong in Flagstaff, Arizona, because _____ (the air was polluted, his eyes didn't water, he began coughing).

2. The fresh air in Flagstaff made Buchwald _____ (sneeze constantly, feel dizzy, want to move there).

3. To solve his fresh air "problem," the author _____ (decided to move to a hut in the mountains, tried not to breathe, breathed truck exhaust fumes).

4. This article suggests that a major cause of air pollution is _____ (diesel buses, airplanes, industry).

Interpreting. Write the answer to each question on your paper.

1. Why was Buchwald so happy to get to Los Angeles?

2. What did Buchwald really mean when he said the air in Flagstaff smelled funny?

3. Does Buchwald really believe that fresh air will kill people?

4. What point is Buchwald trying to make about pollution?

5. Which parts of the article seem funny or crazy?

For Thinking and Discussing

1. Can you think of any other problems and bad conditions that people have accepted as normal?

2. Why do you think the author decided to use humor to make his point? How is satire particularly effective here?

UNDERSTANDING LITERATURE

Satire and Irony. Writing that makes fun of some situation or person to make a point is called *satire*. Writers use satire to expose what seems wrong or foolish to them.

One technique that writers of satire often use is *irony*. Irony is a contrast of ideas. In an ironic situation, one thing would seem to be true, but something very different occurs. For example, it would be ironic if a judge were arrested for law-breaking. In "Fresh Air Will Kill You," it is ironic that fresh air makes the author uncomfortable.

Art Buchwald used an ironic situation to make the point that people have learned to put up with air pollution. Read each of the following quotations from "Fresh Air Will Kill You." Then, on your paper, explain what is ironic about each quotation.

1. "Tests have proved that you can breathe fresh air day and night without its doing any harm to the body."

2. "Nobody who has lived in a major city can stand fresh air for a very long time."

3. "If I'd known I was coming to a place that had nothing but fresh air, I would have brought a surgical mask."

4. "Flagstaff can't seem to attract industry. I guess we're really behind the times."

5. ". . . when I got off the plane, I took one big deep breath of the smog-filled air, my eyes started to water, I began to sneeze, and I felt like a new man again."

WRITING

Clip an editorial cartoon that uses satire or irony from a newspaper. Then, in one or two paragraphs, explain the point of the cartoon. How has the cartoonist used satire or irony to make the point?

And They Lived Happily Ever After for a While

by John Ciardi

It was down by the Dirty River
    As the Smog was beginning to thin
Because we had been so busy
    Breathing the worst of it in,

That the worst remained inside us
    And whatever we breathed back
Was only—sort of—grayish,
    Or at least not entirely black.

It was down by the Dirty River
    That flows to the Sticky Sea
I gave my heart to my Bonnie,
    And she gave hers to me.

I coughed: "I love you, Bonnie,
    And do you love me true?"
The tears of joy flowed from my eyes
    When she sneezed back: "Yes—
    Achoo!"

It was high in the Garbage Mountains
    In Saint Snivens by the Scent,
I married my darling Bonnie
    And we built our Oxygen Tent.

And here till the tanks are empty
    We sit and watch TV
And dream of the Dirty River
    On its way to the Sticky Sea.

Here till the needles quiver
    Shut on the zero mark
We sit hand in hand while the TV screen
    Shines like a moon in the dark.

I cough: "I love you, Bonnie,
    And do you love me true?"
And tears of joy flow from our eyes
    When she sneezes: "Yes—Achoo!"

1. How would you describe the mood of this poem? How do the people in it feel?

2. Why is this poem in the "Humor" section of this book?

3. What will happen when the "needles quiver shut on the zero mark"?

4. In what ways is this poem like "Fresh Air Will Kill You"?

The Cow Who Liked to Kick

by Ambrose Bierce

"The Cow Who Liked to Kick" is a tall tale. Early settlers made up these stories or "yarns," to entertain one another. Bierce uses the tall tale to poke fun at the people on a small farm. He creates humor by exaggerating what happens in their daily lives.

My Aunt Patience, who ran a small farm in Michigan, had a favorite cow. This creature was not a good cow or a profitable one. Instead of producing milk, she spent all her time kicking.

She would kick all day, and then get up in the middle of the night to kick. She would kick at anything—hens, pigs, even birds in the sky. To Phoebe, all were equal.

It was amusing to see Phoebe clear a path through the crowded barnyard. She would kick out—right and left—first with one leg and then another. On good days, Phoebe would have many animals in the air all at once.

Her kicks were wonderful. Phoebe always gave an exciting performance. Let me tell you about one of them.

Phoebe was standing in the road, pretending to be asleep. A big black hog came up beside her. The hog, Elmer, looked like a young rhinoceros.

Suddenly, without a visible movement from Phoebe, Elmer was gone. But where? I looked into the sky, only to see a small black speck. It was traveling as fast as a meteor. That speck was Elmer.

Combing and brushing cows is not a common practice, even in Michigan. But my aunt decided Phoebe needed daily brushing. Phoebe didn't think so.

This didn't stop Aunt Patience from demanding that every new farmhand must brush Phoebe every morning. I say new because the farmhands usually didn't last very long.

They announced their plans to quit by pounding Phoebe half to death. This was after she had given several swift kicks in their direction.

The ex-farmhands would then limp home, never to return. I don't know how many employees my aunt lost that way. But there were a good many lame men in that part of the country.

400

On the other hand, my aunt's farm labor cost her nothing. All the farmhands left before their first paychecks. But as Phoebe's fame spread, it became impossible to hire anyone new.

People gossiped that the cow had kicked the farm to pieces. The land was not well kept. And the buildings and fences badly needed repairs.

Since my aunt was a widow, she couldn't depend on a husband to run the farm. And Aunt Patience hadn't been interested in getting married again. Her heart belonged to Phoebe.

But there was no one to plant her crops. And even if there had been, who would harvest them? My aunt soon began to change her mind about getting married again.

Aunt Patience made it known that she was now looking for a husband. There was much excitement. Every man who was single suddenly wanted to get married. But none of them wanted to marry my aunt.

Men married their cooks, their enemies' sisters—whomever they could find. Anyone but Aunt Patience would do.

There was one eligible male left, and my aunt set her heart on him. His name was Huggins—Jeremiah Huggins. He was probably the most unlucky mortal in the whole northern half of America. Jeremiah was stiff and pale and much too serious for his own good. He was terribly tall, and his clothes didn't fit.

Jeremiah usually wore a black hat. It was set so far down upon his head that he had trouble seeing. His boots were unpolished, and his coattails hung to the ground. Whenever he went into a cornfield, the crows would fight to sit on his shoulders.

None of this stopped my Aunt Patience from marrying him. The day after the wedding, she told him: "Now, Jeremiah, dear, I'll tell you what there is to do about the place.

"First, you must repair all the fences. Clear out the weeds. Mend the wagon. Plow the fields. And get things shipshape. This will keep you out of mischief for at least two years. Oh, I almost forgot poor Phoebe. . . ."

"This sister you mention," interrupted Jeremiah, "do I know her? The name sounds familiar, but . . ."

"Why you old fool!" yelled my aunt. "Phoebe is cow! You will have to comb and brush her every morning for the rest of your life!"

Now, it is necessary to explain that Jeremiah had known from the first who Phoebe was. He had already secretly visited her. For over an hour, he had let Phoebe examine him from every direction.

In short, he and Phoebe had studied each other. They had planned their battle

strategy. Both were ready for action.

To his new home, Jeremiah had brought a cast-iron pump. It stood about seven feet high. He now fastened it to a platform above the well in the barnyard.

Jeremiah took off his long coat. He buttoned it loosely around the pump. His high black hat was the final touch. An observer might have said that Jeremiah had never looked better.

The good man then carefully closed the barnyard gate. He knew how stubborn Phoebe was. If she saw the gate

When Phoebe was within speaking distance, she put out her nose. Phoebe acted as if she wanted to be petted. She came a little closer, as if to shake hands. Suddenly, she turned around. With the speed of lightning, Phoebe gave a terrible kick.

But instead of sending Jeremiah into orbit, Phoebe herself began spinning like a top. Finally, she slowed down, swaying and wobbling from side to side.

Phoebe ended up on her back with her four feet in the air. It seemed to Phoebe that the world had somehow gotten on top of her. Then she fainted.

She lay unconscious for a great while. But, at last, her eyes opened, and Phoebe caught sight of the open door of her stall. Nothing had ever looked better to her. She struggled up and limped, brokenhearted, into her home.

For several weeks, Phoebe's right hind leg was greatly swollen. My aunt nursed her faithfully, and Phoebe soon recovered.

But Phoebe had changed. She had stopped kicking everything in sight. And Phoebe was nice to the other animals. She even allowed Jeremiah to brush and comb her.

Aunt Patience couldn't get over it. One day, she went up to Phoebe with a pan of turnips. My aunt had never dared get this close to her beloved cow before.

Phoebe looked at the turnips. Then she looked at my aunt. Out went Phoebe's hind leg.

I looked for my aunt and couldn't find her. Then I noticed the stone wall. Something was thinly spread out across it. It was Aunt Patience. You could not have done it so evenly with a trowel.

closed, she would want to jump right over it.

Jeremiah was right. Phoebe was soon in the barnyard. He watched Phoebe through a knothole in the barnyard fence.

At first, Phoebe pretended not to see the figure on the platform. She pretended to be asleep. When this didn't work, she began chewing her cud.

But it was clear that Phoebe was thinking very hard. Then she began nosing along the ground. All the time, she drew closer and closer to the figure.

READING COMPREHENSION

Summarizing. Choose the best phrase to complete each sentence. Then write the complete statements on your paper.

1. Phoebe was known for _____ (driving off farmhands before they were paid, producing excellent milk and cream, chasing away Aunt Patience's husband).

2. Aunt Patience married Jeremiah because _____ (her friends wanted her to, she wanted someone to do the farm work for her, she loved him very much).

3. Jeremiah tricked Phoebe by _____ (pretending to be nice to her, putting his own clothes on a cast-iron pump, dressing up as a cow).

Interpreting. Write the answer to each question on your paper.

1. What were the circumstances that led to Aunt Patience's decision to get married again?

2. How had Phoebe changed by the end of the story?

3. Think about how the story ended. In what way does the ending show that justice was finally achieved and Aunt Patience got what she deserved?

For Thinking and Discussing. What sort of people were Aunt Patience and Jeremiah? How were they alike or different?

UNDERSTANDING LITERATURE

Exaggeration. In a satire, a writer often uses *exaggeration* to make a point. Exaggeration involves overstating an idea beyond the limits of truth. The overstatement makes the writer's meaning clear.

Ambrose Bierce used exaggeration in "The Cow Who Liked to Kick" to poke fun at life on a farm. Exaggeration makes the story funny and a bit unkind at the same time.

Here are some statements from the story. On your paper, indicate which are exaggerations. Then indicate whether each exaggeration was meant to be mostly funny or unkind.

1. "This creature was not a good cow or a profitable one."

2. "On good days, Phoebe would have many animals in the air all at once."

3. "Men married their cooks, their enemies' sisters—whomever they could find."

4. "Whenever he went into a cornfield, the crows would fight to sit on his shoulders."

5. "My aunt had never dared get this close to her beloved cow before."

WRITING

Go back to the story and find at least five examples of exaggeration. Then rewrite each one to make it realistic. Is it still funny? Why or why not?

Who's on First?

by Bud Abbott & Lou Costello

Q.: What's your name?
A.: Hugh Who.
Q.: You don't have to call me. I'm right here.

*That's the formula for one of the best-known comedy
routines of all time, "Who's on First?" Bud Abbott and Lou
Costello performed it on the stage, in the movies, on radio,
and on TV. And now, you too can go crazy with confusion. . . .*

Abbott: You know, strange as it may seem, they give ballplayers nowadays very peculiar names. . . . Now, on the St. Louis team, Who's on first, What's on second, I Don't Know is on third—

Costello: That's what I want to find out. I want you to tell me the names of the fellows on the St. Louis team.

Abbott: I'm telling you. Who's on first, What's on second, I Don't Know is on third—

Costello: You know the fellows' names?

Abbott: Yes.

Costello: Well, then, who's playin' first?

Abbott: Yes.

Costello: I mean the fellow's name on first base.

Abbott: Who.

Costello: The fellow playin' first base.

Abbott: Who.

Costello: The guy on first base.

Abbott: Who is on first.

Costello: Well, what are you askin' *me* for?

Abbott: I'm not asking you—I'm telling you. Who is on first.

Costello: I'm asking you—who's on first?

Abbott: That's the man's name!

Costello: That's who's name?

Abbott: Yes.

Costello: Well, go ahead, tell me!

Abbott: Who.

Costello: Have you got a first baseman on first?

Abbott: Certainly.

Costello: Then who's playing first?

Abbott: Absolutely.

Costello: Well, all I'm trying to find out is what's the guy's name on first base.

Abbott: Oh, no, no. What is on second base.

Costello: I'm not asking you who's on second.

Abbott: Who's on first.

Costello: That's what I'm trying to find out.

Abbott: Now, take it easy.

Costello: What's the guy's name on first base?

Abbott: What's the guy's name on second base.

Costello: I'm not askin' ya who's on second.

Abbott: Who's on first.

Costello: I don't know.

Abbott: He's on third.

Costello: If I mentioned the third baseman's name, who did I say is playing third?

Abbott: No, Who's playing first.

Costello: Stay offa first, will ya?

Abbott: Well, what do you want me to do?

Costello: Now, what's the guy's name on first base?

Abbott: What's on second.

Costello: I'm not asking ya who's on second.

Abbott: Who's on first.

Costello: I don't know.

Abbott: He's on third.

Costello: There I go back to third again.

Abbott: Please. Now, what is it you want to know?

Costello: What is the fellow's name on third base?

Abbott: What is the fellow's name on second base.

Costello: I'm not askin' ya who's on second.

Abbott: Who's on first.

Costello: I don't know. You got an outfield?

Abbott: Oh, sure.

Costello: The left fielder's name?

Abbott: Why.

Costello: I just thought I'd ask.

Abbott: Well, I just thought I'd tell you.

Costello: Then tell me who's playing left field.

Abbott: Who's playing first.

Costello: Stay out of the infield. I want to know what's the fellow's name in left field.

Abbott: What is on second.

Costello: I'm not asking you who's on second.

Abbott: Now, take it easy, take it easy.

Costello: And the left fielder's name?

Abbott: Why.

Costello: Because.

Abbott: Oh, he's center field.

Costello: Wait a minute. You got a pitcher?

Abbott: Wouldn't this be a fine team without a pitcher?

Costello: Tell me the pitcher's name.

Abbott: Tomorrow.

Costello: You don't want to tell me today?

Abbott: I'm telling you, man.

Costello: Then go ahead.

Abbott: Tomorrow.

Costello: What time tomorrow are you gonna tell me who's pitching?

Abbott: Now listen. Who is not pitching. Who is on—

Costello: I'll break your arm if you say who's on first.

Abbott: Then why come up here and ask?

Costello: I want to know what's the pitcher's name.

Abbott: What's on second.

Costello: Ya gotta catcher?

Abbott: Yes.

Costello: The catcher's name?

Abbott: Today.

Costello: Today. And Tomorrow's pitching.

Abbott: Yes.

Costello: I'm a good catcher, too, you know.

Abbott: I know that.

Costello: I would like to catch. Tomorrow's pitching and I'm catching.

Abbott: Yes.

Costello: Tomorrow throws the ball and the guy up bunts the ball.

Abbott: Yes.

Costello: Now when he bunts the ball—me being a good catcher—I want to throw the guy out at first base, so I pick up the ball and throw it to who?

Abbott: Now, that's the first thing you've said right.

Costello: I DON'T EVEN KNOW WHAT I'M TALKING ABOUT!

Abbott: Well, that's all you have to do.

Costello: Is to throw it to first base.

Abbott: Yes.

Costello: Now who's got it?

Abbott: Naturally.

Costello: Who has it?

Abbott: Naturally.

Costello: Okay.

Abbott: Now you've got it.

Costello: I pick up the ball and I throw it to Naturally.

Abbott: No you don't. You throw the ball to first base.

Costello: Then who gets it?

Abbott: Naturally.

Costello: I throw the ball to Naturally.

Abbott: You don't. You throw it to Who.

Costello: Naturally.

Abbott: Well, naturally. Say it that way.

Costello: I said I'd throw the ball to Naturally.

Abbott: You don't. You throw it to Who.

Costello: Naturally.

Abbott: Yes.

Costello: So I throw the ball to first base and Naturally gets it.

Abbott: No. You throw the ball to first base—

Costello: Then who gets it?

Abbott: Naturally.

Costello: That's what I'm saying.

Abbott: You're not saying that.

Costello: I throw the ball to first base.

Abbott: Then Who gets it.

Costello: He better get it.

Abbott: That's it. All right now, don't get excited. Take it easy.

Costello: Now I throw the ball to first base, whoever it is grabs the ball, so the guy runs to second.

Abbott: Uh-huh.

Costello: Who picks up the ball and throws it to What. What throws it to I Don't Know. I Don't Know throws it back to Tomorrow—a triple play.

Abbott: Yeah. It could be.

Costello: Another guy gets up and it's a long fly ball to center. Why? I don't know. And I don't care.

Abbott: What was that?

Costello: I said, I don't care.

Abbott: Oh, that's our shortstop. *(Costello steps close to Abbott and they glare at each other.)*

READING COMPREHENSION

Summarizing. Choose the best phrase to complete each sentence. Then write the complete statements on your paper.

1. When Bud Abbott said, "On the St. Louis team, Who's on first," he meant that _____ (he really didn't know the player's name, he had forgotten the player's name, the player's name was Who).

2. When Lou Costello asked, "Then, who's playin' first?" and Abbot said, "Yes," Abbott meant that _____ (Costello had named the first baseman correctly, Yes was the first baseman's name, he didn't know the answer).

3. When Costello said, "I don't care," he was _____ (trying to identify the shortstop, saying what he meant, naming the pitcher).

Interpreting. Write the answer to each question on your paper.

1. What was Bud Abbott's role in this comedy routine? What did Lou Costello do in the routine?

2. How did their two roles fit together?

3. How did all the puns in "Who's on First?" cause Lou Costello's complete confusion?

For Thinking and Discussing. Do you think someone who didn't speak English well would understand this routine? Why or why not?

UNDERSTANDING LITERATURE

Puns. "Who's on First?" is based on puns. A *pun* is a play on words. It is a funny way of using words that sound the same but have different meanings.

Here is a list of jokes, preceded by a list of words which complete each joke with a pun. Choose the word that belongs in each blank. Write your answers on your paper.

quackers	cents
stories	pane
Pharaoh's	

1. "Why did the window call the doctor?"
   "Because it had a _____."

2. "Everything in my uncle's store costs a penny."
   "That makes a lot of _____."

3. "Which building has the most _____?"
   "The public library."

4. "If you put six ducks in a crate, what do you have?"
   "A box of _____."

5. "What was the most popular ride in the king of Egypt's amusement park?"
   "The _____ wheel."

WRITING

Write a short dialogue of your own in which you introduce two or three puns. One character should set up the jokes while the other one presents the puns.

How Beautiful With Mud

by Hildegarde Dolson

Hildegarde read an ad. It told her what to buy to make herself beautiful. She saved her money and bought the product. But things turned out to be harder than she'd expected. Here is a woman remembering something embarrassing that happened when she was a teenager. At the time, it seemed terrible. But, years later, she sees how funny it was—and so do we.

There is a sure way to tell when a female goes over the boundary from childhood into meaningful adolescence. Just watch how long it takes her to get to bed at night. My own crossover was summed up in our family as "What on earth is Hildegarde doing in the bathroom?" It must have occurred when I was a freshman in high school. Until then, I fell into bed dog-tired each night. But then I became aware of the Body Beautiful, as shown in advertisements in women's magazines. I, too, would be beautiful. I would also be Flower-Fresh, Fastidious, and Dainty—virtues obviously prized above pearls by the entire male sex.

Somehow, out of my dollar-a-week allowance, I managed to buy Mum, Odorono, Listerine, and something called Nipso. The latter was guaranteed to remove hair from arms and legs. It would make a man think, "Oooo, what a flawless surface." It's true that I was not a particularly hairy child. Still, I applied the Nipso painstakingly in the bathroom one night with my sister Sally as my audience. After Sally had been watching me for a few minutes, she began holding her nose. Finally she asked me to unlock the door and let her out. "Don't you want to see me wash it off?" I asked, rather hurt.

"No," Sally said. "It smells funny."

In the next hour, as my father, mother, and brothers followed their noses to the upstairs hall, Jimmy, being a simple child, merely said, "Pugh," and went away. My father thought it was most like the odor of rotten eggs. Bobby said that no, it was more like a mouse that's been dead quite a while. Mother was more tactful. She only remarked that Nipso obviously wasn't meant to be applied in

a house people lived in. I was prevailed upon to throw the rest of the can away.

I didn't mind too much. I already had my eye on something that sounded far more fascinating. This was a miraculous substance called Beauty Clay. Even the story of its discovery was a masterpiece. Seems this girl was traveling in a European country and ran out of powder and makeup lotion. She really *needed* them to cover up bumps. She had the presence of

mind to go to a nearby hamlet, pick up a handful of mud, and plaster it on her face. Then she lay dozing in the sun, by a brook. When she came to, she washed the clay-like mud off her face. When she looked at her reflection in the brook, she knew she had hit the jackpot. Boy, was she beautiful.

Looking at the before-and-after pictures, I could well understand why a jar of the Clay cost $4.98. In fact, it was dirt cheap at the price. My only problem was how to lay my hands on $4.98.

Each month, the high school honor roll was published in the *Franklin News Herald*. And each month, my own name was absent. Appeals to my better nature, my pride, and the honor of the family did no good. I meant well. But freshman algebra, implying as it did that x equals y, was simply beyond me. Finally my father said that if I got on the honor roll, he'd give me five dollars. The price of the Beauty Clay. From there on in, I was straining every muscle. When I say that I got 89 in algebra and climbed to the bottom rung of the honor roll, I am stating a miracle simply. What is more important, I got the five bucks.

I made my way, on foot, to Riesenman's drugstore. When Mr. Riesenman said he had no Beauty Clay, I felt sad. When he said he'd never even heard of the stuff, I was appalled. It took three trips to convince him that he must order it immediately, money on the line.

Then I went home and waited. I waited five days. After that, I made daily inquiries on my way home from school.

Finally came the wonderful afternoon when Mr. Riesenman said, "Here you are, Hildegarde."

It took a week more before I could achieve the needed privacy for my quick-change act. Mother was taking Jimmy and Sally downtown to get new shoes, Bobby was going skiing, and my father, as usual, would be at the office. I got home to the empty house at 20 minutes of four, and made a beeline for the Beauty Clay. According to the directions, I then washed off all makeup. In my own case, that was a faint dash of powder on my nose. I wrapped myself in a sheet. Then I took a small wooden paddle the manufacturer had provided, and dug into the jar.

The Beauty Clay was a rather peculiar shade of grayish-green. I spread this all over my face and neck—"even to the hairline where telltale wrinkles hide." The directions also urged me not to talk or smile during the 20 minutes it would take the clay to dry. The last thing in the world I wanted to do was talk or smile.

The thick green clay dried firmly in place. My face and neck felt as if they'd been cast in cement. Obviously, something was happening. I sat bolt upright in a chair and let it happen.

After 15 minutes of this, the doorbell rang. I decided to ignore it. The doorbell rang again and again. Nobody at our house ever ignored doorbells, and I was relieved when it stopped. In my eagerness to see who had been calling on us, I ran to my window, opened it, and leaned out. The departing guest was the man who brought us country butter each week. Hearing the sound of the window opening above him, he looked up. When he saw me leaning out, his mouth dropped open and he let out an awful sound. Then he turned and ran down the steep hill. I couldn't imagine what had struck him.

I remembered the clay and went to look in a mirror. I understood. Swathed in a sheet, my skin a sickly gray-green, I scared even myself.

According to the clock, the Beauty Clay had been on the required 20 minutes. It was now ready to be washed off. It occurred to me that if 20 minutes was enough to make me beautiful, 30 minutes or even 40 minutes would make me twice as beautiful.

By the time my face was so rigid that even my eyeballs felt yanked from their sockets, I knew I must be done. As I started back to the bathroom, I heard Bobby's voice downstairs yelling, "Mom!" I ran back and just managed to bolt myself inside the bathroom as Bobby leaped up the stairs. Then I turned on the water and set to work. The directions had warned, "Use only gentle splashes to remove the mask. No rubbing or washcloth." It took several minutes of gentle splashing to make me realize this was getting me nowhere fast. It was like splashing at the Rock of Gibraltar. Maybe it wouldn't hurt if I rubbed the beauty mask just a little, with a nailbrush. This hurt only the nailbrush.

By this time, I was getting worried. Mother would be home very soon. I needed a face—any old face. It occurred to me that a silver knife would be a big help. I ran down to the sideboard, tripping over my sheet as I went, and got the knife. Unfortunately, just as I was coming back through the upstairs hall, Bobby met me, face to face. To do him justice, he realized almost instantly that this was his own sister, and not, as he at first imagined, a sea monster.

I had often imagined how my family would look at me after the Beauty Clay had taken effect. Now it had taken effect—and Bobby was certainly reacting.

"Wh—what?" he finally managed to croak, pointing at my face. I tried to explain what had happened. The sounds that came out alarmed him even more.

I dashed into the bathroom and began hitting the handle of the knife against my rocky visage. To my heavenly relief, it began to crack. After repeated blows, the stuff had broken up enough to allow me to wiggle my jaw. Bobby stood at the door watching.

I dug the blade of the knife in, and by scraping, gouging, digging, and prying, I got part of my face clear. As soon as I could talk, I turned on Bobby. "If you tell anybody about this, I'll kill you," I said fiercely.

Bobby said, "Cross my heart and hope to die."

He then pointed out that spots of the gray-green stuff were still very much with me. As I grabbed up the nailbrush again, he asked in a hushed voice, "But what is it?"

"Beauty Clay," I said. "I sent away for it."

I now looked into the mirror expecting to see results that would wipe out all memory of suffering. The reflection that met my eye was certainly changed, all right. It varied between an angry scarlet where the skin had been rubbed off, to the greenish splotches still clinging.

Maybe if I got it all off, I thought. When it was all off, except those portions wedded to my hair, I gazed at myself wearily. My face was my own—but raw. Instead of the Body Beautiful I looked like the Body Boiled. Even worse, my illusions had been cracked wide open, and not by a silver knife.

"You look awfully red," Bobby said. I did indeed. To add to my troubles, we could now hear the family downstairs. Mother's voice came up, "Hildegarde, will you come set the table right away, dear?"

I moved numbly.

"You'd better take off the sheet," Bobby said.

I took off the sheet.

Just as I reached the stairs, he whispered, "Why don't you say you were frostbitten and rubbed yourself with snow?"

I looked at him with limp gratitude.

When Mother saw my scarlet, splotched face, she exclaimed in concern, "Why, Hildegarde, are you feverish?" She made a move as if to feel my forehead, but I backed away. I was burning up, but not with fever.

"I'm all right," I said. With my face half in the china cupboard, I mumbled that I'd been frostbitten and had rubbed myself with snow.

"Oh, Cliff," Mother called. "Little Hildegarde was frostbitten."

My father immediately came out to the kitchen. "How could she be frostbitten?" he asked reasonably. "It's 34 degrees above zero."

"But her ears still look white," Mother said.

They probably did, too, compared to the rest of my face. By some oversight, I had neglected to put Beauty Clay on my ears. "I'm all right," I insisted again. "I rubbed hard to get the circulation going."

Bobby had followed me out to the kitchen to see how the frostbite story went over. As Mother kept exclaiming over my condition, he now said staunchly, "She's all right. Let her alone."

"Bobby, did you and your friends knock Hildegarde down and rub her face with snow?" my father asked.

"Me?" Bobby squeaked. He gave me a dirty look, as if to say, "You'd better talk fast."

I denied hotly that Bobby had done any such thing. In fact, I proceeded to build him up as my sole rescuer. A great big St. Bernard of a brother who had come bounding through the snowdrifts to bring me life and hope.

Bobby looked so gratified at what he'd been through in my story that I knew my secret was safe.

Sally, always an affectionate child, began to sob. "She might have died. Bobby saved her from freezing."

My father and mother remained dry-eyed. They were suspicious, but inclined to do nothing.

And in a way I *had* been frostbitten. Lying in bed that night, still smarting, I tried to think up ways to get even. It wasn't clear to me exactly whom or what I had to get even with. All I knew was that I was sore and unbeautiful, and out five dollars. I suddenly conceived my plan for revenge. It was so simple and logical and yet brilliant that my mind relaxed at last. Some day I, too, would write advertisements.

READING COMPREHENSION

Summarizing. Choose the best phrase to complete each sentence. Then write the complete statements on your paper.

1. When Hildegarde became a teenager, she _____ (met her first boyfriend, got her first job, wanted to become beautiful).

2. When Hildegarde was a freshman in high school, she started spending more time _____ (in school, asleep, in the bathroom).

3. The problem with Nipso was that it _____ (didn't work, smelled terrible, cost too much).

4. Hildegarde thought Beauty Clay was worth $4.98 because _____ (it made the woman in the ad so beautiful, most creams cost more, it had worked for her friends).

5. Hildegarde left the Beauty Clay on longer than the suggested 20 minutes because she _____ (didn't read the directions correctly, thought she would become even more beautiful, didn't watch the clock).

6. When Hildegarde left the clay on her face too long, it _____ (turned purple, made her more beautiful, became very hard to remove).

7. When Hildegarde finally removed the clay, her face was _____ (red and sore, frostbitten, very pretty).

Interpreting. Write the answer to each question on your paper.

1. What did Hildegarde plan to do with the money she got for making the school honor roll?

2. Why did Hildegarde become interested in beauty products?

3. What part of the Beauty Clay ad convinced Hildegarde to buy the product?

416

4. Why didn't Hildegarde answer the doorbell, even though it rang again and again?

5. Why did the man who delivered butter to Hildegarde's house run away when he saw Hildegarde lean out of the window?

6. Why did the Beauty Clay become so hard?

7. What did Hildegarde learn from her experience with Beauty Clay?

8. Why did Hildegarde decide to become an advertisement writer?

For Thinking and Discussing

1. When she saw the results of the Beauty Clay, the author said, "My illusions had been cracked wide open—and not by a silver knife." What did she mean by this statement?

2. Do you think Hildegarde's experience with Beauty Clay changed her thinking about becoming beautiful? Why or why not?

3. Can you think of any ads like the one for Beauty Clay? How do they sell the product? Why do people respond to this kind of advertising?

UNDERSTANDING LITERATURE

Ironic Situations. Writers of humor sometimes use irony to make a point. At other times, they use irony just to make readers laugh.

"How Beautiful With Mud" contained many ironic situations. In each situation, Hildegarde expected something good to happen. The results, however, were anything but good. Every time she tried some new beauty treatment, something went wrong, and the harder she tried, the worse things became. Each of these situations was not only ironic, but funny.

Here are five things that Hildegarde tried to do to become beautiful. Write each number on your paper. Next to it, write what she hoped would happen. Then write what actually occurred.

1. She spent hours in the bathroom every night.

2. She tried Nipso on her legs.

3. She went to the drugstore with $5.

4. She left the Beauty Clay on twice as long as suggested.

5. She finally removed the Beauty Clay.

WRITING

Make up two products and write an advertisement for each. Promise your readers anything, as long as you persuade them to buy the product. (This is probably what Hildegarde had in mind when she planned to become an ad writer.) Then tell about an ironic situation that could occur when each product is used. Be sure that the results of using the product are not what you would expect from the advertisement.

Section Review

VOCABULARY

Idioms. You have already learned that writers use similes and metaphors to give words more than their exact, literal meaning. *Idioms* are everyday expressions, such as *raining cats and dogs*. The meaning of the whole idiom is different from its word-for-word, literal meaning.

Each of the following sentences from selections in this section contains an idiom. Write each idiom on your paper. Then write what people mean when they use the idiom.

1. ". . . I *felt like a new man* again."

2. "I *gave my heart* to my Bonnie . . ."

3. "*Her heart belonged* to Phoebe . . ."

4. "And get things *shipshape*."

5. "With the *speed of lightning,* Phoebe gave a terrible kick."

6. "Phoebe herself began *spinning like a top*."

7. "It took three trips to convince him he must order it immediately, money *on the line*."

8. "In fact, it was *dirt cheap* at the price."

9. "I got home to the empty house at 20 minutes of four, and *made a beeline for* the Beauty Clay."

READING

Author's Purpose. Writers of fiction or nonfiction may have a number of purposes in writing stories, plays, articles, or books. Their purpose may be to describe, inform, entertain, instruct, or persuade. Writers of humor often have other, specialized purposes. They may want to make fun of something, to get people to laugh at themselves and change their ways, or just to show how confusing life can be. To carry out these purposes, writers of humor may use satire, exaggeration, irony, puns, or a combination of these and other techniques.

Here is a list of purposes for the selections you read in this section. On your paper, write each purpose. Then write the title of the selection or selections that fit each purpose.

1. to show how advertisements sometimes trick people

2. to make people aware of the problems of air pollution

3. to use words in a funny way

4. to make fun of life on a farm

5. to show how people learn to live with problems rather than try to correct them

6. to convince people to change their way of life

7. to show that people usually get what they deserve in the long run

8. to create confusion

418

WRITING

A Description. A description is a word picture. When you describe something—a scene, an event, a person—you want the readers to "experience" your subject in their imaginations. One way to create a vivid picture is to include sensory details in your description. Sensory details appeal to the five senses: sight, hearing, taste, smell, and touch.

Step 1: Set Your Goal

"How Beautiful with Mud" includes the following description of Nipso hair remover:

> My father thought it was most like the odor of rotten eggs. Bobby said that no, it was more like a mouse that's been dead quite a while.

This description appeals to the sense of smell. Choose one of the following topics for a description:

1. In "How Beautiful With Mud," Hildegarde does not describe her room. Write a description of her bedroom as you imagine it to be. Try to include details that will appeal to the visual sense so that your readers can "see" the room.

2. Write a description of a baseball game or other sports event. The event could be one you participated in. Describe the scene as fully as possible by including details that appeal to the senses.

Step 2: Make a Plan

Now you are ready to make a list of details about your topic. Think of how you want readers to "experience" what you are describing, and list details that will help them do that. For example, Hildegarde wanted the reader to know just what her face looked like with the Beauty Clay on it. She therefore included details such as her "sickly gray-green" skin. Details can be expressed in a single word, in a phrase, or in a sentence.

Suppose Hildegard Dolson had made a list of details before writing "How Beautiful with Mud." Her list might have included the following items:

SUBJECT: Hildegarde's face after using Beauty Clay

DETAILS: angry scarlet
greenish splotches of clay still clinging
sore and unbeautiful

Once you have completed your list of details, you can decide how you want to organize them. If you are describing an event such as a baseball game, you will probably want to use chronological order, the order in which each aspect of the event actually took place. If you are describing a person, place, or thing, however, you may want to use natural order or spatial order.

When you use natural order, you begin your description with an overall impression and then focus in on more specific details. If you were describing a room, for example, you might begin by saying that it was large, dim, and drafty and continue by describing the color of the walls, the drapes, the size and shape of the windows, and other details.

When you use spatial order, you guide the reader from one place to another. In a spatial description of that same room, for example, you might start with the heavy drapes on the windows, move on to the rows of bookshelves on the wall next to the windows, and then go to the desk in front of the bookshelves.

Step 3: Write a First Draft
When you write your first draft, keep in mind the impression you want readers to get. Try to follow the organization you planned, and use your list of details as a guide. Try to make your details vivid and clear. A draft of a description of that room might begin like this:

> It was a large, drafty room, dim and shadowy. The windows were covered with dark drapes. The walls on each side of the windows had dark, wooden bookshelves from floor to ceiling.

Step 4: Revise
When you revise your draft, think about how to make the description more vivid. Remember, you want to appeal to your reader's senses. Ask yourself if you can see, hear, touch, taste, or smell each detail.

One way to make a description clear is to use specific nouns and verbs. For example, *mansion* is more specific than *house,* and *shouted* is more specific than *said.* The author of the description of the room might decide to replace *dark* with *maroon velvet* and might decide to add details such as that the drapes were heavy and overpowering.

Ask yourself these questions:

1. Are the details in my description sharp and vivid?

2. Are the details presented in an order that makes sense?

3. Have I used words that appeal to the senses?

After revising your first draft, proofread it for mistakes in spelling, grammar, and punctuation. Then copy it over.

QUIZ

The following is a quiz for Section 9. Write the answers in complete sentences on your paper.

Reading Comprehension

1. What did Art Buchwald notice about the air in Flagstaff, Arizona? How did he deal with this?

2. In the poem "And They Lived Happily Ever After for a While," why did the couple need an oxygen tent?

3. How did Phoebe the cow treat Jeremiah differently from everyone else in "The Cow Who Liked to Kick"? Why?

4. What were the names of some of the players and their positions in "Who's on First?"

5. How did Hildegarde explain the way she looked to her parents after she had used Beauty Clay?

Understanding Literature

6. What problem did Art Buchwald satirize in "Fresh Air Will Kill You"? What point did he make?

7. How is the title of the poem "And They Lived Happily Ever After for a While" ironic?

8. What technique did Ambrose Bierce use in "The Cow Who Liked to Kick"?

9. What is a pun? How do puns cause confusion in "Who's on First?"

10. In what way is Hildegarde's experience with Beauty Clay an example of irony?

ACTIVITIES

Word Attack

1. Some compound words are written with a hyphen between the words that make up the compound. At other times, the compound is made up of separate words. An example of such an open compound is *ice cream*. The following examples of compounds are from this section. Are they written with hyphens or open? You may use a dictionary or find the compound in the story to check.

dog tired   high school
air pollution   honor roll
dry eyed   gray green

Write four sentences using these compound words. Try to use more than one compound in the same sentence.

2. The word *visage* appears in "How Beautiful with Mud." This word contains the Latin root *vis*, which means "to see." A person's *visage*, his or her face, is probably the first thing we see when we look at someone. There are a number of other words that contain this root. For each definition below, write the word that contains the root *vis*.
   a. sense of sight
   b. to go to see
   c. able to be seen
   d. part of a cap that shades the eyes
   e. apparatus on which images can be seen

Speaking and Listening. Get together with a classmate and act out all or a part of "Who's On First?" Remember that in the routine, Lou Costello is getting more and more frustrated and upset because he can't understand the answers to his questions. Be prepared to perform the routine for the class.

Research. "Fresh Air Will Kill You" was published in 1966. Go to the library and research the answers to the following questions about air pollution. Use the almanac and data from charts and graphs.
   a. What are *emission standards*?
   b. What are the provisions of the Clean Air Amendments of 1970?

Creating. Think of a beauty product, either real or imaginary. Write an advertisement that you think would appeal to people your age. If you like, write your ad as a script to be acted out on TV. Or you might design a print ad for a magazine or newspaper. Use pictures and different sizes and styles of print for different parts of the ad.

IDENTITY

Everybody is a star
I can feel it when you shine on me
I love you for who you are
Not the one you feel you need to be. . . .

— Sylvester (Sly Stone) Stewart

Birthday
Marc Chagall (1887–1985).
Museum of Modern Art,
Acquired through the Lillie P. Bliss Bequest.

Identity

What are you really like? What special qualities identify you? Establishing your identity and maintaining it in the face of challenges may be the most difficult tasks you will face in life.

Throughout history, writers have been fascinated with the problem of identity—how we discover who we are and how we present ourselves to others. Some authors have written about people discovering their "roots," or struggling to be themselves when other people want them to change. Many authors have written about people's self-discovery through happiness or hardship. Still others have written about characters who battle their own limitations or fears to accomplish something important.

The five writers whose works you will read in this section all focus on identity. They describe the efforts of characters to discover and to be themselves. The characters strive to assert their identity in a world filled with such identity-robbing "enemies" as prejudice, loss of parents, poverty, old age, and blindness.

Your "Self"

Being yourself starts with getting to know the "self" you are. Your identity is made up of two parts. The first part you are born with, or given by your parents. The second part you develop as you grow up. You are given your name, nationality, family history, race, and parts of your personality. Over time, you develop the rest of your personality, your values or beliefs, your personal history, and your relationships with others.

Some parts of a person's "self" remain constant; others change. All people grow older and become wiser through experience. Their bodies and lives change over time. They begin to look at everything, including themselves, differently.

New situations also cause people to change. A child starts school, for example, and has to learn to fit in with a large group of children. Or a divorce causes a child and the parents to make major mental and physical adjustments. Or a person fails at something and must learn to accept the failure and work harder to succeed the next time. All of these changes are part of personal growth.

Writing About Identity

The five selections in this section deal with the issue of personal growth at different stages of a person's development. Santha Rama Rau writes about an incident from her early childhood in "By Any Other Name." Doris Halman focuses on a young man in "The Rocking Horse." Hugh Garner's "A Trip for Mrs. Taylor" deals with the problems of an elderly woman. Edna St. Vincent Millay's poem, "Dirge Without Music," focuses on the loss of identity at death. In "Stevie Wonder: Growing Up in a World of Darkness," James Haskins relates a young black boy's struggle with blindness.

The selections in this section also deal with different aspects of a person's struggle to establish his or her identity.

How important is a name? Can changing a person's name change his or her identity? The headmistress of a British school in "By Any Other Name" tries to change the names of the two Indian girls. As the narrative continues, Santha realizes that the school and the headmistress are trying to change more than just her name.

Corky, in "The Rocking Horse," has been trying to shape his identity ever since he was deserted by his mother at the age of four. One day, a coincidence leads Corky back to his childhood, his first home, and his rocking horse. It also leads him to a conflict—and to knowledge about himself.

In "A Trip for Mrs. Taylor," an older woman struggles to do something important for herself. She doesn't want to let her age or her poverty "lock" her into her apartment, away from the world of other people. Her desire for change, for new sights, and for excitement is so great that she saves up for a trip. Mrs. Taylor's story

illustrates that directing one's own life is a very important part of a person's struggle for identity.

"Dirge Without Music" deals with the ultimate threat to a person's identity—death. The poem suggests that a person is more than a body, that people's identities don't die when their bodies do.

In "Stevie Wonder: Growing Up in a World of Darkness," a young boy learns he can live with his lack of sight. By accepting himself and developing his other senses, Stevie finds his identity. He also discovers a talent within himself that opens up a whole new world.

Reading About Identity

In a story about personal growth, the characters are usually more important than the plot. The plot provides situations in which the characters' identities are challenged. They must react to the challenges and change and grow.

As you read the selections in this section, think carefully about the main characters. Ask yourself what they are learning about themselves and what each is trying to say about his or her identity as a person.

Reading about other people's struggles to be themselves may help you learn more about yourself. Challenge yourself. Turn the page and start reading.

By Any Other Name

by Santha Rama Rau

Events in your childhood can be very important. In fact, some early experiences may affect the way you grow up and think about things later.

In this selection, the author writes about something that happened to her when she was only five years old.

My sister and I were sent to an Anglo-Indian school when she was eight and I was five. On the first day of school, our names were changed.

"So you're the new girls," the headmistress said to us. "What are your names?"

My sister answered for us. "I am Premila." Then she nodded at me. "She is Santha."

The English headmistress had been in India for about 15 years, I suppose. But she still smiled helplessly when she heard Indian names.

"Oh, my dears," she said. "Those names are much too hard for me. Suppose we give you pretty English names. Pamela for you," she said to my sister. To me she said, "How about Cynthia for you? Isn't that nice?"

My sister was harder to push around than I was. She did not answer. I said, "Thank you," in a tiny voice.

We were sent to that school because our family had moved. My father, who worked for the government, now had his headquarters in that town. His job was to inspect villages in the area. Just a week before, he had left on one of his tours.

Up to then, my mother had refused to send Premila to a school run by the British. She used to say, "You can bury a dog's tail for seven years, and it still comes out curly. You can take the British away from their country for a lifetime, and they still remain British."

In those days, a degree from an Indian school was not worth much. So at first, our mother taught us at home. When her health broke down, we were sent to the Anglo-Indian school.

I'll never forget that first day of school. If your name is changed at that age, you develop another personality. I remember wondering how "Cynthia" would act. But I did not feel responsible for what she did.

There were about 40 students at the school. About a dozen were Indians —

four of them in my class. They all sat at the back of the room, and I went to join them.

I sat next to a small, serious girl who didn't smile at me. She had long braids and wore a cotton dress—in the English style. But she still kept on her Indian jewelry. The cotton dress must have looked strange to me. But I planned to ask my mother if I could wear a cotton dress to school, too.

After I sat down, the teacher pointed to me and asked me to stand up. She said, "Now, dear, tell the class your name." I stood up and said nothing.

"What is your name?" she insisted.

"I don't know," I finally said.

There were about nine English children at the front of the class. They giggled and turned to look at me. I sat down quickly. I opened my eyes very wide to keep the tears from falling. The

little girl with the braids reached out and lightly touched my arm. She still didn't smile.

After that, I was fairly bored. I looked at the children's drawings that were pinned to the wall. Then I watched a lizard that was on the ledge outside a window. Once in a while it would shoot out its tongue for a fly. Then it would rest with its eyes closed.

The lessons were mostly about reading, writing, and simple numbers. They were things my mother had already taught me. So I paid very little attention.

When the teacher wrote some words on the chalkboard, only the word *apple* was new to me. I had never seen an apple before. I didn't know what it meant.

At lunchtime, I followed the little girl with the braids out onto the porch. Children from the other classes were there already. I saw Premila and ran over to her. She was in charge of our lunchbox.

I noticed that the other children were beginning to eat sandwiches. Premila and I were the only ones who had brought Indian food. Premila quickly handed me my lunch. Then she whispered that I should go and sit with my class. That was what the others were doing.

"She is the youngest," Mother would explain to Premila. "We have to allow for that."

I had often heard her say this. It made sense to me. But because of this, I had no clear idea of what "winning" meant.

We played tag at school that afternoon. I let one of the little English boys catch me. Then I was surprised when the other children would not let *me* catch *them.*

I ran around for what seemed like hours. I did not catch anyone. Later I learned that I was "not being a good sport." I stopped letting myself be caught. But it was many years before I really learned what it meant to compete.

When I saw our car come up to the school gate, I rushed toward it. I yelled to our nursemaid, who had come to take us home. It seemed like years since I had seen her that morning.

Premila quietly followed me. She told me on the way home never to do that again in front of the other children.

When we got home, we went to Mother's room to have tea with her. I climbed onto the bed and bounced up and down gently. Mother asked how we liked our first day of school.

I was so glad to be home — and to have left Cynthia behind — that I said nothing. But I did ask her what *apple* meant.

Premila told Mother about her class. She added that they had weekly tests to see if they had learned their lessons.

I asked, "What is a test?"

Premila said, "You're too small to have them. You won't have them in your

The little Indian girl from my class looked at my food with longing. I offered her some, but she shook her head and quietly ate her sandwiches.

I was very sleepy after lunch. At home we always took a nap after lunch. It was usually a pleasant time of day. Mother would read a story to us, and we would drift into sleep. Later our nursemaid would wake us, and we would have tea.

At school we rested for a short time on cots. Then we had to play games.

I had never really learned how to compete in games. Whenever we played tag at home, I was always allowed to "win."

class for donkey's years." She had learned the expression *donkey's years* that day. She was using it for the first time, and we all laughed at it.

She also told Mother that we should take sandwiches to school from now on. It wasn't that *she* cared, she said. But sandwiches would be easier for me to handle.

A week later, the day of Premila's first test, our lives changed. I was sitting at the back of my class next to the girl with the braids. Her name, I had learned, was Nalini. But she was called Nancy in school. I had started a friendship with her.

As I sat beside her that day, the door opened and Premila marched in. The teacher smiled and said, "You're Cynthia's sister, aren't you?"

Premila didn't even look at the teacher. She looked at me and said, "Get up. We're going home."

I didn't know what had happened. But I knew it was something serious. I stood up and started to walk toward my sister.

"Bring your pencils and your notebook," she said.

I went back for them, and we left the room together. The teacher started to say something as Premila closed the door, but I didn't hear what it was.

Without saying a word, we started to walk home. Finally I asked Premila what was wrong. All she said was, "We're going home—for good."

It was a very long walk for a child who was five. I dragged along behind Premila. I wondered if we would ever reach home.

From time to time I shouted, "Wait for me!"

When we got to our house, the nurse-maid was taking a tray of lunch to Mother's room. She asked us why we were home at this hour. Premila wouldn't tell her.

Mother looked very surprised and worried. She asked Premila what had happened.

Premila said, "We had our test today. The teacher made me and the other Indians sit at the back of the room, with a desk between each of us."

Mother asked, "Why was that?"

"She said it was because Indians cheat," Premila answered. "So I don't think we should go back to that school."

Mother was silent for a long time. Then she said, "Of course not, darling." She sounded both unhappy and angry.

We all shared the curry she was having for lunch. Then I went to my bedroom for my nap. I could hear Mother and Premila talking through the open door.

Mother said, "Do you think she understood all that?"

Premila said, "I don't think so. She's a baby."

Mother said, "Well, I hope it won't bother her."

Of course, they were both wrong. I understood what had happened. I remember it all very clearly. But I put it aside, because it all happened to a girl called Cynthia. And I was never very interested in her.

Corky: Well, I told you. I was waitin' for him to be old enough!

Jane: Yes, but . . . if it was in your mind. . . . How long has it been in your mind?

Corky: I guess since he was born.

Jane: Oh, Corky, then it meant something very important, didn't it, dear? Will you tell me what?

Corky: You'd just laugh.

Jane: No, I wouldn't. Try me.

Corky: Okay. I want Tommy to have a rockin' horse because I had one and I loved it better'n anything in the world, and I wasn't so old either, Jane. I was only four when I went to the orphanage, and I had him before that. . . .

Jane: *Before.* . . . But, Corky, I thought you didn't remember *anything* before the orphanage!

Corky: I didn't, anything else. Just Wag. Wag was his name. The horse. *(Rises and crosses downstage.)* I don't remember my name, but that was his, Jane . . . and I know what Wag looked like, too. He was big and white, prancin' and gallopin' with his mane flyin' and his tail . . . and he had a saddle on his back, with a red blanket underneath it, and on the blanket, see, in gold letters, there it was . . . the name "Wag." . . . And I used to ride him every place a little kid wants to go. On the wind, see, I thought I did, Jane. . . . You laughin'?

Jane: Turn around and see if I am.

Corky *(turns and crosses to her):* Thanks. It sounds crazy, but that's how it was. . . . Wag and me ridin' places on the wind . . . where I wanted to go, and so . . . one day I was in the orphanage without my mother, and I wanted her. . . . I thought Wag would come and take me to her on his back . . . because he always had, see, where I wanted? . . .

Jane: Yes, dear. Yes, Corky.

Corky: But he didn't come. I kept lookin' for him, but he didn't, and when he didn't, I cried myself to sleep nights. And then I'd have the dream, Jane, about Wag. . . .

Jane: Did he get there in the dream?

Corky: Yeah, gallopin'! . . . Up to my bed. With his white mane streamin' out behind him, to take me to my mother, only he never did.

Jane: But you didn't forget him. . . .

Corky: Uh-uh. Never. He was my friend. *(Sits.)* Even after the Corcorans took me, and I was seven then, and I'd been told my . . . my mother'd gone away and left me . . . for good . . . I still . . . kind of . . . expected Wag to come some day . . . *(Puts his arm around her.)* because I was lonesome, I guess. The Corcorans were awful good to me, Jane, but they were old folks that didn't know what to do about a little kid. . . . I'm a grown man, now, with a boy of my own, Jane, but once in a while Wag comes gallopin' to me in that old crazy dream. . . . Silly, huh?

Jane: I don't think so. And I think the nicest thing in the world to give Tommy for his birthday is a rocking horse!

Corky: Oh, now, lookit, just because I. . . .

Jane: But I do, Corky! Only not a great big one like Wag, dear . . . a little one for a little bit of a boy . . . that it won't hurt him to fall off of?

Corky: Yeah. A little one. Thanks.

Jane: And I think you're the person to pick it out for him, Corky, so will you?

Corky: If you want me to. A little white one, huh?

Jane: Yes. You could go down to the stores tomorrow in your lunch hour.

Corky: I got a rush job on tomorrow at the warehouse, and I may have to skip my lunch hour! A little white one, eh?

From the corridor, all that can be seen of 247 is a bare floor and one bare board partition. Sound: fade up man's heavy tread on concrete floor.

McElroy comes in.

McElroy *(calls):* Anybody here?

Corky *(coming out of door):* Yeah. That you, Mac? (Corky enters from 247 with a sewing machine which he brings out and sets down in the nearest open space. Takes big rag from overalls pocket, starts wiping dust off machine.) I'm almost through.

McElroy: Fine, Corky. Where's Dan?

Corky: Quit for lunch.

McElroy: *You* had lunch?

Corky: I'll grab some in a minute, Mac. There's only a bunch of little stuff left in there. *(Into other room)* One more trip, and I'll have it all out.

McElroy: I'll help you.

Corky *(laughs):* No, don't bother, thanks just the same. It's just a couple of screens, Mac, propped up against somethin' or other. (Corky, with both hands, takes hold of screens, starts to move them.) I don't need any help with . . . (He has the screens away from the corner now, and behind them is a huge, once very expensive but now dust-covered, battered white rocking horse.) with . . . (And the letters, suddenly wiped clean, are obviously initials: W.A.G. Corky, standing transfixed, whispers.) Wag. . . .

McElroy *(appears in doorway):* What's the matter, Corky?

Corky: Huh? Oh. Nothin', Mac, nothin'.

McElroy: Well, what are you doing? What's keepin' you?

Corky: Nothin', I said! I been workin' since before eight this mornin', I can stop to get my breath, can't I? I can get tired, can't I?

McElroy: Sure, sure, Corky. Keep your shirt on, I only asked. And give me those screens. . . . (McElroy tries to take screens from Corky, who resists, still not daring to turn and face him.)

Corky: No, I'm sorry, Mac, I'm okay, I'll. . . .

McElroy: Give 'em to me, Corky!

Corky: Well . . . okay. . . . (Corky yields the screens. He has to turn, and McElroy sees his face.)

McElroy: You're sick, boy, why didn't you tell me?

Corky: I'm not sick. . . .

McElroy: Don't kid me, you look like death. You been overworkin', Corky, you better knock off and go home!

Corky: Home? Now? Not a chance, I want. . . . I got to be here this afternoon, when this . . . this Mrs. Grayson comes.

McElroy: I'll take care of her myself . . .

Corky: No, you won't, Mac, it's my job, and I want to stay on it, I want to get a good look at a woman who . . . who put everythin' she had away from her in cold storage for 25 years . . . like that rocking horse.

McElroy: . . . Darned expensive one, too! Red and gold doodads all over it, and even the kid's initials!

Corky: Yeah! Sure it's initials, isn't it—

G for Grayson. But a little bit of a kid mightn't know that, Mac. I bet if my Tommy saw it, he'd think it was the horse's name, huh? Wag? And the grown-ups wouldn't let him know the difference, because they'd think it was cute and funny . . . Wag . . . so they'd let him. . . .

McElroy: If it is, the joke's beyond me. Look, Corky, you're so tired you're talkin' half out of your head.

Corky: I'll be okay, Mac! Let me stay on the job. Soon's I grab me a bite to eat, I'll feel swell.

McElroy: Then the sooner you grab it, the better, Corky, so come on. . . . I'll take these, and you bring the horse. . . . *(McElroy goes out with the screens.)*

Corky *(voice up):* Yeah, sure. . . . Thanks, Mac, I'm comin'. *(Corky turns to Wag, lifts him under one arm, starts slowly with him across the floor of 247. Free fist comes up to take a gentle swipe at the draggled mane, and his voice is very low and filled with a terrible bitterness.)* Okay, Wag, giddyap, take me to my mother!

Fade in.

McElroy's office. The two men in it are still as statues. McElroy seated behind the desk, Corky at file cabinet.

McElroy: You all right, now, Corky? You still look awful pale around the gills to me.

Corky: Oh, for Pete's sake, Mac, quit worryin', will you?

(The shadow of a tall woman falls across the ground glass. Corky stops short. McElroy follows his glance.

(Sound: knock on door.)

McElroy *(rises):* Come in. *(Mrs. Alexander Grayson opens door. Mrs. Grayson stands for a moment looking from one man to the other.)*

Mrs. Grayson: Superintendent McElroy?

McElroy: That's right. And you're Mrs. Grayson.

Mrs. Grayson: Yes.

McElroy: We've got your things ready for you. This is Bill Corcoran, who'll go upstairs with you and help you.

Mrs. Grayson *(crossly):* If . . . Mr. Corcoran will just show me the way, I shan't need any more help.

McElroy: Oh, but you will, Mrs. Grayson! To move the things around for you, and make a list of what you want done. . . .

Mrs. Grayson: When I finish, I'll come and tell you.

McElroy: I'm sorry. But it's a rule of the warehouse to have a man in attendance while a customer's goods are out in the open.

Mrs. Grayson: Oh, I see. Very well, Mr. McElroy, but I should have preferred being left alone.

McElroy: Corky won't bother you . . . will you, Corky?

Corky: I wouldn't think of it, Mr. McElroy.

Mrs. Grayson: I should like to start at once, so that I may finish as soon as possible. I . . . don't suppose that will be today?

McElroy: You better count on closer to a week.

Mrs. Grayson: A week! I took the hotel room for one night only, Mr. McElroy, and I have no other place to go. . . .

McElroy *(exchanges a glance):* Well, Corky, save Mrs. Grayson all the time you can, huh?

Corky: Okay, Mr. McElroy. If you want to come with me, Mrs. Grayson, your stuff's up on the second floor. . . .

Mrs. Grayson: Thank you. *(McElroy follows them to door. Pauses thoughtfully, turns back to desk.)*

(The corridor. Mrs. Grayson and Corky walk into the light from the outer edge of dimness.)

Corky: This is it, Mrs. Grayson.

Mrs. Grayson *(crossing to him):* Yes, I . . . just at first. It's . . . hard . . . to recognize . . . anything. . . .

Corky: Why not, after 25 years? Nobody'd know what they got rid of that long ago.

Mrs. Grayson *(crossing in):* I didn't get rid of it, Mr. Corcoran. And I shall know it in a moment. I only meant that with everything piled up indiscriminately. . . . *(Breaks off.)*

(Mrs. Grayson suddenly sees a tall, slender vase of tarnished silver, which stands with other bric-a-brac atop a chest of drawers at the head of the aisle. Mrs. Grayson takes a step toward it, half reaches up her arm to touch it, lets arm fall as Corky speaks.)

Corky: Recognize somethin'?

Mrs. Grayson: Yes. Mr. Corcoran. . . .

Corky: What?

Mrs. Grayson: I understand the warehouse rule, but . . . since I myself am here to protect my property, would you please leave me just for an hour?

Corky: Sorry, I can't. You go ahead and look around, and decide what you want to keep.

Mrs. Grayson: I shall keep nothing, Mr. Corcoran. I'm here to dispose of my goods.

Corky: Okay. Then decide what you want destroyed, and what you want put up for sale, and I'll make a list and move the stuff into separate piles.

Mrs. Grayson: The stuff. Yes.

Corky *(crossing behind her to trunks):* Want to get the trunks out of the way first? A lot of people do, because I guess it's the toughest part of the job, lookin' over what's inside. . . . You got the keys, Mrs. Grayson?

Mrs. Grayson: Yes. . . .

Corky: Okay, then you want me to move. . . .

Mrs. Grayson: No. No!

Corky: But you can't unpack 'em where. . . .

Mrs. Grayson: I shall not unpack the trunks, Mr. Corcoran. I shall have them destroyed just . . . as they are now.

Corky: Okay, then I'll shove 'em out of. . . .

Mrs. Grayson: Don't touch those trunks!

Corky: But lookit, Mrs. Grayson. . . .

(Sound: fade up footsteps coming along the corridor. And in the silence, McElroy enters with the young matron, Mrs. Brown.)

McElroy *(off):* Now, along here on this floor, Mrs. Brown, are the private rooms. *(Crossing in)* Oh, excuse me a minute. How's it going, Corky?

(Mrs. Brown crosses downstage right, looking at things.)

Corky: Okay.

McElroy: Mrs. Grayson, you gettin' along all. . . .

Corky: She doesn't want to be disturbed, Mac.

McElroy: Oh . . . all right. Sure, Corky. Well, then, Mrs. Brown, I'm sorry I kept you waiting. . . .

Mrs. Brown: I didn't mind. I'm interested, Mr. McElroy. Is this furniture being stored, too?

McElroy: No, it's . . . goin' out. Shall we. . . .

Mrs. Brown: Looks like it's been here a long time.

McElroy: Quite a while. If you'll come. . . .

Mrs. Brown: Oh, really? *Mine* won't be here quite a while, I can tell you! It's *bad* for things to keep them in storage, isn't it? Why just look at *these* things, they. . . .

Mrs. Grayson: Mr. McElroy, if you don't mind.

Mrs. Brown: Oh! I'm sorry, I didn't realize . . . anyone was. . . . Excuse me. . . . Do let's go, Mr. McElroy. . . . *(Sound: footsteps, gradually fading.)*

Mrs. Brown *(fading off):* I was only thinking about my own. . . . Well, I mean, I just couldn't bear. . . .

Mrs. Grayson: Mr. Corcoran. . . .

Corky: Yeah?

Mrs. Grayson: I think if you'll kindly come here, I can at least make a start.

Corky *(crossing to her. Takes a pad and pencil from his overalls pocket, ready to list her instructions):* Okay.

Mrs. Taylor turned and saw a thin young woman trying to hold a young baby in her arms while she tugged at a little boy. The boy was trying very hard to break away.

"Here, young man, where do you think you're going?" Mrs. Taylor said sternly. The child stopped struggling and looked at her in surprise.

"He's been a little devil all morning," his mother said. "He knows I can't do much with him while I've got the baby in my arms."

"Now you just stand still!" Mrs. Taylor warned, letting him go and smiling at the young woman.

"He'll stop for you," the young woman said. "At home he'll do anything for his grandma, but when he knows I've got the baby to look after, he takes advantage of it."

She learned that the young woman's name was Rawlinson. She was on her way to join her husband. Her mother had wanted to come down to the station with her, but her arthritis had kept her at home. She also learned that the baby's name was Ian, and that his mother was 22 years old.

She in turn told the girl that she had lived alone since her oldest boy's marriage. She explained that Johnnie now lived with his wife and a young daughter in Montreal. She also told the young woman that her husband and youngest son were dead, that she received the old-age pension, and that it wasn't enough in these days of high prices.

Mrs. Taylor realized that she had been starved for conversation. She was so glad to have met the young woman with the children.

"They should be opening the gates pretty soon," said the girl, looking at her watch. "The train is due to leave in 22 minutes."

The little boy, Garry, said that he wanted to go to get some candy.

Mrs. Taylor said eagerly, "I'll hold the baby while you take him, if you like."

"Will you? Wonderful!" the young woman exclaimed. She handed the baby over.

Mrs. Taylor pulled back the blanket from the baby's face and saw that he was awake. She placed her finger on his chin and smiled at him. He smiled back at her. The moment took her back more years than she cared to remember. She was filled with the happiness of those days.

She thought, "I'd give up every minute more I have to live just to be young again and have my boys as babies for one more day." Then, to hide the tears that were starting from her eyes, she began talking to the baby in her arms, rocking back and forth on her heels.

When the woman and the little boy returned, she gave up the baby sadly. She and the young woman stood talking together like old friends. They were talking so much that they didn't notice when the man opened the gates.

The crowd began pushing them from behind. Mrs. Taylor picked up her suitcase in one hand and grasped Garry's hand with the other. Then, followed by Mrs. Rawlinson and the baby, they climbed the set of iron stairs to the platform.

Mrs. Taylor's feet were hurting after the long wait at the gates, but her face shone with happiness as she and the small boy walked alongside the train. The boy's mother caught up with them. A trainman waited to help them aboard.

"You've got your hands full there, Granny," he said, picking up the little boy. She was pleased that he thought she was the children's grandmother.

Inside the train Mrs. Taylor led the way to a pair of seats that faced each other. She dropped into one with a tired sigh. Then she held the baby while his mother placed her small case on the rack above.

"Am I ever glad to get aboard!" Mrs. Rawlinson exclaimed. "I wasn't looking forward to the wait at the station. Now I've only got to change trains in Montreal and I'll be all set." She laid the baby on the seat beside her. Then she sat back and relaxed. The train soon filled up.

When the train started, Mrs. Taylor moved over close to the window and pointed out sights to the little boy. Young Garry loved every moment.

"We won't be getting into Montreal until supper time," Mrs. Rawlinson said.

"No."

"I'll bet you'll be glad to get there and see your granddaughter."

Mrs. Taylor shook her head. "I'm not going to Montreal today," she said sadly. "I can't afford to go that far."

"But—but couldn't your son send you the money?" asked the girl.

She had to protect Johnnie, who wasn't really mean, just forgetful. "Oh, he could, but I've never really cared to go that far," she lied.

"Well—well, where are you going then?" the young woman asked.

"Not very far. Just up the line a bit," Mrs. Taylor answered, smiling. "It's just a short trip."

Mrs. Taylor loved the sight of the rows of houses as seen from the back—yards with drying clothes, and every house having an identity of its own. She only recognized some of the streets after the train had passed them. They looked so different when seen from the speeding train.

In a few minutes the train began to slow down for a station. The conductor came along collecting tickets. When Mrs. Taylor handed him hers, he asked, "Are you getting off here, Madam?"

"Yes, I am," Mrs. Taylor replied, red with embarrassment.

"Have you any luggage?"

She pointed to the suitcase at her feet, ashamed to face the stares of those who were watching her.

"Fine. I'll carry it off for you," the conductor said calmly, as if old ladies took such short train rides every day of the week.

She stood up then and said good-bye to the little boy, letting her hand rest for a long minute on his head. She warned him to be a good boy and do what his mother told him.

"You must think I'm crazy just coming this far," she said to Mrs. Rawlinson. "You see, I've wanted to take a trip for so long, and this was sort of—pretending."

The young woman shook the surprised look from her face. "No I don't, Mrs. Taylor," she said. "I wish you were coming all the way. I don't know what I'd have ever done without you to help me with Garry."

"It was nice being able to help. You'll never know how much I enjoyed it," Mrs. Taylor answered, her face breaking into a shy smile. "Good-bye, dear. Have a nice journey."

"Good-bye," the young woman said. "Thanks! Thanks a lot!"

Mrs. Taylor stood on the station platform and waved at the young woman and her son. They waved at her as the train began to move again. Then she picked up her bag and walked along the platform to the street.

When she got on the bus, the driver said, "You look happy. You must have had a great vacation."

She smiled at him. "I had a wonderful trip," she answered.

And it *had* been wonderful! While all the others in the train would get bored and tired after a few hours of travel, she could go back to her room and lie down on the bed, remembering only the excitement and thrill of going away, and the new friends she had made. Perhaps next month, if she could afford it, she would take a trip to the suburbs on the Winnipeg train!

READING COMPREHENSION

Summarizing. Choose the best phrase to complete each sentence. Then write the complete statements on your paper.

1. Mrs. Taylor got the idea for her trip from _____ (an ad she read in the local newspaper, seeing the holiday crowds in the train station, her daughter-in-law).

2. Mrs. Taylor was proud of being independent, but she wished that someone would _____ (offer her an exciting and fulfilling job, move in with her, need her help).

3. Mrs. Taylor's son and his family lived in _____ (New York, Montreal, Winnipeg).

4. As Mrs. Taylor waited for the train to arrive at the station, she felt _____ (happy and excited, disappointed and bitter, lonely).

5. The woman and the children that Mrs. Taylor met at the train station _____ (made her feel needed again, made the trip difficult, begged her to go to Montreal with them).

6. On her trip, Mrs. Taylor went _____ (all the way to her son's house, as far as Mrs. Rawlinson and her children were going, just up the line to the suburbs).

7. Mrs. Taylor did not go to Montreal on her trip because _____ (she didn't have enough time, she couldn't afford it, she was on the wrong train).

Interpreting. Write the answer to each question on your paper.

1. What made life difficult for Mrs. Taylor?

2. Why had Mrs. Taylor decided not to live in Montreal with her son and his wife?

3. What details in the story show that Mrs. Taylor was excited about the trip she had planned?

4. How did Mrs. Rawlinson and her young son, Garry, make Mrs. Taylor feel needed?

5. Why was Mrs. Taylor embarrassed when she got off the train?

6. Why did Mrs. Taylor feel good after her trip, even though it was a short one?

For Thinking and Discussing. What does the story reveal about the problems older people sometimes face in our society? How did Mrs. Taylor cope with these problems?

UNDERSTANDING LITERATURE

Character Motivation. When you read a story, you can find clues to what motivates a character. Note the character's words and deeds or the words of other characters. At times, the narrator explains the motivation by revealing the character's thoughts and feelings.

Look back in the story at each of the actions listed below. On your paper, write at least one sentence to explain the motivation behind each action. Then indicate whether you learned about the motivation from the *character's words* or from the *narrator*.

1. Mrs. Taylor had decided to go on a train trip.

2. Mrs. Taylor was ready two hours ahead of time.

3. Garry acted up in the train station.

4. Garry behaved when Mrs. Taylor told him to.

5. Mrs. Taylor made friends with the young mother.

6. Mrs. Taylor cried when she held the baby.

7. Mrs. Taylor went on a short trip and not all the way to Montreal.

8. Mrs. Taylor smiled as she boarded the bus to return home.

WRITING

Imagine that you are Mrs. Taylor and that you keep a diary. Write a diary entry about your trip. Tell about some of the events of the day and explain your reactions. For instance, you might write about how you felt toward Mrs. Rawlinson. In each case, try to explain your motivation and some of your thoughts and feelings.

Dirge Without Music

by Edna St. Vincent Millay

I am not resigned to the shutting away of loving hearts in the hard ground.
So it is, and so it will be, for so it has been, time out of mind:
Into the darkness they go, the wise and the lovely.
Crowned with lilies and with laurel they go; but I am not resigned.

Lovers and thinkers, into the earth with you.
Be one with the dull, the indiscriminate dust.
A fragment of what you felt, of what you knew,
A formula, a phrase remains,—but the best is lost.

The answers quick and keen, the honest look, the laughter, the love,—
They are gone. They are gone to feed the roses. Elegant and curled
Is the blossom. Fragrant is the blossom. I know. But I do not approve.
More precious was the light in your eyes than all the roses in the world.

Down, down, down into the darkness of the grave
Gently they go, the beautiful, the tender, the kind;
Quietly they go, the intelligent, the witty, the brave.
I know. But I do not approve. And I am not resigned.

---

1. A *dirge* is a funeral song or a song about grief or death. What do you think the poet means when she says, "I do not approve. I am not resigned"? In the phrase "but the best is lost," what is the "best"?

2. The "indiscriminate dust" is the dust of the grave. It doesn't single out anyone. What does the speaker say are the things in life that make someone special or precious and not like everyone else?

Stevie Wonder: Growing Up in a World of Darkness

by James Haskins

The following selection, from a biography of Stevie Wonder, tells about Stevie when he was first learning to cope with his blindness. Read to find out how music brings Stevie out of the world of darkness.

"**S**ee, about sound . . . ," Stevie Wonder says, "there's one thing you gotta remember about sound—sound happens all the time, *all* the time. If you put your hands right up to your ears, if you close your eyes and move your hands back and forth, you can hear the sound getting closer and farther away. . . . Sound bounces off everything, there's always something happening."

Stevie Wonder was born Steveland Morris on May 13, 1950, in Saginaw, Michigan. He was the third boy in a family that would eventually include five boys and one girl. All except Stevie were born without handicaps. He was born prematurely, and his early birth led to his total blindness.

"I have a dislocated nerve in one eye and a cataract [a milky film] on the other," Stevie explains. "It may have happened from being in the incubator too long and receiving too much oxygen. You see, I was premature by one full month.

But a girl who was born on the same day that I was was also put into the incubator, and she died. I personally think that I'm lucky to be alive."

Stevie had retrolental fibroplasia, which was indeed produced by too much oxygen in his incubator. At the time, the role of oxygen in producing this kind of blindness had not been discovered. The condition is permanent and cannot be corrected.

Stevie has never seen, and never will see, a tree, a cloud, a butterfly, or the faces of people he loves. But, as he says, "In my mind I can see all these things in my own way, in the manner that we [blind people] can see them." A blind infant has ways of "seeing" the world around him through hearing and touch and inner feeling. In this way, Stevie could "see" his mother and sense her feelings.

Stevie was too young at the time to understand what being blind was all about. Understanding came when he was

about seven years old. A doctor explained that while others could see, he could not, and that this fact would make his life different from that of other little boys. When he was about two or three years old, he began to notice that he could not do certain things that others could do. For example, he seemed to bump into furniture and doors more than other people. When he began walking with his arms stretched out in front of him—so he would bump his hands rather than his head—his mother made him stop. But he did not realize he would never be able to walk about without danger of bumping into things. He just thought his brothers and his adult relatives were better at walking around because they were older than he was or grown up.

"I guess that I first became aware that I was blind," Stevie recalls "—and I just vaguely remember this—when I'd be wallowing around in the grass back of the house, and I'd get myself and my clothes soiled. My mother would get on me about that. She explained that I couldn't move about so much, that I'd have to try and stay in one place."

It was then that Stevie first began to realize he was blind, although he did not really understand what it meant. His two older brothers, Calvin and Milton, who were also very young, didn't really understand it either. They understood that Stevie could not see with his eyes, but he seemed to be able to "see" with his hands. They knew he could not play catch, but they saw no reason why he could not climb trees.

Stevie did indeed climb trees and, with a passenger to steer, ride a bicycle. He also joined his brothers in jumping from one woodshed roof to another! It seems hard to believe, but it is true. Stevie merely used his "sonar." This is the ability to locate an object by listening to the echo a sound makes as it bounces off it. Thus, Stevie had learned to call out and then listen to his call. If a woodshed rooftop was very close, his call would sound different than if the rooftop was farther away. Everyone who can hear has this same ability. But those who are sighted do not need to develop it. They can *see* how close or far away an object like a woodshed rooftop is. Blind children probably develop this ability at about one year of age.

They were just children together, the two who could see and the one who could not. They played together, they fought together, they were gullible together. "I think back to when we were little kids in Saginaw," Stevie recalls. "My father used to tell us that Saginaw was only twelve miles from the North Pole, and me and my brother Calvin used to go around telling people that we were born twelve miles from the North Pole. I believed that for a long time." Later on, Stevie's brother Calvin would be able to look at a globe or a map and understand how far away the North Pole was from Saginaw, Michigan. Stevie would be unable to do so.

"When I was young," he says, "my mother taught me never to feel sorry for myself, because handicaps are really things to be used, another way to benefit yourself and others in the long run." This was the best possible advice Stevie's mother could have given. He learned to regard his blindness in more than one way. It could be a hindrance, but it could also be a special gift. He was able to accept this idea, sometimes better than his mother could.

"I know it used to worry my mother," Stevie recalls, "and I know she prayed for me to have sight someday, and so finally I just told her that I was *happy* being blind, and I thought it was a gift from God, and I think she felt better after that."

Stevie was a lucky child in many ways. He was lucky to have two brothers close enough to him in age not to understand at first about his blindness and to expect him to do many of the things they did. He was also lucky to have a mother and a father, and occasionally an uncle, who understood how important sound was to him, and how important it was for him to learn to identify things he could not see by their sound. He recalls:

"I remember people dropping money on the table and saying, 'What's that, Steve?' That's a dime—buh-duh-duh-da; that's a quarter—buh-duh-duh-duh-da; that's a nickel. I could almost always get it right except a penny and a nickel confused me.

"I don't really feel my hearing is any better than yours," Stevie says now; "we all have the same abilities, you know. The only difference is how much you use it."

Encouraged by his family, Stevie used his hearing more and more as he grew older. He learned how to tell birds apart by their call, and to tell trees apart by the sound their leaves made as they rustled in the wind. He learned to tell when people were tired or annoyed or pleased by listening to the tone of their voices. His world of sound grew larger and larger, and the most frightening experience for him was silence. He depended so on sound that silence, for him, was like total darkness for deaf children. It is hard for sighted and hearing people to understand this. Perhaps the best way to understand is to imagine being shut up in a dark, sound-proof box. People need to feel that they are part of the world around them. It is hard enough to do so when one cannot see, or when one cannot hear; but it is doubly hard for a blind person in a silent room or a deaf person in total darkness.

Stevie also learned to use his memory. Sometimes it was his mental memory that helped him find an object. Sometimes it was his "muscle" memory that he used, especially in getting about the house in Saginaw. Sighted people use their muscle memory, too. If we walk around a room long enough and often enough, we can do so even in total darkness. It is like tying shoelaces. After tying our shoelaces hundreds of times, we do not have to think about what we are doing.

It was especially hard for Stevie, then, when his mother and father decided to move from Saginaw to the city of Detroit. The family moved into a house in the black section on the east side of the city. It meant a great deal of adjustment for Stevie—a whole new house to get used to, furniture in different places, strange new sounds, and much less freedom to move around. The out-of-doors was just as new, only more frightening because it was larger. He would have to find out all over again where the trees were, or what was a street and what was an alley. He did not know whether the people in the neighborhood would be friendly or hostile and suspicious.

At first Stevie's mother was afraid to let him go outside, even with his brothers, unless she was with them. She realized that Milton and Calvin were too young to be responsible for their younger brother. They were too likely to be attracted by something across the street, or only a few yards away. "We'll be right back, Stevie," they would say. But Stevie, suddenly all alone and unable to see where his brothers had gone, would be frightened. He would start out to find them, and there was no telling what he might bump into, or trip over, or get in the way of.

So, Stevie's mother kept him inside at first. There he was safer from real harm, but he still was not safe from bumping into things and hurting himself. Stevie was an energetic little boy; he needed to move around. He particularly needed to move around because his lack of sight deprived him of much of the outside stimulation sighted children receive. Yet, Stevie did not like to get hurt. For a while, before he had gotten used to the new house, he did a lot of jumping up and down. He knew the ceiling was too high for him to bump into, and he knew the floor was beneath him. It was much safer activity than moving forward or backward or sideways.

He also spent a lot of time beating on things, to make sounds and to make music. Although his mother was a gospel singer, the family was not especially musical. But Stevie had shown musical interest and ability very young. By the time he was two years old his favorite toys were two spoons, with which he would beat rhythmically on pans and tabletops and anything else his mother would let him beat on. When she began to worry about her furniture, she bought him cardboard drums from the dime store. None of them lasted very long. "I'd beat 'em to death," Stevie says with a chuckle. But there would always be a new drum, and there were other toy instruments as well.

"One day someone gave me a harmonica to put on my key chain, a little four-hole harmonica," Stevie recalls. He managed to get a remarkable range of sounds from that toy instrument.

"Then one day my mother took me to a picnic and someone sat me behind my first set of drums. They put my foot on the pedal and I played. They gave me a quarter. I liked the sound of quarters."

At a very early age, too, Stevie began to sing. All voices were very important to him, for they brought him closer to the world around him, a world he could not see. As he grew older, his own voice became particularly important to him, especially at night when the rest of the house was silent. He learned the endless possibilities of the human voice by experimenting with his own, and by mimicking others'.

Within a year or two after the move to Detroit, Milton, Calvin, and Stevie had a new baby brother, Larry. Stevie was fascinated by the sounds that the baby made and quickly was able to identify their meaning.

Stevie's family encouraged his musical ability, for they understood how much

Street. By this time Stevie had a set of bongo drums, which he had mastered as he had every other instrument to which he had been exposed. Often he would play his bongos; sometimes it would be the harmonica. Everyone would join in the singing, but Stevie's clear, strong voice always took the lead. Without exception the music was rhythm and blues, the kind the people listened to on WCHB.

"I played Jimmy Reed's blues, Bobby Blue Bland's. I used to sit by the radio and listen till sunup. Took a little of everybody's style and made it my own." He played like Ray Charles and tried copying his singing style, to the delight of his listeners.

"We used to get pretty big crowds of people playing on those porches," Stevie recalls. "I remember this one time this lady who was a member of our church came along and she said, 'Oh, Stevie, I'm ashamed of you for playing that worldly music out here. I'm so ashamed of you.' Ha, I really blew it, boy. I'd been a junior deacon in the church and I used to sing solo at the services. But she went and told them what I was doing and they told me to leave."

So much for Stevie's intention to become a minister. He decided to be an engineer instead, or maybe a doctor. If his secret wish was to be an entertainer like Ray Charles, he did not share it with anyone.

Unable now to sing in church, Stevie spent even more time performing on neighbors' porches. One of his favorite singing partners was a boy about his age named John Glover. John had a grown-up cousin named Ronnie White, who lived in another part of the city. Ronnie White was a member of the singing group The Miracles, which had enjoyed great success recording with a company named Hitsville USA. Of course, John was very proud to have a cousin like Ronnie White, and he often boasted about him. John was also proud to have a friend like Stevie. "You oughta hear my friend Stevie," he kept telling his cousin. But naturally White was busy, and he didn't really believe this kid Stevie was anything special. Then, one day in 1960, he happened to drop by to visit his relatives on Horton Street, and Stevie just happened to be having one of his front-porch sessions at the time. White did not have to listen very long to realize that his little cousin was right. This kid was something!

White arranged with the president of Hitsville USA, Berry Gordy, to take Stevie to the company's recording studio and to give him an audition, and one exciting afternoon Stevie was taken to the place that would be like a second home to him for the next ten years.

Stevie will never forget that afternoon. White took him around the studio, helping him to the different instruments and sound equipment, letting him touch them. It seemed to Stevie that every wonderful instrument in the world was right there in that sound studio, and he never wanted to leave it. Then he was introduced to Berry Gordy. Gordy listened to him sing, and play the harmonica and drums, and hired him on the spot, which says a lot for Gordy. Few, if any, other record-company owners would have taken such a chance back in 1960. But then, few, if any, other record companies had or would have the history of Gordy's. No other black-owned label would prevail as his would, perhaps because once they were established, those other labels were too busy holding on to their position to take any risks.

Anyway, signing an artist brought in by a performer already with the company has become a common, and famous, practice of Gordy's. The Supremes were discovered by The Temptations. Diana Ross discovered the Jackson Five.

Of course, Stevie's mother actually signed Stevie's contract with Hitsville, for he was under age. There was little talk of money or other conditions. Stevie's family was so excited, so grateful for this opportunity for him, that they would have agreed to anything!

READING COMPREHENSION

Summarizing. Choose the best phrase to complete each sentence. Then write the complete statements on your paper.

1. Stevie Wonder's blindness was _____ (a birth defect, caused by receiving too much oxygen in his incubator, the result of a car accident).

2. The kind of music Stevie loved to listen to on the radio was _____ (rhythm and blues, country and western, classical).

3. Stevie's professional career in music began when _____ (he sang with John Glover, he started playing like Ray Charles, Ronnie White got him an audition at Hitsville USA).

Interpreting. Write the answer to each question on your paper.

1. In what ways was Stevie able to "see"?

2. Why was Stevie lucky to have two brothers close to him in age?

3. Why was sound and music so important to Stevie?

4. How did school help Stevie adjust to the outside world?

5. How did Stevie show that he was musically gifted at an early age?

For Thinking and Discussing. Which of the frustrations blind people face do you think you would find most difficult?

UNDERSTANDING LITERATURE

Character Motivation. A character's motivation is the reason behind a particular action or way of behaving. Knowing a character's personality traits and the circumstances surrounding the life of the character will help you figure out his or her motivation.

Select the best phrase to complete each of the following statements about Stevie Wonder. Write the complete sentences on your paper.

1. Stevie worked hard to make better use of his sense of touch because _____.
   a. it would help bring the world closer to him
   b. he wanted to be like everyone else
   c. he wanted to get good grades in school

2. Stevie didn't tell anyone that he wanted to be an entertainer like Ray Charles because _____.
   a. he wanted to continue to sing with the church
   b. his friends didn't like rhythm-and-blues music
   c. he probably thought people would laugh at him

WRITING

Imagine that you have a chance to interview Stevie Wonder. Write five questions that ask about his motives for doing certain things in his life.

Section Review

VOCABULARY

Shades of Meaning. Synonyms do not always have exactly the same meaning. You cannot always substitute one synonym for another in your writing. For example, the words *always* and *forever* are synonyms. But only one of the words can fit logically in this sentence: I _____ buy bread when I go to the store. The slight differences in the way synonyms are used in sentences are called *shades of meaning.*

Read each of the following quotes from selections in this section. Choose the synonym below the quote that best completes the sentence. Write your answers on your paper.

1. "The little Indian girl . . . looked at my food with _____."

   longing   wishing

2. "I had never really learned how to _____ in games."

   play   perform

3. "**Corky:** Okay. Then decide what you want _____, and what you want put up for sale . . ."

   ruined   destroyed

4. "She _____ him to be a good boy and do what his mother told him."

   alerted   warned

5. Blind children probably _____ this ability at about one year of age.

   develop   create

READING

Critical Reading. As you read a piece of literature, you develop an understanding of what the author thinks is important, or of the personalities and points of view of the characters. In other words, you begin to understand the values of the author and the characters. Developing this understanding is part of *reading critically.*

Look at the following statements. Decide which of the characters listed below might have said each one. On your paper, write the name of the character and a short explanation of your choice. (You can choose a character more than once.)

Characters

headmistress	Premila
Corky	Mrs. Grayson
Mrs. Taylor	

1. People who are young don't realize how lucky they are.

2. The most important thing you can do for a child is to be there when he or she needs you.

3. People want to be alike, not different.

4. Stand up for your rights, and don't let other people push you around.

5. Even a little joy can make a person genuinely happy.

6. Learning to forgive is a difficult but valuable lesson.

7. Without her child, a mother's life has less meaning.

WRITING

Characters in a Narrative. There are many elements that contribute to a good story. One important element is the characters. As you write a narrative, you try to create interesting and lively characters by describing them fully. You want your readers to "see" the characters in your story.

Step 1: Set Your Goal
Choose one of the following topics for a character description:

1. Imagine what you will be like in ten years and write a description.

2. Write a description of one of your parents, a teacher, or a special friend.

3. Write a description of Corky in "The Riding Horse."

Think about your purpose. You know that you want your readers to picture exactly what your subject looks like. Do you also want them to "see" what *kind* of person he or she is?

Step 2: Make a Plan
Look at the two paragraphs below. They each give a description of the same character.

I sat down next to a little girl. She didn't even look at me. She was Indian. But she was dressed in the English style.

I sat next to a small serious girl who didn't smile at me. She had long braids and wore a cotton dress in the English style. But she still kept on her Indian jewelry.

The second paragraph is an actual description from "By Any Other Name." In it, the character is more fully described. Details about her size, expression, and dress add to the picture in the reader's imagination.

Here are some questions to ask yourself as you plan your character description for your narrative:

1. What does the character look like?

2. What is the character wearing?

3. How does the character behave?

4. What kind of personality does the character have?

Once you have answered these questions, you are ready to make a list of details about your subject. You may want to start your list with details that describe physical characteristics. These details might include such things as "six feet tall," "gray-blue eyes," and "thick-boned hands." To describe the character fully, you will also want to include personality traits, such as "talkative," "hard worker," and "sense of humor." You might also include a list of things the character does or thinks to illustrate his or her personality traits. Instead of saying a character is "talkative," you might say he or she "talks a long time on the phone."

When you are writing your list, write whatever comes to mind. List as many details as you can. Once you have your list of details, you can decide how you want to organize them and which ones you wish to include in your description. You may use natural order or order of importance to organize your narrative.

Remember that when you use natural order, you begin your description with an overall impression and then focus in on more specific details. For example, you might begin by saying that your character was a big man and continue by giving specific details about how tall he was, how big his neck and hands were, or other details.

If you use order of importance, you might begin with what you consider the most important detail and end with the least important. Or you can start with unimportant details and save the most important for last.

Step 3: Write a First Draft

When you write your first draft, keep in mind the impression you want readers to get. Include only those details that will help create that impression. Try to follow the organization you planned, and use your list of details. Keep in mind that, as you write new details, a better method of organization may occur to you. Feel free to make changes as you go along. Try to make your details vivid and clear.

Step 4: Revise

When you revise your draft, ask yourself the following questions:

☐ Have I given readers a clear picture of a person they may be unfamiliar with?

☐ Have I used vivid, colorful adjectives?

☐ Do the details support the general impression I want to make?

☐ Are the details presented in an order that makes sense?

☐ Do I achieve my purpose?

After you have revised your paper, proofread it. Look for mistakes in grammar, punctuation, and spelling. Finally, type your paper or copy it over neatly.

QUIZ

The following is a quiz for Section 10. Write the answers in complete sentences on your paper.

Reading Comprehension

1. How did the headmistress feel about Indian children in "By Any Other Name"? How do you know?

2. What two promises did Corky make to his son in "The Rocking Horse"?

3. What were some of the problems faced by Mrs. Taylor in "A Trip for Mrs. Taylor"?

4. Why was Mrs. Taylor's trip so enjoyable for her?

5. How did Stevie Wonder's family encourage his interest in music?

Understanding Literature

6. Which of Premila's actions were motivated by her desire to fit in with British school children?

7. What drove Mrs. Grayson to put her son up for adoption?

8. Why was Corky so unpleasant to Mrs. Grayson when he first saw her?

9. What are some of the factors that motivated Mrs. Taylor to take her trip?

10. What do you think motivated Edna St. Vincent Millay to write "Dirge Without Music"?

ACTIVITIES

Word Attack

1. Compound words are sometimes written as one word and sometimes with a hyphen between the words that make up the compound. The following examples of compounds are from selections in this section. Are they written as one word or with hyphens? You may use a dictionary or go back to the story to check.

head mistress	tight lipped
life time	nurse maid
good bye	lunch box

Write a sentence for each compound word.

2. In "The Rocking Horse," McElroy describes Wag as an expensive horse. The word *expensive* ends with the suffix *-ive*. Suffixes are groups of letters added to a base word or root. Some suffixes do not add a great deal of meaning to the base word. They act primarily to change the word from one part of speech to another. The addition of suffixes allows you to express an idea in more than one way. Read these two sentences:

a. He bought the jacket at great expense.

b. He bought an expensive jacket. You can see that *expense* is a noun and *expensive* is an adjective. The suffix *-ive* makes the noun an adjective.

The following words are nouns: *instinct, mass, excess*. Add the suffix *-ive* to each word to make it an adjective. Then write one sentence using the word as a noun, and another sentence using the word as an adjective. If you wish, you may refer to a dictionary.

Speaking and Listening. Get together with two classmates and act out the scene in "The Rocking Horse" when Mrs. Grayson arrives at the warehouse and speaks with McElroy and Corky. Be prepared to perform the scene for the class.

Researching. Go to the library and find out more about Stevie Wonder. Answer the following questions:

a. How old was Stevie when he got his first gold record? For what song did he receive it?

b. What other awards has he received?

Creating. Pretend you are Premila. Write two diary entries—one for your first day in the Anglo-Indian School and another for your last day there. Write your impressions and your feelings about the headmistress, the teachers, and the other students.

475

THE NOVEL

The word novel *means "new." And every novel is a new way of looking at an old subject — the way people live.*

The Sponge Diver
Winslow Homer (1836–1910).
Museum of Fine Arts, Boston,
Gift of Mrs. Robert B. Osgood.

Introduction

The final section of this book introduces you to another literary form, the novel. This section contains *The Pearl,* a short novel by U.S. novelist John Steinbeck. The section also contains a brief biography of the author to provide background for reading the novel.

Like all novels, *The Pearl* transports readers into a new environment. In this case, you will move to a small fishing village and live with a poor Indian family — Kino, Juana, and their child Coyotito ("Little Coyote"). The story is basically about Kino, who finds a huge pearl, "the Pearl of the World," and attempts to sell it to finance a better future for himself and his family. But the novel is much more. It is a story of conflicting human qualities and emotions: joy and sorrow, generosity and greed, success and failure.

As you read *The Pearl,* you will be enjoying a new story and observing the techniques that a writer uses in developing a novel. At the same time, you will be reviewing many of the skills and literary elements that you have studied in the other sections of this book.

The Old Ways

In some ways, a novel is a combination of all the elements of other literary forms. It has characters, a setting, plot, conflict, resolution, and theme, the way a short story or drama does. A novel often contains symbols and images, the way a poem does. It may center on the story of a person's life, the way a biography does. In a novel, however, the central character is usually a product of the author's imagination, rather than a real person. Like nonfiction, a novel may deal with actual events, places, or people, but it does so in a fictional way, by altering the facts. A novelist also establishes a certain tone in a narrative, creates a mood, and generally follows a particular point of view throughout the novel.

The New Ways

Yet, the word *novel* means "new," and a novel contains elements that are new and different from other types of literature. For one thing, a novel is longer than a short story and most dramas. The plot of a novel is more complex than that of other forms. In a novel, an author will often present not only events that make up the *main plot,* but also events of one or more inner stories, called *subplots.* The novelist takes the reader through these subplots and then weaves the inner stories into the main plot line. Sometimes the reader may wonder just how the author will finally tie together all the different subplots. But the novelist almost always succeeds. As you read *The Pearl*, notice how Steinbeck weaves the story of Coyotito and the scorpion into the main plot.

Characterization is another way that novels differ from other forms. Novels usually contain more characters than short stories, dramas, or nonfiction selections. In fact, in some novels, the author provides a list of characters at the beginning of the book so that readers can keep track of them all. Novelists also develop their characters more fully than many other writers do. Descriptions of characters are longer. Characters' actions, words, and thoughts are presented in greater detail. Character motivation can be explored more comprehensively. In *The Pearl*, Kino is clearly the main character. But secondary characters such as Juana, Coyotito, the doctor, the priest, Juan Tomás, and the trackers are also very important.

Truths and Messages

Most short stories and dramas convey a theme or message, but a novelist develops the theme more fully and dramatically than other writers. In a novel, the author usually tries to illustrate some general truth about our world, or attempts to teach a moral lesson about how people should act. Because a novel's theme can be developed so fully, it usually has a more powerful effect than does the theme of a short story or play. When you have finished reading *The Pearl*, you will probably be emotionally drained. The book has a powerful message, presented very dramatically.

Novelists also use symbols extensively. Most short stories, plays, or poems focus on only one or two symbols. But a novelist can present a wide variety of symbols to represent human ideas and feelings. Even the individual characters in a novel can symbolize human qualities. As you read *The Pearl*, think about such symbols as the songs Kino hears in his mind, the ants and ant lions, the scorpion, the doctor, the pearl buyers, the canoe, and even the pearl itself. Ask yourself what these symbols represent and what truths or lessons they illustrate about our world.

An Old/New Story

In his introduction to *The Pearl* (p. 482), Steinbeck tells readers that the story of his novel is an old one, often retold. It is a story of "good and evil things and no in-between anywhere." The story of *The Pearl* and its message may be old, but Steinbeck has developed them in an entirely new way.

Biography   John Steinbeck

John Steinbeck worked at many jobs in his life. He was a ranch hand, a bricklayer, a fruit picker, and a marine biologist. But most of all, he was a writer. All of his jobs helped him develop the char-

acters and themes of his novels and short stories.

Steinbeck was born in Salinas, California, in 1902. He spent most of his life in this area. Many of his books and stories were set in the Salinas Valley—California's lush farmlands—or along the Monterey coast which he knew and loved so well.

In 1962, Steinbeck's writing earned him the Nobel Prize for Literature, one of the highest honors an author can achieve. He is one of only eight Americans in history to win a Nobel Prize in literature. But his writing career did not start out very successfully. He really did not make much money from his writing until he was in his thirties.

Tortilla Flat, published in 1935, was Steinbeck's first financially successful literary work. Then in 1937, he published *Of Mice and Men,* a novel that became a best seller. It was made into a Broadway play and a movie that you still may see on TV late at night.

Sympathy and understanding for the poor, the oppressed, the underdogs, and the losers run through many of Steinbeck's works. *Of Mice and Men* is about two poor ranch hands, one of them slightly retarded, who travel throughout the Salinas Valley looking for work. *The Pearl,* the novel you will read in this section, is about a poor Mexican-Indian family and how their lives are changed by finding a valuable pearl. It was published in 1947.

Another group of poor people that Steinbeck felt great sympathy for were the "Okies." The Okies were farmers, mostly from Oklahoma, who were driven off their land by severe dust storms in the mid-1930's. Many of them came to California to seek jobs as fruit pickers. Their lives were filled with hardships and misery. Steinbeck described their problems in vivid words in his most famous book, *The Grapes of Wrath*, published in 1939.

The Grapes of Wrath became an outstanding and attention-getting best seller. For it, Steinbeck was awarded the Pulitzer Prize, an award for excellence in writing. Steinbeck was soon to become one of the best-known and most popular writers of the 20th century.

Fame was not always an easy thing for Steinbeck to deal with. Although his words and written images were bold, he was basically a shy, private person. At one point, he escaped from public view and attention by leading an expedition to the Galápagos Islands for a study of marine life there. Steinbeck had studied marine biology in college. He put his studies to work in the Galápagos. Afterward, Steinbeck and E. F. Ricketts, another member of the expedition, wrote *The Sea of Cortes* about their trip and findings.

Throughout Steinbeck's works, he shows his careful study and understanding of nature. He blends his scientific knowledge and strong feelings about the natural universe in all of his writings.

Natural forces are at the heart of *The Pearl*. As the book opens, the main character, Kino, awakens and observes all of the animals and plants and life around him. Kino's own life is tied to nature. He hears a Song of Nature playing in his mind. He makes his living on the sea, and finds and loses his fortune on the sea.

While Steinbeck studied nature and natural forces carefully, his real focus was always people. Steinbeck was a careful observer of people. His writings realistically present the actions, words, and thoughts of people. In one of his last works, *Travels with Charley*, published in 1961, Steinbeck described a tour of the U.S. that he took with his poodle Charley. He wrote about the people and places he saw, and gave readers an inside view of what America and Americans are really like.

When Steinbeck won the Nobel Prize for Literature in 1962, his presenter said, "We find the American temperament . . . expressed, in his great feeling for nature, for the tilled soil, the wasteland, the mountains, and the ocean coasts . . . in the midst of and beyond the world of human beings."

Steinbeck died in 1968, but many of his works continue to touch and entertain readers. Among these works are *Tortilla Flat, Of Mice and Men, The Grapes of Wrath, The Pearl, Travels with Charley, Cannery Row, East of Eden, The Winter of Our Discontent, The Moon Is Down,* and *The Red Pony.*

The Pearl

by John Steinbeck

In the town they tell the story of the great pearl—how it was found and how it was lost again. They tell of Kino, the fisherman, and of his wife, Juana, and of the baby, Coyotito. And because the story has been told so often, it has taken root in every man's mind. And, as with all retold tales that are in people's hearts, there are only good and bad things and black and white things and good and evil things and no in-between anywhere.

"If this story is a parable, perhaps everyone takes his own meaning from it and reads his own life into it. In any case, they say in the town that . . . "

Chapter 1

Kino awakened in the near dark. The stars still shone and the day had drawn only a pale wash of light in the lower sky to the east. The roosters had been crowing for some time, and the early pigs were already beginning their ceaseless turning of twigs and bits of wood to see whether anything to eat had been overlooked. Outside the brush house in the tuna clump, a covey of little birds chittered and flurried with their wings.

Kino's eyes opened, and he looked first at the lightening square which was the door and then he looked at the hanging box where Coyotito slept. And last he turned his head to Juana, his wife, who lay beside him on the mat, her blue head shawl over her nose and over her breasts and around the small of her back.

Juana's eyes were open too. Kino could never remember seeing them closed when he awakened. Her dark eyes made little reflected stars. She was looking at him as she was always looking at him when he awakened.

Kino heard the little splash of morning waves on the beach. It was very good—Kino closed his eyes again to listen to his music. Perhaps he alone did this and perhaps all of his people did it. His people had once been great makers of songs so that everything they saw or thought or did or heard became a song. That was very long ago. The songs remained; Kino knew them, but no new songs were added. That does not mean that there were no personal songs. In Kino's head there was a song now, clear and soft, and

if he had been able to speak of it, he would have called it the Song of the Family.

His blanket was over his nose to protect him from the dank air. His eyes flicked to a rustle beside him. It was Juana arising, almost soundlessly. On her hard bare feet she went to the hanging box where Coyotito slept, and she leaned over and said a little reassuring word. Coyotito looked up for a moment and closed his eyes and slept again.

Juana went to the fire pit and uncovered a coal and fanned it alive while she broke little pieces of brush over it.

Now Kino got up and wrapped his blanket about his head and nose and shoulders. He slipped his feet into his sandals and went outside to watch the dawn.

Outside the door he squatted down and gathered the blanket ends about his knees. He saw the specks of Gulf clouds flame high in the air. And a goat came near and sniffed at him and stared with its cold yellow eyes. Behind him Juana's fire leaped into flame and threw spears of light through the chinks of the brush-house wall and threw a wavering square of light out the door. A late moth blus-

tered in to find the fire. The Song of the Family came now from behind Kino. And the rhythm of the family song was the grinding stone where Juana worked the corn for the morning cakes.

The dawn came quickly now, a wash, a glow, a lightness, and then an explosion of fire as the sun arose out of the Gulf. Kino looked down to cover his eyes from the glare. He could hear the pat of the corncakes in the house and the rich smell of them on the cooking plate. The ants were busy on the ground, big black ones with shiny bodies, and little dusty quick ants. Kino watched with the detachment of God while a dusty ant frantically tried to escape the sand trap an ant lion had dug for him. A thin, timid dog came close and, at a soft word from Kino, curled up, arranged its tail neatly over its feet, and laid its chin delicately on the pile. It was a black dog with yellow-gold spots where its eyebrows should have been. It was a morning like other mornings and yet perfect among mornings.

Kino heard the creak of the rope when Juana took Coyotito out of his hanging box and cleaned him and hammocked him in her shawl in a loop that placed him close to her breast. Kino could see these things without looking at them. Juana sang softly an ancient song that had only three notes and yet endless variety of interval. And this was part of the family song too. It was all part. Sometimes it rose to an aching chord that caught the throat, saying this is safety, this is warmth, this is the *Whole*.

Across the brush fence were other brush houses, and the smoke came from them too, and the sound of breakfast, but those were other songs, their pigs were other pigs, their wives were not Juana. Kino was young and strong and his black hair hung over his brown forehead. His eyes were warm and fierce and bright and his mustache was thin and coarse. He lowered his blanket from his nose now, for the dark poisonous air was gone and the yellow sunlight fell on the house. Near the brush fence two roosters bowed and feinted at each other with squared wings and neck feathers ruffed out. It would be a clumsy fight. They were not game chickens. Kino watched them for a moment, and then his eyes went up to a flight of wild doves twin-kling inland to the hills. The world was awake now, and Kino arose and went into his brush house.

As he came through the door Juana stood up from the glowing fire pit. She put Coyotito back in his hanging box and then she combed her black hair and braided it in two braids and tied the ends with thin green ribbon. Kino squatted by the fire pit and rolled a hot corncake and dipped it in sauce and ate it. And he drank a little pulque and that was breakfast. That was the only breakfast he had ever known outside of feast days and one incredible fiesta on cookies that had nearly killed him. When Kino had finished, Juana came back to the fire and ate her breakfast. They had spoken once, but there is not need for speech if it is only a habit anyway. Kino sighed with satisfaction—and that was conversation.

The sun was warming the brush house, breaking through its crevices in long streaks. And one of the streaks fell on the hanging box where Coyotito lay, and on the ropes that held it.

It was a tiny movement that drew their eyes to the hanging box. Kino and Juana froze in their positions. Down the rope that hung the baby's box from the roof support a scorpion moved slowly. His stinging tail was straight out behind him, but he could whip it up in a flash of time.

Kino's breath whistled in his nostrils and he opened his mouth to stop it. And then the startled look was gone from him and the rigidity from his body. In his mind a new song had come, the Song of Evil, the music of the enemy, of any foe of the family, a savage, secret, dangerous melody, and underneath, the Song of the Family cried plaintively.

The scorpion moved delicately down the rope toward the box. Under her breath Juana repeated an ancient magic to guard against such evil, and on top of that she muttered a Hail Mary between clenched teeth. But Kino was in motion. His body glided quietly across the room, noiselessly and smoothly. His hands were in front of him, palms down, and his eyes were on the scorpion. Beneath it in the hanging box Coyotito laughed and reached up his hand toward it. It sensed danger when Kino was almost within reach of it. It stopped, and its tail rose up over its back in little jerks and the curved thorn on the tail's end glistened.

Kino stood perfectly still. He could hear Juana whispering the old magic again, and he could hear the evil music of the enemy. He could not move until the scorpion moved, and it felt for the source of the death that was coming to it. Kino's hand went forward very slowly, very smoothly. The thorned tail jerked upright. And at that moment the laughing Coyotito shook the rope and the scorpion fell.

Kino's hand leaped to catch it, but it fell past his fingers, fell on the baby's shoulder, landed and struck. Then, snarling, Kino had it, had it in his fingers, rubbing it to a paste in his hands. He threw it down and beat it into the earth floor with his fist, and Coyotito screamed with pain in his box. But Kino beat and stamped the enemy until it was only a fragment and a moist place in the dirt. His teeth were bared and fury flared in his eyes and the Song of the Enemy roared in his ears.

But Juana had the baby in her arms now. She found the puncture with redness starting from it already. She put her lips down over the puncture and sucked hard and spat and sucked again while Coyotito screamed.

Kino hovered; he was helpless, he was in the way.

The screams of the baby brought the neighbors. Out of their brush houses they poured—Kino's brother Juan Tomás and his fat wife Apolonia and their four children crowded in the door and blocked the entrance, while behind them others tried to look in, and one small boy crawled among legs to have a look. And those in front passed the word back to those behind—"Scorpion. The baby has been stung."

Juana stopped sucking the puncture for a moment. The little hole was slightly enlarged and its edges whitened from the sucking, but the red swelling extended farther around it in a hard lymphatic mound. And all of these people knew about the scorpion. An adult might be very ill from the sting, but a baby could easily die from the poison. First, they knew, would come swelling and fever and tightened throat, and then cramps in the stomach, and then Coyotito might die if enough of the poison had gone in. But the stinging pain of the bite was going away. Coyotito's screams turned to moans.

Kino had wondered often at the iron in his patient, fragile wife. She, who was obedient and respectful and cheerful and patient, she could arch her back in child pain with hardly a cry. She could stand fatigue and hunger almost better than Kino himself. In the canoe she was like a strong man. And now she did a most surprising thing.

"The doctor," she said. "Go to get the doctor."

The word was passed out among the neighbors where they stood close packed in the little yard behind the brush fence. And they repeated among themselves, "Juana wants the doctor." A wonderful thing, a memorable thing, to want the doctor. To get him would be a remarkable thing. The doctor never came to the cluster of brush houses. Why should he, when he had more than he could do to take care of the rich people who lived in the stone and plaster houses of the town.

"He would not come," the people in the yard said.

"He would not come," the people in the door said, and the thought got into Kino.

"The doctor would not come," Kino said to Juana.

She looked up at him, her eyes as cold as the eyes of a lioness. This was Juana's first baby — this was nearly everything there was in Juana's world. And Kino saw her determination and the music of the family sounded in his head with a steely tone.

"Then we will go to him," Juana said, and with one hand she arranged her dark blue shawl over her head and made of one end of it a sling to hold the moaning baby and made of the other end of it a shade over his eyes to protect him from the light. The people in the door pushed against those behind to let her through. Kino followed her. They went out of the gate to the rutted path and the neighbors followed them.

The thing had become a neighborhood affair. They made a quick soft-footed procession into the center of the town, first Juana and Kino, and behind them Juan Tomás and Apolonia, her big stomach jiggling with the strenuous pace, then all the neighbors with the children trotting on the flanks. And the yellow sun threw their black shadows ahead of them so that they walked on their own shadows.

They came to the place where the brush houses stopped and city of stone and plaster began, the city of harsh outer walls and inner cool gardens where a little water played and the bougainvillaea crusted the walls with purple and brick-red and white. They heard from the secret gardens the singing of caged birds and heard the splash of cooling water on hot flagstones. The procession crossed the blinding plaza and passed in front of the church. It had grown now, and on the outskirts the hurrying newcomers were being softly informed how the baby had been stung by a scorpion, how the father and mother were taking it to the doctor.

And the newcomers, particularly the beggars from the front of the church who were great experts in financial analysis, looked quickly at Juana's old blue skirt, saw the tears in her shawl, appraised the green ribbon on her braids, read the age of Kino's blanket and the thousand washings of his clothes, and set them down as poverty people and went along to see what kind of drama might develop. The four beggars in front of the church knew everything in town. They were students of the expressions of young women as they went in to confession, and they saw them as they came out and read the nature of the skin. They knew every little scandal and some very big crimes. They slept at their posts in the shadow of the church so that no one crept in for consolation without their knowledge. And they knew the doctor. They knew his ignorance, his cruelty, his avarice, his appetites, his sins. They knew his clumsy abortions and the little brown pennies he gave sparingly for alms. They had seen his corpses go into the church. And, since early Mass was over and business was slow, they followed the procession, these endless searchers after perfect knowledge of their fellow men, to see what the fat lazy doctor would do about an indigent baby with a scorpion bite.

The scurrying procession came at last to the big gate in the wall of the doctor's house. They could hear the splashing water and the singing of caged birds and the sweep of the long brooms on the flagstones. And they could smell the frying of good bacon from the doctor's house.

Kino hesitated a moment. This doctor was not of his people. This doctor was of a race which for nearly four hundred years had beaten and starved and robbed and despised Kino's race, and frightened it too, so that the indigent came humbly to the door. And as always when he came near to one of this race, Kino felt weak and afraid and angry at the same time. Rage and terror went together. He could kill the doctor more easily than he could talk to him, for all of the doctor's race spoke to all of Kino's race as though they were simple animals. And as Kino raised his right hand to the iron ring knocker in the gate, rage swelled in him, and the pounding music of the enemy beat in his ears, and his lips drew tight against his teeth—but with his left hand he reached to take off his hat. The iron ring pounded against the gate. Kino took off his hat and stood waiting. Coyotito moaned a little in Juana's arms, and she spoke softly to him. The procession crowded close the better to see and hear.

After a moment the big gate opened a few inches. Kino could see the green coolness of the garden and little splashing fountain through the opening. The man who looked out at him was one of his own race. Kino spoke to him in the old language. "The little one—the first born—has been poisoned by the scorpion," Kino said. "He requires the skill of the healer."

The gate closed a little, and the servant refused to speak in the old language. "A little moment," he said. "I go to inform myself," and he closed the gate and slid the bolt home. The glaring sun threw the bunched shadows of the people blackly on the white wall.

In his chamber the doctor sat up in his high bed. He had on his dressing gown of red watered silk that had come from Paris, a little tight over the chest now if

it was buttoned. On his lap was a silver tray with a silver chocolate pot and a tiny cup of eggshell china, so delicate that it looked silly when he lifted it with his big hand, lifted it with the tips of thumb and forefinger and spread the other three fingers wide to get them out of the way. His eyes rested in puffy little hammocks of flesh and his mouth drooped with discontent. He was growing very stout, and his voice was hoarse with the fat that pressed on his throat. Beside him on a table was a small Oriental gong and a bowl of cigarettes. The furnishings of the room were heavy and dark and gloomy. The pictures were religious, even the large tinted photograph of his dead wife, who, if Masses willed and paid for out of her own estate could do it, was in Heaven. The doctor had once for a short time been a part of the great world and his whole subsequent life was memory and longing for France. "That," he said, "was civilized living"—by which he meant that on a small income he had been able to keep a mistress and eat in restaurants. He poured his second cup of chocolate and crumbled a sweet biscuit in his fingers. The servant from the gate came to the open door and stood waiting to be noticed.

"Yes?" the doctor asked.

"It is a little Indian with a baby. He says a scorpion stung it."

The doctor put his cup down gently before he let his anger rise.

"Have I nothing better to do than cure insect bites for 'little Indians'? I am a doctor, not a veterinary."

"Yes, Patron," said the servant.

"Has he any money?" the doctor demanded. "No, they never have any money. I, I alone in the world am supposed to work for nothing—and I am tired of it. See if he has any money!"

At the gate the servant opened the door a trifle and looked out at the waiting people. And this time he spoke in the old language.

"Have you money to pay for the treatment?"

Now Kino reached into a secret place somewhere under his blanket. He brought out a paper folded many times. Crease by crease he unfolded it, until at last there came to view eight small misshapen seed pearls, as ugly and gray as little ulcers, flattened and almost valueless. The servant took the paper and closed the gate again, but this time he was not gone long. He opened the gate just wide enough to pass the paper back.

"The doctor has gone out," he said. "He was called to a serious case." And he shut the gate quickly out of shame.

And now a wave of shame went over the whole procession. They melted away. The beggars went back to the church steps, the stragglers moved off, and the neighbors departed so that the public shaming of Kino would not be in their eyes.

For a long time Kino stood in front of the gate with Juana beside him. Slowly he put his suppliant hat on his head. Then, without warning, he struck the gate a crushing blow with his fist. He looked down in wonder at his split knuckles and at the blood that flowed down between his fingers.

Chapter 2

The town lay on a broad estuary, its old yellow plastered buildings hugging the beach. And on the beach the white and blue canoes that came from Nayarit were drawn up, canoes preserved for generations by a hard shell-like waterproof plaster whose making was a secret of the fishing people. They were high and graceful canoes with curving bow and stern and a braced section midships where a mast could be stepped to carry a small lateen sail.

The beach was yellow sand, but at the water's edge a rubble of shell and algae took its place. Fiddler crabs bubbled and sputtered in their holes in the sand, and in the shallows little lobsters popped in and out of their tiny homes in the rubble and sand. The sea bottom was rich with crawling and swimming and growing things. The brown algae waved in the gentle currents and the green eel grass swayed and little sea horses clung to its stems. Spotted botete, the poison fish, lay on the bottom in the eel-grass beds, and the bright-colored swimming crabs scampered over them.

On the beach the hungry dogs and the hungry pigs of the town searched endlessly for any dead fish or sea bird that might have floated in on a rising tide.

Although the morning was young, the hazy mirage was up. The uncertain air that magnified some things and blotted out others hung over the whole Gulf so that all sights were unreal and vision could not be trusted; so that sea and land had the sharp clarities and the vagueness of a dream. Thus it might be that the people of the Gulf trust things of the spirit and things of the imagination, but they do not trust their eyes to show them distance or clear outline or any optical exactness. Across the estuary from the town one section of mangroves stood clear and telescopically defined, while another mangrove clump was a hazy black-green blob. Part of the far shore disappeared into a shimmer that looked like water. There was no certainty in seeing, no proof that what you saw was there or was not there. And the people of the Gulf expected all places were that way, and it was not strange to them. A copper haze hung over the water, and the hot morning sun beat on it and made it vibrate blindingly.

The brush houses of the fishing people were back from the beach on the right-hand side of the town, and the canoes were drawn up in front of this area.

Kino and Juana came slowly down to the beach and to Kino's canoe, which was the one thing of value he owned in the world. It was very old. Kino's grandfather had brought it from Nayarit, and he had given it to Kino's father, and so it had come to Kino. It was at once property and source of food, for a man with a boat can guarantee a woman that she will eat something. It is the bulwark against starvation. And every year Kino refinished his canoe with the hard shell-like plaster by the secret method that had

also come to him from his father. Now he came to the canoe and touched the bow tenderly as he always did. He laid his diving rock and his basket and the two ropes in the sand by the canoe. And he folded his blanket and laid it in the bow.

Juana laid Coyotito on the blanket, and she placed her shawl over him so that the hot sun could not shine on him. He was quiet now, but the swelling on his shoulder had continued up his neck and under his ear and his face was puffed and feverish. Juana went to the water and waded in. She gathered some brown seaweed and made a flat damp poultice of it, and this she applied to the baby's swollen shoulder, which was as good a remedy as any and probably better than the doctor could have done. But the remedy lacked his authority because it was simple and didn't cost anything. The stomach cramps had not come to Coyotito. Perhaps Juana had sucked out the poison in time, but she had not sucked out her worry over her first-born. She had not prayed directly for the recovery of the baby — she had prayed that they might find a pearl with which to hire the doctor to cure the baby, for the minds of people are as unsubstantial as the mirage of the Gulf.

Now Kino and Juana slid the canoe down the beach to the water, and when the bow floated, Juana climbed in, while Kino pushed the stern in and waded beside it until it floated lightly and trembled on the little breaking waves. Then in co-ordination Juana and Kino drove their double-bladed paddles into the sea, and the canoe creased the water and hissed with speed. The other pearlers were gone out long since. In a few moments Kino could see them clustered in the haze, riding over the oyster bed.

Light filtered down through the water to the bed where the frilly pearl oysters lay fastened to the rubbly bottom, a bottom strewn with shells of broken, opened oysters. This was the bed that had raised the King of Spain to be a great power in Europe in past years, had helped to pay for his wars, and had decorated the churches for his soul's sake. The gray oysters with ruffles like skirts on the shells, the barnacle-crusted oysters with little bits of weed clinging to the skirts and small crabs climbing over them. An accident could happen to these oysters, a grain of sand could lie in the folds of muscle and irritate the flesh until in self-protection the flesh coated the grain with a layer of smooth cement. But once started, the flesh continued to coat the foreign body until it fell free in some tidal flurry or until the oyster was destroyed. For centuries men had dived down and torn the oysters from the beds and ripped them open, looking for the coated grains of sand. Swarms of fish lived near the bed to live near the oysters thrown back by the searching men and to nibble at the shining inner shells. But the pearls were accidents, and the finding of one was luck, a little pat on the back by God or the gods or both.

Kino had two ropes, one tied to a heavy stone and one to a basket. He stripped off his shirt and trousers and laid his hat in the bottom of the canoe.

The water was oily smooth. He took his rock in one hand and his basket in the other, and he slipped feet first over the side and the rock carried him to the bottom. The bubbles rose behind him until the water cleared and he could see. Above, the surface of the water was an undulating mirror of brightness, and he could see the bottoms of the canoes sticking through it.

Kino moved cautiously so that the water would not be obscured with mud or sand. He hooked his foot in the loop on his rock and his hands worked quickly, tearing the oysters loose, some singly, others in clusters. He laid them in his basket. In some places the oysters clung to one another so that they came free in lumps.

Now, Kino's people had sung of everything that happened or existed. They had made songs to the fishes, to the sea in anger and to the sea in calm, to the light and the dark and the sun and the moon, and the songs were all in Kino and in his people — every song that had ever been made, even the ones forgotten. And as he filled his basket the song was in Kino, and the beat of the song was his pounding heart as it ate the oxygen from his held breath, and the melody of the song was the gray-green water and the little scuttling animals and the clouds of fish that flitted by and were gone. But in the song there was a secret little inner song, hardly perceptible, but always there, sweet and secret and clinging, almost hiding in the counter-melody, and this was the Song of the Pearl That Might Be,

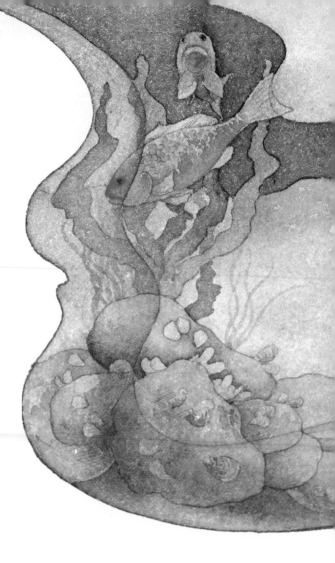

for every shell thrown in the basket might contain a pearl. Chance was against it, but luck and the gods might be for it. And in the canoe above him Kino knew that Juana was making the magic of prayer, her face set rigid and her muscles hard to force the luck, to tear the luck out of the gods' hands, for she needed the luck for the swollen shoulder of Coyotito. And because the need was great and the desire was great, the little secret melody of the pearl that might be was

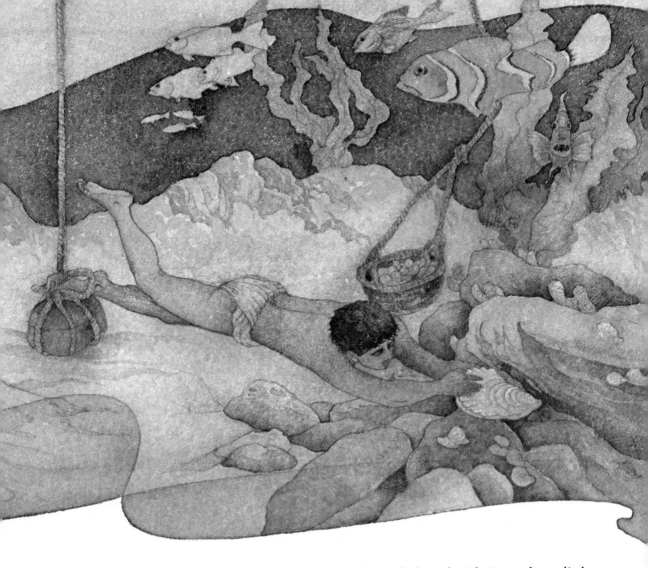

stronger this morning. Whole phrases of it came clearly and softly into the Song of the Undersea.

Kino, in his pride and youth and strength, could remain down over two minutes without strain, so that he worked deliberately, selecting the largest shells. Because they were disturbed, the oyster shells were tightly closed. A little to his right a hummock of rubbly rock stuck up, covered with young oysters not ready to take. Kino moved next to the hum-mock, and then, beside it, under a little overhang, he saw a very large oyster lying by itself, not covered with its cling-ing brothers. The shell was partly open, for the overhang protected this ancient oyster, and in the lip-like muscle Kino saw a ghostly gleam, and then the shell closed down. His heart beat out a heavy rhythm and the melody of the maybe pearl shrilled in his ears. Slowly he forced the oyster loose and held it tightly against his breast. He kicked his foot free from the rock loop, and his body rose to the surface and his black hair gleamed in the sunlight. He reached over the side of the canoe and laid the oyster in the bottom.

Then Juana steadied the boat while he climbed in. His eyes were shining with excitement, but in decency he pulled up his rock, and then he pulled up his basket of oysters and lifted them in. Juana sensed his excitement, and she pretended to look away. It is not good to want a thing too much. It sometimes drives the luck away. You must want it just enough, and you must be very tactful with God or the gods. But Juana stopped breathing. Very deliberately Kino opened his short strong knife. He looked speculatively at the basket. Perhaps it would be better to open *the* oyster last. He took a small oyster from the basket, cut the muscle, searched the folds of flesh, and threw it in the water. Then he seemed to see the great oyster for the first time. He squatted in the bottom of the canoe, picked up the shell and examined it. The flutes were shining black to brown, and only a few small barnacles adhered to the shell. Now Kino was reluctant to open it. What he had seen, he knew, might be a reflection, a piece of flat shell accidently drifted in or a complete illusion. In this Gulf of uncertain light there were more illusions than realities.

But Juana's eyes were on him and she could not wait. She put her hand on Coyotito's covered head. "Open it," she said softly.

Kino deftly slipped his knife into the edge of the shell. Through the knife he could feel the muscle tighten hard. He worked the blade lever-wise and the closing muscle parted and the shell fell apart. The lip-like flesh writhed up and then subsided. Kino lifted the flesh, and there it lay, the great pearl, perfect as the moon. It captured the light and refined it and gave it back in silver incandescence. It was as large as a sea-gull's egg. It was the greatest pearl in the world.

Juana caught her breath and moaned a little. And to Kino the secret melody of the maybe pearl broke clear and beautiful, rich and warm and lovely, glowing and gloating and triumphant. In the surface of the great pearl he could see dream forms. He picked the pearl from the dying flesh and held it in his palm, and he turned it over and saw that its curve was perfect. Juana came near to stare at it in his hand, and it was the hand he had smashed against the doctor's gate, and the torn flesh of the knuckles was turned grayish white by the sea water.

Instinctively Juana went to Coyotito where he lay on his father's blanket. She lifted the poultice of seaweed and looked at the shoulder. "Kino," she cried shrilly.

He looked past his pearl, and he saw that the swelling was going out of the baby's shoulder, the poison was receding from its body. Then Kino's fist closed over the pearl and his emotion broke over him. He put back his head and howled. His eyes rolled up and he screamed and his body was rigid. The men in the other canoes looked up, startled, and then they dug their paddles into the sea and raced toward Kino's canoe.

READING COMPREHENSION

Summarizing. Choose the best phrase to complete each sentence. Then write the complete statements on your paper.

1. The first time Kino sensed the Song of Evil was when he _____ (watched the sun rise out of the Gulf, waited for the doctor, saw a scorpion above the baby's bed).

2. The baby did not receive medical attention because _____ (Kino decided it wasn't necessary, the doctor refused to treat a poor Indian, the doctor was too busy).

3. Kino's family went out on the boat to look for _____ (a cure for the sick baby, a pearl, escape from the towns-people).

Interpreting. Write the answer to each question on your paper.

1. What were the different songs that Kino heard?

2. Why did Kino feel weak, afraid, and angry when he approached the doctor's door?

3. What does Juana's behavior tell you about the kind of person she was?

For Thinking and Discussing. Do you think that the pearl will bring good fortune to Kino, his wife, and child, or do you think it might bring them problems as well?

UNDERSTANDING LITERATURE

Characterization. Authors reveal characters to the reader in several ways. They can describe how the characters look, act, think, and what they say, or what other characters say or think about them, or how they react to them.

Read the following passages from *The Pearl*. For each passage, write on your paper which character is being described and what method(s) of characterization is being used. Then write one or two sentences explaining what you learn about the character from the passage.

1. "His eyes were warm and fierce and bright and his mustache was thin and coarse."

2. "Kino sighed with satisfaction—and that was conversation."

3. "Kino had wondered often at the iron in his patient, fragile wife."

4. "Have I nothing better to do than cure insect bites for 'little Indians'? I am a doctor, not a veterinary."

5. "And he shut the gate quickly out of shame."

6. "In the surface of the great pearl he could see dream forms."

WRITING

Write two paragraphs about Kino. In the first, describe how Kino looks. In the second, describe his feelings. Find details in chapters 1 and 2 of *The Pearl*.

Chapter 3

A town is a thing like a colonial animal. A town has a nervous system and a head and shoulders and feet. A town is a thing separate from all other towns, so that there are no two towns alike. And a town has a whole emotion. How news travels through a town is a mystery not easily to be solved. News seems to move faster than small boys can scramble and dart to tell it, faster than women can call it over the fences.

Before Kino and Juana and the other fishers had come to Kino's brush house, the nerves of the town were pulsing and vibrating with the news—Kino had found the Pearl of the World. Before panting little boys could strangle out the words, their mothers knew it. The news swept on past the brush houses, and it washed in a foaming wave into the town of stone and plaster. It came to the priest walking in his garden, and it put a thoughtful look in his eyes and a memory of certain repairs necessary to the church. He wondered what the pearl would be worth. And he wondered whether he had baptized Kino's baby, or married him for that matter. The news came to the shopkeepers, and they looked at men's clothes that had not sold so well.

The news came to the doctor where he sat with a woman whose illness was age, though neither she nor the doctor would admit it. And when it was made plain who Kino was, the doctor grew stern and judicious at the same time. "He is a client of mine," the doctor said. "I am treating his child for a scorpion sting." And the doctor's eyes rolled up a little in their fat hammocks and he thought of Paris. He remembered the room he had lived in there as a great and luxurious place, and he remembered the hard-faced woman who had lived with him as a beautiful and kind girl, although she had been none of these three. The doctor looked past his aged patient and saw himself sitting in a restaurant in Paris and a waiter was just opening a bottle of wine.

The news came early to the beggars in front of the church, and it made them giggle a little with pleasure, for they knew that there is no almsgiver in the world like a poor man who is suddenly lucky.

Kino has found the Pearl of the World. In the town, in little offices, sat the men who bought pearls from the fishers. They waited in their chairs until the pearls came in, and then they cackled and fought and shouted and threatened until they reached the lowest price the fisherman would stand. But there was a price below which they dared not go, for it had happened that a fisherman in despair had given his pearls to the church. And when the buying was over, these buyers sat alone and their fingers played restlessly with the pearls, and they wished they owned the pearls. For there were not many buyers really—there was only one, and he kept these agents in separate

offices to give a semblance of competition. The news came to these men, and their eyes squinted and their fingertips burned a little, and each one thought how the patron could not live forever and someone had to take his place. And each one thought how with some capital he could get a new start.

All manner of people grew interested in Kino—people with things to sell and people with favors to ask. Kino had found the Pearl of the World. The essence of pearl mixed with essence of men and a curious dark residue was precipitated. Every man suddenly became related to Kino's pearl, and Kino's pearl went into the dreams, the speculations, the schemes, the plans, the futures, the wishes, the needs, the lusts, the hungers, of everyone, and only one person stood in the way and that was Kino, so that he became curiously every man's enemy. The news stirred up something infinitely black and evil in the town; the black distillate was like the scorpion, or like hunger in the smell of food, or like loneliness when love is withheld. The poison sacs of the town began to manufacture venom, and the town swelled and puffed with the pressure of it.

But Kino and Juana did not know these things. Because they were happy and excited they thought everyone shared their joy. Juan Tomás and Apolonia did, and they were the world too. In the afternoon, when the sun had gone over the mountains of the Peninsula to sink in the outward sea, Kino squatted in his house with Juana beside him. And the brush house was crowded with neighbors. Kino held the great pearl in his hand, and it was warm and alive in his hand. And the music of the pearl had merged with the music of the family so that one beautified the other. The neighbors looked at the pearl in Kino's hand and they wondered how such luck could come to any man.

And Juan Tomás, who squatted on Kino's right hand because he was his brother, asked, "What will you do now that you have become a rich man?"

Kino looked into his pearl, and Juana cast her eyelashes down and arranged her shawl to cover her face so that her excitement could not be seen. And in the incandescence of the pearl the pictures formed of the things Kino's mind had considered in the past and had given up as impossible. In the pearl he saw Juana and Coyotito and himself standing and kneeling at the high altar, and they were being married now that they could pay. He spoke softly, "We will be married—in the church."

In the pearl he saw how they were dressed — Juana in a shawl stiff with newness and a new skirt, and from under the long skirt Kino could see that she wore shoes. It was in the pearl—the picture glowing there. He himself was dressed in new white clothes, and he carried a new hat—not of straw but of fine black felt—and he too wore shoes—not sandals but shoes that laced. But Coyotito he was the one—he wore a blue sailor suit from the United States and a little yachting cap such as Kino had seen once when a pleasure boat put into the estuary. All of these things Kino saw in the lucent pearl and he said, "We will have new clothes."

And the music of the pearl rose like a chorus of trumpets in his ears.

Then to the lovely gray surface of the pearl came the little things Kino wanted: a harpoon to take the place of one lost a year ago, a new harpoon of iron with a ring in the end of the shaft; and — his mind could hardly make the leap — a rifle—but why not, since he was so rich. And Kino saw Kino in the pearl, Kino holding a Winchester carbine. It was the wildest daydreaming and very pleasant. His lips moved hesitantly over this—"A rifle," he said. "Perhaps a rifle."

It was the rifle that broke down the barriers. This was an impossibility, and if he could think of having a rifle whole horizons were burst and he could rush on. For it is said that humans are never satisfied, that you give them one thing and they want something more. And this is said in disparagement, whereas it is one of the greatest talents the species has and one that has made it superior to animals that are satisfied with what they have.

The neighbors, close pressed and silent in the house, nodded their heads at his wild imaginings. And a man in the rear murmured, "A rifle. He will have a rifle."

But the music of the pearl was shrilling with triumph in Kino. Juana looked up, and her eyes were wide at Kino's courage and at his imagination. And electric strength had come to him now the horizons were kicked out. In the pearl he saw Coyotito sitting at a little desk in a school, just as Kino had once seen it through an open door. And Coyotito was dressed in a jacket, and he had on a white collar and a broad silken tie. Moreover, Coyotito was writing on a big piece of paper. Kino looked at his neighbors fiercely. "My son will go to school," he said, and the neighbors were hushed. Juana caught her breath sharply. Her eyes were bright as she watched him, and she looked quickly down at Coyotito in her arms to see whether this might be possible.

But Kino's face shone with prophecy. "My son will read and open the books, and my son will write and will know writing. And my son will make numbers, and these things will make us free because he will know—he will know and through him we will know." And in the pearl Kino saw himself and Juana squatting by the little fire in the brush hut while Coyotito read from a great book. "This is what the pearl will do," said Kino. And he had never said so many words together in his life. And suddenly he was afraid of his talking. His hand closed down over the pearl and cut the light away from it. Kino was afraid as a man is afraid who says, "I will," without knowing.

Now the neighbors knew they had witnessed a great marvel. They knew that time would now date from Kino's pearl, and that they would discuss this moment for many years to come. If these things came to pass, they would recount how Kino looked and what he said and how his eyes shone, and they would say, "He was a man transfigured. Some power was given to him, and there it started. You see what a great man he has become, starting from that moment. And I myself saw it."

And if Kino's planning came to nothing, those same neighbors would say, "There it started. A foolish madness came over him so that he spoke foolish words. God keep us from such things. Yes, God punished Kino because he rebelled against the way things are. You see what has become of him. And I myself saw the moment when his reason left him."

Kino looked down at his closed hand and the knuckles were scabbed over and tight where he had struck the gate.

Now the dusk was coming. And Juana looped her shawl under the baby so that he hung against her hip, and she went to the fire hole and dug a coal from the ashes and broke a few twigs over it and fanned a flame alive. The little flames danced on the faces of the neighbors. They knew they should go to their own dinners, but they were reluctant to leave.

The dark was almost in, and Juana's fire threw shadows on the brush walls when the whisper came in, passed from mouth to mouth. "The Father is coming —the priest is coming." The men uncovered their heads and stepped back from the door, and the women gathered their shawls about their faces and cast down their eyes. Kino and Juan Tomás, his brother, stood up. The priest came in—a graying, aging man with an old skin and a young sharp eye. Children, he considered these people, and he treated them like children.

"Kino," he said softly, "thou art named after a great man—and a great Father of the Church." He made it sound like a benediction. "Thy namesake tamed the desert and sweetened the minds of thy people, didst thou know that? It is in the books."

Kino looked quickly down at Coyotito's head, where he hung on Juana's hip. Some day, his mind said, that boy would know what things were in the books and what things were not. The music had gone out of Kino's head, but now, thinly, slowly, the melody of the morning, the music of evil, of the enemy sounded, but it was faint and weak. And Kino looked at his neighbors to see who might have brought this song in.

But the priest was speaking again. "It has come to me that thou hast found a great fortune, a great pearl."

Kino opened his hand and held it out, and the priest gasped a little at the size and beauty of the pearl. And then he said, "I hope thou wilt remember to give thanks, my son, to Him who has given thee this treasure, and to pray for guidance in the future."

Kino nodded dumbly, and it was Juana who spoke softly. "We will, Father. And we will be married now. Kino has said so." She looked at the neighbors for confirmation, and they nodded their heads solemnly.

The priest said, "It is pleasant to see that your first thoughts are good thoughts. God bless you, my children." He turned

and left quietly, and the people let him through.

But Kino's hand had closed tightly on the pearl again, and he was glancing about suspiciously, for the evil song was in his ears, shrilling against the music of the pearl.

The neighbors slipped away to go to their houses, and Juana squatted by the fire and set her clay pot of boiled beans over the little flame. Kino stepped to the doorway and looked out. As always, he could smell the smoke from many fires, and he could see the hazy stars and feel the damp of the night air so that he covered his nose from it. The thin dog came to him and threshed itself in greeting like a wind-blown flag, and Kino looked down at it and didn't see it. He had broken through the horizons into a cold and lonely outside. He felt alone and unprotected, and scraping crickets and shrilling tree frogs and croaking toads seemed to be carrying the melody of evil. Kino shivered a little and drew his blanket more tightly against his nose. He carried the pearl still in his hand, tightly closed in his palm, and it was warm and smooth against his skin.

Behind him he heard Juana patting the cakes before she put them down on the clay cooking sheet. Kino felt all the warmth and security of his family behind him, and the Song of the Family came from behind him like the purring of a kitten. But now, by saying what his future was going to be like, he had created it. A plan is a real thing, and things projected are experienced. A plan once made and visualized becomes a reality along with other realities — never to be destroyed but easily to be attacked. Thus Kino's future was real, but having set it up, other forces were set up to destroy it, and this he knew, so that he had to prepare to meet the attack. And this Kino knew also — that the gods do not love men's plans, and the gods do not love success unless it comes by accident. He knew that the gods take their revenge on a man if he be successful through his own efforts. Consequently Kino was afraid of plans, but having made one, he could never destroy it. And to meet the attack, Kino was already making a hard skin for himself against the world. His eyes and his mind probed for danger before it appeared.

Standing in the door, he saw two men approach; and one of them carried a lantern which lighted the ground and the legs of the men. They turned in through the opening of Kino's brush fence and came to his door. And Kino saw that one was the doctor and the other the servant who had opened the gate in the morning. The split knuckles on Kino's right hand burned when he saw who they were.

The doctor said, "I was not in when you came this morning. But now, at the first chance, I have come to see the baby."

Kino stood in the door, filling it, and hatred raged and flamed in back of his eyes, and fear too, for the hundreds of years of subjugation were cut deep in him.

"The baby is nearly well now," he said curtly.

The doctor smiled, but his eyes in their little lymph-lined hammocks did not smile.

He said, "Sometimes, my friend, the scorpion sting has a curious effect. There will be apparent improvement, and then without warning—pouf!" He pursed his lips and made a little explosion to show how quick it could be, and he shifted his small black doctor's bag about so that the light of the lamp fell upon it, for he knew that Kino's race love the tools of any craft and trust them. "Sometimes," the doctor went on in a liquid tone, "sometimes there will be a withered leg or a blind eye or a crumpled back. Oh, I know the sting of the scorpion, my friend, and I can cure it."

Kino felt the rage and hatred melting toward fear. He did not know, and perhaps this doctor did. And he could not take the chance of putting his certain ignorance against this man's possible knowledge. He was trapped as his people were always trapped, and would be until, as he had said, they could be sure that the things in the books were really in the books. He could not take a chance—not with the life or with the straightness of Coyotito. He stood aside and let the doctor and his man enter the brush hut.

Juana stood up from the fire and backed away as he entered, and she covered the baby's face with the fringe of her shawl. And when the doctor went to her and held out his hand, she clutched the baby tight and looked at Kino where he stood with the fire shadows leaping on his face.

Kino nodded, and only then did she let the doctor take the baby.

"Hold the light," the doctor said, and when the servant held the lantern high, the doctor looked for a moment at the wound on the baby's shoulder. He was thoughtful for a moment and then he rolled back the baby's eyelid and looked at the eyeball. He nodded his head while Coyotito struggled against him.

"It is as I thought," he said. "The poison has gone inward and it will strike soon. Come look!" He held the eyelid down. "See — it is blue." And Kino, looking anxiously, saw that indeed it was a little blue. And he didn't know whether or not it was always a little blue. But the trap was set. He couldn't take the chance.

The doctor's eyes watered in their little hammocks. "I will give him something to try to turn the poison aside," he said. And he handed the baby to Kino.

Then from his bag he took a little bottle of white powder and a capsule of gelatine. He filled the capsule with the powder and closed it, and then around the first capsule he fitted a second capsule and closed it. Then he worked very deftly. He took the baby and pinched its lower lip until it opened its mouth. His fat fingers placed the capsule far back on the baby's tongue, back of the point where he could spit it out, and then from the floor he picked up the little pitcher of pulque and gave Coyotito a drink, and it was done. He looked again at the baby's eyeball and he pursed his lips and seemed to think.

At last he handed the baby back to Juana, and he turned to Kino. "I think the poison will attack within the hour," he said. "The medicine may save the baby from hurt, but I will come back in an hour. Perhaps I am in time to save him." He took a deep breath and went out of the hut, and his servant followed him with the lantern.

Now Juana had the baby under her shawl, and she stared at it with anxiety and fear. Kino came to her, and he lifted the shawl and stared at the baby. He moved his hand to look under the eyelid, and only then saw that the pearl was still in his hand. Then he went to a box by the wall, and from it he brought a piece of rag. He wrapped the pearl in the rag, then went to the corner of the brush house and dug a little hole with his fingers in the dirt floor, and he put the pearl in the hole and covered it up and concealed the place. And then he went to the fire where Juana was squatting, watching the baby's face.

The doctor, back in his house, settled into his chair and looked at his watch. His people brought him a little supper of chocolate and sweet cakes and fruit, and he stared at the food discontentedly.

In the houses of the neighbors the subject that would lead all conversations for a long time to come was aired for the first time to see how it would go. The neighbors showed one another with their thumbs how big the pearl was, and they made little caressing gestures to show how lovely it was. From now on they would watch Kino and Juana very closely to see whether riches turned their heads, as riches turn all people's heads. Everyone knew why the doctor had come. He was not good at dissembling and he was very well understood.

Out in the estuary a tight woven

school of small fishes glittered and broke water to escape a school of great fishes that drove in to eat them. And in the houses the people could hear the swish of the small ones and the bouncing splash of the great ones as the slaughter went on. The dampness rose out of the Gulf and was deposited on bushes and cacti and on little trees in salty drops. And the night mice crept about on the ground and the little night hawks hunted them silently.

The skinny black puppy with flame spots over his eyes came to Kino's door and looked in. He nearly shook his hind quarters loose when Kino glanced up at him, and he subsided when Kino looked away. The puppy did not enter the house, but he watched with frantic interest while Kino ate his beans from the little pottery dish and wiped it clean with a corncake and ate the cake and washed the whole down with a drink of pulque.

Kino was finished and was rolling a cigarette when Juana spoke sharply. "Kino." He glanced at her and then got up and went quickly to her for he saw fright in her eyes. He stood over her, looking down, but the light was very dim. He kicked a pile of twigs into the fire hole to make a blaze, and then he could see the face of Coyotito. The baby's face was flushed and his throat was working and a little thick drool of saliva issued from his lips. The spasm of the stomach muscles began, and the baby was very sick.

Kino knelt beside his wife. "So the doctor knew," he said, but he said it for himself as well as for his wife, for his mind was hard and suspicious and he was remembering the white powder. Juana rocked from side to side and moaned out the little Song of the Family as though it could ward off the danger, and the baby vomited and writhed in her arms. Now uncertainty was in Kino, and the music of evil throbbed in his head and nearly drove out Juana's song.

The doctor finished his chocolate and nibbled the little fallen pieces of sweet cake. He brushed his fingers on a napkin, looked at his watch, arose, and took up his little bag.

The news of the baby's illness traveled quickly among the brush houses, for sickness is second only to hunger as the enemy of poor people. And some said softly, "Luck, you see, brings bitter friends." And they nodded and got up to go to Kino's house. The neighbors scuttled with covered noses through the dark until they crowded into Kino's house again. They stood and gazed, and they made little comments on the sadness that this should happen at a time of joy, and they said, "All things are in God's hands." The old women squatted down beside Juana to try to give her aid if they could and comfort if they could not.

Then the doctor hurried in, followed by his man. He scattered the old women like chickens. He took the baby and examined it and felt its head. "The poison has worked," he said. "I think I can defeat it. I will try my best." He asked for water, and in the cup of it he put three drops of ammonia, and he pried open the baby's mouth and poured it down. The baby spluttered and screeched under the treatment, and Juana watched him with haunted eyes. The doctor spoke a little as he worked. "It is lucky that I know about the poison of the scorpion, otherwise—" and he shrugged to show what could have happened.

But Kino was suspicious, and he could not take his eyes from the doctor's open bag, and from the bottle of white powder there. Gradually the spasms subsided and the baby relaxed under the doctor's hands. And then Coyotito sighed deeply and went to sleep, for he was very tired with vomiting.

The doctor put the baby in Juana's arms. "He will get well now," he said. "I have won the fight." And Juana looked at him with adoration.

The doctor was closing his bag now. He said, "When do you think you can pay this bill?" He said it even kindly.

"When I have sold my pearl I will pay you," Kino said.

"You have a pearl? A good pearl?" the doctor asked with interest.

And then the chorus of the neighbors broke in. "He has found the Pearl of the World," they cried, and they joined forefinger with thumb to show how great the pearl was.

"Kino will be a rich man," they clamored. "It is a pearl such as one has never seen."

The doctor looked surprised. "I had not heard of it. Do you keep this pearl in a safe place? Perhaps you would like me to put it in my safe?"

Kino's eyes were hooded now, his cheeks were drawn taut. "I have it secure," he said. "Tomorrow I will sell it and then I will pay you."

The doctor shrugged, and his wet eyes never left Kino's eyes. He knew the pearl would be buried in the house, and he thought Kino might look toward the place where it was buried. "It would be a shame to have it stolen before you could sell it," the doctor said, and he saw Kino's eyes flick involuntarily to the floor near the side post of the brush house.

When the doctor had gone and all the neighbors had reluctantly returned to their houses, Kino squatted beside the little glowing coals in the fire hole and listened to the night sound, the soft sweep of the little waves on the shore and the distant barking of dogs, the creeping of the breeze through the brush house roof and the soft speech of his neighbors in their houses in the village. For these people do not sleep soundly all night; they awaken at intervals and talk a little and then go to sleep again. And after a while Kino got up and went to the door of his house.

He smelled the breeze and he listened for any foreign sound of secrecy or creeping, and his eyes searched the darkness, for the music of evil was sounding in his head and he was fierce and afraid. After he had probed the night with his senses he went to the place by the side post where the pearl was buried, and he dug it up and brought it to his sleeping mat, and under his sleeping mat he dug another little hole in the dirt floor and buried his pearl and covered it up again.

And Juana, sitting by the fire hole, watched him with questioning eyes, and when he had buried his pearl she asked, "Who do you fear?"

Kino searched for a true answer, and at last he said, "Everyone." And he could feel a shell of hardness drawing over him.

After a while they lay down together on the sleeping mat, and Juana did not put the baby in his box tonight, but cradled him on her arms and covered his face with her head shawl. And the last light went out of the embers in the fire hole.

But Kino's brain burned, even during his sleep, and he dreamed that Coyotito could read, that one of his own people could tell him the truth of things. And in his dream, Coyotito was reading from a book as large as a house, with letters as big as dogs, and the words galloped and played on the book. And then darkness spread over the page, and with the darkness came the music of evil again, and Kino stirred in his sleep; and when he stirred Juana's eyes opened in the darkness. And then Kino awakened, with the evil music pulsing in him, and he lay in the darkness with his ears alert.

Then from the corner of the house came a sound so soft that it might have been simply a thought, a little furtive movement, a touch of a foot on earth, the almost inaudible purr of controlled breathing. Kino held his breath to listen, and he knew that whatever dark thing was in his house was holding its breath too, to listen. For a time no sound at all came from the corner of the brush house. Then Kino might have thought he had imagined the sound. But Juana's hand came creeping over to him in warning, and then the sound came again! The whisper of a foot on dry earth and the scratch of fingers in the soil.

And now a wild fear surged in Kino's breast, and on the fear came rage, as it always did. Kino's hand crept into his breast where his knife hung on a string, and then he sprang like an angry cat, leaped striking and spitting for the dark thing he knew was in the corner of the house. He felt cloth, struck at it with his knife and missed, and struck again and felt his knife go through cloth, and then his head crashed with lightning and exploded with pain. There was a soft scurry in the doorway, and running steps for a moment, and then silence.

Kino could feel warm blood running down from his forehead, and he could hear Juana calling to him. "Kino! Kino!" And there was terror in her voice. Then coldness came over him as quickly as the rage had, and he said, "I am all right. The thing has gone."

He groped his way back to the sleeping mat. Already Juana was working at the fire. She uncovered an ember from the ashes and shredded little pieces of cornhusk over it and blew a little flame into the cornhusks so that a tiny light danced through the hut. And then from a secret place Juana brought a little piece of consecrated candle and lighted it at the flame and set it upright on a fireplace stone. She worked quickly, crooning as she moved about. She dipped the end of her head shawl in water and swabbed the blood from Kino's bruised forehead. "It is nothing," Kino said, but his eyes and his voice were hard and cold and a brooding hate was growing in him.

Now the tension which had been growing in Juana boiled up to the surface and her lips were thin. "This thing is evil," she cried harshly. "This pearl is like a sin! It will destroy us," and her voice rose shrilly.

"Throw it away, Kino. Let us break it between stones. Let us bury it and forget the place. Let us throw it back into the sea. It has brought evil. Kino, my husband, it will destroy us." And in the firelight her lips and her eyes were alive with her fear.

But Kino's face was set, and his mind and his will were set. "This is our one chance," he said. "Our son must go to school. He must break out of the pot that holds us in."

"It will destroy us all," Juana cried. "Even our son."

"Hush," said Kino. "Do not speak any more. In the morning we will sell the pearl, and then the evil will be gone, and only the good remain. Now hush, my wife." His dark eyes scowled into the little fire, and for the first time he knew that his knife was still in his hands, and he raised the blade and looked at it and saw a little line of blood on the steel. For a moment he seemed about to wipe the blade on his trousers but then he plunged the knife into the earth and so cleansed it.

The distant roosters began to crow and the air changed and the dawn was coming. The wind of the morning ruffled the water of the estuary and whispered through the mangroves, and the little waves beat on the rubbly beach with an increased tempo. Kino raised the sleeping mat and dug up his pearl and put it in front of him and stared at it.

And the beauty of the pearl, winking and glimmering in the light of the little candle, cozened his brain with its beauty. So lovely it was, so soft, and its own music came from it — its music of promise and delight, its guarantee of the future, of comfort, of security. Its warm lucence

510

promised a poultice against illness and a wall against insult. It closed a door on hunger. And as he stared at it Kino's eyes softened and his face relaxed. He could see the little image of the consecrated candle reflected in the soft surface of the pearl, and he heard again in his ears the lovely music of the undersea, the tone of the diffused green light of the sea bottom. Juana, glancing secretly at him, saw him smile. And because they were in some way one thing and one purpose, she smiled with him.

And they began this day with hope.

Chapter 4

It is wonderful the way a little town keeps track of itself and of all its units. If every single man and woman, child and baby, acts and conducts itself in a known pattern and breaks no walls and differs with no one and experiments in no way and is not sick and does not endanger the ease and peace of mind or steady unbroken flow of the town, then that unit can disappear and never be heard of. But let one man step out of the regular thought or the known and trusted pattern, and the nerves of the townspeople ring with nervousness and communication travels over the nerve lines of the town. Then every unit communicates to the whole.

Thus, in La Paz, it was known in the early morning through the whole town that Kino was going to sell his pearl that day. It was known among the neighbors in the brush huts, among the pearl fishermen; it was known among the Chinese grocery-store owners; it was known in the church, for the altar boys whispered about it. Word of it crept in among the nuns; the beggars in front of the church spoke of it, for they would be there to take the tithe of the first fruits of the luck. The little boys knew about it with excitement, but most of all the pearl buyers knew about it, and when the day had come, in the offices of the pearl buyers, each man sat alone with his little black velvet tray, and each man rolled the pearls about with his fingertips and considered his part in the picture.

It was supposed that the pearl buyers were individuals acting alone, bidding against one another for the pearls the fishermen brought in. And once it had been so. But this was a wasteful method, for often, in the excitement of bidding for a fine pearl, too great a price had been paid to the fishermen. This was extravagant and not to be countenanced. Now there was only one pearl buyer with many hands, and the men who sat in their offices and waited for Kino knew what price they would offer, how high they would bid, and what method each one would use. And although these men would not profit beyond their salaries, there was excitement among the pearl buyers, for there was excitement in the hunt, and if it be a man's function to break down a price, then he must take joy and satisfaction in breaking it as far down as possible. For every man in the world functions to the best of his ability, and no one does less than his best, no matter what he may think about it. Quite apart from any reward they might get, from any word of praise, from any promotion, a pearl buyer was a pearl buyer, and the best and happiest pearl buyer was he who bought for the lowest prices.

The sun was hot yellow that morning, and it drew the moisture from the estuary and from the Gulf and hung it in shimmering scarves in the air so that the air vibrated and vision was insubstantial. A vision hung in the air to the north of

513

the city — the vision of a mountain that was over two hundred miles away, and the high slopes of this mountain were swaddled with pines and a great stone peak arose above the timber line.

And the morning of this day the canoes lay lined up on the beach; the fishermen did not go out to dive for pearls, for there would be too much happening, too many things to see when Kino went to sell the great pearl.

In the brush houses by the shore Kino's neighbors sat long over their breakfasts, and they spoke of what they would do if they had found the pearl. And one man said that he would give it as a present to the Holy Father in Rome. Another said that he would buy Masses for the souls of his family for a thousand years. Another thought he might take the money and distribute it among the poor of La Paz; and a fourth thought of all the good things one could do with the money from the pearl, of all the charities, benefits, of all the rescues one could perform if one had money. All of the neighbors hoped that sudden wealth would not turn Kino's head, would not make a rich man of him, would not graft onto him the evil limbs of greed and hatred and coldness. For Kino was a well-liked man; it would be a shame if the pearl destroyed him. "That good wife Juana," they said, "and the beautiful baby Coyotito, and the others to come. What a pity it would be if the pearl should destroy them all."

For Kino and Juana this was the morning of mornings of their lives, comparable only to the day when the baby had been born. This was to be the day from which all other days would take their arrangement. Thus they would say, "It was two years before we sold the pearl," or, "It was six weeks after we sold the pearl." Juana, considering the matter, threw caution to the winds, and she dressed Coyotito in the clothes she had prepared for his baptism, when there would be money for his baptism. And Juana combed and braided her hair and tied the ends with two little bows of red ribbon and she put on her marriage skirt and waist. The sun was quarter high when they were ready. Kino's ragged white clothes were clean at least, and this was the last day of his raggedness. For tomorrow, or even this afternoon, he would have new clothes.

The neighbors, watching Kino's door through the crevices in their brush houses, were dressed and ready too. There was no self-consciousness about their joining Kino and Juana to go pearl selling. It was expected, it was an historic moment, they would be crazy if they didn't go. It would be almost a sign of unfriendship.

Juana put on her head shawl carefully, and she draped one long end under her right elbow and gathered it with her right hand so that a hammock hung under her arm, and in this little hammock she placed Coyotito, propped up against the head shawl so that he could see everything and perhaps remember. Kino put on his large straw hat and felt it with his hand to see that it was properly placed, not on the back or side of his head, like a rash, unmarried, irresponsible man, and not flat as an elder would

514

wear it, but tilted a little forward to show aggressiveness and seriousness and vigor. There is a great deal to be seen in the tilt of a hat on a man. Kino slipped his feet into his sandals and pulled the thongs up over his heels. The great pearl was wrapped in an old soft piece of deerskin and placed in a little leather bag, and the leather bag was in a pocket in Kino's shirt. He folded his blanket carefully and draped it in a narrow strip over his left shoulder, and now they were ready.

Kino stepped with dignity out of the house, and Juana followed him, carrying Coyotito. And as they marched up the freshet-washed alley toward the town, the neighbors joined them. The houses belched people; the doorways spewed out children. But because of the seriousness of the occasion, only one man walked with Kino, and that was his brother, Juan Tomás.

Juan Tomás cautioned his brother. "You must be careful to see they do not cheat you," he said.

And, "Very careful," Kino agreed.

"We do not know what prices are paid in other places," said Juan Tomás. "How can we know what is a fair price, if we do not know what the pearl buyer gets for the pearl in another place."

"That is true," said Kino, "but how can we know? We are here, we are not there."

As they walked up toward the city the crowd grew behind them, and Juan Tomás, in pure nervousness, went on speaking.

"Before you were born, Kino," he said, "the old ones thought of a way to get more money for their pearls. They thought it would be better if they had an agent who took all the pearls to the capital and sold them there and kept only his share of the profit."

Kino nodded his head. "I know," he said. "It was a good thought."

"And so they got such a man," said Juan Tomás, "and they pooled the pearls, and they started him off. And he was never heard of again and the pearls were lost. Then they got another man, and they started him off, and he was never heard of again. And so they gave the whole thing up and went back to the old way."

"I know," said Kino. "I have heard our father tell of it. It was a good idea, but it was against religion, and the Father made that very clear. The loss of the pearl was a punishment visited on those who tried to leave their station. And the Father made it clear that each man and woman is like a soldier sent by God to guard some part of the castle of the Universe. And some are in the ramparts and some far deep in the darkness of the walls. But each one must remain faithful to his post and must not go running about, else the castle is in danger from the assaults of Hell."

"I have heard him make that sermon," said Juan Tomás. "He makes it every year."

The brothers, as they walked along, squinted their eyes a little, as they and their grandfathers and their great-grandfathers had done for four hundred years, since first the strangers came with argument and authority and gunpowder to back up both. And in the four hundred years Kino's people had learned only one defense—a slight slitting of the eyes and a slight tightening of the lips and a retirement. Nothing could break down this wall, and they could remain whole within the wall.

The gathering procession was solemn, for they sensed the importance of this day, and any children who showed a tendency to scuffle, to scream, to cry out, to steal hats and rumple hair, were hissed to silence by their elders. So important was this day that an old man came to see, riding on the stalwart shoulders of his nephew. The procession left the brush huts and entered the stone and plaster city where the streets were a little wider and there were narrow pavements beside the buildings. And as before, the beggars joined them as they passed the church; the grocers looked out at them as they went by; the little saloons lost their customers and the owners closed up shop and went along. And the sun beat down on the streets of the city and even tiny stones threw shadows on the ground.

The news of the approach of the procession ran ahead of it, and in their little dark offices the pearl buyers stiffened and grew alert. They got out papers so that they could be at work when Kino appeared, and they put their pearls in the desks, for it is not good to let an inferior pearl be seen beside a beauty. And word of the loveliness of Kino's pearl had come to them. The pearl buyers' offices were clustered together in one narrow street, and they were barred at the windows, and wooden slats cut out the light so that only a soft gloom entered the offices.

A stout slow man sat in an office waiting. His face was fatherly and benign, and his eyes twinkled with friendship. He was a caller of good mornings, a ceremonious shaker of hands, a jolly man

who knew all jokes and yet who hovered close to sadness, for in the midst of a laugh he could remember the death of your aunt, and his eyes could become wet with sorrow for your loss. This morning he had placed a flower in a vase on his desk, a single scarlet hibiscus, and the vase sat beside the black velvet-lined pearl tray in front of him. He was shaved close to the blue roots of his beard, and his hands were clean and his nails polished. His door stood open to the morning, and he hummed under his breath while his right hand practiced legerdemain. He rolled a coin back and forth over his knuckles and made it appear and disappear, made it spin and sparkle. The coin winked into sight and as quickly slipped out of sight, and the man did not even watch his own performance. The fingers did it all mechanically, precisely, while the man hummed to himself and peered out the door. Then he heard the tramp of feet of the approaching crowd, and the fingers of his right hand worked faster and faster until, as the figure of Kino filled the doorway, the coin flashed and disappeared.

"Good morning, my friend," the stout man said. "What can I do for you?"

Kino stared into the dimness of the little office, for his eyes were squeezed from the outside glare. But the buyer's eyes had become as steady and cruel and unwinking as a hawk's eyes, while the rest of his face smiled in greeting. And secretly, behind his desk, his right hand practiced with the coin.

"I have a pearl," said Kino. And Juan Tomás stood beside him and snorted a little at the understatement. The neighbors peered around the doorway, and a line of little boys clambered on the window bars and looked through. Several little boys, on their hands and knees, watched the scene around Kino's legs.

"You have a pearl," the dealer said. "Sometimes a man brings in a dozen. Well, let us see your pearl. We will value it and give you the best price." And his fingers worked furiously with the coin.

Now Kino instinctively knew his own dramatic effects. Slowly he brought out the leather bag, slowly took from it the soft and dirty piece of deerskin, and then he let the great pearl roll into the black velvet tray, and instantly his eyes went to the buyer's face. But there was no sign, no movement, the face did not change, but the secret hand behind the desk missed in its precision. The coin stumbled over a knuckle and slipped silently into the dealer's lap. And the fingers behind the desk curled into a fist. When the right hand came out of hiding, the forefinger touched the great pearl, rolled it on the black velvet; thumb and forefinger picked it up and brought it near to the dealer's eyes and twirled it in the air.

Kino held his breath, and the neighbors held their breath, and the whispering went back through the crowd. "He is inspecting it — No price has been mentioned yet — They have not come to a price."

Now the dealer's hand had become a personality. The hand tossed the great pearl back in the tray, the forefinger poked and insulted it, and on the dealer's face there came a sad and contemptuous smile.

"I am sorry, my friend," he said, and his shoulders rose a little to indicate that the misfortune was no fault of his.

"It is a pearl of great value," Kino said.

The dealer's fingers spurned the pearl so that it bounced and rebounded softly from the side of the velvet tray.

"You have heard of fool's gold," the dealer said. "This pearl is like fool's gold. It is too large. Who would buy it? There is no market for such things. It is a curiosity only. I am sorry. You thought it was a thing of value, and it is only a curiosity."

Now Kino's face was perplexed and worried. "It is the Pearl of the World," he cried. "No one has ever seen such a pearl."

"On the contrary," said the dealer, "it is large and clumsy. As a curiosity it has interest; some museum might perhaps take it to place in a collection of sea-shells. I can give you, say, a thousand pesos."

Kino's face grew dark and dangerous. "It is worth fifty thousand," he said. "You know it. You want to cheat me."

And the dealer heard a little grumble go through the crowd as they heard his price. And the dealer felt a little tremor of fear.

"Do not blame me," he said quickly. "I am only an appraiser. Ask the others. Go to their offices and show your pearl —or better let them come here, so that you can see there is no collusion. Boy," he called. And when his servant looked through the rear door, "Boy, go to such a one, and such another one and such a third one. Ask them to step in here and do not tell them why. Just say that I will be pleased to see them." And his right hand went behind the desk and pulled another coin from his pocket, and the coin rolled back and forth over the knuckles.

Kino's neighbors whispered together. They had been afraid of something like this. The pearl was large, but it had a strange color. They had been suspicious of it from the first. And after all, a thousand pesos was not to be thrown away. It was comparative wealth to a man who was not wealthy. And suppose Kino took a thousand pesos. Only yesterday he had nothing.

But Kino had grown tight and hard. He felt the creeping of fate, the circling of wolves, the hover of vultures. He felt the evil coagulating about him, and he was helpless to protect himself. He heard in his ears the evil music. And on the black velvet the great pearl glistened, so that the dealer could not keep his eyes from it.

The crowd in the doorway wavered and broke and let the three pearl dealers through. The crowd was silent now, fearing to miss a word, to fail to see a gesture or an expression. Kino was silent and watchful. He felt a little tugging at his back, and he turned and looked in Juana's eyes, and when he looked away he had renewed strength.

The dealers did not glance at one another nor at the pearl. The man behind the desk said, "I have put a value on this pearl. The owner here does not think it fair. I will ask you to examine this—this thing and make an offer. Notice," he said to Kino, "I have not mentioned what I have offered."

The first dealer, dry and stringy, seemed now to see the pearl for the first time. He took it up, rolled it quickly between thumb and forefinger, and then cast it contemptuously back into the tray.

"Do not include me in the discussion," he said dryly. "I will make no offer at all. I do not want it. This is not a pearl—it is a monstrosity." His thin lips curled.

Now the second dealer, a little man with a shy soft voice, took up the pearl, and he examined it carefully. He took a glass from his pocket and inspected it under magnification. Then he laughed softly.

"Better pearls are made of paste," he said. "I know these things. This is soft and chalky, it will lose its color and die in a few months. Look —." He offered the glass to Kino, showed him how to use it, and Kino, who had never seen a pearl's surface magnified, was shocked at the strange-looking surface.

The third dealer took the pearl from Kino's hands. "One of my clients likes such things," he said. "I will offer five hundred pesos, and perhaps I can sell it to my client for six hundred."

Kino reached quickly and snatched the pearl from his hand. He wrapped it in the deerskin and thrust it inside his shirt.

The man behind the desk said, "I'm a fool, I know, but my first offer stands. I still offer one thousand. What are you doing?" he asked, as Kino thrust the pearl out of sight.

"I am cheated," Kino cried fiercely. "My pearl is not for sale here. I will go, perhaps even to the capital."

Now the dealers glanced quickly at one another. They knew they had played too hard; they knew they would be disciplined for their failure, and the man at the desk said quickly, "I might go to fifteen hundred."

But Kino was pushing his way through the crowd. The hum of talk came to him dimly, his rage blood pounded in his ears, and he burst through and strode away. Juana followed, trotting after him.

When the evening came, the neighbors in the brush houses sat eating their corncakes and beans, and they discussed the great theme of the morning. They did not know, it seemed a fine pearl to them, but they had never seen such a pearl before, and surely the dealers knew more about the value of pearls than they. "And mark this," they said. "Those dealers did not discuss these things. Each of the three knew the pearl was valueless."

"But suppose they had arranged it before?"

"If that is so, then all of us have been cheated all of our lives."

Perhaps, some argued, perhaps it would have been better if Kino took the one thousand five hundred pesos. That is a great deal of money, more than he has ever seen. Maybe Kino is being a pigheaded fool. Suppose he should really go to the capital and find no buyer for his pearl. He would never live that down.

And now, said other fearful ones, now that he had defied them, those buyers will not want to deal with him at all. Maybe Kino has cut off his own head and destroyed himself.

And others said, Kino is a brave man, and a fierce man; he is right. From his courage we may all profit. These were proud of Kino.

In his house Kino squatted on his sleeping mat, brooding. He had buried his pearl under a stone of the fire hole in his house, and he stared at the woven tules of his sleeping mat until the crossed design danced in his head. He had lost one world and had not gained another. And Kino was afraid. Never in his life had he been far from home. He was afraid of strangers and of strange places. He was terrified of that monster of strangeness they called the capital. It lay over the water and through the mountains, over a thousand miles, and every strange terrible mile was frightening. But Kino had lost his old world and he must clamber on to a new one. For his dream of the future was real and never to be destroyed, and he had said, "I will go," and that made a real thing too. To determine to go and to say it was to be halfway there.

Juana watched him while he buried his pearl, and she watched him while she cleaned Coyotito and nursed him, and Juana made the corncakes for supper.

Juan Tomás came in and squatted down beside Kino and remained silent for a long time, until at last Kino demanded, "What else could I do? They are cheats."

Juan Tomás nodded gravely. He was the elder, and Kino looked to him for wisdom. "It is hard to know," he said. "We do know that we are cheated from birth to the overcharge on our coffins. But we survive. You have defied not the pearl buyers, but the whole structure, the whole way of life, and I am afraid for you."

"What have I to fear but starvation?" Kino asked.

But Juan Tomás shook his head slowly. "That we must all fear. But suppose you are correct — suppose your pearl is of great value—do you think then the game is over?"

"What do you mean?"

"I don't know," said Juan Tomás, "but I am afraid for you. It is new ground you are walking on, you do not know the way."

"I will go, I will go soon," said Kino.

"Yes," Juan Tomás agreed. "That you must do. But I wonder if you will find it any different in the capital. Here, you have friends and me, your brother. There, you will have no one."

"What can I do?" Kino cried. "Some deep outrage is here. My son must have a chance. That is what they are striking at. My friends will protect me."

"Only so long as they are not in danger of discomfort from it," said Juan Tomás. He arose, saying, "Go with God."

And Kino said, "Go with God," and did not even look up, for the words had a strange chill in them.

Long after Juan Tomás had gone Kino sat brooding on his sleeping mat. A lethargy had settled on him, and a little gray hopelessness. Every road seemed blocked against him. In his head he heard only the dark music of the enemy. His senses were burningly alive, but his mind went back to the deep participation with all things, the gift he had from his people. He heard every little sound of the gathering night, the sleepy complaint of settling birds, the love agony of cats, the strike and withdrawal of little waves on the beach, and the simple hiss of distance. And he could smell the sharp odor of exposed kelp from the receding tide. The little flare of the twig fire made the design on his sleeping mat jump before his entranced eyes.

Juana watched him with worry, but she knew him and she knew she could help him best by being silent and by being near. And as though she too could hear the Song of Evil, she fought it, singing softly the melody of the family, of the safety and warmth and wholeness of the family. She held Coyotito in her arms and sang the song to him, to keep the evil out, and her voice was brave against the threat of the dark music.

Kino did not move nor ask for his supper. She knew he would ask when he wanted it. His eyes were entranced, and he could sense the wary, watchful evil outside the brush house; he could feel the dark creeping things waiting for him to go out into the night. It was shadowy and dreadful, and yet it called to him and threatened him and challenged him. His right hand went into his shirt and felt his

knife; his eyes were wide; he stood up and walked to the doorway.

Juana willed to stop him; she raised her hand to stop him, and her mouth opened with terror. For a long moment Kino looked out into the darkness and then he stepped outside. Juana heard the little rush, the grunting struggle, the blow. She froze with terror for a moment, and then her lips drew back from her teeth like a cat's lips. She set Coyotito down on the ground. She seized a stone from the fireplace and rushed outside, but it was over by then. Kino lay on the ground, struggling to rise, and there was no one near him. Only the shadows and the strike and rush of waves and the hiss of distance. But the evil was all about, hidden behind the brush fence, crouched beside the house in the shadow, hovering in the air.

Juana dropped her stone, and she put her arms around Kino and helped him to his feet and supported him into the house. Blood oozed down from his scalp and there was a long deep cut in his cheek from ear to chin, a deep, bleeding slash. And Kino was only half conscious. He shook his head from side to side. His shirt was torn open and his clothes half pulled off. Juana sat him down on his sleeping mat and she wiped the thickening blood from his face with her skirt. She brought him pulque to drink in a little pitcher, and still he shook his head to clear out the darkness.

"Who?" Juana asked.

"I don't know," Kino said. "I didn't see."

Now Juana brought her clay pot of water and she washed the cut on his face while he stared dazed ahead of him.

"Kino, my husband," she cried, and his eyes stared past her. "Kino, can you hear me?"

"I hear you," he said dully.

"Kino, this pearl is evil. Let us destroy it before it destroys us. Let us crush it between two stones. Let us—let us throw it back in the sea where it belongs. Kino, it is evil, it is evil!"

And as she spoke the light came back in Kino's eyes so that they glowed fiercely and his muscles hardened and his will hardened.

"No," he said. "I will fight this thing. I will win over it. We will have our chance." His fist pounded the sleeping mat. "No one shall take our good fortune from us," he said. His eyes softened then and he raised a gentle hand to Juana's shoulder. "Believe me," he said. "I am a man." And his face grew crafty.

"In the morning we will take our canoe and we will go over the sea and over the mountains to the capital, you and I. We will not be cheated. I am a man."

"Kino," she said huskily, "I am afraid. A man can be killed. Let us throw the pearl back into the sea."

"Hush," he said fiercely. "I am a man. Hush." And she was silent, for his voice was command. "Let us sleep a little," he said. "In the first light we will start. You are not afraid to go with me?"

"No, my husband."

His eyes were soft and warm on her then, his hand touched her cheek. "Let us sleep a little," he said.

Summarizing. Choose the best phrase to complete each sentence. Then write the complete statements on your paper.

1. The doctor came to see Coyotito because _____ (Juana called him and begged him to come, the family was now rich, the baby's condition had not improved).

2. The first person who tried to steal the pearl from Kino was probably sent by the _____ (doctor, pearl buyers, priest).

3. When Kino said, "I am a man," he meant he _____ (was the person in charge of his family, expected to be treated fairly, was not afraid to travel to the capital).

Interpreting. Write the answer to each question on your paper.

1. What were some of the things Kino imagined for the future when he looked into the pearl?

2. How did Kino know that the pearl buyers were trying to cheat him?

3. Why did Juana think the pearl was evil and should be destroyed?

For Thinking and Discussing

1. Why do you think Kino could not give up the pearl?

2. What changes took place in Kino as the story progressed?

Plot and Subplots. In a long piece of writing, such as a novel, the author often presents a main plot and one or more subplots. A *subplot* is a less important story that occurs within the main story.

In *The Pearl*, the main plot line deals with Kino's finding the great pearl and attempting to sell it. The subplot of the novel is the story of Coyotito's scorpion bite and treatment.

Below is a list of plot events from the first four chapters of *The Pearl*. The events are out of order. On your paper, indicate whether each event is part of the *main plot*, the *subplot*, or *both*. Then arrange the events in the proper order.

1. The doctor came to Kino's house.

2. Someone broke into Kino's house and tried to steal the pearl.

3. Juana said, "Go to get the doctor."

4. Kino decided to travel to the capital.

5. The doctor refused to treat the baby.

6. Kino was told his pearl was valueless.

7. Kino dreamed of the great things the future would hold for his son.

8. Kino and Juana searched for pearls.

Write a paragraph in which you predict several plot events you think will occur in the last part of *The Pearl*. How do you think the main plot will end? Why?

Chapter 5

The late moon arose before the first rooster crowed. Kino opened his eyes in the darkness, for he sensed movement near him, but he did not move. Only his eyes searched the darkness, and in the pale light of the moon that crept through the holes in the brush house Kino saw Juana arise silently from beside him. He saw her move toward the fireplace. So carefully did she work that he heard only the lightest sound when she moved the fireplace stone. And then like a shadow she glided toward the door. She paused for a moment beside the hanging box where Coyotito lay, then for a second she was black in the doorway, and then she was gone.

And rage surged in Kino. He rolled up to his feet and followed her as silently as she had gone, and he could hear her quick footsteps going toward the shore. Quietly he tracked her, and his brain was red with anger. She burst clear out of the brush line and stumbled over the little boulders toward the water, and then she heard him coming and she broke into a run. Her arm was up to throw when he leaped at her and caught her arm and wrenched the pearl from her. He struck her in the face with his clenched fist and she fell among the boulders, and he kicked her in the side. In the pale light he could see the little waves break over her, and her skirt floated about and clung to her legs as the water receded.

Kino looked down at her and his teeth were bared. He hissed at her like a snake, and Juana stared at him with wide unfrightened eyes, like a sheep before the butcher. She knew there was murder in him, and it was all right; she had accepted it, and she would not resist or even protest. And then the rage left him and a sick disgust took its place. He turned away from her and walked up the beach and through the brush line. His senses were dulled by his emotion.

He heard the rush, got his knife out and lunged at one dark figure and felt his knife go home, and then he was swept to his knees and swept again to the ground. Greedy fingers went through his clothes, frantic fingers searched him, and the pearl, knocked from his hand, lay winking behind a little stone in the pathway. It glinted in the soft moonlight.

Juana dragged herself up from the rocks on the edge of the water. Her face was a dull pain and her side ached. She steadied herself on her knees for a while and her wet skirt clung to her. There was no anger in her for Kino. He had said, "I am a man," and that meant certain things to Juana. It meant that he was half insane and half god. It meant that Kino would drive his strength against a mountain and plunge his strength against the sea. Juana, in her woman's soul, knew that the mountain would stand while the man broke himself; that the sea would surge while the man drowned in it. And yet it was this thing that made him a man, half insane and half god, and Juana had need of a man; she could not live

without a man. Although she might be puzzled by these differences between man and woman, she knew them and accepted them and needed them. Of course she would follow him, there was no question of that. Sometimes the quality of woman, the reason, the caution, the sense of preservation, could cut through Kino's manness and save them all. She climbed painfully to her feet, and she dipped her cupped palms in the little waves and washed her bruised face with the stinging salt water, and then she went creeping up the beach after Kino.

A flight of herring clouds had moved over the sky from the south. The pale moon dipped in and out of the strands of clouds so that Juana walked in darkness for a moment and in light the next. Her back was bent with pain and her head was low. She went through the line of brush when the moon was covered, and when it looked through she saw the glimmer of the great pearl in the path behind the rock. She sank to her knees and picked it up, and the moon went into the darkness of the clouds again. Juana remained on her knees while she considered whether to go back to the sea and finish her job, and as she considered, the light came again, and she saw two dark figures lying in the path ahead of her. She leaped forward and saw that one was Kino and the other a stranger with dark shiny fluid leaking from his throat.

Kino moved sluggishly, arms and legs stirred like those of a crushed bug, and a thick muttering came from his mouth. Now, in an instant, Juana knew that the old life was gone forever. A dead man in the path and Kino's knife, dark bladed beside him, convinced her. All of the time Juana had been trying to rescue something of the old peace, of the time before the pearl. But now it was gone, and there was no retrieving it. And knowing this, she abandoned the past instantly. There was nothing to do but to save themselves.

Her pain was gone now, her slowness. Quickly she dragged the dead man from the pathway into the shelter of the brush. She went to Kino and sponged his face with her wet skirt. His senses were coming back and he moaned.

"They have taken the pearl. I have lost it. Now it is over," he said. "The pearl is gone."

Juana quieted him as she would quiet a sick child. "Hush," she said, "Here is your pearl. I found it in the path. Can you hear me now? Here is your pearl. Can you understand? You have killed a man. We must go away. They will come for us, can you understand? We must be gone before the daylight comes."

"I was attacked," Kino said uneasily. "I struck to save my life."

"Do you remember yesterday?" Juana asked. "Do you think that will matter? Do you remember the men of the city? Do you think your explanation will help?"

Kino drew a great breath and fought off his weakness. "No," he said. "You are right." And his will hardened and he was a man again.

"Go to our house and bring Coyotito," he said, "and bring all the corn we have. I will drag the canoe into the water and we will go."

He took his knife and left her. He stumbled toward the beach and he came to his canoe. And when the light broke through again he saw that a great hole had been knocked in the bottom. And a searing rage came to him and gave him strength. Now the darkness was closing in on his family; now the evil music filled the night, hung over the mangroves, skirled in the wave beat. The canoe of his grandfather, plastered over and over, and a splintered hole broken in it. This was an evil beyond thinking. The killing of man was not so evil as the killing of a boat. For a boat does not have sons, and a boat cannot protect itself, and a wounded boat does not heal. There was sorrow in Kino's rage, but this last thing had tightened him beyond breaking. He was an animal now, for hiding, for attacking, and he lived only to preserve himself and his family. He was not conscious of the pain in his head. He leaped up the beach, through the brush line toward his brush house, and it did not occur to him to take one of the canoes of his neighbors. Never once did the thought enter his head, any more than he could have conceived breaking a boat.

The roosters were crowing and the dawn was not far off. Smoke of the first fires seeped out through the walls of the brush houses, and the first smell of cooking corncakes was in the air. Already the dawn birds were scampering in the bushes. The weak moon was losing its light and the clouds thickened and curdled to the southward. The wind blew freshly into the estuary, a nervous, restless wind with the smell of storm on its breath, and there was change and uneasiness in the air.

Kino, hurrying toward his house, felt a surge of exhilaration. Now he was not confused, for there was only one thing to do, and Kino's hand went first to the great pearl in his shirt and then to his knife hanging under his shirt.

He saw a little glow ahead of him, and then without interval a tall flame leaped up in the dark with a crackling roar, and a tall edifice of fire lighted the pathway. Kino broke into a run; it was his brush house, he knew. And he knew that these houses could burn down in a very few moments. And as he ran a scuttling figure ran toward him—Juana, with Coyotito in her arms and Kino's shoulder blanket clutched in her hand. The baby moaned with fright, and Juana's eyes were wide and terrified. Kino could see the house was gone, and he did not question Juana. He knew, but she said, "It was torn up and the floor dug—even the baby's box turned out, and as I looked they put the fire to the outside."

The fierce light of the burning house lighted Kino's face strongly. "Who?" he demanded.

"I don't know," she said. "The dark ones."

The neighbors were tumbling from their houses now, and they watched the falling sparks and stamped them out to save their own houses. Suddenly Kino was afraid. The light made him afraid. He remembered the man lying dead in the brush beside the path, and he took Juana by the arm and drew her into the shadow of a house away from the light, for light was danger to him. For a mo-

ment he considered and then he worked among the shadows until he came to the house of Juan Tomás, his brother, and he slipped into the doorway and drew Juana after him. Outside, he could hear the squeal of children and the shouts of the neighbors, for his friends thought he might be inside the burning house.

The house of Juan Tomás was almost exactly like Kino's house; nearly all the brush houses were alike, and all leaked light and air, so that Juana and Kino, sitting in the corner of the brother's house, could see the leaping flames through the wall. They saw the flames tall and furious; they saw the roof fall and watched the fire die down as quickly as a twig fire dies. They heard the cries of warning of their friends, and the shrill, keening cry of Apolonia, wife of Juan Tomás. She, being the nearest woman relative, raised a formal lament for the dead of the family.

Apolonia realized that she was wearing her second-best head shawl and she rushed to her house to get her fine new one. As she rummaged in a box by the wall, Kino's voice said quietly, "Apolonia, do not cry out. We are not hurt."

"How do you come here?" she demanded.

"Do not question," he said. "Go now to Juan Tomás and bring him here and tell no one else. This is important to us, Apolonia."

She paused, her hands helpless in front of her, and then, "Yes, my brother-in-law," she said.

In a few moments Juan Tomás came back with her. He lighted a candle and came to them where they crouched in a corner and he said, "Apolonia, see to the door, and do not let anyone enter." He was older, Juan Tomás, and he assumed the authority. "Now, my brother," he said.

"I was attacked in the dark," said Kino, "And in the fight I have killed a man."

"Who?" asked Juan Tomás quickly.

"I do not know. It is all darkness—all darkness and shape of darkness."

"It is the pearl," said Juan Tomás. "There is a devil in this pearl. You should have sold it and passed on the devil. Perhaps you can still sell it and buy peace for yourself."

And Kino said, "Oh, my brother, an insult has been put on me that is deeper than my life. For on the beach my canoe is broken, my house is burned, and in the brush a dead man lies. Every escape is cut off. You must hide us, my brother."

And Kino, looking closely, saw deep worry come into his brother's eyes and he forestalled him in a possible refusal. "Not for long," he said quickly. "Only until a day has passed and the new night has come. Then we will go."

"I will hide you," said Juan Tomás.

"I do not want to bring danger to you," Kino said. "I know I am like a leprosy. I will go tonight and then you will be safe."

"I will protect you," said Juan Tomás, and he called, "Apolonia, close up the door. Do not even whisper that Kino is here."

They sat silently all day in the darkness of the house, and they could hear the neighbors speaking of them. Through the walls of the house they could watch their neighbors raking through the ashes to find the bones. Crouching in the house of Juan Tomás, they heard the shock go into their neighbors' minds at the news of the broken boat. Juan Tomás went out among the neighbors to divert their suspicions, and he gave them theories and ideas of what had happened to Kino and to Juana and to the baby. To one he said, "I think they have gone south along the coast to escape the evil that was on them." And to another, "Kino would never leave the sea. Perhaps he found another boat." And he said, "Apolonia is ill with grief."

And in that day the wind rose up to beat the Gulf and tore the kelps and weeds that lined the shore, and the wind cried through the brush houses and no boat was safe on the water. Then Juan Tomás told among the neighbors, "Kino is gone. If he went to the sea, he is drowned by now." And after each trip among the neighbors Juan Tomás came back with something borrowed. He brought a little woven straw bag of red beans and a gourd full of rice. He borrowed a cup of dried peppers and a block of salt, and he brought in a long working knife, eighteen inches long and heavy, as a small ax, a tool and a weapon. And when Kino saw this knife his eyes lighted up, and he fondled the blade and his thumb tested the edge.

The wind screamed over the Gulf and turned the water white, and the mangroves plunged like frightened cattle, and a fine sandy dust arose from the land and hung in a stifling cloud over the sea. The wind drove off the clouds and skimmed the sky clean and drifted the sand of the country like snow.

Then Juan Tomás, when the evening approached, talked long with his brother. "Where will you go?"

"To the north," said Kino. "I have heard that there are cities in the north."

"Avoid the shore," said Juan Tomás. "They are making a party to search the shore. The men in the city will look for you. Do you still have the pearl?"

"I have it," said Kino. "And I will keep it. I might have given it as a gift, but now it is my misfortune and my life and I will keep it." His eyes were hard and cruel and bitter.

Coyotito whimpered and Juana muttered little magics over him to make him silent.

"The wind is good," said Juan Tomás. "There will be no tracks."

They left quietly in the dark before the moon had risen. The family stood formally in the house of Juan Tomás. Juana carried Coyotito on her back, covered and held in by her head shawl, and the baby slept, cheek turned sideways against her shoulder. The head shawl covered the baby, and one end of it came across Juana's nose to protect her from the evil night air. Juan Tomás embraced his brother with the double embrace and kissed him on both cheeks. "Go with God," he said, and it was like a death. "You will not give up the pearl?"

"This pearl has become my soul," said Kino. "If I give it up I shall lose my soul. Go thou also with God."

Chapter 6

The wind blew fierce and strong, and it pelted them with bits of sticks, sand, and little rocks. Juana and Kino gathered their clothing tighter about them, and covered their noses and went out into the world. The sky was brushed clean by the wind and the stars were cold in a black sky. The two walked carefully, and they avoided the center of the town where some sleeper in a doorway might see them pass. For the town closed itself in against the night, and anyone who moved about in the darkness would be noticeable. Kino threaded his way around the edge of the city and turned north, north by the stars, and found the rutted sandy road that led through the brushy country toward Loreto where the miraculous Virgin has her station.

Kino could feel the blown sand against his ankles and he was glad, for he knew there would be no tracks. The little light from the stars made out for him the narrow road through the brushy country. And Kino could hear the pad of Juana's feet behind him. He went quickly and quietly, and Juana trotted behind him to keep up.

Some ancient thing stirred in Kino. Through his fear of dark and the devils that haunt the night, there came a rush of exhilaration; some animal thing was moving in him so that he was cautious and wary and dangerous; some ancient thing out of the past of his people was alive in him. The wind was at his back and the stars guided him. The wind cried and whisked in the brush, and the family went on monotonously, hour after hour. They passed no one and saw no one. At last, to their right, the waning moon arose, and when it came up the wind died down, and the land was still.

Now they could see the little road ahead of them, deep cut with sand-drifted wheel tracks. With the wind gone there would be footprints, but they were a good distance from the town and perhaps their tracks might not be noticed. Kino walked carefully in a wheel rut, and Juana followed in his path. One big cart, going to the town in the morning, could wipe out every trace of their passage.

All night they walked and never changed their pace. Once Coyotito awakened, and Juana shifted him in front of her and soothed him until he went to sleep again. And the evils of the night were about them. The coyotes cried and laughed in the brush, and the owls screeched and hissed over their heads. And once some large animal lumbered away, crackling the undergrowth as it went. And Kino gripped the handle of the big working knife and took a sense of protection from it.

The music of the pearl was triumphant in Kino's head, and the quiet melody of the family underlay it, and they wove themselves into the soft padding of sandaled feet in the dust. All night they walked, and in the first dawn Kino searched the roadside for a covert to lie in during the day. He found his place near to the road, a little clearing where deer might have lain, and it was curtained thickly with the dry brittle trees that lined the road. And when Juana had seated herself and had settled to nurse the baby, Kino went back to the road. He broke a branch and carefully swept the footprints where they had turned from the roadway. And then, in the first light, he heard the creak of a wagon, and he crouched beside the road and watched a heavy two-wheeled cart go by, drawn by slouching oxen. And when it had passed out of sight, he went back to the roadway and looked at the rut and found that the footprints were gone. And again he swept out his traces and went back to Juana.

She gave him the soft corncakes Apolonia had packed for them, and after a while she slept a little. But Kino sat on the ground and stared at the earth in front of him. He watched the ants moving, a little column of them near to his foot, and he put his foot in their path. Then the column climbed over his instep and continued on its way, and Kino left his foot there and watched them move over it.

The sun arose hotly. They were not near the Gulf now, and the air was dry and hot so that the brush cricked with heat and a good resinous smell came from it. And when Juana awakened, when the sun was high, Kino told her things she knew already.

"Beware of that kind of tree there," he said, pointing. "Do not touch it, for if you do and then touch your eyes, it will blind you. And beware of the tree that bleeds. See, that one over there. For if you break it the red blood will flow from it, and it is evil luck." And she nodded and smiled a little at him, for she knew these things.

"Will they follow us?" she asked. "Do you think they will try to find us?"

"They will try," said Kino. "Whoever finds us will take the pearl. Oh, they will try."

And Juana said, "Perhaps the dealers were right and the pearl has no value. Perhaps this has all been an illusion."

Kino reached into his clothes and brought out the pearl. He let the sun play

miles around came to drink from the little pools, and the wild sheep and the deer, the pumas and raccoons, and the mice—all came to drink. And the birds which spent the day in the brushland came at night to the little pools that were like steps in the mountain cleft. Beside this tiny stream, wherever enough earth collected for root-hold, colonies of plants grew, wild grape and little palms, maidenhair fern, hibiscus, and tall pampas grass with feathery rods raised above the spike leaves. And in the pool lived frogs and water-skaters, and waterworms crawled on the bottom of the pool. Everything that loved water came to these few shallow places. The cats took their prey there, and strewed feathers and lapped water through their bloody teeth. The little pools were places of life because of the water, and places of killing because of the water, too.

The lowest step, where the stream collected before it tumbled down a hundred feet and disappeared into the rubbly desert, was a little platform of stone and sand. Only a pencil of water fell into the pool, but it was enough to keep the pool full and to keep the ferns green in the underhang of the cliff, and wild grape climbed the stone mountain and all manner of little plants found comfort here. The freshets had made a small sandy beach through which the pool flowed, and bright green watercress grew in the damp sand. The beach was cut and scarred and padded by the feet of animals that had come to drink and to hunt.

The sun had passed over the stone mountains when Kino and Juana struggled up the steep broken slope and came at last to the water. From this step they could look out over the sunbeaten desert to the blue Gulf in the distance. They came utterly weary to the pool, and Juana slumped to her knees and first washed Coyotito's face and then filled her bottle and gave him a drink. And the baby was weary and petulant, and he cried softly until Juana gave him her breast, and then he gurgled and clucked against her. Kino drank long and thirstily at the pool. For a moment, then, he stretched out beside the water and relaxed all his muscles and watched Juana feeding the baby, and then he got to his feet and went to the edge of the step where the water slipped over, and he searched the distance carefully. His eyes set on a point and he became rigid. Far down the slope he could see the two trackers; they were little more than dots or scurrying ants and behind them a larger ant.

Juana had turned to look at him and she saw his back stiffen.

"How far?" she asked quietly.

"They will be here by evening," said Kino. He looked up the long steep chimney of the cleft where the water came down. "We must go west," he said, and his eyes searched the stone shoulder behind the cleft. And thirty feet up on the gray shoulder he saw a series of little erosion caves. He slipped off his sandals and clambered up to them, gripping the bare stone with his toes, and he looked into the shallow caves. They were only a few feet deep, wind-hollowed scoops, but they sloped slightly downward and back.

Kino crawled into the largest one and lay down and knew that he could not be seen from the outside. Quickly he went back to Juana.

"You must go up there. Perhaps they will not find us there," he said.

Without question she filled her water bottle to the top, and then Kino helped her up to the shallow cave and brought up the packages of food and passed them to her. And Juana sat in the cave entrance and watched him. She saw that he did not try to erase their tracks in the sand. Instead, he climbed up the brush cliff beside the water, clawing and tearing at the ferns and wild grape as he went. And when he had climbed a hundred feet to the next bench, he came down again. He looked carefully at the smooth rock shoulder toward the cave to see that there was no trace of passage, and last he climbed up and crept into the cave beside Juana.

"When they go up," he said, "we will slip away, down to the lowlands again. I am afraid only that the baby may cry. You must see that he does not cry."

"He will not cry," she said, and she raised the baby's face to her own and looked into his eyes and he stared solemnly back at her.

"He knows," said Juana.

Now Kino lay in the cave entrance, his chin braced on his crossed arms, and he watched the blue shadow of the mountain move out across the brushy desert below until it reached the Gulf, and the long twilight of the shadow was over the land.

The trackers were long in coming, as though they had trouble with the trail Kino had left. It was dusk when they came at last to the little pool. And all three were on foot now, for a horse could not climb the last steep slope. From above they were thin figures in the evening. The two trackers scurried about on the little beach, and they saw Kino's progress up the cliff before they drank. The man with the rifle sat down and rested himself, and the trackers squatted near him, and in the evening the points of their cigarettes glowed and receded. And then Kino could see that they were eating, and the soft murmur of their voices came to him.

Then darkness fell, deep and black in the mountain cleft. The animals that used the pool came near and smelled men there and drifted away again into the darkness.

He heard a murmur behind him. Juana was whispering, "Coyotito." She was begging him to be quiet. Kino heard the

543

baby whimper, and he knew from the muffled sounds that Juana had covered his head with her shawl.

Down on the beach a match flared, and in its momentary light Kino saw that two of the men were sleeping, curled up like dogs, while the third watched, and he saw the glint of the rifle in the match light. And then the match died, but it left a picture on Kino's eyes. He could see it, just how each man was, two sleeping curled up and the third squatting in the sand with the rifle between his knees.

Kino moved silently back into the cave. Juana's eyes were two sparks reflecting a low star. Kino crawled quietly close to her and he put his lips near to her cheek.

"There is a way," he said.

"But they will kill you."

"If I get first to the one with the rifle," Kino said, "I must get to him first, then I will be all right. Two are sleeping."

Her hand crept out from under her shawl and gripped his arm. "They will see your white clothes in the starlight."

"No," he said. "And I must go before moonrise."

He searched for a soft word and then gave it up. "If they kill me," he said, "lie quietly. And when they are gone away, go to Loreto."

Her hand shook a little, holding his wrist.

"There is no choice," he said. "It is the only way. They will find us in the morning."

Her voice trembled a little. "Go with God," she said.

He peered closely at her and he could see her large eyes. His hand fumbled out and found the baby, and for a moment his palm lay on Coyotito's head. And then Kino raised his hand and touched Juana's cheek, and she held her breath.

Against the sky in the cave entrance Juana could see that Kino was taking off his white clothes, for dirty and ragged though they were they would show up against the dark night. His own brown skin was a better protection for him. And then she saw how he hooked his amulet neck-string about the horn handle of his great knife, so that it hung down in front of him and left both hands free. He did not come back to her. For a moment his body was black in the cave entrance, crouched and silent, and then he was gone.

Juana moved to the entrance and looked out. She peered like an owl from the hole in the mountain, and the baby slept under the blanket on her back, his face turned sideways against her neck and shoulder. She could feel his warm breath against her skin, and Juana whispered her combination of prayer and magic, her Hail Marys and her ancient intercession, against the black unhuman things.

The night seemed a little less dark when she looked out, and to the east there was a lightning in the sky, down near the horizon where the moon would show. And, looking down, she could see the cigarette of the man on watch.

Kino edged like a slow lizard down the smooth rock shoulder. He had turned his neck-string so that the great knife hung down from his back and could not clash against the stone. His spread fingers gripped the mountain, and his bare toes found support through contact, and even his chest lay against the stone so that he would not slip. For any sound, a rolling pebble or a sigh, a little slip of flesh on rock, would rouse the watchers below. Any sound that was not germane to the night would make them alert. But the night was not silent; the little tree frogs that lived near the stream twittered like birds, and the high metallic ringing of the cicadas filled the mountain cleft. And Kino's own music was in his head, the music of the enemy, low and pulsing, nearly asleep. But the Song of the Family had become as fierce and sharp and feline as the snarl of a female puma. The family song was alive now and driving him down on the dark enemy. The harsh cicada seemed to take up its melody, and the twittering tree frogs called little phrases of it.

And Kino crept silently as a shadow down the smooth mountain face. One bare foot moved a few inches and the toes touched the stone and gripped, and the other foot a few inches, and then the palm of one hand a little downward, and then the other hand, until the whole body, without seeming to move, had moved. Kino's mouth was open so that even his breath would make no sound, for he knew that he was not invisible. If the watcher, sensing movement, looked at the dark place against the stone which was his body, he could see him. Kino must move so slowly he would not draw the watcher's eyes. It took him a long time to reach the bottom and to crouch behind a little dwarf palm. His heart thundered in his chest and his hands and his face were wet with sweat. He crouched and took great slow long breaths to calm himself.

Only twenty feet separated him from the enemy now, and he tried to remember the ground between. Was there any stone which might trip him in his rush? He kneaded his legs against cramp and found that his muscles were jerking after their long tension. And then he looked apprehensively to the east. The moon would rise in a few moments now, and he must attack before it rose. He could see the outline of the watcher, but the sleeping men were below his vision. It was the watcher Kino must find — must find quickly and without hesitation. Silently he drew the amulet string over his shoulder and loosened the loop from the horn handle of his great knife.

He was too late, for as he rose from his crouch the silver edge of the moon slipped above the eastern horizon, and Kino sank back behind his bush.

It was an old and ragged moon, but it threw hard light and hard shadow into the mountain cleft, and now Kino could see the seated figure of the watcher on the little beach beside the pool. The watcher gazed full at the moon, and then he lighted another cigarette, and the match illumined his dark face for a moment. There could be no waiting now; when the watcher turned his head, Kino must leap. His legs were as tight as wound springs.

And then from above came a little murmuring cry. The watcher turned his head to listen and then he stood up, and one of the sleepers stirred on the ground and awakened and asked quietly, "What is it?"

"I don't know," said the watcher. "It sounded like a cry, almost like a human —like a baby."

The man who had been sleeping said, "You can't tell. Some coyote bitch with a litter. I've heard a coyote pup cry like a baby."

The sweat rolled in drops down Kino's forehead and fell into his eyes and burned them. The little cry came again and the watcher looked up the side of the hill to the dark cave.

"Coyote maybe," he said, and Kino heard the harsh click as he cocked the rifle.

"If it's a coyote, this will stop it," the watcher said as he raised the gun.

Kino was in mid-leap when the gun crashed and the barrel-flash made a picture on his eyes. The great knife swung and crunched hollowly. It bit through neck and deep into chest, and Kino was a terrible machine now. He grasped the rifle even as he wrenched free his knife. His strength and his movement and his speed were a machine. He whirled and struck the head of the seated man like a melon. The third man scrabbled away like a crab, slipped into the pool, and then he began to climb frantically, to climb up the cliff where the water penciled down. His hands and feet threshed in the tangle of the wild grapevine, and he whimpered and gibbered as he tried to get up. But Kino had become as cold and deadly as steel. Deliberately he threw the lever of the rifle, and then he raised the gun and aimed deliberately and fired. He saw his enemy tumble backward into the pool, and Kino strode to the water. In the moonlight he could see the frantic frightened eyes, and Kino aimed and fired between the eyes.

And then Kino stood uncertainly. Something was wrong, some signal was trying to get through to his brain. Tree frogs and cicadas were silent now. And then Kino's brain cleared from its red concentration and he knew the sound— the keening, moaning, rising hysterical cry from the little cave in the side of the stone mountain, the cry of death.

Everyone in La Paz remembers the return of the family; there may be some old ones who saw it, but those whose fathers and whose grandfathers told it to them remember it nevertheless. It is an event that happened to everyone.

It was late in the golden afternoon when the first little boys ran hysterically in the town and spread the word that Kino and Juana were coming back. And everyone hurried to see them. The sun was settling toward the western mountains and the shadows on the ground were long. And perhaps that was what left the deep impression on those who saw them.

The two came from the rutted country road into the city, and they were not walking in single file, Kino ahead and

Juana behind, as usual, but side by side. The sun was behind them and their long shadows stalked ahead, and they seemed to carry two towers of darkness with them. Kino had a rifle across his arm and Juana carried her shawl like a sack over her shoulder. And in it was a small limp heavy bundle. The shawl was crusted with dried blood, and the bundle swayed a little as she walked. Her face was hard and lined and leathery with fatigue and with the tightness with which she fought fatigue. And her wide eyes stared inward on herself. She was as remote and as removed as Heaven. Kino's lips were thin and his jaws tight, and the people say that he carried fear with him, that he was as dangerous as a rising storm. The people say that the two seemed to be removed from human experience; that they had gone through pain and had come out on the other side; that there was almost a magical protection about them. And those people who had rushed to see them crowded back and let them pass and did not speak to them.

Kino and Juana walked through the city as though it were not there. Their eyes glanced neither right nor left nor up nor down, but stared only straight ahead. Their legs moved a little jerkily, like well-made wooden dolls, and they carried pillars of black fear about them. And as they walked through the stone and plaster city, brokers peered at them from barred windows and servants put one eye to a slitted gate and mothers turned the faces of their youngest children inward against their skirts. Kino and Juana strode side by side through the stone and plaster city and down among the brush houses, and the neighbors stood back and let them pass. Juan Tomás raised his hand in greeting and did not say the greeting and left his hand in the air for a moment uncertainly.

In Kino's ears the Song of the Family was as fierce as a cry. He was immune and terrible, and his song had become a battle cry. They trudged past the burned square where their house had been without even looking at it. They cleared the brush that edged the beach and picked their way down the shore toward the water. And they did not look toward Kino's broken canoe.

And when they came to the water's edge they stopped and stared out over the Gulf. And then Kino laid the rifle down, and he dug among his clothes, and then he held the great pearl in his hand. He looked into its surface and it was gray and ulcerous. Evil faces peered from it into his eyes, and he saw the light of burning. And in the surface of the pearl he saw the frantic eyes of the man in the pool. And in the surface of the pearl he saw Coyotito lying in the little cave with the top of his head shot away. And the pearl was ugly; it was gray, like a malignant growth. And Kino heard the music of the pearl, distorted and insane. Kino's hand shook a little, and he turned slowly to Juana and held the pearl out to her. She stood beside him, still holding her dead bundle over her shoulder. She looked at the pearl in his hand for a moment and then she looked into Kino's eyes and said softly, "No, you."

And Kino drew back his arm and flung the pearl with all his might. Kino and Juana watched it go, winking and glimmering under the setting sun. They saw the little splash in the distance, and they stood side by side watching the place for a long time.

And the pearl settled into the lovely green water and dropped toward the bottom. The waving branches of the algae called to it and beckoned to it. The lights on its surface were green and lovely. It settled down to the sand bottom among the fern-like plants. Above, the surface of the water was a green mirror. And the pearl lay on the floor of the sea. A crab scampering over the bottom raised a little cloud of sand, and when it settled the pearl was gone.

And the music of the pearl drifted to a whisper and disappeared.

READING COMPREHENSION

Summarizing. Choose the best phrase to complete each sentence. Then write the complete statements on your paper.

1. Juana took the pearl and _____ (tried to sell it on her own, hid it in Coyotito's sleeping box, tried to throw it into the sea).

2. The trackers hunting Kino _____ (managed to steal the pearl, killed the baby accidentally, chased Kino down the mountain).

3. Kino and Juana threw the pearl back into the sea because _____ (it was worthless, they didn't want anyone else to have it, it had brought them only trouble).

Interpreting. Write the answer to each question on your paper.

1. What did Kino do when Juana tried to throw the pearl back into the sea?

2. Why was Kino so disturbed when he saw that his boat had been damaged?

3. Why was Kino's brother, Juan, reluctant to hide Kino and Juana?

For Thinking and Discussing. What do you think would have happened if Juana had thrown the pearl back into the sea earlier? How would the family's life have changed? Do you think they could have returned to the life they knew before Kino found the pearl?

UNDERSTANDING LITERATURE

Theme. The *theme* of a work of literature is the author's message about the way people do live or should live.

What theme do you think Steinbeck was trying to convey in *The Pearl*? The statements below will help you think about the novel's theme. On your paper, select the best choice to complete each statement.

1. According to Steinbeck's introduction, the retold story has become a tale _____.
   a. people often tell their children at night
   b. of good and evil and nothing in between
   c. about the poor against the rich

2. Kino's Song of the Family and Song of Evil suggest that _____.
   a. Indians love music
   b. music affects a person's life
   c. life has conflicting forces

3. Kino's experience with the pearl suggests that _____.
   a. wealth doesn't guarantee happiness
   b. poor people can never become rich
   c. people usually get what they deserve

WRITING

Pretend you are either Kino or Juana. Write a paragraph describing your feelings as you watched the pearl hit the water. Write another paragraph about your hopes for the future.

Section Review

VOCABULARY

Using Context Clues. The way a word is used in a sentence and the other words around it give you clues to the word's meaning. These clues are called *context clues.*

The following sentences from *The Pearl* present context clues to help you understand the meaning of the word in italics. Read the sentences. Then, on your paper, write a definition for each italicized word. Use a dictionary to check your definitions.

1. "Behind him, Juana's fire leaped into flame and threw spears of light through the *chinks* of the brush-house wall. . . ."

2. "He was growing very *stout,* and his voice was hoarse with the fat that pressed on his throat."

3. "The town lay on a broad *estuary,* its old yellow plastered buildings hugging the beach."

4. "Spotted *botete,* the poison fish, lay on the bottom in the eel-grass beds. . . ."

5. "Kino moved cautiously so that the water would not be *obscured* with mud or sand."

6. "Kino lay as *rigid* as the tree limb. He barely breathed. . . ."

Cloze Exercise. In a cloze exercise, blanks are substituted for certain words in a selection. Your job is to fill in the blanks with the correct words. Each word you choose should make sense in its context.

Here are three incomplete sentences from *The Pearl.* Following each sentence are three words. On your paper, write the word that best fits in the blank.

1. "A town is a thing separate from all other towns, so that there are no two towns _____."

   different   alike   around

2. "His face was fatherly . . . and his eyes twinkled with _____."

   hatred   dizziness   friendship

3. "In his mind a new song had come, the Song of Evil, the music of the _____. . . ."

   friend   enemy   morning

Read this passage carefully. Then, on your paper, write the missing words. When you have finished, refer to the story and compare your words to the ones Steinbeck used.

"Hush," said Kino. "Do not _____ anymore. In the morning we will _____ the pearl, and then the _____ will be gone, and only the good remain. Now hush, my wife." His dark eyes scowled into the little fire, and for the first _____ he knew that his _____ was still in his _____, and he raised the blade and looked at it and _____ a little line of blood on the steel.

WRITING

A Story. You have read many stories in this book. You have learned about the different elements of a story: plot, characters, conflict, setting, point of view, theme, and mood.

Step 1: Set Your Goal

Think of an *event* you would like to write about. It can be something that actually happened to you or to someone you know. It can be an idea that came from something you read—a newspaper article, perhaps, or another story. After reading *The Pearl*, for example, you might wonder what happened to Kino and Juana after they threw the pearl away. You could write a story telling how they began to build a new life for themselves.

Or you might begin by thinking of a *character*, *setting*, or *theme* you want to write about. For example, you might decide to write a story based on the theme of *The Pearl*—that money doesn't always bring happiness. If you do decide to write about a character, setting, or theme, you should then choose the main events of the story before going on to Step 2. After all, something important has to happen in a story, or it isn't a story at all.

Step 2: Make a Plan

To make a plan for your story, think about the following elements. On your paper, write the appropriate information for each.

Plot/Climax: List the events that take place. What is the major problem, or conflict, in the story? What obstacles stand in the way of solving the problem? Which event is the climax, or turning point? How is the conflict finally resolved?

Characters: Describe each major character. List his or her physical characteristics and personality traits. Describe how each sounds and acts. Tell how the characters are related to each other.

Setting: Where and when does the story take place?

Point of View: Who is telling the story?

Theme: What message do you want to get across?

Mood: What feeling do you want the story to give the reader?

Step 3: Write a First Draft

Remember that a story has a beginning, a middle, and an end. The beginning should capture the reader's interest so that he or she will want to continue reading. The middle should develop the action of the story. And the end should tell how the story's conflict is resolved. Try using this approach:

- ☐ Start with a description of your setting.

- ☐ Describe each main character when he or she first appears.

- ☐ Start the action and introduce the conflict as early as possible.

- ☐ Tell the events in chronological order. Build the action towards the highest point of interest or climax.

☐ Wind down the action. End the story by telling what, if anything, has changed because of the story's events.

☐ Choose a title for your story. The title may refer to an important event, character, setting, or idea from your story.

As you write, remember that there are different ways to give information to the reader. You may wish to review some of the stories in this book for examples. Your story will probably contain a mixture of description, action, and dialogue. Dialogue will make your story more realistic and more exciting. Look at dialogue in this book to help you punctuate your conversations correctly.

Step 4: Revise

Put your story away for a few days before you revise it. Then try to read it as if you've never seen it before. Does your story convey your message? Will the reader become caught up in it and want to read it to the end? If not, you may need to rewrite. You may have to change something as basic as the behavior of a central character. Or you may just need to take out some unnecessary descriptions or add more dialogue. It's your story, and you're free to make whatever changes you wish.

You should probably reread your story several times over a number of days. Once you are satisfied with it, proofread it and copy it over neatly.

QUIZ

The following is a quiz for Section 11. Write the answers in complete sentences on your paper.

Reading Comprehension

1. How did the doctor treat Kino and Juana when they first came to see him? Why did the doctor act that way?

2. Why was Kino reluctant at first to open the large oyster shell that contained the great pearl?

3. What were some of the things Kino hoped to do with the money he would receive from selling the pearl?

4. What happened when Kino tried to sell the pearl to the dealers? What did he decide to do with the pearl?

5. When the trackers shot at the "coyote," what happened? What did Kino and Juana do next?

Understanding Literature

6. How did Kino and Juana react after the baby was bitten by the scorpion? What do their actions reveal about their individual characters?

7. What kind of person was the doctor? How do you know what he was like?

8. When did Kino first hear the Song of Evil? At what other times did the song come to his mind?

9. What is the main plot of *The Pearl*? What is its subplot? What is one event that is part of both the main plot and the subplot?

10. How do the events in the novel convey the theme that wealth doesn't always bring happiness?

ACTIVITIES

Word Attack

1. In Chapter 3 of *The Pearl*, when the priest spoke to Kino, he made it sound like a benediction. A *benediction* is a blessing. Look at how the word is formed. The prefix *bene-* means "well" or "good." *Dict* is a word part that comes from a Latin word meaning "to say." When you say a blessing, you are asking for good fortune. List two other words beginning with the prefix *bene-* and two words beginning with the word part *dict*. Write the meaning of each word, and use the word in a sentence. You may use a dictionary if you need help.

2. In Chapter 6 of *The Pearl*, "the family went on monotonously, hour after hour." The word *monotonously* means "in a way that is unchanging," or "dull because of a lack of variety." The word gets its meaning from the prefix *mono-*, meaning "one, single, alone." Write the meaning of each of the following words that begin with *mono-*. You may use the dictionary to help you.

monocle	monorail
monosyllabic	monologue
monopoly	monolith

Speaking and Listening

1. Get together with some classmates, and act out the scene in Chapter 4 between Kino and the pearl dealers. You will need people for the speaking parts of Kino and the four dealers. Other members of the class can play Juana, Juan Tomás, and other onlookers. Perform your scene for the rest of the class.

2. Prepare a speech in which you are Juana, trying to convince Kino to throw away the pearl. Or you may be Kino, arguing to keep the pearl. Read your speech to the class.

Researching

1. Use the library to find out about pearls. Answer the following questions:
   a. What makes a pearl valuable?
   b. Where are natural pearls found? How are they harvested?
   c. What are cultured pearls? How and where are they made?

2. Find *The Red Pony*, or one of Steinbeck's other works, in the library. Read it and write a short book report.

Creating

1. Draw a floor plan of Kino's and Juana's brush house. Show where the fire pit is, where Kino's and Juana's sleeping blankets are, and the three places in the house where Kino buried the pearl.

2. Chapter 1 of *The Pearl* contains a detailed description of morning in Kino's family. Write a description of some of the sights, sounds, smells, and actions of a morning in your own household. Make your description two paragraphs long.

LEVEL FOUR
Glossary

PRONUNCIATION KEY

ă	pat	j	judge	sh	dish, ship
ā	aid, fey, pay	k	cat, kick, pique	t	tight
â	air, care, wear	l	lid, needle	th	path, thin
ä	father	m	am, man, mum	*th*	bathe, this
b	bib	n	no, sudden	ŭ	cut, rough
ch	church	ng	thing	û	circle, firm, heard, term,
d	deed	ŏ	horrible, pot		turn, urge, word
ĕ	pet, pleasure	ō	go, hoarse, row, toe	v	cave, valve, vine
ē	be, bee, easy, leisure	ô	alter, caught, for, paw	w	with
f	fast, fife, off, phase, rough	oi	boy, noise, oil	y	yes
g	gag	ou	cow, out	yōo	abuse, use
h	hat	ŏŏ	took	z	rose, size, xylophone, zebra
hw	which	ōo	boot, fruit	zh	garage, pleasure, vision
ĭ	pit	p	pop	ə	about, silent, pencil, lemon,
ī	by, guy, pie	r	roar		circus
î	dear, deer, fierce, mere	s	miss, sauce, see	ər	butter

PART OF SPEECH LABELS

n.	(noun)	*conj.*	(conjunction)
adj.	(adjective)	*prep.*	(preposition)
adv.	(adverb)	*v.*	(verb)
pron.	(pronoun)	*interj.*	(interjection)

The additional italicized labels below are used as needed to show inflected forms:

pl. (plural)   *sing.* (singular)

STRESS

Primary stress ′
bi · ol′o · gy | bī ŏl′əjē |
Secondary stress ′
bi′o · log′i · cal | bī′ə lŏj′ĭ kəl |

In this glossary, definitions were chosen to show the meanings of the words as they are used in the selections. Unless otherwise indicated, entries based on © 1977 by Houghton Mifflin Company. Reprinted by permission from The American Heritage School Dictionary.

*© 1983 by Scholastic, Inc.

a·cute | ə kyōōt′ | *adj.* **1.** Keen; perceptive: *an acute sense of hearing; an acute awareness of one's surroundings.*

a·dept | ə dĕpt′ | *adj.* Skillful and effective; proficient: *adept at sewing; an adept mechanic.*

ag·i·tated |ăj′ ə tāt′ ĭd | *adj.* Excited; stirred up emotionally.*

a·li·en | ā′ lē ən | *or* | āl′ yən | *adj.* **2.** In science fiction, an intelligent being from anywhere other than Earth.

am·u·let | ăm′ yə lĭt | *n.* A charm worn to ward off evil or injury, especially one worn around the neck.

an·aes·thet·ic | ăn′ ĭs thĕt′ ĭk | *n.* A drug that deadens the senses, especially the sense of touch.*

an·a·tom·i·cal | ăn′ ə tŏm′ ĭ kal | *or* **an·a·tom·ic** | ăn′ ə tŏm′ ĭk | *adj.* **1.** Of or concerned with anatomy or dissection.

an·o·nym·i·ty | ăn′ ə nĭm′ ĭ tē | *n.* The condition of being nameless or unnamed.

an·ti·dote | ăn′ tĭ dōt′ | *n.* **1.** A substance that counteracts the effects of a poison.

anx·i·e·ty | ăng zī′ ĭ tē | *n., pl.* **anx·i·e·ties. 1.** A feeling of uneasiness and distress about something in the future; worry: *He was filled with anxiety about his mother's return.*

ap·palled | ə pôld′ | *adj.* Filled with horror and amazement; shocked.*

ap·par·el | ə păr′ əl | *n.* Clothing; attire: *children's apparel.*

ap·pren·tice |ə prĕn′ tĭs | *n.* **3.** Any beginner.

ap·ti·tude | ăp′ tə tōōd′, ăp′ tə tyōōd′ | *n.* A natural ability for something.*

ar·chi·tect | är′ kĭ tĕkt′ | *n.* **1.** A person who designs and directs the construction of buildings and other large structures.

ar·ter·y | är′ tə rē | *n., pl.* **ar·ter·ies. 1.** Any of the blood vessels that carry blood from the heart to the capillaries.

ar·thri·tis | är thrī′ tĭs | *n.* Inflammation and stiffness of a joint or joints in the body.

ar·ti·fice |är′ tə fĭs | *n.* A clever device or stratagem; a ruse.

as·sump·tion | ə sump′ shən | *n.* **2.** An idea or statement accepted as fine without any proof: *acting on the assumption that Russia was also interested in world peace.*

au·di·tion | ô dĭsh′ ən | *n.* A test or trial performance, as of a musician who is applying for employment.

au·thor·i·ta·tive | ə thôr′ ĭ tā′ tiv | *or* | ə thŏr- | *adj.* **1.** Having or arising from the proper authority; official: *the general's authoritative manner.*

bea·con | bē′ kən | *n.* **1.** A fire, light, radio signal, or any other signaling device used to guide ships, airplanes, etc. **2.** A tower or other installation bearing such a device.

be·stowed | bĭ stōd′ | *v.* Gave or presented, especially as a gift or honor; confer: *an award bestowed on the nine best defensive players each season.*

big·ot·ry | bĭg′ ə trē | *n.* Intolerance of other creeds or beliefs; prejudice.

board | bôrd | *or* | bōrd | *n.* **4. b.** Food served daily to paying guests: *room and board.*

bond·age | bŏn′ dĭj | *n.* The condition of a slave or serf; servitude.

bos'n | bō′ sən | *n.* An officer on a ship who is responsible for the rigging and anchors and directs the work of the crew.*

bran·dish | brăn′ dĭsh | *v.* To wave or exhibit in a dramatic or threatening way: *The cave man brandished a club.*

broach | brōch | *v.* **1.** To talk or write about for the first time; begin to discuss: *He did not know how to broach the subject tactfully.*

bul·wark | bool′ wərk | *or* | bŭl′- | *n.* **2.** Any protection or defense: *calling on all friends of the Union to form a bulwark around the Constitution that cannot be shaken.*

cal·cu·lat·ing | kăl′ kyə lā′ tĭng | *adj.* Sly; crafty.*

can·teen | kăn tēn′ | *n.* A container for carrying drinking water.

ca·per | kā′ pər | — *n.* **1.** A playful leap or hop: *the capers of a frisky pony.* **2. a.** An antic; prank.

cap·i·tal | kăp′ ĭ tl | *adj.* **2.** Excellent: *a capital fellow.*

cas·u·al·ty | kăzh′ oo əl tē | *n., pl.* **cas·u·al·ties. 1. a.** A person who is killed or injured in an accident. **b.** A person who is killed, wounded, captured, or missing during a military action.

col·lu·sion | kə loo′ zhən | *n.* Secret agreement between two or more persons seeking to deceive or cheat another or others.

com·pen·sa·tion | kŏm′ pən sā′ shən | *n.* **1.** Something given as payment or amends, as for work, loss, or injury: *honest labor with just compensation; a pension granted as compensation for bodily injury.*

con·ceive | kən sēv | *v.* **con·ceived, con·ceiv·ing. 2. a.** To have an idea or concept; think: *People in ancient times conceived of the earth as flat.* **b.** To imagine; consider: *We could not conceive that such a strange and beautiful place really existed.*

con·cert·ed | kən sûr′ tĭd | *adj.* Planned or accomplished together with others; combined: *a concerted fund-raising drive.*

con·so·la·tion | kŏn′ sə lā′ shən | *n.* **1.** Comfort during a time of disappointment or sorrow.

con·sole | kən sōl′ | *v.* **con·soled, con·sol·ing.** To comfort in time of disappointment or sorrow.

con·spir·a·cy | kən spĭr′ ə sē | *n., pl.* **conspiracies.** A secretive agreement to act with others in an illegal action.*

cope | kōp | *v.* To deal with successfully.*

crave | krāv | *v.* **craved, crav·ing, craves.** To desire or yearn for something with great longing.*

crev·ice | krĕv′ ĭs | *n.* A narrow crack or opening; a fissure; cleft.

cri·te·ri·on | krī tîr′ ē ən | *n., pl.* **cri·te·ri·a** | krī tîr′ ē ə | or **cri·te·ri·ons.** A rule or standard on which a judgment can be based: *What are your criteria for judging the quality of his work?*

cru·cial | kroo′ shəl | *adj.* Extremely important.*

crypt | krĭpt | *n.* An underground vault or chamber, especially one that is used as a tomb beneath a church.

cur·ry | kûr′ ē | *or* | kŭr′ ē | *n., pl.* **cur·ries. 1.** Also **curry powder.** A sharp-flavored mixture of powdered spices. **2.** A pungent sauce or dish seasoned with curry.

dap·per | dăp′ ər | *adj.* **1.** Neatly dressed; trim; spruce: *a dapper bridegroom.*

de·scend·ant | dĭ sĕn′ dənt | *n.* A person or animal considered as descended from specified ancestors.

de·ter·rent | dĭ tûr′ ənt | *or* | -tŭr′- | *n.* Someone or something that prevents something from happening.*

de·vise | dĭ vīz′ | *v.* **de·vised, de·vis·ing.** To form or arrange in the mind; plan, invent; contrive.

dip·lo·mat | dĭp′ lə măt | *n.* **1.** A person appointed to represent his government in its dealings with other governments. **2.** A person who has skill in dealing with others.

dis·sect | dĭ sĕkt′ | *or* | dī- | *v.* **2.** To examine, analyze, or criticize with great care.

dis·tem·per | dĭs tĕm′ pər | *n.* An infectious, often fatal disease of dogs, cats, and other animals.

dis·tinc·tive | dĭs tĭngk′ tĭv | *adj.* Being especially different; unlike others.*

do·mes·tic | də mĕs′ tĭk | *adj.* **2.** Enjoying or interested in home life and household affairs.

dor·sal | dôr′ səl | *adj.* Of, toward, on, in, or near the back of an animal.

drought | drout | *n.* A long period with little or no rain.

ef·fi·cient | ĭ fĭsh′ ənt | *adj.* Acting or producing effectively with a minimum of waste, expense, or effort: *James Watt designed the first efficient steam engine. She is an efficient secretary.*

e·la·tion | ĭ lā′ shən | *n.* An intense feeling of happiness or joy.

e·lic·it | ĭ lĭs′ ĭt | *v.* To bring out; evoke: *He elicited the truth from the witness.*

e·lim·i·na·tion | ĭ lĭm′ ə nā′ shən | *n.* The removal one by one of people, things, or ideas.*

e·lude | ĭ lood′ | *v.* **e·lud·ed, e·lud·ing. 1.** To avoid or escape, as by artfulness, cunning, or daring; evade: *He eluded the attacks of the beast. The fox eludes as the dogs pursue.*

em·bark | ĕm bärk′, ĭm bärk′ | *v.* **em·barked, em·bark·ing, em·barks.** To begin a journey or voyage.*

es·sence | ĕs′ əns | *n.* **1.** The quality or qualities of a thing that give it its identity: *The essence of democracy is faith in the people.*

es·sen·tial | ĭ sĕn′ shəl | *adj.* **1.** Of the greatest importance; indispensable; basic: *Each part is essential to the whole. The microscope is an essential tool of science.*

es·tu·ar·y | ĕs′ choo ĕr′ ē | *n., pl.* **es·tu·ar·ies.** The wide lower part of a river where its current is met and influenced by the tides of the ocean.

ex·cru·ci·at·ing | ĭk skroo′ shē ā′ tĭng | *adj.* Intensely painful; agonizing: *excruciating pain in his left hand; an excruciating headache.*

ex·hil·a·ra·tion | ĭg zĭl′ ə rā′ shŭn | *n.* **1.** Extreme happiness; elation.*

ex·ile | ĕg′ zīl | *or* | ĕk′ sīl | *v.* **ex·iled, ex·il·ing.** To send (someone) away from his or her native country; banish.*

ex·qui·site | ĕk′ skwĭz ĭt | *or* | ĭk skwĭz′ ĭt | *adj.* Of special beauty, charm, or elegance: *an exquisite vase.*

fate | fāt | *n.* A force or power that brings about future events.*

fil·a·ment | fĭl′ ə mənt | *n.* **1. a.** A fine wire that is enclosed in the bulb of an electric lamp and that is heated by the passage of current until it gives off light. **b.** An electrically heated wire that heats the cathode of some electric tubes.

flick·er | flĭk ər | **1.** To give off light that burns or shines unsteadily: *The candles flickered in the breeze.*

flit | flĭt | *v.* **flit·ted, flit·ting, flits.** To dart about lightly and quickly.*

frus·tra·tions | frŭs trā′ shənz | *n.* Feelings of discouragement at being prevented from achieving one's objective.*

fur·tive | fûr′ tĭv | *adj.* Done or marked by stealth; shifty; sly: *a furtive glance.*

gas·tron·o·my | gă stron′ ə mē | *n.* The art or science of good eating.

ger·mane | jər mān′ | *adj.* Closely or naturally related to the thing in question; appropriate.

gnarled | närld | *adj.* Having gnarls; knotty and misshapen.

grope | grōp | *v.* To feel around in an uncertain way.*

gul·li·ble | gŭl′ ə bəl | *adj.* Easily tricked or fooled.*

har·ass | hăr′ əs | *or* | hə răs′ | *v.* **1.** To bother or torment with repeated interruptions, attacks, etc.: *harass a speaker with whistles and shouts.*

hatch | hăch | *v.* **hatched, hatch·ing, hatches.** To plot and plan; to cook up a scheme.*

her·o·ine | hĕr′ ō ĭn | *n.* **1.** The female counterpart of a hero. **2.** The main female character in a novel, poem, movie, etc.

hy·brid | hī′ brid | *n.* A plant or animal that is the offspring of parents of different varieties or strains within a species or of different species.

il·lu·sion | ĭ loo′ zhən | *n.* **1.** An appearance or impression that has no real basis; false perception: *creating the illusion of depth in a painting.* **2.** A mistaken notice or belief.

im·par·tial·ly | ĭm pär′ shə lē | *adv.* Not favoring either side: *an impartial witness.*

in·can·des·cent | ĭn′ kən dĕs′ ənt | *adj.* **1.** Giving off visible light as a result of being raised to a high temperature.

in·di·gent | ĭn′ di jənt | *adj.* Lacking the means to live; very poor; needy.

in·dis·crim·i·nate | ĭn′ dĭ skrĭm′ ə nĭt | *adj.* **2.** Not sorted out or put in order; confused: *an indiscriminate pile of letters.*

in·fa·mous | ĭn′ fə məs | *adj.* **2.** Deserving universal condemnation; shocking; outrageous: *infamous deeds.*

in·no·cence | ĭn′ ə səns | *n.* The quality of being inexperienced or free of guilt.*

in·nu·mer·a·ble | ĭ noo′ mər ə bəl | *or* | ĭ nyoo′- | *adj.* Too numerous to be counted: *innumerable difficulties.*

in·stinc·tive | ĭn stĭngk′ tĭv | *adj.* Natural, not learned; spontaneous.*

in·tact | ĭn tăkt′ | *adj.* Not impaired, injured, or damaged.

in·tent·ly | ĭn tĕnt′ lē | *adv.* Fastening attention closely on a particular purpose; in an attentive way.*

in·tol·er·ance | ĭn tŏl′ ər əns | *n.* Prejudice.*

in·trigue | ĭn trēg′ | *v.* **in·trigued, in·tri·gu·ing, in·trigues.** To be greatly interested; to have one's curiosity aroused.*

jour·nal·ism | jûr′ nə lĭz′ əm | *n.* The gathering and presentation of news, especially by newspapers and magazines.

ju·di·cious | joo dĭsh əs | *adj.* Showing forethought and caution; prudent; sensible: *a more judicious use of resources.*

kin·ship | kĭn′ shĭp′ | *n.* **1.** The condition of being related by blood or common origin: *the kinship of man with all other vertebrates.*

lav·ish·ly | lăv′ ĭsh lē | *adv.* Abundantly; extravagantly.*

leg·a·cy | lĕg′ ə sē | *n.* **1.** Money or property left to someone in a will.

leg·end | lĕj′ ənd | *n.* **1. a.** A story of uncertain truthfulness handed down from earlier times. **b.** A group of such stories or all such stories of the remote past: *a giant in Norse legend.*

leth·ar·gy | lĕth′ ər jē | *n., pl.* **leth·ar·gies. 1.** Drowsy or sluggish indifference; apathy.

lit·er·al·ly | lĭt ər əl ē | *adv.* In the sense of corresponding word for word.

log·ic | lŏj′ ĭk | *n.* Clear thinking.*

mam·mal | măm′ əl | *n.* Any of a group of animals that have hair or fur on their bodies and, in the females, special glands that produce milk for feeding their young. Cats, dogs, cows, elephants, mice, bats, whales, and human beings are all mammals.

man·u·al | măn′ yoo əl | *adj.* **2.** Used by or operated with the hands: *a manual keyboard; manual controls.* **3.** Requiring physical rather than mental effort: *manual labor.*

mar·a·thon | măr ə thŏn′ | *n.* **2.** Any longdistance race: *a swimming marathon.*

mat·i·nee or **mat·i·née** | măt′ n ā′ | *n.* A theatrical performance given in the afternoon.

max·im | măk′ sĭm | *n.* A brief formulation of a basic principle or rule of conduct; for example, *Early to bed, early to rise, makes a man healthy, wealthy, and wise* is a maxim.

me·di·e·val | mē′ dē ē′val | *or* | mĕd′ ē- *or* | mĭd′ē- *or* | mĭ dē′ vəl | *adj.* Of or characteristic of the period in European history from the fall of the Roman Empire (about A.D. 500) to the rise of the Renaissance (about 1400).

men·ace | mĕn′ əs | *n.* **2.** Someone or something that threatens harm; a threat: *a reef that is a menace to passing ships.* **3.** A dangerous or annoying person.

miffed | mĭft | *adj.* Offended or annoyed.*

mim·ic | mĭm′ ĭk | *v.* To imitate or copy certain things about a person, such as speech or gestures.*

mi·rage | mĭ räzh′ | *n.* An optical illusion in which nonexistent bodies of water and upside-down reflections of distant objects are seen.

mon·o·tone | mŏn′ ə tōn′ | *n.* **1.** A succession of sounds or words uttered in a single tone of voice.

ne·go·ti·a·tion | nĭ gō′ shē ā′ shən | *n.* Often **negotiations.** The act or process of negotiating: *secret negotiations between the two nations.*

ob·scure | ŏb skyoor′, əb skyoor′ | *adj.* Not well-known or understood.*

op·ti·cal | ŏp′ ti kəl | *adj.* **1.** Of or having to do with sight.

or·deal | ôr dēl′ | *n.* A very difficult or painful experience.

o·va·tion | ō vā shən | *n.* A loud and enthusiastic display of approval, usually in the form of shouting or hearty applause.

par·a·ble | păr′ə bəl | *n.* A simple, realistic story illustrating a moral or religious lesson.

par·af·fin | păr′ ə fĭn | *adj.* Wax.*

pa·ral·y·sis | pə răl′ ĭ sĭs | *n.* **2.** An inability to act or move normally.

pat·ent | păt′ nt | *n.* A grant made by a government to an inventor, assuring him the exclusive right to manufacture, use, and sell his invention for a stated period of time.

pen·sion | **pĕn′** shən | *n.* A sum of money paid regularly as a retirement benefit or by way of patronage.

per·spec·tive | pər **spĕk′** tĭv | *n.* Point of view.*

plan·ta·tion | plăn **tā′** shən | *n.* **1.** A large farm or estate on which crops such as cotton, sugar, or rubber are tended and gathered by workers who often live on the same property.

pol·lu·ted | pə **loo′** tĭd | *adj.* Unfit or harmful to living things.*

pon·dered | **pŏn′** dərd | *v.* Thought or considered carefully and at length: *she pondered over the decision.*

pre·miere | prĭ **mîr′** | *n.* The first public performance of a play, motion picture, or other theatrical work.

prom·i·nent | **prŏm′** ə nənt | *adj.* **3.** Well-known; leading, eminent: *a prominent career in public service.*

proph·e·cy | **prŏf′** ĭ sē | *n., pl.* **proph·e·cies. 2.** A declaration or warning of something to come; a vivid, pointed, or solemn prediction: *prophecies of financial disaster that were fulfilled many years later.*

proph·et | **prŏf′** ĭt | *n.* A person who predicts what the future might hold.*

ra·tion | **răsh′** ən, **rā′** shən | *v.* To supply a limited or fixed amount of something.*

re·cede | rĭ **sēd′** | *v.* **re·ced·ed, re·ced·ing. 1.** To move back or away from a limit, point, or mark: *after the flood had receded.*

rel·e·vant | **rĕl′** ə vənt | *adj.* To the point; related; pertinent.*

re·luc·tant | rĭ **lŭk′** tənt | *adj.* Not eager; unwilling.*

rem·i·nisce | **rĕm′** ə **nĭs′** | *v.* **rem·i·nisced, rem·i·nisc·ing.** To remember and tell of past experiences or events.

re·mote | rĭ **mōt′** | *adj.* **re·mot·er, re·mot·est. 5.** Distant in manner; aloof.

re·pose | rĭ **pōz′** | *n.* Rest; relaxation; calmness.*

res·ig·na·tion | rĕz′ ĭg **nā′** shən | *n.* Total, patient acceptance.*

re·sis·tance | rĭ **zĭs′** təns | *n.* The act of working

against or trying to stop; the act of opposing.*

re·source·ful | rĭ **sors′** fəl | *or* | **-sōrs′-** | *adj.* Clever and imaginative, especially in finding ways to deal with a difficult situation.

res·ur·rect | rĕz′ ə **rĕkt′** | *v.* **1.** To bring back to life; raise from the dead.

re·venge | rĭ **vĕnj′** | *n.* The act of inflicting punishment in return for an injury or insult.

rev·er·ence | **rĕv′** ər əns | *n.* A feeling of very deep respect; awe.*

riv·u·let | **rĭv′** yə lĭt | *n.* A small stream; brook.

seep | sēp | *v.* **seeped, seep·ing, seeps.** To leak; to trickle slowly.*

sick·le | **sĭk′** əl | *n.* A tool for cutting grain or tall grass, consisting of a semicircular blade attached to a short handle.

so·nar | **sō′** när | *n.* **1.** A system, similar in principle to radar, that uses reflected sound waves to detect and locate underwater objects.

spit·toon | spĭ **toon′** | *n.* A bowl-shaped receptacle for spitting into.

spurn | spûrn | *v.* To reject or refuse with disdain; scorn.

steth·o·scope | **stĕth′** ə skōp | *n.* An instrument used to listen to sounds made within the body.

sul·fur | **sŭl′** fər | *n.* Symbol **S** One of the elements, a pale yellow substance that occurs in nature in both free and combined forms and that has several solid forms in which it occurs at normal temperatures.

tact·ful | **tăkt′** fəl | *adj.* Having the ability to say or do the right thing at the right time; considerate.*

taunt | tônt | *n.* A scornful remark.*

taunt | tônt | *v.* **taunt·ed, taunt·ing, taunts.** To mock; to jeer at a person.

ten·ta·tive | **tĕn′** tə tĭv | *adj.* Not certain or permanent; not definite: *tentative plans; a tentative production schedule.*

ter·mi·nal | **tûr′** mə nəl | *adj.* Resulting in death.*

thread·bare | **thrĕd′** bâr′ | *adj.* **2.** Wearing old, shabby clothes: *a threadbare tramp.*

tithe | tīth | *n.* **1.** A tenth part of one's annual income, paid to a church.

tol·er·ance | tŏl' ər əns | *n.* **1.** The capacity for or practice of recognizing and respecting the opinions, practices, or behavior of others. **4.** The degree to which an organism resists the effect of a poison or other drug.

trans·mit | trăns mĭt' | *or* | trănz- | *v.* **trans·mit·ted, trans·mit·ting. 1.** To send from one person, place, or thing to another: *transmit a message; transmit an infection.* **3.** To send out (an electric or electronic signal), as by wire or radio.

twinge | twĭnj | *n.* An unexpected, sharp emotional pain.*

ty·coon | tī kōon' | *n.* A wealthy and powerful businessman or businesswoman or industrialist.

u·nan·i·mous·ly | yōo năn' ə məs lē | *adv.* Being in complete agreement with a number of people.*

un·du·lat·ing | ŭn' jə lāt ing | *or* | ŭn' dyə- | *or* | -də- | *adj.* Wavy in appearance or form.*

u·ni·ver·sal | yōo' nə vûr' səl | *adj.* **2.** Of, for, done by, or affecting all.

vague | vāg | *adj.* Indistinct; unclear; not defined.*

van·i·ty | văn' ĭ tē | *n., pl.* **van·i·ties. 1.** Excessive pride, conceit.

var·i·cose | văr' ĭ kōs' | *adj.* Of or designating blood vessels that are abnormally wide and knotted and that follow an abnormally twisted path.

vaude·ville | vôd' vĭl | *or* | vôd'- | *or* | vô' də- | *n.* Stage entertainment offering a variety of short acts.

vig·or | vĭg' ər | *n.* **1.** Physical energy or strength: *a rosy-cheeked, bright-eyed lass full of health and vigor.*

vir·u·lent | vĭr' yə lənt | *or* | vĭr' ə- | *adj.* **2.** Bitterly hostile or malicious: *virulent criticism.*

vi·tal | vīt' l | *adj.* **1.** Of or characteristic of life: *vital processes; vital signs.* **2.** Essential for the continuation of life: *vital organs; vital functions.*

whee·dling | hwēd' lĭng | *v.* Persuading or trying to persuade by pleading or flattery; coaxing.

yield | yēld | *v.* To give up.*

zeal | zēl | *n.* Eager enthusiasm.*

Handbook

of Literature, Reading, Vocabulary, and Research Skills and Terms

The following pages contain information about skills and terms that you will find helpful as you read the selections in this book and other materials as well. The terms are arranged alphabetically, with a brief definition or explanation for each. Examples from this book are used, and the section where a term is taught is indicated.

act   A part of a play. Acts may be divided into *scenes*.

almanac   A book containing many facts. Almanacs are published every year so that the facts will be up to date. The subjects almanacs cover include government leaders of the world, sports records, weather records, awards like the Nobel Prize, and the size and population of different countries. The facts may be given in the form of lists and charts.

When to use an almanac.   Almanacs give facts, but they do not discuss or explain them. Use an almanac when you are looking for a particular name or date, especially if the information is too recent to be in an encyclopedia. For example, if you wanted to find out who won the Nobel Prize for literature in 1986, an almanac would be the best place to find the information.

How to use an almanac.   To find the topic you want in an almanac, look it up in the index. The *index* is a section at the back of the book that lists topics alphabetically. If you were looking for Nobel Prize winners, you would look under *n* for *Nobel*. The index would tell you what page or pages the information is on.

Use the newest almanac you can get to be sure of finding the most recent information.

alphabetical order   The order of the letters in the alphabet. To put words in alphabetical order, look at the first letter of each word first. If the first letters are the same, look at the second letters, and so on.

Many research materials are arranged in alphabetical order, including *card catalogs*, *dictionaries*, *encyclopedias*, and *indexes*.

561

Remember, if you are looking for a person's name in alphabetical order, look for the last name first. If you are looking for a book title, ignore the articles *a, an,* and *the.*

antonyms   Words that have opposite meanings. *Up* and *down* are antonyms. [Section 1]

article   A short, nonfiction work; not a made-up story. Articles appear in newspapers, magazines, and books. (See also news story.)

atlas   A book of maps. Some atlases also give other geographical information, such as the products of various regions, countries, or states.

   When to use an atlas.   Use an atlas when you need information on a map, including directions, locations of particular places, and distances between places. For example, if you wanted to know how far Miami, Florida, is from Gainesville, Florida, you would use an atlas.

   How to use an atlas.   Most atlases have an *index,* a section at the back of the book where the places shown on the maps are arranged in alphabetical order. The indexes will usually tell you both the number of the map you need and the particular section of the map that shows the place you are looking for.

   For example, if you look up *Gainesville, Florida,* in the index, you might see a notation like this after it: "42 E 4." You would turn to map number 42 in the atlas. You would see that the map is divided into squares. You would look along the top of the page until you found the square marked

E. Then you would look along the side of the page for the square marked *4.* Where the two squares meet, in square E 4, you would find Gainesville.

author   The writer of an article, a story, a play, a poem, or a book. If you know who wrote a book, you can find the book in the library by looking at the *author card* in the *card catalog.*

author card   A card in the library's *card catalog* that has the author's name at the top. Author cards are arranged alphabetically by the author's last name. (See also catalog card.)

author's purpose   The author's goal in writing. Authors may wish to *entertain* readers by making them laugh as in "Who's On First?" (page 405), or by scaring them as in "Flight Into Danger" (page 119). Or an author may want to give readers a serious message about life as in "Letter to a Black Boy" (page 260), explain something to readers, or tell a true story about a person as in "Clemente—A Bittersweet Story" (page 312). (See also theme.)   [Section 9]

autobiography   Someone's true account of his or her own life. An autobiography is usually written from the *first-person point of view,* using the pronouns *I* and *me.* It tells important events from the author's life and says how the author feels about those events. "Growing Up" (page 328) is an example of an autobiography.   [Section 7]

bibliography   A list of writings. Many books contain lists of other books and articles on the same subject. Here is part of a bibliography from a book about zoos. Notice that the entries are arranged alphabetically by the authors' last names. After each author's name comes the title of the book, the place where it was published, the publisher, and the date:

Crandall, Lee S. *Management of Wild Mammals in Captivity*. Chicago: University of Chicago Press, 1964.

Elgin, Robert. *The Tiger Is My Brother*. New York: Morrow, 1980.

Bibliographies are usually at the end of a book, although sometimes short bibliographies are given at the end of each chapter.

By looking at a bibliography, you can find the authors and titles of other books that may give you more information about the subject you are interested in.

For a list of bibliographies, look up your subject in *The Bibliographic Index*. It will tell you which publications contain bibliographies on the subject.

biographical dictionary　A special dictionary that gives information about famous people. Some biographical dictionaries are *Webster's Biographical Dictionary*, which includes information about people from many nations; the *Dictionary of American Biography*; and *Who's Who in America*, which is revised every second year and includes only people living at the time of publication.

When to use a biographical dictionary. Use a biographical dictionary when you need brief, factual information about a famous person. Biographical dictionaries usually give information such as birth (and death) dates, birthplaces, and important accomplishments. Many biographical dictionaries do not include details about a person's life. You may be able to find more details in an *encyclopedia*. If there is a *biography*, or book about the person's life, it would contain the most information of all.

How to use a biographical dictionary.　If the person you are looking up became famous recently, make sure the biographical dictionary you are using is new enough to list him or her. Check to see whether the dictionary includes people from your person's country.

In most biographical dictionaries, people are listed in alphabetical order by their last names. If you wanted information about George Washington, you would look for *Washington, George*. However, if you wanted information about Queen Victoria, you would look for *Victoria*. People are not listed by their titles.

biography　A true story about a person's life written by another person. A book-length biography will give you a lot of information about a person. "The Electrical Wizard" (page 306) is a short biography. [Section 7]

To find out whether your library has any biographies about the person you are interested in, look for the person's name in the *subject cards* in the *card catalog*. The person would be listed there in alphabetical order, last name first. On library shelves, biographies are arranged together, alphabetically by subject's names.

Books in Print　A list of books that are available for purchase from publishers doing business in this country. *Books in Print* is published every year in three sets. One set lists books alphabetically by author; another set lists books alphabetically by title; and a third set, *The Subject Guide to Books in Print*, lists books alphabetically by subject.

Books in Print is excellent for finding out what books are available at regular bookstores. Remember, though, that there are millions of books that are no longer "in print" but that can still be found in libraries and second-hand bookstores.

call number The *Dewey Decimal Classification* number. A number written on library books and at the upper left-hand corner of *catalog cards* to show where the books are placed on the library shelves.

card catalog A large cabinet in the library whose drawers, called trays, contain filing cards listing all the books in the library. There are three types of *catalog cards:* author, title, and subject. All are usually combined in the cabinet in alphabetical order. Letters on the front of each drawer, or tray, show which section of the alphabet it contains. The trays themselves are placed in the cabinet in alphabetical order, from top to bottom.

You will see an example of the card catalog on the next page.

When to use the card catalog. Use the card catalog when you want to find out whether your library has a book whose title

you know, or when you want to see what books your library has by a particular author or on a particular subject.

How to use the card catalog. See the next section, catalog card, for information on how to use the card catalog.

catalog card There are at least three cards in the *card catalog* for every nonfiction book in the library: an author card, a title card, and a subject card. Here is an example of an author card:

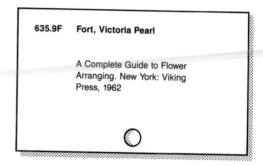

The top of this card tells you the author's name. Her name is Victoria Pearl Fort, but last names are listed first on catalog cards. Below the author's name are the title of the book, the place where it was published, the publisher's name, and the date of publication. At the top of the card is the call number that you should look for on the shelf in order to find the book: 635.9F. This card is called the *author card* because it has the author's name at the top.

The other two catalog cards contain the same information in a different order. Here is an example of a title card for the same book:

635.9F   **FLOWER ARRANGING**

Fort, Victoria Pearl
A Complete Guide to Flower
Arranging. New York: Viking
Press, 1962.

635.9F   **A Complete Guide to Flower
Arranging**

Fort, Victoria Pearl
A Complete Guide to Flower
Arranging, New York: Viking
Press, 1962.

This is called a *title card* because it has the title at the top. Otherwise, the information is the same as on the author card.

Here is an example of a subject card:

This is the *subject card* because it has the subject of the book at the top. If a book covers several subjects, it will have a separate subject card for each subject. Fiction books usually do not have subject cards.

When to use catalog cards. Use catalog cards to find out what books your library has and where they are located on the shelves.

565

How to use catalog cards. If you know the title of a book, you can look in the card catalog for the title card. Remember, all the cards are arranged in alphabetical order. If you were looking for *A Complete Guide to Flower Arranging,* you would look in the catalog drawer containing the letter *c* (for *Complete*), because the articles *a, an,* and *the* are ignored in alphabetizing titles. If you find the card, your library has the book. Note the call number given in the upper left-hand corner of the card. It will help you find the book on the shelves.

If you are looking for books by a particular author, look for author cards with that author's name. In this case, you would look in the *f* drawer *Fort, Victoria Pearl.* There will be a separate card for each book the library has by that author. Make notes of the titles and call numbers.

If you are looking for books on a particular subject, look for subject cards. If you were interested in flower arranging, for example, you would look in the *f* drawer for cards with this heading. There will be a card for each book the library has on the subject. Note the titles, authors, and call numbers.

Now you can find the books on the library shelves. Look at the call numbers you wrote down. For the book we have been discussing, it is 635.9F. This book would probably be on a shelf marked 635. It would come after books with the call number 635.8. (In a library, call numbers are marked on the side of the books, or *spines*.) The *F* in the call number is the initial of the author's name.

There are some exceptions to the rule. *Fiction* books are arranged on the shelves not by call number but alphabetically by the author's last name. *Biographies* are shelved together alphabetically by the subject's name. *Reference books,* including *dictionaries* and *encyclopedias,* are kept on special shelves.

cause Something that makes something else happen. (See also cause and effect.) [Section 3]

cause and effect In some stories and some sentences, there is a cause-and-effect relationship. The *cause* is something that makes another thing happen. What happens is called the *effect.* In "Flight Into Danger" (page 119), Spencer is asked to take over the controls of Flight 714 because he is the only passenger with flying experience. Spencer's experience was the cause. Being asked to take over was the effect.

Effects may have more than one cause. Spencer took over because of his experience, and also because he wanted to save the lives of the people on the plane. Similarly, causes may have more than one effect.

Think about cause and effect relationships as you read. Noticing clue words and phrases such as *because, since, so, so that, as a result of,* and *for this reason* will help you. [Section 3]

character A person or an animal in a story. (See also flat character and round character.)

characterization The way an author informs readers about characters. *Direct characterization* is when the author describes the character directly. For example, in "The Pearl," the author describes Kino: "Kino felt weak and afraid and angry. . . ." *Indirect characterization* is when the author lets readers find out about a character through the character's own thoughts, speech, or actions. For example, the reader can tell Kino was angry from his actions. The author states ". . . he struck the gate a crushing blow with his fist. He looked down in wonder at his split knuckles. . . ."

Pay attention to the characters' thoughts, words, and actions when you read a story. They may be related to the message or *theme* that the author wants you to discover.   [Sections 1, 2, 10, 11]

chart   An orderly list of facts. Here is an example of a chart:

Noun	Adjective
Danger	Dangerous
Beauty	Beautiful
Remark	Remarkable

You can read this chart down or across. If you read down each column, you see a list of nouns and a list of adjectives. If you read across, you see which nouns and adjectives are similar.

climax   The highest point of action in a story. The climax is the same as the *turning point.*   [Section 3]

cloze exercise   A reading test in which words are left out of a selection and the reader is asked to fill in the blanks.   [Section 11]

compare   To say how two or more people or things are alike. Comparing often uses the words *like* or *as.* In "A Red, Red Rose" (page 225), Robert Burns compares his love to a rose in this way: "O, my love is like a red, red rose . . ." (See also comparison and contrast.)   [Section 5]

comparison and contrast   Comparison involves identifying how two people or things are alike. Contrast involves finding out how they are different. Comparisons add emphasis to reading and writing.

If you say that "Butterfly" (page 224) and "Thief" (page 231) are both poems, you are making a comparison. If you say that "Butterfly" is a poem about love but "Thief" is about anger, you are making a contrast.

In your writing, you will often be asked to compare and contrast two people or things; to say both how they are alike and how they differ.   [Sections 1, 5, 10]

comparison of unlike things   See figurative language.

composition   See writing.

compound word   A word made up of two or more smaller words. *Cowboy* is an example of a compound word. It is made up of the words *cow* and *boy.* Notice that the meaning of the compound word is different from the meaning of each word alone. [Section 9]

conclusion   1. The end of an article, a story, a play, a poem, or a book. 2. An opinion or judgment. To find out how to form opinions about stories and characters, see drawing conclusions.

conflict   A struggle or fight. Many selections contain conflict, because conflict helps make a story interesting. Readers want to find out who or what will win the struggle.

There are several types of conflict: (1) *Conflict of a person against another person or group.* For example, in "Take Over, Bos'n" (page 284), Snyder and the others have a conflict. (2) *Conflict of a person against nature.* This type of conflict is found in "Leiningen Versus the Ants" (page 108). (3) *Inner conflict.* A person struggles with his or her own different feelings. Dr. Sadao Hoki in "The Enemy" (page 41), has this type of conflict.   [Section 3]

contents   See table of contents.

context   The selection or part of a selection that contains a particular word or group of words. The context can affect the meaning of words or sentences. If you just read the sentence "Laura was hurt," you might think that Laura had been injured. However, if the sentence was in a story about someone refusing a present Laura had bought, you would know it meant she was insulted.   [Sections 2, 11]

context clues   Other words in a sentence, a paragraph, or lines of poetry that help you figure out the meaning of a word you do not know. Here is an example: "The teacher's *lucid* explanation helped the students understand." The explanation helped the students understand, so it must have been clear.   [Sections 2, 11]

contrast   To say how two or more people or things are different. (See also comparison and contrast.)

copyright date   The date a book was published. The date is usually printed like this:

© 1987. If you need up-to-date information, be sure the book was published recently.

critical reading   Making judgments about what you read. To read critically, you must try to find the author's message and understand how the characters think and feel. You must read the author's descriptions and the characters' words and actions.

Here are some of the questions you might think about as you read critically: What is the *author's purpose,* and how well does he or she accomplish it?

In a story, does the *plot* make the message clear?

If *facts* are presented, are they correct?

Are the *characters* in a story believable? [Section 10]

decoding   Figuring out unfamiliar words from the sounds of the letters they contain. Knowing the sounds that different letters and groups of letters may make is important in decoding. Here are some examples:

a The letter *a* usually stands for the short *a* sound when it is followed by two consonants, as in *batter,* or by one consonant and no vowel, as in *tag.* A usually stands for the long *a* sound when it is followed by *i, y,* or a consonant and a vowel, as in *daily, day,* and *race.*

ch When the letters *ch* come together in a word, they may stand for the sounds at the beginning of *child.* That is the sound they always make when a *t* comes before the *ch,* as in *patch.* At other times, though, the letters *ch* together make a sound like *k,* as in *character.* If you are not sure which sound *ch* stands for, try saying the word both ways. See which way sounds like a word you know.

ea When the vowels *ea* come together, they usually stand for the long *e* sound, as in *teach.* However, sometimes they stand for the short *e* sound *thread,* the long *a* sound *great,* the vowel sound in *her, heard,* or the vowel sound in *here, beard.* If you are not sure which sound *ea* makes in a word you are reading, try pronouncing the word different ways until one pronunciation sounds like a word you know.

-ed Many words end with the suffix *-ed.* Sometimes the suffix is pronounced like a *t,* as in *skipped.* Sometimes it sounds like a *d,* as in *demand.* At other times it stands for the *ed* sound, as in *batted.* If you know the base word, you can figure out which sound *-ed* has.

g The letter *g* usually stands for the sound at the beginning of *go.* However, when *g* is followed by an *e, i,* or *y,* it may make a *j* sound, as in *badge, giant,* or *gym.* Often when a *g* and an *h* come together, they are both silent, as in *night.*

i The letter *i* usually stands for the long *i* sound when it is followed by a consonant and then a vowel, as in *kite.* It usually stands for the short *i* sound when it is followed by two consonants, as in *kitten,* or by one consonant and no vowel, as in *him.* When *i* is followed by the letters *gh,* the *i* usually stands for the long *i* sound, as in *night.*

-ly Some words end with the suffix *-ly.* When the letters *-ly* come together at the end of a word, they make the sound *lee,* as in *slowly.*

-ous When the letters *-ous* come together at the end of a word, the suffix is usually pronounced like the word *us. Dangerous* is an example.

-tion Some words end with the suffix *-tion.* The letters *-tion* almost always make the sound shun, which rhymes with *run. Perfection* is an example.

y When the letter *y* comes at the beginning of the word, it usually stands for the sound you hear at the beginning of *yes.* When *y* comes at the end or in the middle of a word, it may stand for a vowel sound, as in *my, flying,* or *city.* When *y* comes after a vowel, it usually helps the vowel make a vowel sound, as in *say, joy,* or *saying.*

definition The meaning of a word or term. Definitions are given in *dictionaries.*

description A word picture of what someone or something is like. Authors include details about the person, place, or thing being described to help the readers form pictures in their minds. [Section 9]

detail A small piece of information. In a paragraph, the *main idea* tells what the paragraph is about, and the details give information to support or explain the main idea.

Sometimes important details are called *significant details. Significant* means "important" or "meaningful." For example, a significant detail in "The Haunted Chess Set" is that the little bottle of "Silver Night" perfume struck Angelica on the cheek. [Sections 1, 7]

Dewey Decimal Classification System   A system of arranging books according to their subject matter that was invented by Melvil Dewey. The subjects are divided into nine main classes and many sub-classes. The *call number* that is written on library books and *catalog cards* is the number the book is given in this system.

diagram   A drawing that shows the parts of something or shows how something works.

dialect   The way a character would speak in person. Spoken language is often different from standard written language. It is informal. It may contain expressions, slang, or pronunciations that are casual. (See also expressions.)

dialogue   The conversation in a story or a play. The exact words the characters say. In a story, quotation marks point out the dialogue.   [Section 2]

dictionary   A book that lists words in alphabetical order and gives their meanings, pronunciations, and other information.

When to use a dictionary.   Use a dictionary to find out any of the following things: the meaning of a word; how a word is spelled; how it is pronounced; where it is divided into syllables; where it comes from; synonyms (words that mean the same) and antonyms (opposites) for a word; the meanings of prefixes (word parts added to the beginning of a word) and the meanings of suffixes (word parts added to the ending of a word.)

How to use a dictionary.   Look up your word in alphabetical order. Guide words at the top of each dictionary page will tell you the first and last words contained on that page. Following a word are letters and symbols that tell you how to pronounce it. If you are not sure what the symbols stand for, turn to the pronunciation key at the beginning of the dictionary. That explains the meanings of the symbols.

direct characterization   An author's direct description of a person or an animal in the story. Readers do not have to form an opinion about the character from his or her thoughts, speech, or actions, because the author says what the character is like. An example is in "Marigolds," when the author says that "Miss Lottie didn't like people who bothered her, especially children."   [Sections 1, 11]

drawing conclusions   Making your own decisions about a story and its characters. The happenings and details in a story help you draw conclusions. For example, in "The Third Level," when the narrator says, "Everyone in the station was dressed like the 1890's. I never saw so many beards, sideburns, and fancy mustaches in my life," you can assume that he has gone back in time.   [Section 4]

editorial   An item in a newspaper or magazine that expresses the opinions or beliefs of the editors.

effect   Something that happens as a result of a cause. (See also cause and effect.)   [Section 3]

elements of plot   The plot is the sequence, or order, of important events in a story or a play. The plot usually has four elements, or parts: (1) the *problem* that the characters face; (2) the *rising action* as the characters try to solve the problem; (3) the *turning point*, the highest point of the action, as the characters find a solution; and (4) the *resolution*, when readers learn how the solution affects the characters. (See also plot.) [Section 1]

encyclopedia   A book or set of books containing information about many topics.

When to use an encyclopedia. Use an encyclopedia when you need a lot of information about a subject. For example, if you wanted to find out the history of libraries, the names of some famous modern libraries, and how libraries arrange their books, it would be a good idea to look up *library* in an encyclopedia.

How to use an encyclopedia. The articles in encyclopedias are arranged in alphabetical order. If the encyclopedia you are using is in more than one book or *volume*, be sure to look in the volume that includes the letter you are looking for.

entertain   To give readers enjoyment by making them laugh or by scaring them. An *author's purpose* in writing may be to entertain readers.   [Section 9]

essay   A brief discussion of a particular subject or idea.

explain   To state how or why something happens. An *author's purpose* may be to explain.   [Section 9]

explanation   An account of how or why something happens. When you write an explanation, help your readers understand by stating the events clearly and in the correct order.

expression   A word or a group of words with a specific meaning; an idiom. For example, *hanging around* is an expression that means "waiting."   [Section 9]

fact   Something that can be proved or observed. For example, in "Dolphins" (page 365), the author says that an adult bottle-nosed dolphin can keep 20 pounds of fish inside his body and go without eating again for about a week. This is a fact that can be proved. You can look up dolphins in the encyclopedia to see if the information is correct. Dr. John Lilly has made records of dolphins imitating their human friends. This is a fact that was observed. [Section 8]

When you read, think about which statements are facts and which are *opinions* (ideas, beliefs, or feelings that cannot be proved).

fiction   Made-up stories. Many of the stories in this book are fiction. Fiction that contains imaginary characters and events that are very much like people and happenings in real life is called *realistic fiction*. "Marigolds" (page 32) is an example of realistic fiction.

"The Cow Who Liked to Kick" (page 400) is not realistic fiction because it contains a character that could not exist in real life.

figurative language   Words used in a fresh, new way to appeal to the imagination. The words take on more than their usual meanings.

Figurative language often compares two things that are not usually thought of as alike. Here are some examples:

The man's hair was as smooth as velvet. (The man's hair is compared to velvet.)

His voice was thunder. (His voice is compared to thunder.)

The clouds frowned at the earth. (The clouds' appearance is compared to a person's frown.) (See also simile, metaphor, and personification.)   [Section 5]

first-person point of view   Telling a story by using the pronouns *I* and *me*. Some stories told from the first-person point of view are *autobiographies,* or true accounts of a person's life. "Growing Up" (page 328) is an example. Other stories told in this way are *fiction,* or made-up stories, but the author pretends to be a character in the story and writes as if the events had happened to him or her. "Marigolds" (page 32) is an example.   [Section 7]

finding facts   First decide what kind of fact you are looking for. For facts about words, you would look in a *dictionary.* For facts about places, you might use an *atlas,* an *encyclopedia,* or an *almanac.* For facts about people, you might use a *biography,* an *autobiography,* a *biographical dictionary,* an *encyclopedia,* or a *newspaper.* Sometimes you will want to read a *nonfiction* book to find facts. The *catalog cards* in the library's *card catalog* will tell you what books the library has and where to find them on the shelves.

flat character   A person in a story who is described only briefly. The author does not provide much information about the character. Sometimes that is because the character does not have a big part in the story. Other characters are more important. In "Future Tense" (page 54), Dani is an example of this. At other times, even the main characters in a story are flat, because the author wants readers to concentrate on other things.

folktale   A story that has been handed down from generation to generation. Originally, folktales were spoken rather than written. Many folktales contain these elements:

They happened long ago and far away.

They contain unusual characters.

There is a *moral,* or lesson, to be learned from the story.

foreshadowing   Clues in a story that hint at what is to happen at the end. In "The Haunted Chess Set" (page 173), clues in the story hint at the discovery Angelica finally made.   [Section 4]

form   The particular way in which an author chooses to write a story, an article, or a poem. For example, an author may choose to write a modern story as though it were an old folktale. Or an author may choose to write an article by stating the main idea and then giving examples that support it.

glossary   A list of important or hard words in a book, with their meanings. A glossary is usually at the end of a book. Not every book has a glossary.

graph   A drawing that shows how two kinds of information are related. There are several kinds of graphs. Here is a bar graph that shows average summer temperatures in Juneau, Alaska.

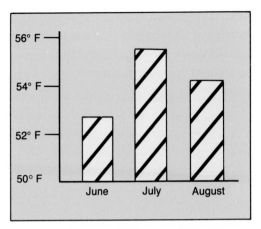

The two kinds of information that are related on this graph are the months, shown at the bottom of the graph, and the temperatures, shown at the left.

Here is a line graph that shows the same things:

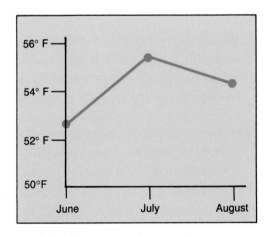

guide words   Words printed at the top of dictionary and encyclopedia pages to let you know the first and last words or topics on that page.

homophone   Words that sound alike but are spelled differently. The words *whole* and *hole* in the following sentences are homophones:

The whole family will be here.
Be careful you don't fall into the hole.

humor   The quality of being funny. An *author's purpose* or goal may be to entertain readers by making them laugh. In other cases, the author's main purpose may be to teach readers a message about life, but he or she uses humor to keep readers interested. In "Fresh Air Will Kill You" (page 394), the characters speak with humor. Through these characters, the author gives the reader the message about the value of clever thinking.

Authors can create humor in several ways. They may use funny events or situations. They may use funny characters. They may use *word play*, such as nonsense words and words with double meanings. "Who's On First?" (page 405) contains humorous characters and word play.   [Section 9]

imagery   Words that appeal to the senses of sight, hearing, taste, touch, or smell. "The saw screeched through the wood," for example, is an image that appeals to the sense of hearing. Imagery is used in all forms of writing, but it is most common in poetry.   [Section 5]

index   A section at the back of a nonfiction book that lists the topics in the book in alphabetical order and tells what pages they are on. Use an index to see if facts you need are in the book.

Indexes in atlases usually give map numbers and sections instead of page numbers; see *atlas* to find out how to use this type of index. Indexes in newspapers are usually printed on the first page. They list sections and pages of regular features in the newspaper, such as the crossword puzzle.

indirect characterization   Instead of describing a character directly, the author tells about the character's thoughts, speech, and actions and leaves it up to the reader to decide what the person is like.

For example, in indirect characterization, an author would not say, "Ken was helpful." He or she might say, "When Ken had finished eating, he immediately cleared the table." Readers should be able to see for themselves that Ken was helpful. [Sections 1, 2, 11]

inference   A conclusion or guess based on the information presented. When you make an inference, you recognize clues the author gives as well as information he or she presents directly.

For example, in "Very Special Shoes" (page 254), you read that Mrs. Johnson seemed to need more and more sleep each day. You could infer that Mrs. Johnson was not in good health and that she was not improving.   [Section 6]

inform   To give readers information about some topic. An *author's purpose* may be to inform.

inner conflict   A person's struggle with his or her own different feelings. If you love pizza but you are on a diet, you may have an inner conflict when you are offered a slice of pizza. (See also conflict.)   [Section 3]

interview   A meeting in order to get information from a person.

When to use an interview.   Interviews are a good way of getting first-hand information from somebody with special experience or knowledge. For example, if you were interested in becoming a teacher, you might interview one of your teachers and ask about the advantages and disadvantages of teaching as a career.

How to interview.   Before the interview, make a list of the questions you want to ask. Make an appointment for the interview, and tell the person what the purpose of the interview is. Ask permission to take notes. Notes will help you remember what the person said. If you have a recorder, you can use that instead of taking notes, but again you will need the person's permission. Ask permission to use the person's name if you are going to write about the interview.

ironic turn of events   When something happens that is different from what was expected. For example, in "How Beautiful With Mud" (page 410), Hildegarde expects the beauty treatments to improve her looks, but the effects are just the opposite. [Section 9]

joint author   A book with more than one author is said to have joint authors. There is an author card for each author in the *card catalog.*

journal   1. A diary. 2. A magazine, newspaper, or other work that is published every day, every week, or at other intervals.

judgment   An opinion based on facts. Your own knowledge and experience help you make good judgments. (See also critical reading.)   [Section 10]

legend   A story handed down from earlier times that tries to explain how or why something in nature came to be. Every country and group of people has legends.

librarian A person who works in a library.

library 1. A collection of books and/or other materials. 2. The place where such a collection is kept. For information on finding books in a library, see catalog card.

library card A card that allows a person to borrow books from a library.

Library of Congress system A way of classifying and arranging books that is used in the National Library in Washington, D.C., and some other large libraries. The system is different from the *Dewey Decimal Classification System,* which is used in most school libraries.

magazine A publication that contains stories, articles, pictures, and/or other features written by different authors. Magazines are published weekly, monthly, or at other intervals.

main idea The most important idea in a paragraph; the sentence that tells what the paragraph is about. The main idea may be at the beginning, the middle, or the end of a paragraph. In this paragraph from "The Green Door" (page 20), the main idea is given in the first sentence: "Rudolph Steiner was a true adventurer. During the day he sold pianos. In the evening he went out in search of the unexpected. The most interesting thing in life, he thought, might lie just around the next corner." [Sections 1, 6]

map A drawing or diagram of a place. Here is a map of California.

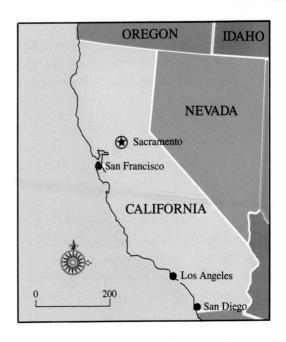

On the map, a special symbol stands for the capital city. You can tell that the capital of California is Sacramento.

Most maps contain a *compass rose* that shows directions. You can tell that San Diego is southeast of Sacramento.

The above map is called a *political map*. Political maps show divisions such as countries, states, and boundaries. There are other kinds of maps as well. For example, *physical maps* show physical features of the earth's surface, such as mountains and valleys.

For information about books of maps, see atlas.

meaning in poetry Because poets often use words in special ways that appeal to your senses and allow you to form mental pictures, it is important to read the whole poem and examine all the words and ideas carefully so that you can understand the full meaning of the poem. [Section 5]

message   An important idea about life that the author wants to tell readers. An author's purpose in writing may be to give readers such a message. (See also *theme*.) [Sections 5, 6, 9, 11]

metaphor   A comparison of two things that are not usually thought of as alike. Metaphors do not contain words such as *like* or *as*. Here is an example of a metaphor: "The football player's legs were tree trunks." The author does not mean the legs were really tree trunks. He or she is just comparing them to tree trunks.

   Metaphors are a type of *figurative language*.

mood   The strongest feeling or emotion in a work of literature. Plots, descriptions, conversations, and actions contribute to the mood. Examples of mood are *humor* and *suspense*.   [Sections 4, 5]

moral   A message or lesson about right and wrong. In some works, the moral is stated directly. In other works, readers can figure it out for themselves from the plot and the actions, thoughts, and speeches of the characters. Not every work has a moral.

multiple meaning of words   Some words have more than one meaning. From the context clues, or the way a word is used in a sentence, you can decide which meaning is correct. For example, *bat* can mean "a flying mammal" or "a stick." In the sentence "Joanne stepped up to the mound and lifted her bat," you can tell that *bat* means "a stick."   [Section 4]

mystery   A story or a play that contains a puzzle that the characters and the readers try to solve.   [Section 4]

myth   A story told by people in ancient times to explain life and nature. Many myths, including the Greek myths, are about gods and goddesses.

narration   Writing or speaking that tells a story.

narrative essay   See personal narrative essay.   [Section 7]

narrative poem   A poem that tells a story. Like a story, a narrative poem has characters and a *plot* (a sequence of important events). The events occur in a particular order, or *sequence*. The poem has a beginning, a middle, and an end.   [Section 5]

narrator   A person who tells a story. Some stories, poems, and plays have a narrator who is a character in the work. For example, in "The Sneeze" (page 70), the writer assumes the part of the play's narrator. On the stage, an actor or actress would play the part of the narrator.

newspaper   A paper that contains news, editorials, (writings giving the editors' opinions), and features, and that usually is published every day or every week.

   When to use a newspaper.   Use a newspaper to find out about important recent happenings and about sports and entertainment events. Use newspaper advertisements to find products that are for sale and jobs that are available.

   How to use a newspaper.   Most newspapers have indexes on the front page that tell the sections and the pages of regular features, such as movie listings.

   Libraries usually have old copies of

newspapers. Sometimes they have been reduced in size and copied on film called *microfilm*. Libraries have special machines for viewing these films.

news story   A nonfiction story that appears in a newspaper or news magazine; an article. A news story should answer these questions: *Who? What? When? Where? Why? How?*   [Sections 2, 3]

nonfiction   Writing about real people and real events. Articles, essays, biographies, and autobiographies are examples of nonfiction. Some nonfiction works such as encyclopedias and dictionaries, give information used for reference.

Among the nonfiction selections in this book are "Growing Up" (page 328), "400 Mulvaney Street" (page 319), and "Dolphins" (page 365).   [Section 8]

notes   When you are doing research, it helps to take notes on what you read so that you will remember it. Write down the important information and the title, author, and page number of the book where you got it.

novel   A book-length piece of writing that tells a story. Novels are *fiction;* that is, they are made-up stories.   [Section 11]

numbers   In alphabetical order, numbers appear as though they were spelled out. For example, if you were looking for a catalog card for a book title that started with *12*, you would look under *t* for *twelve*.

opinion   A statement about a person's ideas, beliefs, or feelings. Opinions cannot be proved true or false. Another person may have a different opinion. For example, in "The Enemy" (page 41), the author says, "The Americans were full of prejudice." This statement is an opinion. You may agree or disagree.

Authors often support their opinions with *facts* (statements that can be proved) that they hope will convince readers to share their beliefs.   [Section 8]

out-of-print book   A book that is no longer available for sale from the publisher or regular bookstores. You can often find out-of-print books in libraries or second-hand bookshops.

parts of a book   The front cover of a book gives the title and author and perhaps the person who did the pictures. The *spine* of the book is the side that shows on the library shelves. The spine also gives the title and author. In libraries, the call number of the book is marked on the spine so that you can find the book on the shelf.

Inside the book, one of the first pages is the *title page,* which again gives the title and author. Next to it is the *copyright page,* which tells when the book was published. If you need up-to-date facts, be sure the book was published recently.

Two parts of a book help you find out what topics are covered in the book. The *table of contents,* which is in the front of many books, lists all the chapters in the book. The index, which is at the back of many nonfiction books, is an alphabetical list of the topics in the book and the pages they are on. Use the table of contents to find out what broad subjects are covered in the book. Use the index to see whether facts you need are in the book.

periodical A publication that comes out daily, weekly, monthly, or at other intervals. Magazines are periodicals.

personal narrative essay A brief, nonfiction work in which an author expresses his or her own beliefs about a particular subject or idea. [Section 7]

personification Writing about a nonhuman thing as if it were human. For example, an author might say, "The wind grabbed at my coat." Personification really compares a nonhuman thing to a human being. In the example, the wind is compared to a person, who can grab a coat.

Personification is a type of *figurative language.* [Section 5]

persuasion Convincing people to share your beliefs.

persuasive writing Writing that tries to convince people to share the author's beliefs. The author usually states his or her opinions, or beliefs, and then supports them with facts, or true statements, and examples that may convince readers.
[Sections 1, 8]

places You can find information about places in *atlases, encyclopedias,* and *almanacs.*

play Something written to be performed before an audience. A play may be divided into parts called *acts.* The acts are often divided into smaller parts called *scenes. Stage directions* tell the director or actors how the stage should look and how the characters should act, move, and speak.

Like stories, plays have plots, characterization, and settings. The *plot* is the sequence, or order, of important events. *Characterization* is the way an author informs the reader or the audience about the characters. In a play, you can learn about the characters through their speech and actions or through a narrator's descriptions. *Setting* is the time when and the place where the events of the story happen. The characters' speeches, the narrator's descriptions, and the stage directions all may give information about the setting.

Four plays in this book are "The Sneeze" (page 70), "I Remember Mama" (page 78), "Sudden Death" (page 87), and "The Rocking Horse (page 433). [Section 2]

plot The sequence, or order, of important events in a story, that makes a point or brings out a reaction in the reader. The plot has a beginning, a middle, and an end. The events are planned to get the reader interested and to show what the *theme,* or most important idea in the selection, is.

Usually the events that make up the plot can be divided into three elements, or parts:

1. *Rising Action* is the part of the plot where a problem situation develops and the action builds up. In "The Pearl" (page 482), Kino and Juana have a happy life together wih their baby Coyotito. But they begin to have problems when Kino finds the Pearl of the World.

2. The *turning point* is the highest point of the action. The characters find a way to solve the problem. In "The Pearl," Kino and Juana decide to travel north to sell the pearl.

3. The *resolution* is the last part of the plot. The problem is solved, and readers learn

how the characters react. In "The Pearl," Kino and Juana return home with the pearl. They decide to throw the pearl back into the sea where it came from. [Sections 1, 4, 11]

poem A written or spoken work with language chosen for its sound, beauty, and power to express feelings. (See also poetry.)

poet The author of a poem.

poetry Poems. Poetry looks and sounds different from other forms of writing. It looks different because poets arrange their words in lines instead of sentences and group these lines into stanzas instead of paragraphs. It sounds different because poets often use rhythm, rhyme, imagery, and figurative language.

Rhythm is the arrangement of the syllables in a line to make a particular sound pattern, or beat, as in music. You can hear the rhythm of a line of poetry best when you read it aloud. The punctuation and capitalization in a poem will help you decide when to pause and what to stress in order to hear the rhythm.

Rhyme is an element that many poems have. Two words rhyme when they end with the same sound: *cat, fat.* Two lines rhyme when they end with rhyming words. Here are rhyming lines from "Could Be" (page 222):

"Hastings Street is weary,
Also Lenox Avenue.
Any place is dreary
Without my watch and you."

Imagery is language that appeals to the senses of sight, hearing, taste, touch, or smell.

Figurative language means words that are used in a new way to appeal to the imagination. Two things that do not seem alike may be compared. In "Butterfly" (page 224), for example, love is compared to a butterfly.

There are other elements poets may use. For instance, *humor.*

The words and elements a poet chooses are part of the poet's *style.*   [Section 5]

point of view The position from which a story is told. In the *first-person point of view,* an author tells a true story about his or her own life; or, in a made-up story, the author pretends to be one of the characters. The first-person point of view uses the pronouns *I* and *me* in telling the story. In the *third-person point of view,* the story-teller is not a character in the story. The author uses the pronouns *he, she,* and *they* to tell the story.

"Marigolds" (page 32) is an example of a story told from the first-person point of view. "The Green Door" (page 20) is an example of a story told from the third-person point of view.   [Sections 4, 7, 11]

predicting outcomes Guessing what will happen next in a story. You have a better chance of being right if you keep in mind what has already happened and what the characters are like.

prefix A word part added to the beginning of a word. Each prefix has its own meaning. For example, the prefix *un-* means "not." If you add a prefix to a word, you change the meaning of the word. For example, *done* means finished. Add the prefix *un-* and you get *undone,* meaning "not finished."

If you do not know a word, look at the word parts. The meaning of each part can help you figure out the word. [Sections 6, 7]

problem   A difficult situation that the characters in a story have to solve. The problem is the first part of the *plot*. In "The Pearl" (page 482), for example, the problem is how to sell the pearl in order to pay for the doctor.

prose   Written work that is not poetry.

pun   A humorous play on words, usually using a word or phrase with a double meaning.   [Section 9]

publisher   A person or company that prints and sells books, newspapers, magazines, and/or other written materials.

realistic fiction   Stories that contain made-up characters and events that are similar to people and happenings in real life. "Marigolds" (page 32) is an example of realistic fiction.   [Section 1]

Readers' Guide to Periodical Literature   A guide that comes out once or twice a month and lists recent magazine articles by their subjects. If you wanted to see what magazine articles had been written recently about whales, you would take a recent copy of the *Readers' Guide* and look under *w* for *whales*. If you wanted to read one of the listed articles, you might be able to borrow the magazine from the library. Large libraries have copies of many old and new magazines.

reference books   Books that are not meant to be read from cover to cover like a story but instead are used to look up particular facts.

Dictionaries, encyclopedias, atlases, almanacs, and biographical dictionaries are important types of reference books.

Reference books are kept on special shelves in the library.

research   Investigation to find facts.

resolution   The last part of the *plot*, when the problem is solved, and you learn how the solution affects the characters. In "The Pearl" (page 482), the resolution comes when Kino and Juana return to the village after Coyotito has been killed. They throw the pearl back into the sea because it has brought them nothing but trouble. [Sections 3, 11]

rhyme   An element found in many, though not all, poems. Words rhyme when they end with the same sound. Lines rhyme when they end with rhyming words. [Section 5]

rhythm   The arrangement of the syllables in a line of poetry so that they make a particular sound pattern, or beat, as in music. When you read poetry aloud, listen for the rhythm. The punctuation and capitalization in a poem will help you decide when to pause and what words to stress to make the rhythm clear.   [Section 5]

rising action   The first part of a *plot*. The action builds up and a problem situation develops. In "The Pearl" (page 482), Kino and Juana must find help for Coyotito, who has been stung by a scorpion. [Sections 3, 11]

root word   A word from which other words can be made. By adding a *prefix* to the beginning of a root word or a *suffix* to the end, you can change the word's meaning. For example, if you add the prefix *re-* to the root word *play*, you form the word *replay*, which means "play again." If you add the suffix *-ful* to the end of the root word, you get *playful*, which means "full of play" or "fun-loving." [Section 6]

round character A character that is described fully. The author includes details that help you understand how the character thinks, acts, looks, and feels. Dr. Sadao Hoki in "The Enemy" (page 41) is a round character. [Sections 1, 10, 11]

scene Part of a play. Plays are often divided into parts called *acts*, which, in turn, may be divided into smaller parts, the scenes. [Section 2]

sensory imagery Words that appeal to the senses of sight, hearing, taste, touch, or smell. [Section 5]

sequence of events The order in which events occur in a story or play. The events are put in a particular order, or sequence, so that the reader will understand what the story is about. The order of important events in a story makes up the *plot*. [Section 1]

setting The time when and the place where the events of the story happen. You can tell what the setting is by looking for words or phrases that tell when and where.

Pay attention to time and place words throughout the selection, because the setting may change as the story or play goes on. For example, in "The Third Level" (page 190), the setting shifts in time from the present to the past and back again. [Sections 1, 4]

short story A brief work of *fiction* (made-up story).

significant detail A small but important bit of information. (See also detail.) [Sections 1, 5]

simile A comparison. Usually similes contain the word *like* or the word *as*. Examples of similes are "her hands were like ice" and "her hands were as cold as ice." [Section 5]

speaking and listening (See decoding.)

speech A formal talk given in public before an audience. Speeches may present facts or opinions or both.

spine The part of a book that shows on the library shelf. The spine tells the book's title and author and, in a library, is marked with the book's *call number*.

stanza A division of a poem that is longer than a line. Lines in poetry are grouped into stanzas in much the same way that sentences in other works are grouped into paragraphs.

The following stanza is a part of the poem "Could Be" (page 222):

"Could be you love me
Could be that you don't.
Might be that you'll come back
Like as not you won't."
[Section 5]

stage directions Directions in a play that tell the director or actors how the stage should look and how the characters are to act, move, and speak. Stage directions are not meant to be spoken out loud to the audience. [Section 2]

style The words an author uses and the type of sentences he or she writes. For example, some authors use more *imagery,* or words that appeal to the senses, than other authors. Some authors write in short sentences, while others prefer to use long sentences. An author may change his or her style for different types of writing. In poetry, for instance, the author might use more imagery than when he or she was writing a nonfiction article.

suffix A word part added to the ending of a word. Each suffix has its own meaning. For example, the suffix *-less* means "without." If you add a suffix to a word, you change the meaning of the word. For example, *care* means "concern." Add the suffix *-less* and you get *careless,* which means "without concern."

If you do not know a word, look at the word parts. The meaning of each part can help you figure out the word. Here are some other examples of suffixes: *-less,* "without"; *-ful,* "filled with"; and *-able,* "able." [Section 6]

subject card A card in the library's *card catalog* that has the subject at the top.

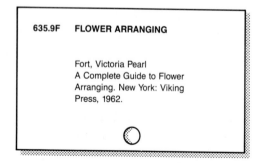

635.9F   **FLOWER ARRANGING**

Fort, Victoria Pearl
A Complete Guide to Flower
Arranging. New York: Viking
Press, 1962.

The subject tells what the book is about. Subject cards are arranged alphabetically in the card catalog. *Fiction* books do not have subject cards.

(For more information about subject cards, see catalog cards.)

summary A brief retelling of a story. A summary tells the main events. In order for people who have not read the story to understand it, the events should be in the correct order, or *sequence.*

surprise ending An ending that is different from what readers have been led to believe would happen. In most stories, the ending follows logically from the rest of the plot, or sequence of events. However, in stories with a surprise ending, the story takes an unexpected twist at the end.

In "Take Over Bos'n" (page 284), the ending comes as a surprise to the reader and the characters in the story.   [Section 6]

suspense A quality that produces feelings of curiosity and tension in the reader, because the reader is not sure what will happen next. The suspense keeps you reading the story. The stories in Section 4 are written with suspense.

synonyms Synonyms are words that have the same or almost the same meaning. *Try* and *attempt* are synonyms.   [Sections 1, 2]

symbol Something that stands for something else. For example, a heart may be a symbol of love. In "A Work of Artifice" (page 232), the bonsai tree is a symbol for women.   [Sections 5, 6]

table of contents A section at the front of many books that lists all the chapters in the order in which they appear in the book.

The table of contents tells you what broad subjects are covered in the book.

telephone directory　A list of names, addresses, and telephone numbers.

theme　The author's message; the most important idea in a written work. The *plot,* or sequence of important events in a story, helps to show what the theme is. So does the *characterization,* or what the author lets readers know or discover about the characters. Even if the author does not state the theme directly, you can figure out the message by thinking about the events in the story and the characters' thoughts, words, and actions.

In "The Pearl" (page 482), the theme is that the forces of evil can be hidden in what seems to be a thing of beauty. The events in the story lead the readers to understand that Kino's life has changed from simplicity and joy to confusion and sorrow.

In "Letter to a Black Boy" (page 260), the theme is that cooperation among family members could help to make dreams for a better life come true.

In some stories, readers learn a lesson about life while laughing at the characters or the situations. The author uses humor to develop the theme. "Fresh Air Will Kill You" (page 394) is an example of this. The theme of the story is that pollution is harmful and dangerous. The author makes his point with his satirical style of writing. [Sections 6, 11]

third-person point of view　Telling a story by using the pronouns *he, she,* and *they.* Most *biographies,* or true accounts of another person's life, are written from the third-person point of view. Most (though not all) made-up stories are also written in a third-person point of view. (See also first-person point of view.)　[Section 7]

title card　A card in the library's *card catalog* that has the book's title at the top.

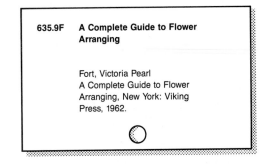

> 635.9F　**A Complete Guide to Flower Arranging**
>
> Fort, Victoria Pearl
> A Complete Guide to Flower Arranging, New York: Viking Press, 1962.

Title cards are arranged alphabetically in the card catalog. The articles *a, an,* and *the* are ignored in alphabetizing the cards. (For more information about title cards, see catalog cards.)

title page　A page at the beginning of a book that gives the book's title and author.

turning point　The highest point of the action in a story. At the turning point, or climax, the characters finally find a way to solve the problem they have been facing. In "The Pearl" (page 482), the turning point comes when Kino and Juana leave the village to find a city in the north. (See also plot.)　[Section 3]

volume　1. A book. 2. One book in a set of books. 3. A group of issues of a magazine or other periodical.

word meaning　A definition. The best place to find the meaning of a word is in a dictionary. (See also context.) [Sections 3, 4, 5, 8, 9, 10]

word origin Where a word comes from. Most dictionaries include this information. [Section 7]

word parts Root words, prefixes, and suffixes. A *root word* is a word from which other words can be made. A *prefix* is a word part added to the beginning of a word. A *suffix* is a word part added to the ending of a word. If you know the meaning of each word part, you can figure out the word.

For example, in the word *prepayable,* the prefix *pre-* means "before"; the root word *pay* means "to give money"; and the suffix *-able* means "able to be." By putting all these meanings together, you can see that *prepayable* means "able to be given money for, in advance." [Sections 6, 7]

word play A humorous use of words. In order to be funny, authors sometimes use nonsense words and *puns,* or words with double meanings. [Section 9]

writing These four steps will help you in your writing:

Step 1: Set Your Goal
Choose the topic that you will write about.

Step 2: Make a Plan
Plan what you are going to say. Often this involves making a list.

Step 3: Write a First Draft
Use your plan to write a first draft.

Step 4: Revise
Read what you have written. Make sure that it says what you want to say in a clear way. Correct any errors in spelling, grammar, and punctuation. Make a final, neat copy.

Here are the main writing assignments given in this book:

character sketch For step 2, you list details that describe your subject. [Section 10]

comparison and contrast of two characters For step 2, you make one list of ideas from the story that shows how the characters or their lives are alike, and another list that shows how they are different. [Section 1]

description For step 2, you list the details about your subject that appeal to the senses of sight, hearing, taste, smell, and touch. [Section 9]

personal narrative For step 2, you identify the action, conflict, climax, and resolution of your story. [Section 7]

persuasive writing For step 2, you list the reasons that support your purpose [Section 8]

poem For step 2, you list the words that come into your mind when you think of your subject. [Section 5]

report For step 2, you gather information through observations and interviews. [Section 4] *a review* For step 2, you decide your standards and apply them. [Section 2]

social letter For step 2, you list the facts and ideas you want to tell your friend. [Section 6]

story For step 2, you list the elements of plot, characters, conflict, setting, point of view, and mood. [Section 11]

the writing process: paragraphs For step 2, you list ideas and details and organize them into paragraphs. [Section 3]

AUTHOR AND TITLE

Abbott, Bud, 405
Acorn People, The, 353
ADVENTURE (Section 3), 104
  Introduction, 106
Adventure of the Copper Beeches, The, 179
And They Lived Happily Ever After for a
    While, 398
Appleman, Philip, 236

Baker, Russell, 328
Bierce, Ambrose, 400
Blue Eyes Far Away, 24
Brand, Joshua, 87
Buchwald, Art, 394
Buck, Pearl S., 41
Burns, Marjorie, 240, 242
Burns, Robert, 225
Butterfly, 224
By Any Other Name, 426

Callaghan, Morley, 254
Celebration, 266
Central Park, 344
Ch'ang Ch'u Ling, 275
Chehak, Tom, 87
Chekhov, Anton, 70
Ciardi, John, 398
Clemente—A Bittersweet Story, 312
Colgrass, Michael, 228
Collier, Eugenia, 32
Costello, Lou, 405
Could Be, 222
Cow Who Liked to Kick, The, 400
Cryer, Gretchen, 215

de Saavedra, Guadalupe, 283
Dirge Without Music, 454
Dolphins, 365
Dolson, Hildegarde, 410
Do Not Go Gentle Into That Good Night,
    238
Dos Passos, John, 306
Doyle, Sir Arthur Conan, 179
DRAMA (Section 2), 66
  Introduction, 68

Earth's a Baked Apple, The, 228
Electrical Wizard, The, 306
Emotion Twists Issues—Stick to the Facts,
    370
Enemy, The, 41

Field, Edward, 212
Finney, Jack, 190
Flight Into Danger, 119
Food Processor, 242
Forbes, Kathryn, 79
Ford, Nancy, 215
Found Poems and Concrete Poems, 240
400 Mulvaney Street, 319
Frankenstein, 212
Fresh Air Will Kill You, 394
Future Tense, 54

Gardner, Sandra, 210
Garner, Hugh, 446
Gentleman of Río en Medio, 28
Ghosts, 210
Giovanni, Nikki, 319, 326
Greenbank, Fiona, 296

Green Door, The, 20
Growing Up, 328
Guns: A Serious Problem, 375

Hailey, Arthur, 119
Halman, Doris, 433
Haskins, James, 456
Haunted Chess Set, The, 173
Hector the Collector, 217
Henry, O., 20
Herriot, James, 268, 380
Homecoming of Ulysses, The, 150
Homer, 150
How Beautiful With Mud, 410
Hughes, Langston, 222
HUMOR (Section 9), 390
    Introduction, 392

I Remember Mama, 79
IDENTITY (Section 10), 422
    Introduction, 424
If You Hear That a Thousand People Love
    You, 283
In the Shadow of a Rainbow, 139
Izenberg, Jerry, 312

Jones, Ron, 353

Kantor, Mackinlay, 24
Keady, Susan, 234
Kitten for Mrs. Ainsworth, A, 380
Knoxville, Tennessee, 326
Kostelanetz, Richard, 244

Landers, Ann, 375
Last Day at the Job, 215
Lehrer, Alice Herman, 365
Leiningen Versus the Ants, 108
Leslie, Robert Franklin, 139
Letter to a Black Boy, 260
Libby, Larry, 276
Ling Chung, 226
Lipsyte, Robert, 54
Long Walk to Forever, 277
Lopez, Alonzo, 266
Lyric Poems, 217

Marigolds, 32
Medicine, 220
Memo to the 21st Century, 236
Message Poems, 231
Millay, Edna St. Vincent, 454
Mind Over Water, 134
Morrison, Lillian, 218
MYSTERY (Section 4), 168
    Introduction, 170

Narrative Poems, 210
NONFICTION (Section 8), 340
    Introduction, 342
NOVEL, THE (Section 11), 476
    Introduction, 478
Nyad, Diana, 134

Of Kings and Things, 218

Pearl, The, 482
PERSONAL NARRATIVE (Section 7), 292
    Introduction, 294
Piercy, Marge, 232
Piggin, Julia Remine, 173
Player Piano, 227
POETRY (Section 5), 206
    Introduction, 208
President Regrets, The, 196
Purificasion, Andrés, 221

Queen, Ellery, 196

Rama Rau, Santha, 426
Red, Red Rose, A, 225
RELATIONSHIPS (Section 6), 250
    Introduction, 252
Rexroth, Kenneth, 226
Right of Way, 240
Rive, Richard, 235
Road, 276
Rocking Horse, The, 433

Schisgall, Oscar, 284
Sedillo, Juan A.A., 28
SHORT STORIES (Section 1), 16
    Introduction, 18

Silverstein, Shel, 217
Simon, Neil, 70
Since You Left, 275
Sneeze, The, 70
Solomon, Donald James, 224
St. Croix, Spike, 243
Starting at Dawn, 226
Steele, Kevin E., 370
Steelworker: Mike Lefevre, 347
Steinbeck, John, 482
  Biography, 480
Stephenson, Carl, 108
Stevie Wonder: Growing Up in a World of
    Darkness, 456
Still, 221
Story of Little Sure-Shot, The, 296
Sudden Death, 87
Sun Yün-feng, 226

Take Over, Bos'n, 284
Teague, Bob, 260

Telephone Conversation, 234
Terkel, Studs, 347
Thief, 231
Third Level, The, 190
Thomas, Dylan, 238
Tribute to Henry Ford—3, 244
Trip for Mrs. Taylor, A, 446
Troublemaker, The, 268

Updike, John, 227, 344
Urban Landscape, 243

Van Druten, John, 79
Very Special Shoes, 254
Vonnegut, Jr., Kurt, 277

Walker, Alice, 220
Where the Rainbow Ends, 235
Whitecloud, Tom, 231
Who's On First?, 405
Work of Artifice, A, 232

ACKNOWLEDGMENTS

Grateful acknowledgment is made to the following authors and publishers for the use of copyrighted materials. Every effort has been made to obtain permission to use previously published material. Any errors or omissions are unintentional.

Akwesasne Notes for "Thief" by Tom Whitecloud.

Ann Elmo Agency Inc. for an adaptation of "Leiningen Versus the Ants" by Carl Stephenson.

Bantam Books, Inc. for an adaptation from *The Acorn People* by Ron Jones. Copyright © 1976 by Ron Jones.

Congdon & Weed, Inc. for "Growing Up" by Russell Baker from the book *Growing Up* by Russell Baker. Copyright © 1982 by Russell Baker.

Darien House, Inc. for "Who's on First?"; Edited by Richard J. Anobile. Copyright © 1972 by Darien House, Inc.

Delacorte Press for "Future Tense" by Robert Lipsyte. Copyright © 1984 by Robert Lipsyte, excerpted from the book *Sixteen: Short Stories by Outstanding Writers for Young Adults*, edited by Donald R. Gallo.

Delacorte Press/Seymour Lawrence for "Long Walk To Forever" excerpted from *Welcome to the Monkey House* by Kurt Vonnegut, Jr. Copyright © 1960 by Kurt Vonnegut, Jr. Originally published in *The Ladies' Home Journal*.

Doubleday & Company, Inc. for "Clemente: A Bittersweet Memory" from *Great Latin Sports Figures: The Proud People* by Jerry Izenberg. Copyright © 1976 by Jerry Izenberg: "Celebration" by Alonzo Lopez from *The Whispering Wind* by Terry Allen. Copyright © 1972 by The Institute of American Indian Arts; an adaptation from "The Green Door" from *The Four Million* by O. Henry; an adaptation of "Blue Eyes Far Away." Copyright 1932 by Liberty Magazine, Inc. from *Story Teller* by MacKinlay Kantor.

Norma Millay Ellis for "Dirge Without Music" by Edna St. Vincent Millay from *Collected Poems*, Harper & Row, Publishers, Inc. Copyright 1921, 1928, 1948, 1955 by Edna St. Vincent Millay and Norma Millay Ellis.

Esquire Publishing, Inc. for an adaptation of "Mind Over Water" from *Esquire* Magazine (October 1975), by Diana Nyad. Copyright © 1975 by Esquire Publishing, Inc.

ACKNOWLEDGMENTS

Pantheon Books, a Division of Random House, Inc. for "Steelworker: Mike Lefevre" from *Working: People Talk About What They Do All Day and How They Feel About What They Do,* by Studs Terkel. Copyright © 1972, 1974 by Studs Terkei.

Mrs. Elizabeth A. Dos Passos for an edited version of "The Electrical Wizard" by John Dos Passos. Copyright 1930, 1960 by Houghton-Mifflin.

Prentice-Hall, Inc. for "If You Hear That a Thousand People Love You" by Guadelupe de Saavedra from *Love Me, Love Me Not* by A. Daigon. Copyright © 1977 by Prentice-Hall, Inc.

Andrés Purificasion for his poem "Still."

G. P. Putnam's Sons for "Fresh Air Will Kill You" from *Have I Ever Lied to You?* by Art Buchwald. Copyright © 1966, 1967, 1968 by Art Buchwald.

Random House, Inc. for "How Beautiful With Mud" from *We Shook the Family Tree,* by Hildegarde Dolson. Copyright 1941, 1942, 1946 and renewed 1970 by Hildegarde Dolson; "The Sneeze" from *The Good Doctor* by Neil Simon. Copyright © 1974 by Neil Simon and Albert I. Da Silva as Trustee.

Oscar Schisgall for "Take Over, Bos'n!" by Oscar Schisgall. Copyright 1950 by the United Newspapers Magazine Corporation.

Scott Meredith Literary Agency, Inc. and the author's estate for the adaptation of "The President Regrets" by Ellery Queen. Copyright © 1965 by Ellery Queen.

Juan A. A. Sedillo for "Gentleman of Río En Medio." Published by New Mexico Quarterly.

St. Martin's Press, Inc. for "Troublemaker" from *All Things Wise and Wonderful* by James Herriot, copyright © 1976, 1977 by James Herriot; for "A Kitten for Mrs. Ainsworth" from *The Best of James Herriot,* copyright © 1976, 1977.

Kevin E. Steele and *Guns* Magazine "Emotion Twists Issues—Stick to the Facts." Copyright © 1980 (July): Publishers' Development Corp., All rights reserved.

Bob Teague for an adaptation of "Letters to a Black Boy" by Robert L. Teague. Copyright © 1968 by Lancer Books.

Viking Penguin Inc. for *The Pearl* by John Steinbeck. Copyright 1945 by John Steinbeck. Coyright renewed 1973 by Elaine Steinbeck, Thom Steinbeck, and John Steinbeck IV.

Warner Bros. Music for "Everybody Is a Star" by Sylvester Stewart. Copyright © 1976 by Warner-Tamerlane Publishing Corp. and Stone Flower Music. All rights reserved.

Wesleyan University Press for "Skinny Poem" from *Cold Water* by Lou Lipsitz. Copyright © 1966 by Lou Lipsitz.

William Morris Agency, Inc. for "By Any Other Name" by Santha Rama Rau. Copyright © 1951, 1961 by Vasanthi Rama Rau Bowers.

William Morrow & Company, Inc. for "Knoxville, Tennessee" from *Black Feeling, Black Talk, Black Judgment* by Nikki Giovanni. Copyright © 1968, 1970 by Nikki Giovanni.

W. W. Norton & Company, Inc. for *In The Shadow of a Rainbow, The True Story of a Friendship Between Man and Wolf,* by Robert Franklin Leslie. Copyright © 1974 by W. W. Norton & Company, Inc.; "Memo to the 21st Century" from *Open Doorways, Poems,* by Philip Appleman. Copyright © 1976 by W. W. Norton & Company, Inc.

Scholastic Inc. for "Telephone Conversation" by Susan Keady (Scholastic Awards); "Butterfly" by Donald James Solomon (Copyright © 1976); "Dolphins" by Alice Herman Lehrer; "The Haunted Chess Set" by Julia Remine Piggin; "The Story of Little Sure-Shot" by Fiona Greenbank; "Urban Landscape" by Spike St. Croix; and Four Winds Press, Inc. for "The Road" by Larry Libby, from *Story: The Yearbook of Discovery* edited by Whit and Hallie Burnett. Copyright © 1971 by Scholastic Inc.; for "The Homecoming of Ulysses." Copyright © 1983.

ILLUSTRATION AND PHOTOGRAPHY CREDITS

Illustration: p. 21, Kathryn Yingling; p. 26, Jas Szygiel; pp. 29, 192, 411, 412, 415, Tom Leonard; pp. 34, 38-39, Gerry Hoover; pp. 43, 46-47, 49, 50, 269, 270, Steve Tanis; pp. 57, 60, Brian Cody; pp. 72-73, Tim Raglin; pp. 88, 91, 94, 96-97, Bill Purdom; pp. 122-123, 126, 130-131, Frederick Porter; pp. 140, 143, 146-147, Jon Friedman; pp. 152, 157, 161, 162, Floyd Cooper; pp. 176, Will Kefauver; pp. 199, 200, Konrad Hack; p. 217, Cathy Johnson; p. 242, Don Madden; pp. 256-257, Ivan Powell; pp. 261, 262-263, 254, Walter Brooks; pp. 278, 281, 354-355, 357, 361, Robert Steele; pp. 285, 286, Jim Pearson; pp. 320, 323, Lyle Miller; pp. 326-327,

Greg Voth; pp. 330, 333, 334, Susan Magurn; pp. 380, 383, 384, 427, 428-429, 431, Sue Rother; pp. 401, 402-403, Rosekrans Hoffman; pp. 437, 440-441, Arieh Zeldich; pp. 483, 484, 489, 492, 494-495, 499, 503, 506-507, 511, 513, 516-517, 520, 523, 527, 530, 534-535, 538, 542-543, 547, Arvis Stewart.

Photography: 81, 213, 218, 307, 308-309, The Bettmann Archive; 84, 114-115, 116, Culver Pictures/Photo Coloration: Marc Tauss; 110-111, Ross Hutchins/Photo Researchers; 136-137, Frank Zarino/Black Star Photos; 171, 298, 303, 407, The Granger Collection; 180, 185, Adam Wolfitt/Woodfin Camp & Associates; 182, Russ Kinne/Photo Researchers; 210, Michal Heron/Woodfin Camp & Associates; 220, 225, 275, Farrell Grehan/Photo Researchers; 221, National Museum of American Art/Smithsonian Institution; 222-223, 235, Richard Hutchings/Photo Researchers; 224, H. Uible/Photo Researchers; 238, Judy Gurevitz/Photo Researchers; 226, Hans Reinhard/Bruce Coleman; 227, Elie Nadelman/Museum of Modern Art; 228-229, NASA/Photo Researchers; 231, Richard Weiss/Peter Arnold; 232-233, Jack Daly; 234, Michael Morre/DPI; 237, Momatiuk-Eastcott/Woodfin Camp & Associates; 240-241, Elihu Blotnick/Woodfin Camp & Associates; 266-267, Robert Frereck/Woodfin Camp & Associates; 276, Virginia Carleton/Photo Researchers; 277, Alon Reininger/Contact; 313, 316, Focus on Sports; 345, Herman Emmet/Photo Researchers; 349, Lowell Georgia/Photo Researchers; 350, Ray Ellis/Photo Researchers; 351, Junebug Clark/Photo Researchers; 366, E. R. Degginger/Bruce Coleman; 371, Tim Eagan/Woodfin Camp & Associates; 372, Louis Anderson/Black Star Photos; 376, Ira Berger/Woodfin Camp & Associates; 378, Earl Dotter/Magnum Photos; 394-395, Tom McHugh/Photo Researchers; 398-399, Arthur Tress/Photo Researchers; 448-449, Wayne Miller/Magnum Photos; 454, Meike Maas/The Image Bank; 457, Yoram Kahana/Shooting Star; 468, Al Satterwhite/Camera 5; 469 (tl), Wide World; (tr), Ken Regan/Camera 5; (b), Gamma Liaison; 470, Sam Emerson-Naras/Gamma Liaison; 480, Erich Hartman/Magnum Photos.